AF606054

MASCULINITIES AND REPRESENTATION

The Eroticized Male in Early Modern Italy and England

Masculinities and Representation

The Eroticized Male in Early Modern Italy and England

EDITED BY KONRAD EISENBICHLER

UNIVERSITY OF TORONTO PRESS
Toronto Buffalo London

Toronto Buffalo London
utorontopress.com
Printed in the USA

ISBN 978-1-4875-5697-6 (cloth)
ISBN 978-1-4875-5699-0 (EPUB)
ISBN 978-1-4875-5698-3 (PDF)

Library and Archives Canada Cataloguing in Publication

Title: Masculinities and representation : the eroticized male in early modern Italy and England / edited by Konrad Eisenbichler.
Names: Eisenbichler, Konrad, editor.
Description: Includes bibliographical references and index.
Identifiers: Canadiana (print) 20240370244 | Canadiana (ebook) 20240370279 | ISBN 9781487556976 (cloth) | ISBN 9781487556990 (EPUB) | ISBN 9781487556983 (PDF)
Subjects: LCSH: Masculinity – Italy – History. | LCSH: Masculinity – England – History. | LCSH: Masculinity in literature. | LCSH: Masculinity in art. | LCSH: Masculinity – Religious aspects – Christianity.
Classification: LCC HQ1090.7.I8 M37 2024 | DDC 305.310945–dc23

Cover design: Val Cooke
Cover image: Cosimo I de' Medici (1519–1574), Grand Duke of Tuscany, painting entitled "Portrait of Cosimo I de' Medici as Orpheus," by Agnolo Bronzino (1503–1572), oil on panel, 1540s. IanDagnall Computing / Alamy Stock Photo; AlexZaitsev/Shutterstock.com

We wish to acknowledge the land on which the University of Toronto Press operates. This land is the traditional territory of the Wendat, the Anishnaabeg, the Haudenosaunee, the Métis, and the Mississaugas of the Credit First Nation.

University of Toronto Press acknowledges the financial support of the Government of Canada, the Canada Council for the Arts, and the Ontario Arts Council, an agency of the Government of Ontario, for its publishing activities.

Canada Council for the Arts
Conseil des Arts du Canada

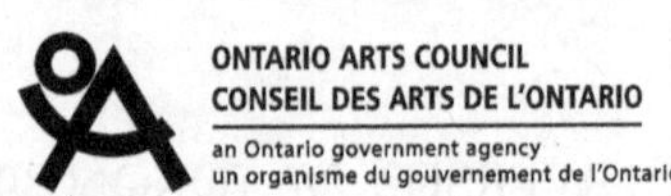

Funded by the Government of Canada
Financé par le gouvernement du Canada

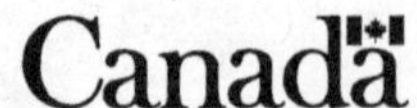

Contents

List of Illustrations vii

Acknowledgments xi

Introduction 3
JAMES M. SASLOW

Part One: Religion, Heavenly Art, Earthly Bodies

1 Bathing and Bonding: Sensual Male Imagery in Italian Paintings of Baptism 23
STEVEN F.H. STOWELL

2 Blasphemous or Beautiful? Leonardo da Vinci's *Saint John the Baptist*: Holy Masculinity and Its Ambiguities ca. 1500 52
ANNE L. WILLIAMS

3 Sharing a Bed with Dominic: Celibacy and Masculinity in the Cult of Saint Vincent Ferrer 77
LAURA ACKERMAN SMOLLER

4 The Body of Christ: Suffering and Desire in Gianfrancesco Pico della Mirandola's *De Venere et Cupidine Expellendis* 97
MARCO PIANA

Part Two: Women and Men: Masculinity, Effeminacy, and Desire

5 *A Dio Zerbini a Dio, a Dio Narcisi*: Satirizing Effeminacy in Margherita Costa's Florentine Works (1638–1641) 117
SARA E. DÍAZ

6 Masculine-Feminine Dichotomy in the Sixteenth Century: Mythological *Donna con Donna* Images from Fontainebleau and Northern Italy 141
TARA WHITE

Part Three: Knowledge and Emotions: Forbidden and Required

7 Wounded Histories on the Stages of Old and New Worlds: Vivaldi's *Motezuma* and the Cries of Conquest 171
KATE DRISCOLL

8 Male Courtly Feeling and the Historical Performativity of Shyness in *A Midsummer Night's Dream* 199
TIFFANY HOFFMAN

9 Latin Epigrams and Early Modern Sexual Knowledge: Or, How Jonson Read His Martial 221
IAN FREDERICK MOULTON

Contributors 245

Index 249

Illustrations

1.1 Masolino da Panicale, *The Baptism of Christ* (top); *The Baptist Preaching on the Banks of the River Jordan* (bottom left); *The Baptist Reproves Herod* (bottom right) (ca. 1435) 24
1.2 *Spinario*, first century 26
1.3 Domenico Ghirlandaio, *The Baptism of Christ* (1485–90) 27
1.4 Masaccio, Masolino da Panicale, and Filippino Lippi, view of Brancacci Chapel showing *St. Peter Baptizing the Neophytes* (top left) and *The Temptation of Adam and Eve* (top right) and other scenes (ca. 1423–8, and 1484–5) 28
1.5 Paris Bordone, *The Baptism of Christ* (1544) 29
1.6 Jacopo and Lorenzo Salimbeni, *Scenes from the Life of John the Baptist: Saint John Baptizing the Neophytes* (1416) 30
1.7 Pisanello (or school of) after Gentile da Fabriano, *Baptism of Christ* (ca. 1430) 33
1.8 Aristotile da Sangallo after Michelangelo, *Battle of Cascina* (1542) 37
1.9 Fra Angelico, Armadio Panels (detail): *Christ Washing His Apostles' Feet* (ca. 1451–5) 41
2.1 Leonardo da Vinci, *Saint John the Baptist* (ca. 1513–16) 53
2.2 Perugino, *Saint Sebastian* (ca. 1485) 56
2.3 Leonardo da Vinci, *The Last Supper* (1495–7). Detail of the left side with Saint John 57

2.4 Marriage of Christ and John the Evangelist at the Marriage of Cana. Libellus for John the Evangelist, Upper Rhine (before 1493) 58
2.5 Jacob Hoefnagel, after Leonardo da Vinci, *Unequal Couple* (1602) 60
2.6 Master of the Amsterdam Cabinet (Housebook Master), *Unequal Couple* (1475–80) 61
2.7 Rosso Fiorentino, *The Dead Christ with Angels* (ca. 1524–7) 62
2.8 Giovanni Antonio de' Sacchis, called Pordenone, *The Blessed Lorenzo Giustiniani between Two Monks and Saints Louis of Toulouse, Francis, Bernardino of Siena, and John the Baptist* (ca. 1528–32) 63
2.9 School of Raphael, *Virgin and Child with Saint John (Madonna of the Veil)* (1483–1520) 64
2.10 Leonardo da Vinci and pupil, *Horses and Soldiers, Mechanics, and the Angel of the Annunciation* (ca. 1503–4) 65
2.11 Leonardo da Vinci (?), *The Angel in the Flesh* (ca. 1510–15) 67
5.1 Jacques Callot (1592–1635), *Scapino and Cap. Zerbino. Balli di Sfessania* series, ca. 1622 121
5.2 Stefano della Bella (1610–1664), *Dwarfs' Tournament* 122
5.3 Margherita Costa, *La chitarra, canzoniere amoroso.* [Frankfurt: Daniel Wastch], 1638 124
5.4 Stefano della Bella, frontispiece to Margherita Costa's *Li buffoni* (Florence, 1641) 128
6.1 Pierre Milan (after Primaticcio), *Jupiter and Callisto* (1537–40) 142
6.2 Master GK (after Luca Penni), *A Satyr Surprising Four Bathing Nymphs* (ca. 1550) 143
6.3 Parmigianino, *Story of Diana and Actaeon* (northern lunettes) (1523–4) 144
6.4 Detail of fig. 6.3 showing lunette with Actaeon in human form 145
6.5 Parmigianino, *Story of Diana and Actaeon* (east lunettes) (1523–4) 146
6.6 Detail of fig. 6.5 showing lunette with nymphs 147
6.7 Fontana Family Workshop, *Dish with Diana and Her Nymphs Bathing* (ca. 1560–70) 148
6.8 Jean Mignon (after Luca Penni), *Women Bathing* (1547–50) 154
6.9 Giovanni Jacopo Caraglio (after Perino del Vaga), *Neptune and Doride* from the *Loves of the Gods* (1515–65) 155
6.10 Attributed to Bernardino Lanino, *Venus and Mars with Cupid* (ca. 1550) 156

7.1 Jan van der Straet, *Allegory of America* (ca. 1600) 189
7.2 Isabella Piccini, "Motezuma" (1699) 190
9.1 Martial, *Epigrams* (Milan, 1490) 224
9.2 Ben Jonson's letter to Richard Briggs, handwritten on sig. A1v in Martial, *Epigrammaton* (London, 1615) 231
9.3 Ben Jonson's copy of Martial, *Nova Editio* [*Epigrams*] (Leiden, 1619) 232
9.4 Ben Jonson's annotations to epigram 1.32 237

Acknowledgments

In bringing together this collection of articles, I have incurred many debts with colleagues and institutions that I now wish to acknowledge.

My first debt is with my dear friend and colleague, Jacqueline Murray, who co-organized with me the international conference "Masculinities in the Premodern World: Continuities, Change, and Contradictions" from which these articles originate. The conference was held on 12–14 November 2020; it was originally meant to be an in-person event at Victoria College in the University of Toronto, but the pandemic obliged us, at the last moment, to morph it into a virtual event. The ever-capable Eva Chivite (Victoria University Events Department) managed the switch and entire virtual side of the conference so well that neither Jacqueline nor I can understate our debt to her for the smooth running of the event.

The conference was made possible by the generous support of many institutions, first among them the Toronto Renaissance and Reformation Colloquium, which sponsored the event. Then the Social Sciences and Humanities Research Council of Canada, whose Connections Grant supported not only the conference but also the editing of this and other volumes that sprang from the conference. The conference received essential support from Victoria University through its President's Office and its Centre for Renaissance and Reformation Studies. We are also grateful to the Office of the President at the University of Saint Michael's College and to the Praeses of the Pontifical Institute for Mediaeval Studies. Many units within the University of Toronto supported the conference, in particular the Emilio Goggio Chair in Italian Studies, the Centre for Medieval Studies, the Bonham Centre for Sexual Diversity Studies, the Centre for Comparative Literature, the departments of English, French, History, Religion, and Spanish and Portuguese, and the Institute for Islamic Studies. We also received considerable support from partners at the University of Guelph through the Dean of the College of Arts, the Department of History, and the Work-Study program. At Saint Jerome's University the Academic Dean and the DRAGEN Lab also came to our assistance. And we are grateful to the Royal Ontario Museum for sponsoring the participation of Professor Patricia Simons and including her plenary presentation in the ROM Connects series of talks.

As editor of this collection, I am deeply indebted to Jacqueline Murray and James M. Saslow, both of whom generously provided me with their vast expertise and valuable advice. I have long admired their scholarship and treasured their friendship, so it is a distinct pleasure for me to now acknowledge their help in this project. My thanks also go to Emma Hoffer-Weinper (University of Guelph), who helped to pre-edit the original submissions.

The double-blind peer reviewers who read through the collection for the University of Toronto Press provided me and the contributors with some excellent suggestions that strengthened the various contributions and improved the volume as a whole. We very much appreciate their sharing their knowledge, wisdom, and time with us.

And I am also grateful to Suzanne Rancourt, Editorial Director at the University of Toronto Press, and to the entire UTP team for their support and expertise in bringing this collection into print.

Finally, I would like to thank all the colleagues who have contributed their research to this volume, as well as all the conference participants whose research fed into this enterprise and continues to inspire and expand this important area of historical research.

Konrad Eisenbichler, CM, OMRI, FRSC

MASCULINITIES AND REPRESENTATION

Introduction

JAMES M. SASLOW

The focus of this collection is the social and psychological dimensions of maleness: how early modern Europeans perceived the male body, what gendered structures they projected onto it both sacred and secular, and how it resonated as a site for both spiritual aspiration and erotic anxiety, for passion and guilt, power and submission. Proper male roles were contested ground, a discursive arena in which those individuals and institutions entrenched in the fortress of established cultural norms contended with reformist assailants bent on breaching its walls and trundling in the Trojan Horse of dissenting ideas.

It's tough to "be a man" at any time, but particularly, as noted by Tiffany Hoffman, "during this especially formative time in the history of masculinity," when "conceptions of masculinity were beginning to be reconfigured."[1] Hoffman contends (following Ronda Arab) that Shakespeare's *Dream* play in particular "takes as one of its central preoccupations the overarching question of 'what it is to be a man.'" Multiple and conflicting answers evolved and spread slowly across time and geography, even into the present. Reflecting the dominant interests of the conference where these papers originated, this collection focuses on two contrasting but interrelated cultural spheres, the English island and the Italian peninsula.

The pivotal start of this long transition had, like most social-historical changes, multiple causes. Among the most suggestive explanations for the early modern gender crisis is one outlined by Hoffman, following social theorist Mikhail Bakhtin: the shift in the archetypal aristocratic male role from warrior to courtier. Broadly, as centralized nation-states superseded the feudal system of military fiefs, the long-established expectations of knightly strength and battlefield aggression grew increasingly superfluous, while demand arose for skills and attitudes more suitable to administrative roles in the increasingly refined and bureaucratized palaces of power. Men were now expected to develop behaviours and emotions formerly assigned only to women – like civility and cooperation – in order to be considered "gentlemanly."

Bakhtin's powerful narrative, which helps illuminate the patterns and conflicts underlying many studies in this volume, was most overtly exemplified in France, where the aristocracy was divided into two distinct castes: the medieval *noblesse d'épée* – the hereditary "nobility of the sword," descended from the land-holding warrior class – and the *noblesse de robe*, appointed government functionaries whose status derived not from the martial arts but from the liberal arts, an education symbolized by their academic-style robes. Not surprisingly, the macho soldiers looked down on the effete civil servants, highlighting the role of social class in this volume's cultural analyses.[2]

This book is not, however, a work of social history. As signalled in the title's evocation of representation, these essays examine questions of eros and gender through the lenses of cultural studies in visual arts, literature, theatre, and religion: creative spaces where systems of gender are clothed in tangible form, propagated, and reinforced. Nor is it a comprehensive history, either temporally or geographically; rather, it offers a sampler of new approaches and themes in selected areas. While each of the essays focuses on specific manifestations of the shifting codes of gender and sexuality in localized contexts, the normative matrix of adult masculinity common across England and Italy (and elsewhere in Europe) shared many assumptions and expectations. Clergy and religious were held to different standards (see below), but the upper-class layman's code, inherited from Antiquity through the Middle Ages (and which trickled down to other social groups), prescribed three characteristics for the masculine role that are relevant to the present studies:

1 Virility: Men are to be sexually active and not passive, to penetrate women and beget offspring.
2 Aggression: They are to build physical strength and martial skills, in order to fight for clan and country.
3 Stoicism: They are to develop self-control, suppressing their own emotions in order to control others with strategic objectivity.

Within this schema of values, demands, and taboos, male beauty and male emotions – particularly male-male desire – posed endless dilemmas. There is by now an abundant and complex bibliography on masculinity and its discontents – to adapt the title of Sigmund Freud's foundational study of the eternal conflict between self and civilization. The present essays were originally presented at the

2020 conference "Masculinities in the Premodern World: Continuities, Change, and Contradictions," at the University of Toronto. In their call for participation, the conference co-organizers Konrad Eisenbichler and Jacqueline Murray welcomed the "bourgeoning of studies on sexuality and gender in the pre-modern world." They went on to frame this current research in terms of methodologies and genres that undergird many of the chapters below: "Building on the theoretical perspectives provided by feminism, Foucault, and cultural studies, the study of men and masculinities is increasingly theoretically inflected and sophisticated."[3]

While a detailed review of recent scholarship is beyond the scope of this volume, we might recall that the evolution of gender and sexuality studies, male division, was unwittingly triggered by feminist scholars of the 1970s, such as the art historian Linda Nochlin, whose 1971 essay "Why Have There Been No Great Women Artists?" opened the gates to interrogation of existing behavioural norms for women.[4] Early feminist scholars in art and literature, who emphasized empirical recuperations of overlooked or suppressed female creativity, then found conceptual allies in the post-structuralism of Michel Foucault and other French theoreticians; Foucault's *History of Sexuality* (4 vols., English translation 1978) inspired numerous further studies of eros and the body, both male and female.[5] Their emphasis on the arbitrary and contingent construction of sexual and gender identities and the controlling power of official discourse sensitized subsequent researchers to the inherent contradictions and anomalies within general normative practices, and the presence of alternative consciousness in the margins and interstices of ostensibly consistent and fixed social and artistic structures.

This epistemic revolution was further complicated by Judith Butler, whose *Gender Trouble: Feminism and the Subversion of Identity* (1990) theorized that gender is not innate or fixed, but rather a self-fashioning performance of specified codes of behaviour (or deliberate violation of them). In the present volume, Butler's insight informs, for example, Sara Diaz's study of Margarita Costa's satire of young male *zerbini*, who assumed an artificial social and gendered role of the aesthetic fop.

It soon became obvious that conceptions of femininity were inextricable from concepts of masculinity, each defined reciprocally by what it is not. This awareness sparked extensive research both on the social history of men's gender and sexuality[6] and on representations of their bodies and acts in the arts.[7] Most recently, three further essay collections on early modern masculinities, stemming, like this volume, from the 2021 Toronto conference, provide a wide range of further examples of contemporary interests and methods, plus ample bibliography.[8]

One salient characteristic of much of this new work is hybridity: the essays in this collection often cross-pollinate between traditional disciplines and methodologies, begetting mixed seedlings like Hoffman's combination of Shakespeare studies with Bakhtinian theory. In the same spirit, Kate Driscoll ("Wounded Histories on the Stages of Old and New Worlds: Vivaldi's *Motezuma* and the Cries of Conquest"; 171–98) views Venetian musical theatre through the lens of colonial studies, while Anne Williams ("Blasphemous or Beautiful? Leonardo da Vinci's *Saint John the Baptist*: Holy Masculinity and Its Ambiguities ca. 1500"; 52–76) unpacks traditional Christian iconography in the light of Leonardo's Aristotelian philosophy. Filtered through the eyes of such diverse cultural observers, the male persona resembles an object seen in a kaleidoscope: broken down into a shifting array of facets, fragments, and partial views, reconfiguring each time we turn the prism. Or, as Driscoll phrases it in musical terms, the "polyphony" of perspectives offered in this collection provides both an overview of current avenues of research and tantalizing suggestions for future directions.

That complex methodological counterpoint weaves together several repeating and overlapping themes that merit some brief prefatory observations, roughly corresponding to the thematic groupings of the essays laid out in the table of contents

Religion: Heavenly Art, Earthly Bodies

Several essays anatomize the tangled nexus between masculinity and religion, examining the role of Catholic (and Anglican) belief and practice in producing anxiety around the male (and female) body and psyche. The Church is omnipresent in discussions of gender because it commissioned so many artworks illustrating scantily clad male saints and divinities and because, were it not for the faith's fundamental hierarchization of spirit over flesh and male over female, there would have been far less controversy surrounding the eroticized and/or feminized male in post-antique Western culture.

Christian theology is profoundly ambivalent about corporeality. The human body, biblically created in the image of God, models an uplifting manifestation of the divine soul within each mortal vessel – a union that reaches its mystical apogee in the handsome young carpenter's body of Jesus himself, whose Incarnation literally injected the godhead into our somatic clay. But it can also become a site of fleshly temptation, a handle for Satan to drag the struggling soul down into the heaven-foreclosing swamp of sinful appetites. Since Christ was male, and God, while officially incorporeal, was traditionally figured and illustrated as the Father, the Church needed a subtle form of "media management" in the arts. Painters were encouraged to exploit the sensuous ideal beauty of a holy figure in order to arouse male churchgoers' passionate identification and devotion, but without straying across the border into the enemy territory of sodomy – which, because it inverted the canonical active male role into a passive one, was among the most reviled of sins.

Both Steven Stowell ("Bathing and Bonding: Sensual Male Imagery in Italian Paintings of Baptism"; 23–51) and Anne Williams explicate the conflicting attitudes towards saintly male bodies by analysing the complex messages men received when gazing upon representations of such young male nudes as John the Baptist, John the Evangelist, Sebastian, and Jesus himself. In "Blasphemous or Beautiful?" Williams assembles period writings testifying to the belief that corporeal beauty symbolizes and celebrates a privileged spiritual relationship with divinity. Both authors focus on the symbolism of androgyny: an ideal fusion of male and female bodily characteristics, alternately viewed as the exemplary outward sign of a pure hybrid soul embracing both masculine and feminine traits, or as an evocation of gender-deviant sexual appeal. The womanized bodies of these paragons evoke their traditionally "feminine" religious virtues of compassion, humility, and piety, helping the male faithful to yearn for these virtuous bodies, elevated to a plane of angelic seductiveness, as "a consummation devoutly to be wished" (giving back to Hamlet's deathly "consummation" its sexualized connotation).

Laura Smoller's "Sharing a Bed with Dominic: Celibacy and Masculinity in the Cult of Saint Vincent Ferrer" (79–96) transposes these issues of holy masculinity from sacred representations to the everyday life of mortal clergy, especially monks and friars, for whom the demands of the flesh clashed with the demands of holy orders. The Dominican missionary-friar Saint Vincent Ferrer's (d. 1419) celebrated vision – in which Saint Dominic sat with him on the bed in his cell, praised his spirituality, and slept with him overnight before vanishing – made his numerous chroniclers squeamish about the whiff of physical intimacy hovering around the encounter. Tracing the historiography of this canonical episode in Ferrer's biographies from the fifteenth through the sixteenth centuries, Smoller tellingly demonstrates the extent of official fears over sexual irregularities in all-male, theoretically celibate institutions.

Churchmen's anxiety was aroused by three intersecting problems: clerical masculinity, the demands of celibacy, and the prevalence of sodomy. On one hand, abstention from women was held to demonstrate an admirably masculine spiritual self-control, while on the other, the obvious sexual alternative, available in every cloister, provided a ready (if equally taboo) outlet for their pent-up erotic energy. Add to the mix the feminization of monks – often assigned such traditional "women's work" as prayer, charity, and caring for the old, sick, and poor – and we see that monastics were simultaneously emasculated and feminized, compounding the reasons to suspect deviant sexuality among them (quite justifiably).

Women and Men: Masculinity, Effeminacy, and Desire

While all the essays aim to trace the contours of masculine roles and rules, two focus mainly on women, as subject or author, emphasizing how notions of masculinity are always already imbricated with conceptions of femininity. As Giuliano de' Medici posits in his discussion of the ideal female in Baldassare Castiglione's *Book of the Courtier* (1528), "Although they [men and women] have in common some qualities, which are as necessary to the man as to the woman, there are yet others befitting a woman rather than a man, and others again which befit a man but which a woman should regard as completely foreign to her."[9] In "*A Dio Zerbini a Dio, a Dio Narcisi*: Satirizing Effeminacy in Margherita Costa's Florentine Works (1638–1641)" (117–40), Sara Díaz parses the writings of the author and performer Costa, notably her savage criticism of a familiar type of foppish young males, nicknamed *zerbini* ("doormats") for their obsequious (and seldom successful) wooing of disdainful females. She compares them unfavourably to such archetypes of youthful, feminized homosexuality as Ganymede and Narcissus, "in ways that reveal the fault lines between transgressive effeminacy and heteronormative masculinity" (117).

By mocking these under-virilized men, Costa arrogates to herself enforcement of the boundaries of masculine behaviour, a tactic in the struggle to establish her own authorial legitimacy against the prevailing male stereotypes of women's intellectual and creative inferiority. Ironically, she builds up the gender-transgressive authority of her "masculine" pronouncements at the expense of a subaltern group whom she castigates for their failure to live up to the standard male role. Costa thus reinscribes the very same masculine-feminine binary that she (like other women of her time) was attempting to loosen for herself. Its content aside, however, Costa's claim on a public voice – by the act of writing about anything at all – was a successful intervention in the long campaign to broaden boundaries of gender permissibility.

While Díaz examines how a woman looked at men, Tara White's essay on "Masculine-Feminine Dichotomy in the Sixteenth Century:

Mythological *Donna con Donna* Images from Fontainebleau and Northern Italy" (141–68) lays out how men looked at groups of women together. She demonstrates that the same traditional hierarchy exploited by Costa is the key to understanding male concepts of intimate relationships between women, as depicted in images of nude females bathing or lounging. She juxtaposes them to period texts about female-female love from Ludovico Ariosto's *Orlando furioso* to Pierre de Brantôme's *Vies des dames galantes* – all by men, since first-person lesbian testimony was scarce and sporadic until later centuries.

White observes that in each female pairing, one partner's skin tone is noticeably darker than the other's, adapting the ancient visual convention for distinguishing ruddy male from pale female bodies; the couples' figural types and body language similarly maintain the social and visual conventions of an active, "masculine" partner and a passive, "feminine" one. Male artists and viewers, she concludes, simply could not imagine female sexuality without one partner, despite being female, taking the traditionally male role of aggressive instigator. Unfortunately, we have precious little first-person testimony to what such women themselves thought they were doing, but in any case, their perspectives mattered far less in both moral discourse and artistic expression than those of phallocentric male theologians, lawmakers, and artists.

As both authors demonstrate, complementary binaries like masculine/feminine can exist only in dialectical relation to one another; whether in love or war, women help to define what a man is by exemplifying what he is not. Moreover, like the females of many other species, early modern women were enlisted to reinforce male social expectations, by evaluating and rewarding prospective mates for achieving the masculine ideal of physical prowess. As the reluctant nymph Astérie, in Henri Desmarest's 1694 opera *Circé*, admonishes her frustrated suitor, Ulysses' fellow warrior Polite, "Glory has a thousand charms for me … Your courage could assure my affection."[10] Hence, despite perpetual discursive attempts to establish two mutually exclusive spheres, each ineluctably depends on the other.

Knowledge and Emotions: Forbidden and Required

However much men and women may be mutually defined by contrast, some of our authors call attention to male behaviour that appropriates elements of the traditionally feminine range of emotions. As Driscoll shows in her analysis of Antonio Vivaldi's 1733 opera about the defeated Aztec ruler Montezuma, the genre of lamentation – of vocal mourning for loss – was traditionally marked as feminine: how women react to what men do. Early modern canons of masculinity espoused a principle still familiar in many a parent's admonition to male children, "Big boys don't cry." Failing to maintain the required façade of stoic invincibility would signal weakness and vulnerability, unacceptable admissions for the impenetrable body and mind. Driscoll examines an exceptional male outburst of sorrow, justified by its historical circumstances: a situation in which "men's actions make other men cry" (177).

Vivaldi's librettist permits the Aztec emperor to indulge the gender-atypical elegiac mode – in part, perhaps, because as a non-European he was already feminized as inferior and subordinate. But also, as Driscoll proposes, because the vanquished can exploit the lament's potential for reparative history, for propagating an alternative counter-narrative of events to the history written (as always) by the victors. We might call this tactic "subversive femininity." If, as the poet Audre Lorde declares, "The master's tools will never dismantle the master's house,"[11] then at least the loser against a master's military tools can appropriate some of the mistress's emotional tools to salvage agency and dignity. Montezuma's "womanish" keening over his people's doomed struggle reframes the theme of what the Spanish "conquistadores" perpetrated, from "their" victory to "our" heroic Aztec resistance.

To grasp the subversive gendered potential of Montezuma's politically revisionist soliloquy, compare it to the ancient heroine Dido's more conventionally self-abnegating lament in Purcell's opera *Dido and Aeneas* (ca. 1685). Despite having good reason to seek revenge on her lover Aeneas, who has broken his promise to live faithfully with her, the queen of Carthage opts for the customary female suicide, out of shame over losing the battle of love. In her final aria, she apologetically forswears any intent to rewrite the thoughts and feelings of her listeners: "When I am laid in earth / May my wrongs create / No trouble in thy breast; / Remember me, but ah! Forget my fate!"[12]

In "Male Courtly Feeling and the Historical Performativity of Shyness in *A Midsummer Night's Dream*," Tiffany Hoffman explores the shifting valence in the male psyche of interlinked emotions – also traditionally classified as female – of timidity, shyness, and stage fright, across the play's broad spectrum of nobles, lovers, and rustics. Hoffman operates within a psychological frame that might classify this constellation of emotional behaviours as components of "performance anxiety." As Judith Butler has emphasized, performance can reference a make-believe theatrical role, or equally, one's real-life social role. Anyone of any sex can experience such nervous self-doubt about meeting society's criteria, but the most revealing characters in Hoffman's analysis are the mechanicals, the humble male craftworkers who, in the course of preparing a mythological playlet to entertain the duke's court, are simultaneously real people *and* actors. It was a daunting enough challenge for upper-class males as their job description shifted from clobbering others to engaging with them in cooperative deliberations and sophisticated verbal entertainments, like the ones memorably captured in Castiglione's *Courtier*. In turn, the lower orders were chronically – and in the mechanicals' case, comically – insecure about their ability to mimic this new genteel, educated standard they thought they should aspire to.

As longstanding values and symbols wore out, many of those elite men were beset by doubts about their masculinity and how to perform or display it to maintain status and prestige. Cervantes' Don Quixote, the would-be knight errant, is a tragicomic character precisely because he alone refuses to acknowledge the utter obsolescence by the 1600s of the chivalric world he dreams of in medieval romances. Most men were more realistic and found ways to adapt, such as the sudden early sixteenth-century fashion for full, showy facial hair – a primary signifier of maleness. The proximate cause was Pope Julius II's decision to let his beard grow as a classical sign of mourning for his military defeats, a form of nonverbal "lament" from a warrior-priest. But his temporary grooming model was copied far, fast, and long because, as Patricia Simons and others have demonstrated, it answered a need for substitute outward signs of virile masculinity to compensate for those that were disappearing. If men could no longer be eagles, they would at least be peacocks.[13]

Audience Response: From Transmitter to Receiver

As a corollary to our authors' interest in emotional norms and how they are internalized, a number of essays, cutting across thematic categories, seek to recuperate the viewer's or reader's subjective reactions to cultural messages. The methodology of spectator response, or reception theory, asks how gender is consciously experienced from within. Its focus is less on epistemology – how conceptions of gender were created and transmitted – than on phenomenology: how these expectations impacted individual men in their spiritual life and their conscious decisions to resist or accommodate profound social changes. These authors' questions move beyond "How did men think?" to "What did men feel?"

Anne Williams expresses most explicitly the impulse behind her re-examination of Leonardo's *Saint John the Baptist*: "attempting to reconstruct the painting's devotional implications for the period viewer" (52). Part of that attempt is a historiographical rebuttal to older, moralizing readings of the figure's androgyny: "[Previous authors] assumed that for his period viewer, Leonardo's *Saint John* was understood to be 'deviant' with respect to both gender and religious norms. However, period accounts of the painting remark not on blasphemy, but beauty" (52). Steven Stowell similarly asks about audience reaction: What did male parishioners see, think, and feel when face to face with images of Christ and the Baptist that were idealized, largely nude, and in which the two beautiful youths look so similar as to conjure extra-biblical associations of sacred twins and *all'antica* love between men? Unfortunately, such internal reactions are notoriously difficult to make out through the historical mists, notably the dearth of first-person testimony from all those who were illiterate, poor, female, or gender-deviant.

In sharp contrast to these attractive, if ambiguous, portrayals of virtuous beauty, Marco Piana's "The Body of Christ: Suffering and Desire in Gianfrancesco Pico della Mirandola's *De Venere et Cupidine Expellendis*" (97–114) unpacks a deliberate attempt to steer viewers' subjective responses to religious art in the opposite direction. Influenced by the fiercely ascetic Ferrarese friar Girolamo Savonarola, Pico's 1493 poem preaches that the widespread devotional practice of meditating on the gruesome suffering and repulsive body of the crucified Jesus – a common subject in visual art – can act as an antidote to physical desire, a form of spiritual exercise potentially strengthening the soul to withstand the ephemeral temptations of earthly beauty.

While the mental universe of most ordinary people is lost to us, the educated elite is better documented, allowing provocative glimpses into the formation of an individual consciousness. Jacobean playwright Ben Jonson's close reading of the multiple handwritten annotations in printed Latin versions of the Roman satirist Martial's blunt, often coarsely sexual *Epigrams* (ca. 100 CE) demonstrates how alternative sources could provide an early modern reader with mental furniture not easily available in the bare text or in bowdlerized translations. Ian Moulton, in "Latin Epigrams and Early Modern Sexual Knowledge: Or, How Jonson Read His Martial" (221–44), notes the irony that, while Martial himself mockingly disapproved of the unorthodox or nonprocreative male sexual practices that he described (anything not active and penetrating), his published editions and learned commentaries constituted a channel for covert transmission of precisely that erotic knowledge, a rare cornucopia of pre-Christian practices. Jonson, like his classical predecessor, also condemned the same behaviours, but the larger point is that a near-encyclopaedic knowledge of transgressive sexuality among the ancients was available to those with the necessary linguistic skills and, with that, the potential for critiquing modern values and cultural forms in a comparative historical perspective.

Past, Present, and Future: Some Personal Reflections

These essays seldom draw overt parallels to the contemporary world, but all scholarship is informed by its time and social context – including this Introduction. Like Williams, I myself have written on the erotic undertones of Saint Sebastian. That, along with being cited in this volume's endnotes, for a book published twenty-five years ago, hopefully justifies some brief personal reminiscences, offering a historical perspective from my now three generations of digging in the trenches of sex and gender.

When I was an art history graduate student in the 1970s, second-wave feminism had only recently opened the door to wider and better-contextualized considerations of both sexes, while the discipline that became known as gay studies, then queer studies, and now shelters under the umbrella of sex, gender, and sexuality studies, was but a twinkle in the eye of scattered academics activated by the Stonewall riots of 1969.

My first published article – which appeared in 1977 in a short-lived journal of the Gay Academic Union (an early professional group for the few hundred scholars across all disciplines who were labouring to lay the foundations of gay/lesbian studies) – attempted to establish Sebastian as a "gay icon" by the fifteenth century. It was rightly criticized for a shortage of period sources attesting to the sentiments I was reading into his images and their audience. The sad truth was that, for that founding generation of gender and sexuality researchers, so little reliable information was then available that we often had to start (as I had) from intuition and informed speculation. This dearth of empirical evidence was especially problematic because many of us came to academia by way of political activism, and (as with women's studies) the discipline retained in its first decades an aura of outsider advocacy that made traditionalists wary of "special pleading."

Thus, I could not help smiling at the gradual shift in consciousness that enabled Stowell's analysis of the homosocial undertones in Masolino's 1437 fresco of John baptizing Jesus. I studied this artist with the beloved septuagenarian Columbia University professor Howard Davis, whose elegant but exclusively formalist analyses never raised such social or psychological questions. Like most established academics then, he was clueless about the fresh breezes blowing through progressive circles – though at least, unlike some scholars and critics who actively resisted or belittled these new approaches, he was not hostile. When I proposed to write a feminist psychoanalysis of (probably homosexual) Sandro Botticelli's images of women, Davis shrugged blankly, "Well, I see no reason why you *can't* do it."

Two generations later, everyone, including the younger authors in this volume, *can* "do it" in gender studies. Subsequent scholars have amply fleshed out our tentative schemata and built upon them, vastly enriching the discipline's depth of accumulated background and historiographic guideposts – and many readers and students see the reasons why they want to. By the late 1980s, a second generation of gender-studies specialists emerged, university-trained, suckled on post-structuralist theory, and adept at deconstructing the often-politicized connections between culture, knowledge, and power. As gender studies grew both more empirically grounded and theoretically sophisticated, it gradually became acceptable within mainstream academic circles – both a cause and effect of the increasing social integration of women and minorities. I was granted tenure in 1991 on the strength of my translation of Michelangelo's poetry, which frankly acknowledged for the first time the artist's homosexual desire and self-expression; at least in educated urban circles, studies of nontraditional gender and sexuality were no longer professional suicide, but a positive career choice.

The satisfaction of witnessing the discipline expand and mature is offset by the wistfulness of missed opportunities: the awareness that my earlier writings could have been more convincing or nuanced "if only I'd known" some subsequently discovered corroborating fact, text, or image back when I was doing related research in less enlightened decades. Five years ago, for example, I published a study of the Italian artist Sodoma, more conclusively homosexual than Botticelli, and painter of one of the best-known and most clearly homoerotic versions of Saint Sebastian, from 1525.[14] This time around, my gender analysis could draw on testimony from many sources – literary, religious, visual, documentary – unearthed in the four decades since my first ill-fated essay; but I wish I had also been able to include the complaint that Williams now recounts from religious reformer Ulrich Zwingli, written in that very same year, warning against the erotic temptation of beautiful nude saints (55).

Similarly, I wish I had read her contextualization of John 3:29 when I was writing about Sodoma's fresco *The Marriage of Alexander the Great and Roxana*, in which the handsome Greek emperor's male beloved, Hephaestion, stands nude in supportive witness as his equally beloved master crowns his new bride. Williams focuses on the official theological meaning of the biblical passage, in which John the Baptist graciously gives way to the greater destiny of his beloved cousin and near-twin, Jesus, who will leave him for a higher love, the symbolic marriage with God: "He who has the bride is the bridegroom; but the friend of the bridegroom, who stands and hears him, rejoices greatly because of the bridegroom's voice. This my joy is therefore fulfilled" (61).

But John's bittersweet sentiments could as easily issue from the mouth of Hephaestion, himself depicted as strikingly similar to Alexander. Such crossover between pagan and Christian symbolism was a time-honoured process, with religious glosses layered onto many classical narratives. Though I leave it to some future scholar to seek any supporting documents, my initial intuition and informed speculation wonders whether Sodoma or his learned, often libertine audience might have had this text in mind when gazing upon his scene of passionate bisexuality. Here, as with the Baptist and the Evangelist, Classical and Christian, body and spirit, male and female swirl together into a dense cloud of fluid, overlapping gender possibilities yet to be fully unpacked.

For my generation, it is immensely gratifying to have helped set academia on a half-century odyssey towards a fuller critical understanding of early modern patterns of sexuality, gender, and representation. At the same time, my smile turns rueful with the concomitant realization that, like Moses gazing into the distant promised land, nature and time will preclude us veterans from witnessing the further unfolding of that historical progress.

Through a Glass, Darkly

To a significant segment of contemporary society, however, this historical fantasia is not a dream but a nightmare. While it is heartening to look back on how much positive evolution has occurred in the social and intellectual realms since the homophobic and misogynistic 1970s, it is disheartening to acknowledge that today's third generation of teachers and researchers face a resurgent tide of resistance, both elite and populist, to the questions and methods of our discipline. Part of a wider distrust of rational discourse and social change, this trend is disturbingly reminiscent of that earlier, tradition-bound era many thought we had left behind. The ivory tower is a misleading metaphor: both yesteryear and today, the academic study of sexuality and gender is encircled by the wider landscape of cultural production. Gazing outward from on high may afford a broader, more sharply focused overview of the historical past, but it cannot escape present conditions down on the ground.

This anthology enters the public forum at a polarized and uncertain historical juncture, marked by the rise of reactionary movements, and even whole nations, that aggressively aim to turn back the clock to narrowly traditional sexual, gender, and other individual limits.

Both Canada and the United States are grappling with belligerently conservative, often violent extremists not unlike those clamping down on Hungary, Russia, and Iran. Outlawing sexual variations like homosexuality and transgender, banning books, and denying women control over reproduction are principal planks in the broader authoritarian agenda: an unquestioned and ahistorical social uniformity in which Driscoll's "polyphony" of potentially destabilizing inquiry into sexual evolution is a heresy to be silenced. Despite Queen Victoria having been dead for well over a century, the puritanical squeamishness of her era about frank, nonjudgmental discussion of sexual topics has been, as her ancestor Charles II apologized, "a most unconscionable time a-dying."

Like it or not, what we do has a political dimension. When forces of moral absolutism, legal proscription, and censorship are intensifying efforts to naturalize and universalize obsolete customs and values, the mission of the academy – to foster open, critical, and objective minds – is more crucial than ever. By exposing fault lines and shifts in gender regimes of the past, the historians in this volume are continuing to transmit the central message of cultural history, increasingly under attack: that "man-made" social conventions have been, and could always become, other than what they are now.

Not all historians are social activists, but all historians know well the potential cultural and psychological impact of literature, art, and theatre: that is what we study, after all. And while we adhere to the canons of professional neutrality, scholars in our field often have some personal investment in their chosen subject. Specialists in, say, early modern Italy and England – like those in this volume – may be neither Italian nor English, and they certainly are not early modern. But everyone has a gender – nowadays, in an era of sexual fluidity, sometimes more than one. After postmodernism, we are admonished to acknowledge our own subject position, and there is no shame in having one. It might even enhance a historian's skills of analysis and empathy towards our long-vanished objects of study to acknowledge, in Sara Driscoll's apt phrase, that "the overlapping concerns of the personal and the political are as resonant today as they were centuries ago" (176).

Half a millennium after the events chronicled in this volume's nine essays, the male body and psyche remain hotly disputed territory within which defenders of the status quo – nostalgic, like Don Quixote, for the vanished fantasy of medieval certainty and uniformity – are fighting zealously to disarm, imprison, or expel "foreign" models of sex and gender. It is not for the historian to urge future action, but to trace the processes of the past that have brought us to this present – the better to comprehend how we got here, and the need for vigilance against those who feel threatened by attempts to rethink the power that sex and gender literally embody.

We may hope that these deeply thought essays, which further extend our lengthening chain of knowledge, will in turn inspire yet another generation to delve ever more deeply into both the early modern gender imaginary and the social reality of that formative stage in an ongoing cultural evolution. May their inquiry expand our comprehension of both the early modern world and its modern descendants, who continue to grapple with the same dilemmas and conflicting emotions. And may they continue to enjoy the freedom to do so.

NOTES

1 Hoffman, "Male Courtly Feeling," 200.

2 See, e.g., Karras, *From Boys to Men*; Shepard, *Meanings of Manhood in Early Modern England*; Bridges and Pascoe, "Hybrid Masculinities"; Thomas, *In Pursuit of Civility*.

3 See the Call for Papers at https://trrc.itergateway.org/2020_conference.

4 Nochlin, "Why Have There Been No Great Women Artists?"; reprinted in Nochlin, *Women, Art, and Power and Other Essays*, 145–78.

5 See, e.g., Matthews-Grieco, *Erotic Cultures of Renaissance Italy*; Levy, *Sex Acts in Early Modern Italy*.

6 For a brief overview, see the relevant chapters in Kent, *Gender: A World History*. See also Gardiner, ed., *Masculinity Studies and Feminist Theory*; Rocke, *Forbidden Friendships*; Traub, *Thinking Sex with the Early Moderns*.

7 Turner, *Sexuality and Gender in Early Modern Europe*, explores connections between social behaviour and cultural representation across media, as does Simons, *The Sex of Men in Premodern Europe*. More specifically on visual arts, see Rubin, *Seen from Behind*; Saslow, "The Desiring Eye." For a detailed case study of a bisexual sculptor, see Gallucci, *Benvenuto Cellini*. In literature: Vaught, *Masculinity and Emotion*; Bates, *Masculinity, Gender and Identity*; Milligan and Tylus, eds., *The Poetics of Masculinity*. Theatre and performance studies date back to, e.g., Kahn, *Man's Estate*; Orgel, *Impersonations*.

8 Eisenbichler and Murray, eds., *Premodern Masculinities in Transition*; Murray, ed., *The Male Body and Social Masculinity*; Murray, *Patriarchy, Honour, and Violence*.

9 Castiglione, *The Book of the Courtier*, 211.

10 Saintonge and Desmarest, *Circé*, act 5, lines 19–22: "La gloire a pour moi mille appas, / Je vous verrais voler au milieu des combats; / Sans vous laisser voir de faiblesse, / Votre valeur pourrait rassurer ma tendresse."

11 Lorde, "The Master's Tools," 110.
12 Tate and Purcell, *Dido and Aeneas*. Online.
13 See Rycroft, *Facial Hair*; Simons, "Marked Differences."
14 Saslow, "Gianantonio Bazzi, Called 'Il Sodoma.'"

WORKS CITED

Printed Sources

Bates, Catherine. *Masculinity, Gender and Identity in the English Renaissance Lyric*. Cambridge: Cambridge University Press, 2007.

Bridges, Tristan, and C.J. Pascoe. "Hybrid Masculinities: New Directions in the Sociology of Men and Masculinities." *Sociology Compass* 8.3 (2014): 246–58.

Butler, Judith. *Gender Trouble: Feminism and the Subversion of Identity*. New York: Routledge, 1990.

Castiglione, Baldassare. *The Book of the Courtier*. Trans. George Bull. Harmondsworth: Penguin, 1967.

Eisenbichler, Konrad, and Jacqueline Murray, eds. *Premodern Masculinities in Transition*. Gender in the Middle Ages. Woodbridge, UK: Boydell & Brewer, forthcoming 2024.

Gallucci, Margaret. *Benvenuto Cellini: Sexuality, Masculinity, and Artistic Identity in Renaissance Italy*. New York: Palgrave, 2003.

Gardiner, Judith Kegan, ed. *Masculinity Studies and Feminist Theory: New Directions*. New York: Columbia University Press, 2002.

Hoffman, Tiffany. "Male Courtly Feeling and the Historical Performativity of Shyness in *A Midsummer Night's Dream*." In Konrad Eisenbichler, ed., *Masculinities and Representation: The Eroticized Male in Early Modern Italy and England*. Toronto: University of Toronto Press, 2024, 199–220.

Kahn, Coppelia. *Man's Estate: Masculine Identity in Shakespeare*. Berkeley: University of California Press, 1981.

Karras, Ruth Mazo. *From Boys to Men: Formations of Masculinity in Late Medieval Europe*. Philadelphia: University of Pennsylvania Press, 2003.

Kent, Susan Kingsley. *Gender: A World History*. New York: Oxford University Press, 2021.

Levy, Allison, ed. *Sex Acts in Early Modern Italy*. Farnham, UK: Ashgate, 2010.

Lorde, Audre. "The Master's Tools Will Never Dismantle the Master's House." In Audre Lorde, *Sister Outsider: Essays and Speeches*. Trumansburg, NY: Crossing Press, 1984, 110–13. (Comments at "The Personal and the Political Panel," Second Sex Conference, New York, 29 September 1979, originally published in 1979.)

Matthews-Grieco, Sara, ed. *Erotic Cultures of Renaissance Italy*. Farnham, UK: Ashgate, 2010.

Milligan, Gerry, and Jane Tylus, eds. *The Poetics of Masculinity in Early Modern Italy and Spain*. Essays and Studies 22. Toronto: Centre for Reformation and Renaissance Studies, 2010.

Murray, Jacqueline, ed. *The Male Body and Social Masculinity in Premodern Europe*. Essays and Studies 56. Toronto: Centre for Renaissance and Reformation Studies, 2022.

– *Patriarchy, Honour, and Violence: Masculinities in Premodern Europe*. Essays and Studies 57. Toronto: Centre for Renaissance and Reformation Studies, 2022.

Nochlin, Linda. "Why Have There Been No Great Women Artists?" *Art News* 69.9 (January 1971): 22–39 and 67–71.

– *Women, Art, and Power and Other Essays*. New York: Harper and Row, 1988.

Orgel, Stephen. *Impersonations: The Performance of Gender in Shakespeare's England*. Cambridge: Cambridge University Press, 1996.

Rocke, Michael. *Forbidden Friendships: Homosexuality and Male Culture in Renaissance Florence*. New York: Oxford University Press, 1996.

Rubin, Patricia Lee. *Seen from Behind: Perspectives on the Male Body and Renaissance Art*. New Haven: Yale University Press, 2018.

Rycroft, Eleanor. *Facial Hair and the Performance of Masculinity*. New York: Routledge, 2019.

Saslow, James M. "The Desiring Eye: Gender, Sexuality, and the Visual Arts." In Babette Bohn and James M. Saslow, eds., *A Companion to Renaissance and Baroque Art*. Chichester: Wiley-Blackwell, 2013, 127–48.

– "Gianantonio Bazzi, Called 'Il Sodoma': Homosexuality in Art, Life, and History." In Jacqueline Murray and Nicholas Terpstra, eds., *Sex, Gender and Sexuality in Renaissance Art*. Oxford: Routledge, 2019, 183–210.

Shepard, Alexandra. *Meanings of Manhood in Early Modern England*. Oxford Studies in Social History. Oxford: Oxford University Press, 2006.

Simons, Patricia. *The Sex of Men in Premodern Europe: A Cultural History*. Cambridge and New York: Cambridge University Press, 2011.

– "Marked Differences: Beards in Renaissance Europe." In Konrad Eisenbichler and Jacqueline Murray, eds. *Premodern Masculinities in Transition*. Gender in the Middle Ages series. Woodbridge, UK: Boydell & Brewer, forthcoming 2024.

Thomas, Keith. *In Pursuit of Civility: Manners and Civilization in Early Modern England*. The Menahem Stern Jerusalem Lectures. New Haven and London: Yale University Press, 2018.

Traub, Valerie. *Thinking Sex with the Early Moderns*. Philadelphia: University of Pennsylvania Press, 2015.

Turner, James Grantham, ed. *Sexuality and Gender in Early Modern Europe: Institutions, Texts, Images*. Cambridge: Cambridge University Press, 1993.

Vaught, Jennifer C. *Masculinity and Emotion in Early Modern English Literature*. New York: Ashgate, 2008.

Electronic Sources

Saintonge, Louise-Geneviève Gillot de (librettist), and Henri Desmarest (composer). *Circé*. Ed. Gilbert Blin, trans. Ellen Hargis. Online at https://issuu.com/bostonearlymusicfestival/docs/bemf_circe_libretto. Accessed 10 July 2023.

Tate, Nahum (librettist), and Henry Purcell (composer). *Dido and Aeneas*. Online at https://home.olemiss.edu/~mudws/courses/dido.html. Accessed 10 July 2023.

PART ONE

Religion, Heavenly Art, Earthly Bodies

1 Bathing and Bonding: Sensual Male Imagery in Italian Paintings of Baptism

STEVEN F.H. STOWELL

Summary: Neophytes undressing in paintings of the Baptism of Christ – sometimes seen in Byzantine images – became common in fifteenth-century Italy, as for example in Masolino da Panicale's fresco at Castiglione Olona (1437). Scholars have proposed that this Byzantine motif may have originated in Italian art during negotiations for the unification of the Eastern and Western Churches, a theory that does not, however, explain its lingering popularity. By tracing the pictorial origins of the Italian neophytes (whose poses may derive from the ancient sculpture the *Spinario*), this article argues that the figures envision and idealize a masculine, homosocial intimacy bordering on eroticism. This is supported by examining Giorgio Vasari's descriptions of such figures in two key passages of his biographies of Renaissance artists, in which the imagery is linked to intergenerational relationships among master artists and apprentices, as well as to bathing more broadly, which was culturally understood as a context for homosocial gathering (sometimes leading to same-sex relations among men). The reappearance of figures in identical poses in contemporaneous images of Christ washing his apostles' feet – an event ritually re-enacted by clergy and confraternities – further suggests that this imagery carried associations of idealized, homosocial relations.

On the right-hand side of his 1437 fresco of *The Baptism of Christ*, Masolino da Panicale depicted a group of neophytes dressing and undressing, preparing for baptism (fig. 1.1). Among them is one who stands in an elegant contrapposto, his back facing the viewer, appearing to pull his white garment over his head, revealing a muscular frame and buttocks covered by a thin loin cloth. In her book on depictions of male

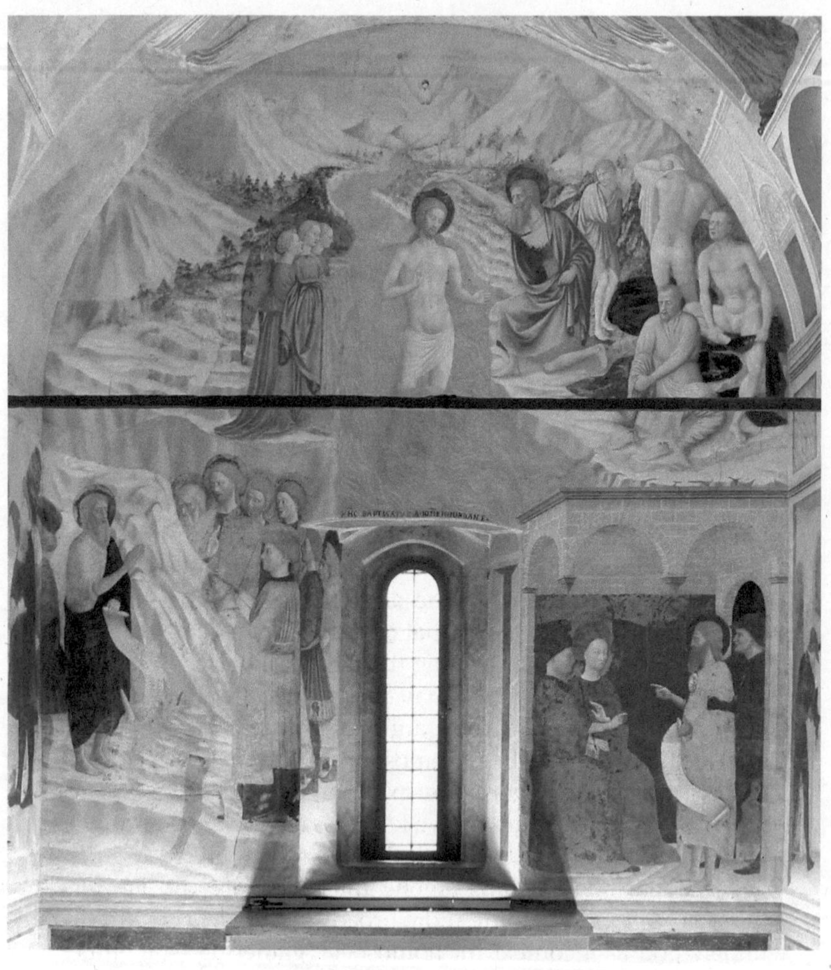

1.1. Masolino da Panicale, *The Baptism of Christ* (top); *The Baptist Preaching on the Banks of the River Jordan* (bottom left); *The Baptist Reproves Herod* (bottom right) (ca. 1435). The Baptistery, Castiglione Olona. Photo credit: Saliko/Wikimedia Commons. Original photo has been cropped by the author.

buttocks, Patricia Rubin described the figure as "one of the most naturalistic and idealized nudes painted to that date."[1] The pose of this figure, Rubin argues, is juxtaposed visually with Christ, whose contrapposto is nearly identical, though seen from the front. In covering his head and turning his back on Christ, the neophyte's pose, in Rubin's words, suggests spiritual blindness: "awaiting spiritual awakening, the perfection of baptism."[2]

Other figures in Masolino's fresco are also posed as opposites or reflections of one another. Farthest to the right, a man naked except for his loin cloth pulls a dark legging off his right foot in a pose reminiscent of the ancient sculpture the *Spinario* (fig. 1.2).[3] Beneath him is a man who is nearly his opposite: mostly dressed and putting *on* his sock. The creases in his stocking show he is straining to pull the fabric over his skin, perhaps because, having just been baptized, his feet are wet. Above these two are another contrasting pair: one huddles and wraps a yellow cloth around his shoulders, perhaps cold from the water, and beside him stands the earlier described neophyte seen from behind, uncovering his shoulders.[4] The variety of contrasting poses suggests at the very least that these figures were thoughtfully composed: they thematize the act of dressing and undressing, prompting us to ask what these bodies might have meant to contemporary viewers.

While Italian depictions of the baptism of Christ had usually figured Jesus, John, and attendant angels, in fifteenth-century images undressed catechumens became more common; they appear in Perugino's *Baptism of Christ* in the Sistine Chapel; Piero della Francesca's altarpiece now in the National Gallery, London; Ghirlandaio's frescos for Santa Maria Novella in Florence (fig. 1.3); and Masaccio's depiction of *St. Peter Baptizing the Neophytes* in the Brancacci chapel, to name a few (fig. 1.4).[5] In the sixteenth century, neophytes displaying their semi-nude bodies become even more elaborate, as in Paris Bordone's version (fig. 1.5), suggesting that the imagery held rich emotional meaning to viewers.

On the spiritual level, most obviously, by picturing the ritual of baptism as a joyous reunion with God, the image draws our attention to the shedding of clothes that represents the stripping off a vice.[6] Likewise, since baptism is necessitated by the original sin of Adam and Eve, taking off clothes to receive the sacrament may recall the clothes humans acquired after their expulsion from Paradise.[7] But this does not explain the particular relevance this imagery acquired in the fifteenth century. Drawing on literary sources and contextual history, this article will argue that these images envision and idealize a masculine, homosocial intimacy that borders on eroticism. I suggest, however, that the use of positive and negative exemplars seen in some of these images – like the

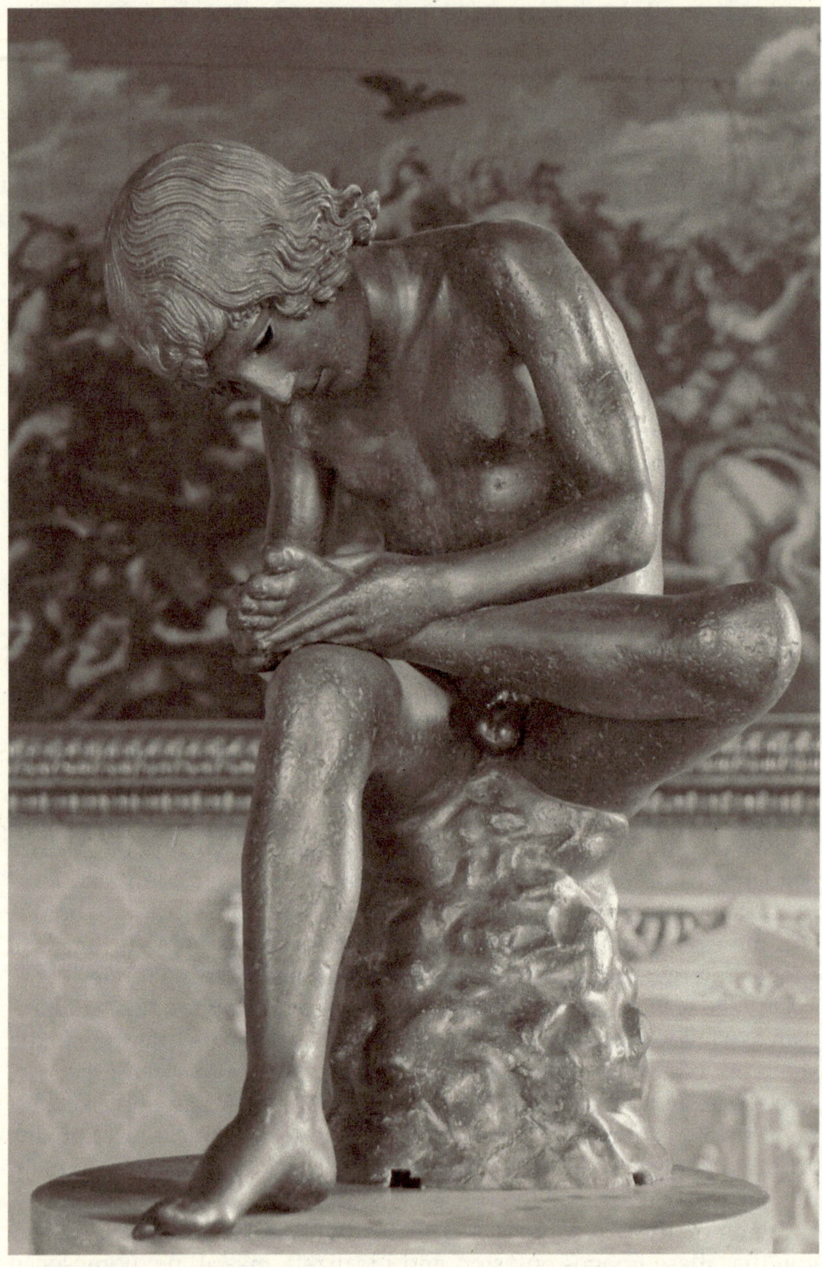

1.2. *Spinario*, first century. Musei Capitolini, Rome. Photo credit: © Marie-Lan Nguyen/Wikimedia Commons.

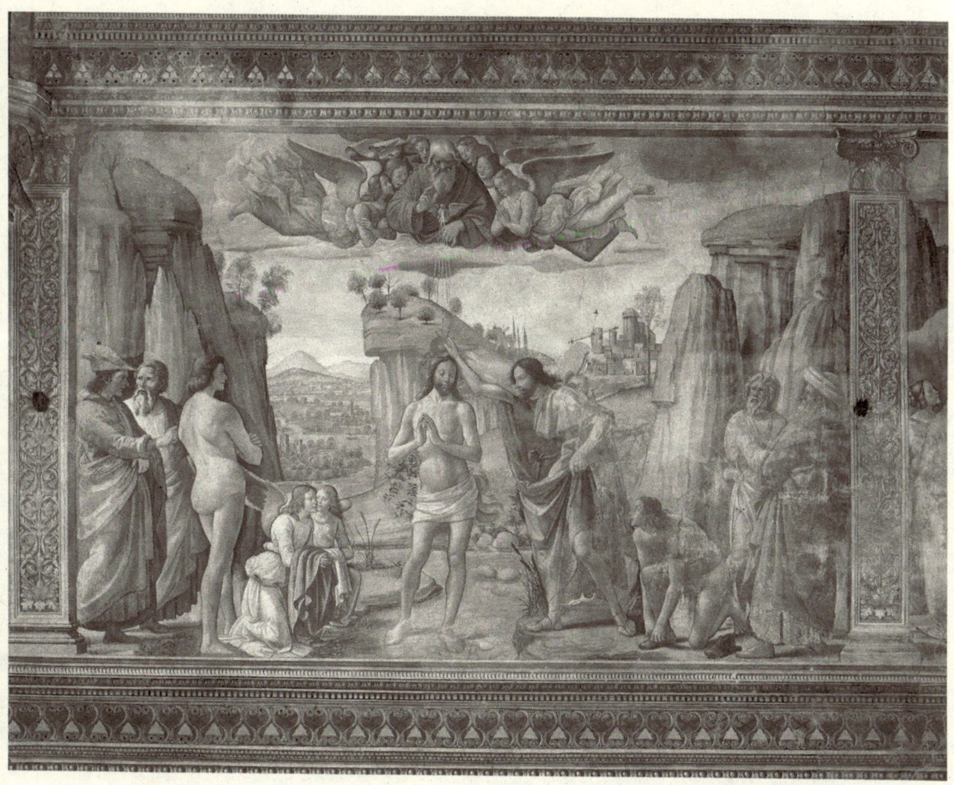

1.3. Domenico Ghirlandaio, *The Baptism of Christ* (1485–90). Tornabuoni Chapel, Santa Maria Novella, Florence. Photo credit: Scala/Art Resource, NY.

contrasting neophytes described above – is a visual device that casts potentially erotic imagery in a spiritual light.

In the fifteenth century, semi-nude neophytes arise in images predominantly created by Florentine artists, or artists who spent a significant amount of time in that city. In addition to the artists named above, this article will explore works by Mantegna, Fra Angelico, Michelangelo, and Andrea del Sarto. These paintings, however, were often created outside Florence, raising the question of how to interpret this imagery – whether in relation to the location where the painting was installed or the artists' culture of origin. While either approach has merits, this article adopts the latter method based on the assumption that artists create works that respond to their formative culture. The contextual material explored here is largely drawn from Florence in the fifteenth century (an important

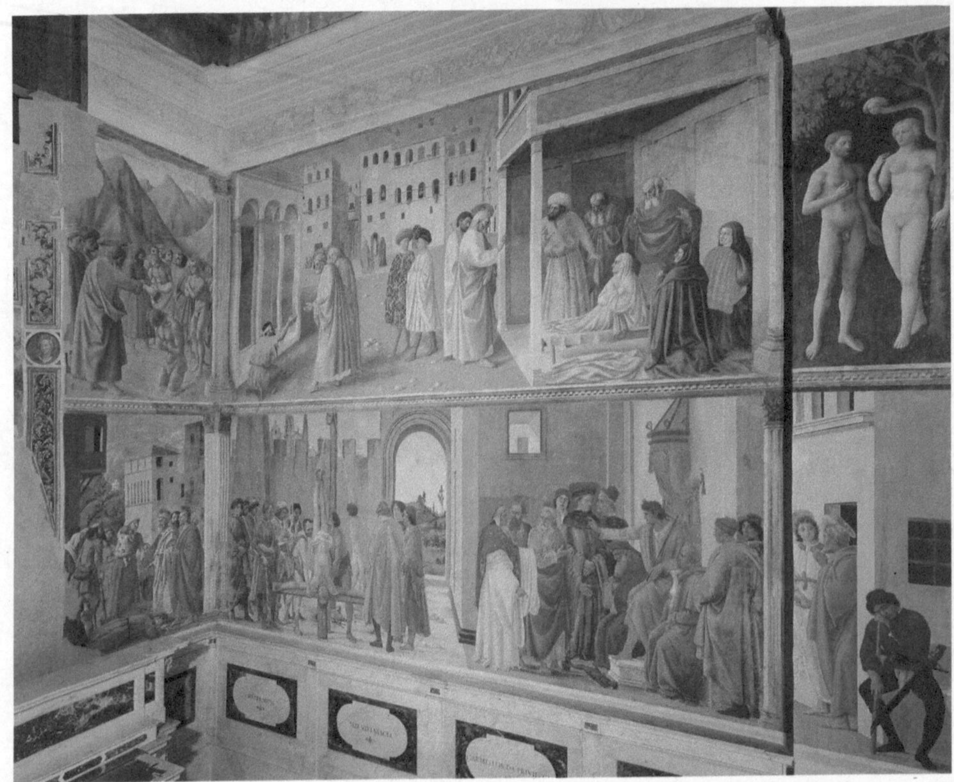

1.4. Masaccio, Masolino da Panicale, and Filippino Lippi, view of Brancacci Chapel showing *St. Peter Baptizing the Neophytes* (top left) and *The Temptation of Adam and Eve* (top right) and other scenes (ca. 1423–8, and 1484–5). Santa Maria del Carmine, Florence. Photo credit: Scala/Art Resource, NY.

exception is Giorgio Vasari's writing from the sixteenth century, though this source is deeply steeped in the artistic traditions of the century that preceded it). This is not to say that the location of the painting or the intended viewers did not play an important role in determining the nature of the imagery, and in fact earlier attempts to understand the neophytes have taken this approach. This study supplements rather than invalidates earlier research; indeed, the widespread nature of the imagery seems to necessitate multiple perspectives. Thus, while the images explored in this article are found in Florence, Rome, Castiglione Olona, and elsewhere, their meanings are explored through the culture of the artists who created them, all of whom spent formative time in Florence.

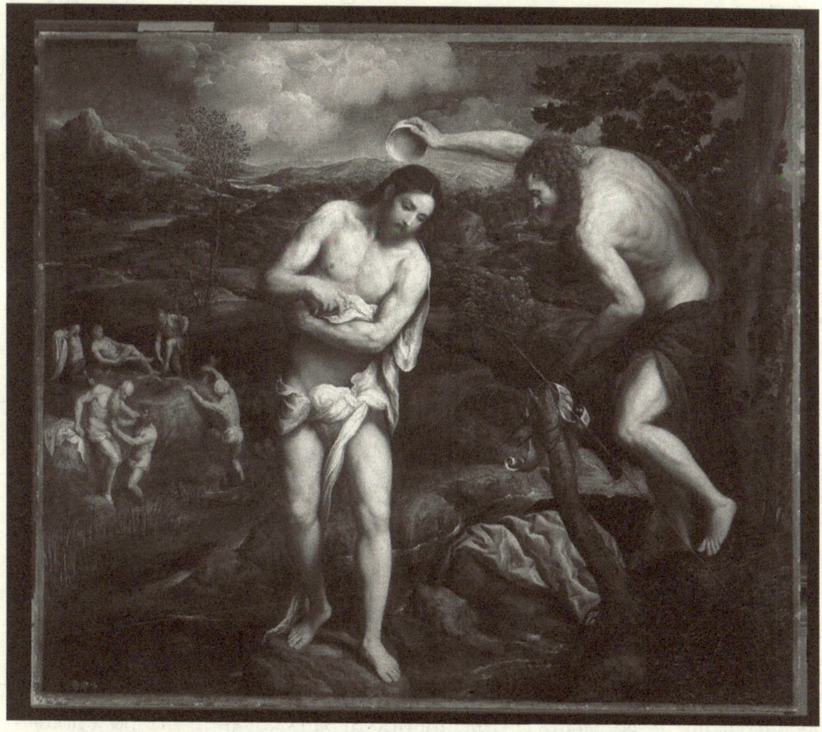

1.5. Paris Bordone, *The Baptism of Christ* (1544). Pinacoteca di Brera, Milan. Photo credit: Pinacoteca di Brera, Milano/Bridgeman Images.

Scholarly Interpretations of the Neophytes

The scriptural accounts of Christ's baptism do not state that he was baptized with others, though the neophytes seen in Masolino's image surely refer to the people of Judea and Jerusalem to whom John the Baptist preached and offered baptism. The Gospel of Matthew reads: "In those days John the Baptist appeared in the wilderness of Judea, proclaiming 'Repent, for the kingdom of heaven has come near' … Then the people of Jerusalem and all Judea were going out to him, and all the region along the Jordan, and they were baptized by him in the river Jordan, confessing their sins" (Matthew 3:1–6).[8] These figures make their first known appearance in Italian art in the 1350 fresco in the Baptistery in Parma, and then again in the 1416 *Saint John Baptizing the Neophytes* by the Salimbeni brothers in the Oratorio of San Giovanni in Urbino (fig. 1.6).[9]

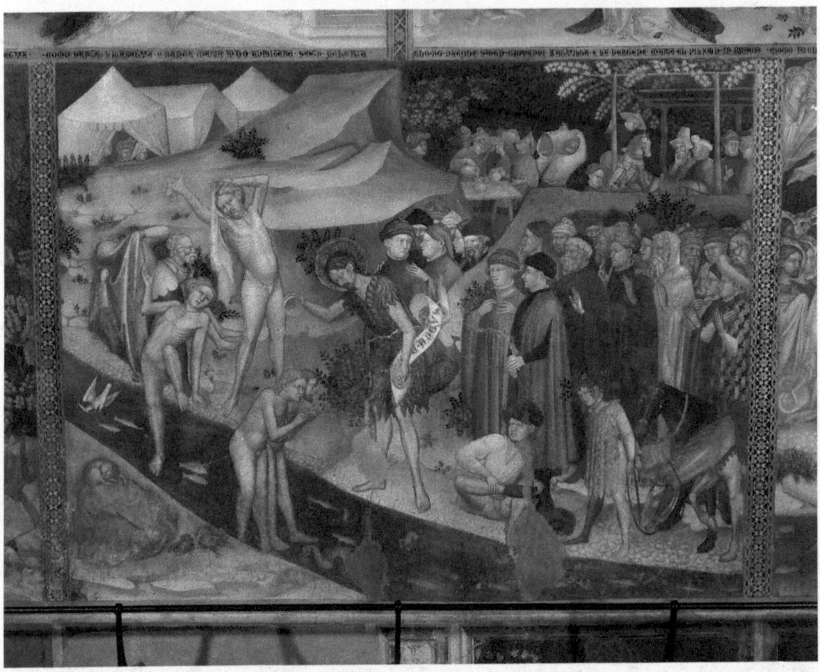

1.6. Jacopo and Lorenzo Salimbeni, *Scenes from the Life of John the Baptist: Saint John Baptizing the Neophytes* (1416). Oratorio di San Giovanni, Urbino. Photo credit: Scala/Art Resource, NY.

Shown in this way, the baptism of Christ might have recalled early Christian rituals in which the sacrament was given to adult catechumens. On Easter Sunday eve, candidates for baptism would participate in a ritual that linked the resurrection of Christ to their own spiritual rebirth as a Christian.[10] In the words of Saint Ambrose, the sacrament was a "passage from sin to life, from fault to grace, from defilement to sanctifications – he who passes through this font does not die but rises."[11] The drama of entering into the spiritual community of Christians is evoked also in Saint Augustine's *Confessions* when he describes the baptism of Victorinus, a rhetor of Rome, who at first was hesitant to be baptized. When he finally presented himself for baptism, Victorinus' high standing in the community caused a minor commotion among the congregation, who "murmured in exaltation" when they saw him and "wanted to clasp him to their hearts, and the hands with which they embraced him were their love and their joy."[12] Clearly, adult baptism was imagined as a moment of connection and intimacy.

In Renaissance Italy, however, baptism was primarily for newborn infants and so would not have created bonds of adult brotherhood and sisterhood in the same way, though it might have on another level. In 1301, for instance, Dino Compagni imagined baptism as a ritual that united the citizens of Florence in brotherhood. At the Baptistery, he exhorted them to recall how they had "each of [them] taken holy baptism from this font" and so "reason forces and constrains [them] to love … [one another] like brothers" ("i quali comunemente tutti prendesti il sacro baptemso di questo fonte, la ragione vi sforza e strigne ad amarvi come cari frategli").[13]

At a less anecdotal level, baptism continued to forge bonds of brotherhood among Florentines through godparenthood. As Christiane Klapisch-Zuber, Louis Haas, John Bossy, and others have noted, Florentines were inclined to acquire large numbers of godparents for their children.[14] In a study of Tuscan records of baptism from the fourteenth to the sixteenth century, Klapisch-Zuber has observed that it was not unusual for a child to have several godparents, "on average three spiritual parents, but 18% of them acquired at least four," and at times many more.[15] Since godparents were normally chosen from outside the natural kinship group, John Bossy has argued that Florentines used godparents to form what he calls a "polyadic horizontal coalition," namely "a kinship-group partly natural and partly artificial."[16] Much as Compagni used the imagery of baptism to encourage brotherly love among Florentines, the actual ritual, which linked fathers to spiritual co-parents, may have strengthened relationships among men in Renaissance Florence; while the same may be true for mothers and co-mothers, the sources consulted by Klapisch-Zuber document mostly godfathers rather than godmothers.[17] Usually men in higher positions offered the honour of godparenthood to socially inferior men; as Louis Haas has noted, "to further intensify the web of clientage."[18] As will be seen below, by forging relationships among men of higher and lower status, the ritual had affinities with its biblical prototype, during which Christ submitted himself to be baptized by John, who in humility confessed that he was "not worthy to carry his sandals" (Matthew 3:11).

It is against this background of fraternal relations among men that I view images of the neophytes. Existing scholarship, however, proposes that their presence in images of the baptism of Christ served a political purpose. Though, as noted above, the imagery appeared in a 1416 fresco by the Salimbeni brothers, its popularity seems to stem from three fifteenth-century frescos, two of which are now lost: Gentile da Fabriano and Pisanello's painting in San Giovanni in Laterano in Rome (begun 1426), undertaken for Pope Martin V; Masolino's fresco in Castiglione Olona

(1435); and Mantegna's fresco in the Belvedere cortile in Rome (1488–90). Though the Roman frescos are lost, some elements of the Lateran composition are preserved in a drawing from Pisanello's circle, which shows indeed that an undressing neophyte was prominent (fig. 1.7).[19] Likewise, the presence of the neophytes in Mantegna's painting is attested by Giorgio Vasari, as discussed below.

Edith Pogány-Balás has proposed that the iconography of the neophytes, common in Byzantine art, served a special purpose amid negotiations to unify the Eastern and Western Churches during which baptism was a concern.[20] Throughout the period beginning with the Council of Constance (1414–18), including the Council of Basel (1431–49), and continuing through the Council of Ferrara-Florence (1438–45), members of the Eastern Church feared that in a unified church their baptism would not be recognized, requiring re-baptism.[21] As such, the imagery of neophytes being baptized communally alongside Christ, familiar in Byzantine art since the twelfth century, may have been meant to assuage their fears.[22]

Pógany-Balás argues that Cardinal Branda Castiglione, a man deeply involved in negotiations between the Eastern and Western Churches throughout this time and also the patron of Masolino's frescos at Castiglione Olona (and at San Clemente in Rome), played an instrumental role in the adoption of this iconography in Italy, possibly becoming aware of Byzantine concerns about re-baptism as early as 1424.[23] According to this theory, therefore, the baptism of neophytes was pictured alongside the baptism of Christ in Rome at San Giovanni in Laterano and then in Castiglione Olona as a response to Byzantines' fears that their baptism would not be recognized in a unified church. If this theory is correct, the presence of the neophytes might again recall the underlying theme of bonding and incorporation expressed in baptism rituals. The possibility that the frescos in Rome and Castiglione Olona expressed a similar intent can be substantiated by the probable similarities between the two works. Gentile da Fabriano's fresco seems to have included neophytes, as can be adduced by Pisanello's drawing of the Lateran painting that shows a neophyte taking a garment off his head, a gesture that is then echoed (though significantly modified) in the standing figure seen from behind at Castiglione Olona.[24] Further connections between the two fresco cycles have also been noted in other scenes, leading Eiko Wakayama to suppose that the majority of the Roman frescos were already finished before Masolino left Rome; Carlo Bertelli further suggests that the frescos at Castiglione Olona were intended to replicate the program in Rome.[25] Wakayama proposes finally that the Castiglione Olona frescos testify to Branda's political and religious

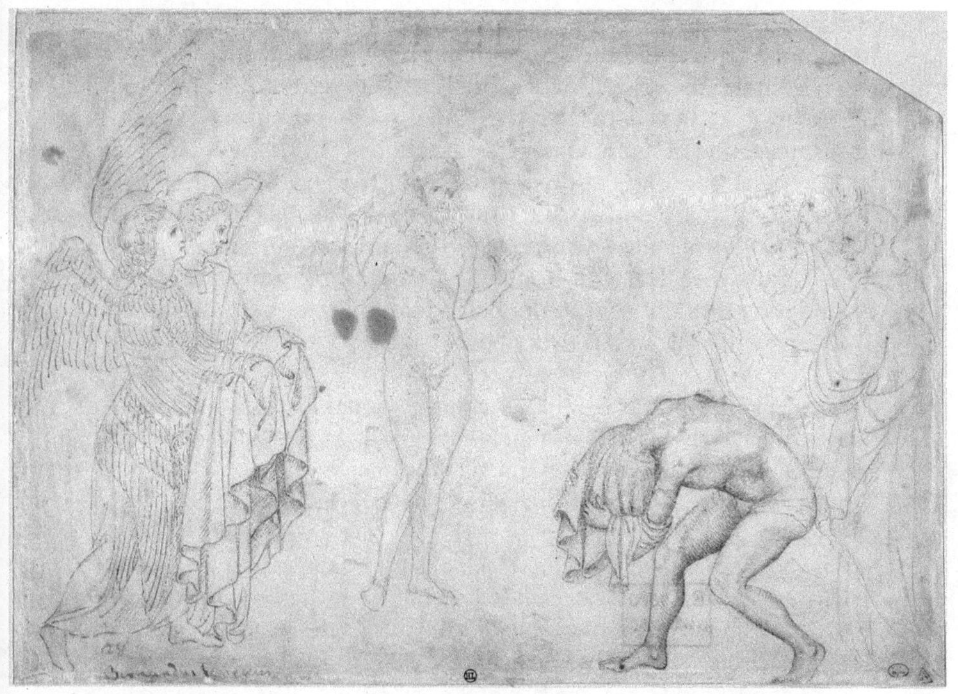

1.7. Pisanello (or school of) after Gentile da Fabriano, *Baptism of Christ* (ca. 1430). Musée du Louvre, Cabinet des Dessins, Paris. Photo credit: © RMN-Grand Palais/Art Resource, NY.

position.[26] This interpretation of the neophytes may be plausible in the context of San Giovanni in Laterano and Branda's chapel. It does not, however, account for the lingering appeal of this iconography well into the sixteenth century and beyond.

Cultural Meanings of Baptism: Brotherhood in Vasari

The many examples in Pogány-Balás' article testify to the longstanding popularity of the neophytes. For instance, the figure bending his knee over one leg and taking off his stocking, found originally in the Salimbeni brothers' image, is repeated by Masolino as well as several later artists. The figure appears to be based on the ancient sculpture the *Spinario*, well known in the Renaissance: at the time Masolino was painting in Rome at San Clemente, this sculpture was installed not far away, in fact outside the Lateran.[27] In the Middle Ages it was at least once interpreted as Priapus, an identification that, if known by Masolino, might have made the sculpture a fitting model for a man preparing to be baptized and cleansed of sin.[28] This figure appears often in Renaissance art and seems to have held a special pertinence to baptism; for instance, one of its most famous iterations is in Brunelleschi's competition panel for doors of the Baptistery of Florence.

According to a detailed description in Giorgio Vasari's *Lives of the Painters, Sculptors, and Architects* (1568), Mantegna's now lost painting of the Baptism of Christ also included a man in a similar pose.[29] Discussing the artist's frescos in the Belvedere in Rome, commissioned by Pope Innocent VIII, Vasari describes:

> uno, che volendosi cavare una calza appiccata per il sudore alla gamba, se la cava a rovescio attraversandola all'altro stinco, con tanta forza e disagio, che l'una e l'altro gli appare manifestamente nel viso; la qual cosa capricciosa recò, a chi la vide in quei tempi, maraviglia.[30]

> one who, seeking to draw off a stocking that has stuck to his leg through sweat, has crossed that leg over the other and is drawing the stocking off inside out, with such great effort and difficulty, that both are seen clearly in his face; which bizarre fancy caused marvel to all who saw it in those times.[31]

When Vasari writes that the neophyte made an impression on viewers, he underscores the cultural significance of this figure, as is evident also by its many iterations. If the neophytes were not strictly necessary in depictions of the baptism of Christ, and if their original inclusion was motivated by efforts to unify the Eastern and Western Churches, their lingering presence indicates that they held meanings beyond the biblical narrative or the temporally limited fifteenth-century purpose.

In the broader context of Vasari's work, the passage about Mantegna's fresco may offer clues as to the larger cultural meaning of the neophytes. Vasari's description resonates with other passages about baptism in his book in which he pays special attention to the poses of neophytes. As I have pointed out elsewhere, Vasari frequently describes young apprentice artists copying images of baptism, many of whom establish themselves as masters after creating successful images of the subject. In Vasari's text, the very imagery of baptism seems to bring about the incorporation of the young artist into the community of masters, just as the actual sacrament initiates the catechumen into the faith.

The archetypal example of this pattern is Masaccio's fresco of *St. Peter Baptizing the Neophytes* in the Brancacci Chapel, famously studied by young Florentine artists, according to Vasari.[32] As in the description of

Mantegna's painting, Vasari describes a semi-nude neophyte in Masaccio's painting "who is trembling and shivering with cold among the others who are being baptized" and states that the figure has "ever been held in reverence and admiration by all craftsmen, both ancient and modern."[33] Vasari emphasizes the impact this neophyte had on artists when he claims that the Brancacci chapel was "frequented continually up to our own day by innumerable draftsmen and masters … [who] have become excellent and famous by exercising themselves and studying this chapel."[34] The artists collected around the painting studying Masaccio mirror the central theme of the image: like the neophytes around Saint Peter, waiting to join the Christian faith, the Brancacci chapel fresco became a vehicle through which artists were incorporated into a brotherhood.

This theme is repeated in other biographies, indicating that it conveys ideas about the cultural significance of baptism beyond its essential theological meanings. To provide another example, Vasari relates that Andrea del Sarto (who had studied Masaccio's image)[35] reached maturity as an artist by creating his own baptismal painting for the Company of the Scalzo:

> Per lo che egli messovi mano, fece nella prima quando San Giovanni battezza Christo, con molta diligenza e tanto buona maniera che gl'acquistò credito, onore e fama per sì fatta maniera, che molte persone si voltarono a fargli fare opere, … il principio del suo operare straordinario …[36]

> Whereupon, setting his hand to this, he painted in the first scene of St. John baptizing Christ, with much diligence and such excellent manner, whereby he gained credit, honor, and fame to such an extent that many persons turned to him with commissions for works [because of] his extraordinary beginning in his profession.[37]

Images of baptism, as suggested by Vasari's biographies, play a special role in the incorporation and maturity of young artists, whereby apprentices learn from images of baptism, are transformed by them, and eventually become masters when they create their own version of the subject.

In Renaissance Florence, becoming an artist was not unlike joining a brotherhood. Painters in Florence belonged to the Guild of Doctors, Apothecaries, and Grocers (Arte dei Medici, Speziali e Merciai), which included practitioners of many different trades and professions; they could also, however, join a spiritual confraternity: the Company of Saint Luke (Compagnia di San Luca).[38] This confraternity, which united painters and sculptors, was among a small number in Florence restricted by trade.

Membership in it, which included both master painters and apprentices (unlike the guild), involved partaking in communal spiritual activities, such as hearing Mass together twice a month, as a statute from 1406 records.[39] In 1550 the confraternity was evicted from its longstanding meeting place in Santa Maria Nuova, but did not disappear – the Compagnia ed Accademia del Disegno, founded in 1563, was widely understood as a revival of the former confraternity, especially since its members also participated in many spiritual activities.[40] It is therefore not unreasonable to suggest that, within the imagination of Florentine artists, achieving artistic maturity was visualized in both religious and fraternal terms.

With this in mind, we can now ask whether the ideas expressed in Vasari's text can help explain more generally the meaning and popularity of the neophytes on a cultural level. Beyond its spiritual meaning as a sacrament, baptism was associated with fraternity and incorporation, and even – as in the case of artists – with coming of age and reaching maturity. But why would artists and viewers visualize baptism in sensual terms, as evident by the undressed neophytes in Masolino's painting? The broader social and historical meaning of the neophytes becomes clearer when Vasari describes Michelangelo's now-lost cartoon for the *Battle of Cascina* (fig. 1.8), in which another figure struggles with his stocking. As reported by Vasari, Michelangelo was yet another artist who drew at the font of Masaccio in the Brancacci chapel;[41] it was in fact a formative event for him, since this is where the artist Pietro Torrigiano broke his nose in jealousy. Having learned from Masaccio, Michelangelo then went on to create, in the early part of his career, his own image of men bathing. Vasari writes:

> Eravi fra l'altre figure un vecchio ... il quale, postosi a sedere per mettersi le calze, e non potevano entrargli per avere le gambe umide dell'acqua ... affrettando tirava per forza una calza; et oltra che tutti i muscoli e ' nervi della figura si vedevano, faceva uno storcimento di bocca, per il quale dimostrava assai quanto e' pativa, e che egli si adoperava fin alle punte de' piedi.[42]

> There was, among other figures, an old man ... who, having sat down in order to put on his hose, into which his legs would not go because they were wet with water ... was struggling to draw on one stocking by force; and besides that all the muscles and nerves of his figure could be perceived, his mouth was so distorted as to show clearly how he was straining and struggling to even to the very tips of his toes.[43]

This passage is strikingly similar to Vasari's description of Mantegna's bather: in both descriptions a man struggles with a damp sock,

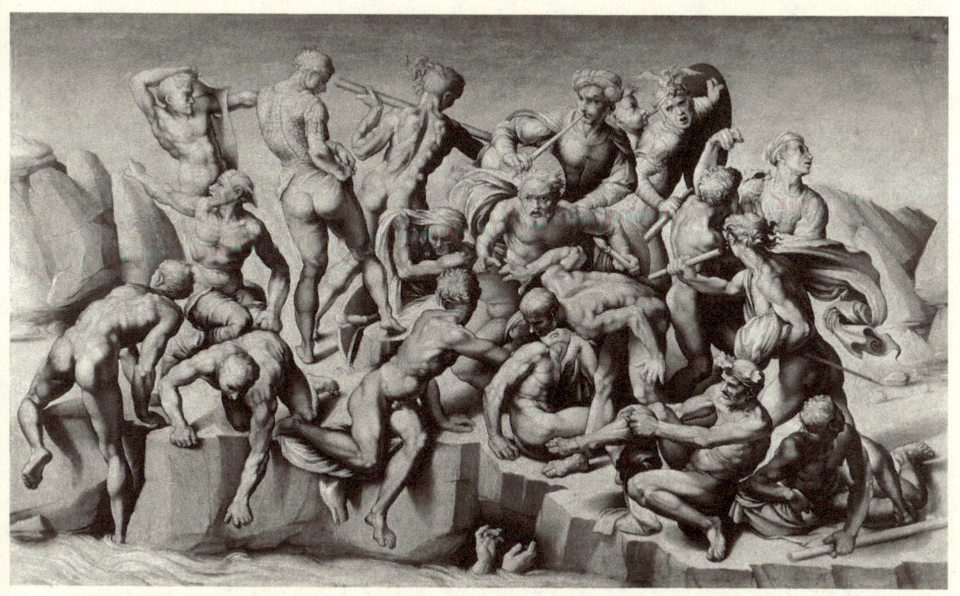

1.8. Aristotile da Sangallo after Michelangelo. *Battle of Cascina* (1542). Holkham Hall, Norfolk. Photo credit: © DeA Picture Library/Art Resource, NY.

though one puts on while the other takes off the garment. Despite this difference, earlier scholars have concluded that Michelangelo drew inspiration from Mantegna's image.[44] Taken together, the two passages about Mantegna and Michelangelo describe quite accurately the pair of neophytes at the bottom right-hand side of Masolino's fresco: one who crosses his leg to pull off his stocking, and the other who pulls upward to put it back on.

The parallel between Michelangelo's cartoon and other baptismal images is deepened when Vasari states that the cartoon was frequently copied by apprentice artists, thereby acquiring a status similar to Masaccio's painting. He writes that:

> tutti coloro che su quel cartone studiarono e tal cosa disegnarono, come poi si seguitò molti anni in Fiorenza per forestieri e per terrazzani diventarono persone in tale arte eccellenti.[45]

> all those who studied from that cartoon and drew those figures – as was afterwards the custom in Florence for many years both for strangers and for natives – became persons eminent in art.[46]

Vasari even notes that Andrea del Sarto (who, as noted, studied the Brancacci chapel) would also "spend the whole day in company with other young men" ("spendeva tutto il dì insieme con altri giovani") drawing Michelangelo's and Leonardo da Vinci's battle cartoons in the Sala del Papa.[47] Later art historians, such as Patricia Rubin, have traced the influence of Michelangelo's drawing through many generations of artists, all the way to Peter Paul Rubens.[48]

Vasari's relatively detailed description of these two figures putting on and taking off stockings suggests that he and his readers imaginatively linked baptism to bathing more generally. Vasari connects bathing and baptism explicitly in a passage from the life of Francesco Salviati when he notes that the artist was asked to paint some "stories of the life of St. John the Baptist," and went "to study nudes from life ... in a bathhouse" ("alcune storie della vita di San Giovanni Battista ... a studiare ignudi di naturale ... in una stufa quivi vicina").[49] Scenes of men bathing together are what the images of the neophytes most clearly resemble. Later examples, such as the painting by Paris Bordone, which includes bathers in the background relatively divorced from the main action of the painting, resemble the carefree figures in Domenico Cresti's (called Passignano) depiction of male bathers at San Niccolò from 1600. This painting, which depicts a multitude of young men bathing in the Arno, shows homosocial intimacy and conviviality in an environment entirely removed from religious or mythological narrative; to some viewers the image strays clearly into eroticism.[50] The existence of this kind of imagery, and the literary and artistic evidence found in Vasari and the images he described, suggest strongly that the neophytes gathered before and after baptism were linked imaginatively to a culture of bathing about which little information remains.

Was bathing similar to baptism not only in its visual appearance, but also because it entailed homosocial bonding among men? The neophytes in all images of which I am aware are exclusively men, and the *Battle of Cascina* of course concerned male soldiers; Rubin has also noted that the painting Michelangelo intended to create would have been in a room entirely used by males.[51] While the contextual and literary sources described above indicate that in many respects baptism still evoked notions of men drawing together in bonds of brotherhood, was this true also for bathing more broadly? The evidence unfortunately is somewhat anecdotal, a consequence of our limited knowledge of baths in Renaissance cities, but some documents do, nonetheless, suggest that visiting a bathhouse was seen as an activity that drew men together in homosocial community. For instance, in an article exploring the culture of bathhouses in northern Europe, Diane Wolfthal has noted that in many cities public baths were separated by sex, even if complete segregation was not always successful;[52] Maria Serena Mazzi notes that similar efforts were made in fifteenth-century Florence.[53] The sexes were isolated to prevent heterosexual intercourse, notably among men and female sex workers, but it may have unintentionally promoted same-sex relations among men.[54] Michael Rocke has noted that in fifteenth-century prosecutions of sodomy in Florence, for instance, certain areas of the city were popular locations for same-sex relations among men, notably in the streets around the public baths at San Michele Bertoldi.[55] Rocke also notes the case of a boy who was sodomized by a friend during swimming lessons at the Arno.[56] During the Savonarolan period, controls on sodomy led the city to order the managers of public baths to keep "suspect boys" out of their establishments or pay a fine.[57] We also know that the baths of San Michele were commonly believed to be a place of sin through the record of a miraculous image of the Virgin across the street that closed its eyes so as to not see what took place there; in his description of this miracle, Luca Landucci records that the place was not fitting for women.[58] Though the area would naturally have been frequented by some women, some of whom were sex workers, Natalie Tomas has described these areas, along with taverns and inns, as "areas of male sociability ... closed to upper-class women."[59] It seems possible therefore that in the imagination of Florentine men, bathing was an activity that connoted time spent among their own sex, but also clandestine sexual encounters, both heterosexual and with other men.

It may have been natural therefore for Florentine artists to imagine baptism as an event that reflected a myriad of linked experiences: the sacrament itself concerned incorporation into the Christian faith; this in turn made it a fitting emblem of fraternal, homosocial bonding; at the same time, for Vasari, baptism was intertwined with the maturity and coming of age of young artists. Likewise, images of neophytes might have evoked public bathing, itself a homosocial activity for men, and one that took place in an atmosphere of physical sensuality.

Baptism and the "Lavanda"

The imagery of neophytes bathing and undressing may have resonated with yet another aspect of fifteenth-century Italian life in which men forged bonds through physical intimacy: the ritual of foot washing, known as the "lavanda," performed among religious communities and members of confraternities in imitation of Christ's washing of his apostles' feet at the Last Supper. This episode is recounted in the Gospel of John:

> Jesus … got up from the table, took off his outer robe, and tied a towel around himself. Then he poured water into a basin and began to wash the disciples' feet and to wipe them with the towel that was tied around him. (John 13:3–6)

The relationship between this moment and Christ's baptism is suggested by some paintings that include figures reminiscent of the neophytes. Several Renaissance examples of Christ washing his apostles' feet include one follower crossing one leg over the other to remove his stocking, recalling both the *Spinario* and the neophyte in Masolino's fresco. Such a figure can be seen, for instance, in the bottom left-hand corner of a fifteenth-century drawing by the Florentine Zanobi di Benedetto Strozzi;[60] likewise, in a small painting by Bernardino Butinone from around 1500.[61] An apostle bending his knee to remove his shoe appears even earlier, in Giotto's Arena Chapel, though it is a bit ambiguous whether the figure crosses his legs. However, the closest comparison between the apostle and the neophyte appears in a section of Fra Angelico's mid-fifteenth-century *Armadio Panels* (fig. 1.9). Here the pose is replicated nearly exactly, with the bent leg being grasped by the right hand, while the left pulls the sock inside out.

In raising these examples, I do not suggest necessarily that Fra Angelico quoted Masolino, though he did spend time in Rome and thus may have seen the *Spinario*. Rather, I believe the figure type carried a culturally understood meaning, as evident by its many iterations and, most notably, by the special attention Vasari pays to it. Indeed, figures that seem to be derived from these early prototypes appear in later paintings of the Last Supper as well: perhaps the most dramatic is a painting of the subject by Tintoretto, which depicts one apostle pulling with both hands on the stocking of a companion who leans on a bench for support.[62]

At an intuitive level, the crossover of imagery from baptism to Last Supper appears self-explanatory: both images require figures taking off their clothes, or their socks, and both are homosocial scenes among men. Baptism and the Last Supper are also theologically linked: as noted above, catechumens being baptized and reborn are thought to mirror the death and resurrection of Christ.[63]

Unlike baptismal images, however, it is very clear that paintings of Christ washing his apostles' feet must have resonated strongly with contemporary religious and confraternal rituals in fifteenth-century Florence. Ronald Weissman writes, for instance, that in celebrations of Holy Thursday, the "most solemn day of confraternal assembly and the day of greatest attendance … the brothers reenacted the archetypal

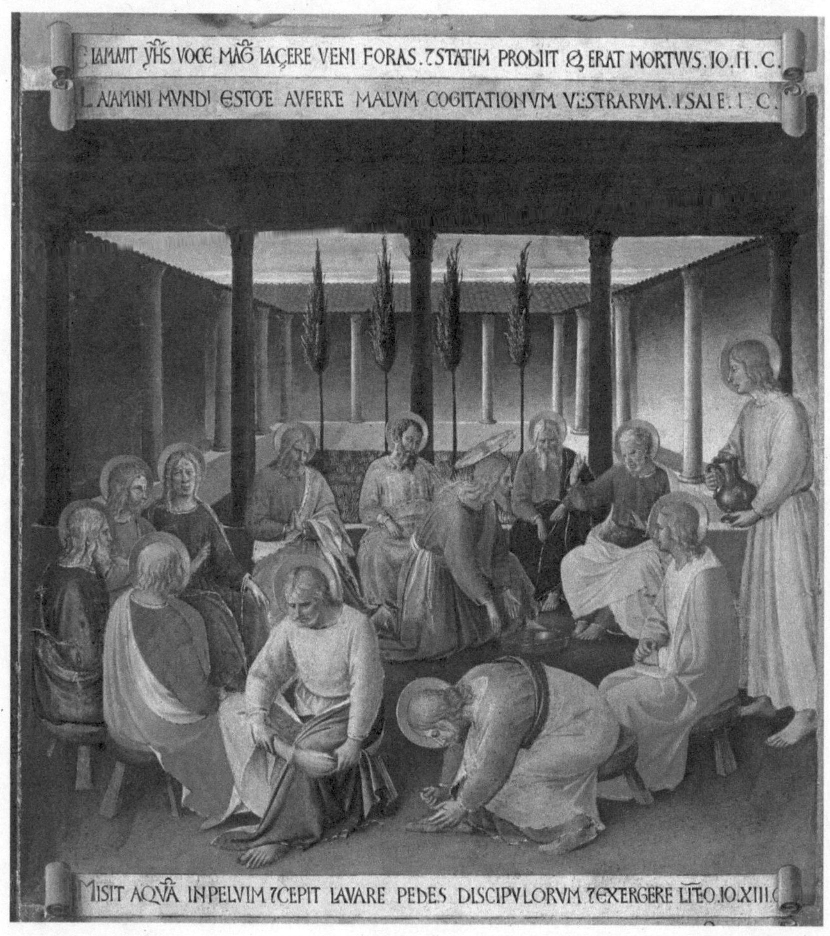

1.9. Fra Angelico, Armadio Panels (detail): *Christ Washing His Apostles' Feet* (ca. 1451–5). Museo Nazionale di San Marco, Florence. Photo credit: Alfredo Dagli Orti/Art Resource, NY.

Christian brotherhood of the Last Supper."[64] This entailed a ritual modelled after a religious rite, in which the governor washed the feet of the confraternity officers, or the officers washed the feet of other members.[65]

In the lavanda ritual, the governor, or the confraternity officers, demonstrated humility by washing the feet of their social inferiors. This imitated the humility of Christ, who says to his apostles: "if I, your Lord and teacher, have washed your feet, you also ought to wash one another's feet ... Very truly, I tell you, servants are not greater than their master" (John 13:14–16). Humility was understood to be one of the principal themes of the fifteenth-century ritual, as evident by a sermon from 1470 by Alamanno Rinuccini, delivered to the company of the Magi on Holy Thursday; Rinuccini stated that the highest grade of humility was found in Christ, who "remained kneeling in front of His own disciples in order to wash the feet of His own servants."[66] Christ's humility at the Last Supper echoes his Baptism in which he submitted himself to Saint John the Baptist. As stated above, the homosocial connections forged at the time of baptism in fifteenth-century Florence – such as the choice of godfathers – also entailed the bonding of men of higher and lower status. Therefore, it is not without reason that artists would imagine Christ washing his apostles' feet with a visual vocabulary also found in baptismal images.

Like baptism, the lavanda was linked to the cleansing and purging of the soul. For instance, in 1476, while delivering a sermon after the lavanda ritual, Giovanni Nesi implored members of the brotherhood of the Nativity to emulate Christ's example of humility by using their tears to "cleanse [their] breast" of their crimes and to "convert enmity into amity, hate and dissimulation into love and benevolence, pride into humility."[67] As these words suggest, the ritual had a purgative effect, allowing men to reconnect with one another, temporarily dissolving tensions, as much as the social distinctions between them. The picture of the apostle removing his stocking in Fra Angelico's painting would naturally have recalled an atmosphere of cleansing and fraternity not dissimilar to the images of the neophytes.

In considering the cultural meanings of images of neophytes in the Renaissance, the evidence suggests that they evoked a rich variety of associations, all of which were connected to the central themes of baptism. Though the actual ritual of baptism itself at this time did not typically involve adult immersion in water, the atmosphere of harmony and fraternity in these images, achieved through the sensual depiction of male beauty, was appropriate to men's experiences of contemporary baptisms, bathing, and homosocial ritual. These images signified not just the coming together of the Eastern and Western Churches, as scholars have previously supposed, but also a larger union of men in brotherhood, with sensual and perhaps even erotic overtones.

Fraternity as Antidote to Sexuality?

The concluding section of this chapter will explore perhaps the most difficult question posed by these images, namely the erotic quality they seem to possess. As noted above, bathing was itself associated with homosexual encounter in fifteenth-century Florence. To what extent might these images have invited erotic interpretations? Thanks to the work of Rocke, we know that homosexual relations were common, even expected, among Florentines in the Renaissance, and so one might suppose that any image of a nearly nude male figure could have aroused erotic feelings: for instance, Masolino's neophyte elegantly lifting his garment over his head, or the figure who turns his back in Ghirlandaio's frescos at Santa Maria Novella, permitting the admiration of his physique.[68] Based on Rocke's work, and subsequent explorations of homoeroticism in Florentine imagery, it may be a given that images of beautiful young men held erotic appeal for a (possibly large) number of male viewers.[69] The question remains what meaning these figures might have had in a religious image. Clearly, even if Florentine men appreciated male beauty, sodomy was officially forbidden and actively persecuted, so the inclusion of potentially erotic imagery in sacred art demands some explanation. Were viewers simply not conscious of the contradiction between religious values and sensual imagery? If this was the case, what permitted these two things to coexist? While the issue of erotic imagery in sacred art has been a vexing problem for art historians for a long time and cannot be examined in full here, in this section I will suggest that, by means of contrasting exempla, Masolino's fresco encouraged viewing male nudity in a spiritual light.[70] In Branda's chapel, Masolino exalts fraternity by juxtaposing the harmonious neophytes against sinful heterosexuality.

It is natural that baptism should be contrasted with sin, since the sacrament cleansed the soul of original sin. This point is implied visually in the Brancacci chapel, for instance, by the fact that Masolino's image of the *Temptation of Adam and Eve* is on the same register as Masaccio's depiction of *St. Peter Baptizing the Neophytes* (fig. 1.4): the viewer is shown both original sin and the sacrament that removes it at opposite sides of one wall. Visual similarities also encourage the viewer to connect these scenes: both scenes show nude (or nearly nude) and unselfconscious figures. While it is natural that baptism should illustrate the path to redemption from the fall of Adam and Eve, by highlighting this connection the paintings also prime the viewer to consider baptism in relation to sexuality. The sins of Adam and Eve had for several centuries been closely related to sexuality, as Joyce E. Salisbury has noted: "For the early Fathers, sexuality was brought into being when Adam and Eve sinned, for Ambrose and Jerome saw the original sin as sexual."[71] Though he diverged from Ambrose and Jerome, Augustine likewise associated original sin with sex; in his view, however, Adam and Eve's sin was disobedience, which in turn brought about the disobedience of human bodies[72] – for instance, "the inability to control one's sexual organs," whereby sexual impulses could not be controlled by one's will.[73] Therefore, when Masaccio and Masolino juxtaposed the harmonious baptism of semi-nude men with the naked and disobedient bodies of Adam and Eve, the early modern viewer may have perceived an implied dichotomy between sinful sexuality and a righteous homosocial encounter.

In Masolino's frescos at Castiglione Olona, the danger of sexuality is raised more obviously. Beneath the baptism of Christ are two moments from John the Baptist's life: *The Baptist Preaching on the Banks of the River Jordan* on the left and *The Baptist Reproving Herod* on the right (fig. 1.1).[74] While the preaching scene precedes the baptism in the narrative sequence, the reproving of Herod is far ahead in the story of the Baptist's life, suggesting that the wall as a whole has a thematic rather than temporal logic. In the right-hand episode, the Baptist, captured by Herod's soldiers, points to and reproves Herod and his wife for incest. Herod and Herodias (formerly the wife of Herod's deceased brother) sit enthroned before John and react to his accusation. Here, the only woman to appear anywhere on a wall otherwise dominated by images of men has a cold, almost defiant, expression. With the gesture of her left hand, she appears to appeal to her husband for protection. Herod in turn points either to the Baptist or to the guard who is about to apprehend him. The Baptist himself stands defiant, with an expression of disgust or anger on his face.

The composition is linked visually with the opposite side of the wall, where John is in a nearly identical pose, though rotated 180 degrees: he holds a scroll on which the words "Ecce agnus dei" are legible, while gesturing with his right hand. His arm is held up not to accuse, but to recognize Christ, who stands opposite him behind the rocky terrain in a position equivalent to Herod on the other side of the wall. Like Herod, Christ also holds up his right hand, though he makes a gesture of benediction. Both scenes have structurally similar compositions, though in one the Baptist gestures to the spiritually pure Christ and in the other he points to a couple who have sinned sexually. This triad of scenes –

preaching, reproving, and baptism – are linked not as a sequence of events in the Baptist's life, but rather by the logic of baptism itself. As the Gospel makes clear, the Baptist preached repentance before baptizing the people, and so repentance is an implied theme on the left-hand side of the wall. Likewise, in the early Christian ritual, catechumens undertook repentance before their initiation.[75] Taken together, therefore, these three scenes are thematically linked: they illustrate man's sexually fallen state, the repentance this requires, and the baptism that cleanses original sin. The juxtaposition suggests subtly how baptism, and the fraternal bonds it creates between men, can be an antidote to sexual sin.

As in the very poses of the neophytes described in the introduction of this article, which playfully reflect or contrast with one another, the use of opposing images of sin and redemption creates an image where the fraternal nudity of men is contrasted with the condemnation of women and their sexuality. While I would not argue that this was meant to tacitly condone homosexuality, it complicates the eroticism of the neophytes. The arrangement of the frescos conveys to the viewer that, whatever rich meaning the bodies of these beautiful men evoked for them, it stands opposite to and separate from the sexuality that led to Adam and Eve's expulsion from Eden, or John the Baptist's condemnation of Herod. The bonds of brotherhood created in baptism are celebrated in such a way that may have diverted attention from their sensuality and eroticism.

NOTES

1 Rubin, *Seen from Behind*, 31.
2 Rubin, *Seen from Behind*, 31.
3 The relationship to the *Spinario*, discussed below, is widely acknowledged. See Roberts, *Masolino da Panicale*, 141; Bertelli, *Masolino: Gli affreschi*, 129.
4 The clenching of this man's left hand strongly suggests pulling off the garment, rather than pulling it on.
5 See Pogány-Balás, "Problems of Mantegna's Destroyed Fresco"; Lavin, *Piero della Francesca's Baptism of Christ*, 109–13.
6 On this interpretation, see Lavin, *Piero della Francesca's Baptism of Christ*, 112.
7 On baptism and original sin, see De Clerck, "Baptism," 152.
8 Biblical citations are to the New Revised Standard Version in *The New Oxford Annotated Bible*.
9 Lavin, *Piero della Francesca's Baptism of Christ*, 73–4.
10 Wharton, "Ritual and Reconstructed Meaning," 361.

11 Ambrose, *The Sacraments: I*, 273. On this source, see also Wharton, "Ritual and Reconstructed Meaning." See also Spinks, *Early and Medieval Rituals*.
12 Augustine, *Confessions*, 137.
13 Translation from Trexler, *Public Life*, 48. Compagni, *Cronica delle cose*, bk. II, ch. 8.
14 Bossy, "Blood and Baptism"; Klapisch-Zuber, "Parrains et filleuls"; Hass, "Il Mio Buono Compare"; Muir, *Ritual in Early Modern Europe*, 22–7.
15 "trois parents spirituels en moyenne, mais 18% d'entre eux en comptent au moins quatre"; Klapisch-Zuber, "Parrains et filleuls," 56.
16 Bossy, "Blood and Baptism," 134.
17 Klapisch-Zuber, "Parrains et filleuls," 56. See also Haas, "Il Mio Buono Compare," 347.
18 Haas, "Il Mio Buono Compare," 345.
19 On this drawing and its relationship to Masolino, see Bertelli, *Masolino: Gli affreschi*, 128.
20 Pogány-Balás, "Problems of Mantegna's Destroyed Fresco," 116–18. On the neophytes in Byzantine art, see also Lavin, *Piero della Francesca's Baptism of Christ*, 109.
21 Pogány-Balás, "Problems of Mantegna's Destroyed Fresco," 116; Gill, *Council of Florence*, 281, 307–8.
22 Pogány-Balás, "Problems of Mantegna's Destroyed Fresco," 116.
23 Pogány-Balás, "Problems of Mantegna's Destroyed Fresco," 116–17. On Branda's involvement in church councils, see Girgensohn, "Castiglione, Branda da." See also Roberts, *Masolino da Panicale*, 132, and on Masolino in Rome, 100. On other Eastern themes in Masolino's painting, see Wakayama, "Il programma iconografico." On Branda's patronage and intellectual formation, see Bertelli, *Masolino: Gli affreschi*, 25–38.
24 On the frescos of Gentile da Fabriano and Pisanello, see De Marchi, "Reconsidering the Traces"; as this article notes, these frescos were frequently praised in the early modern period.
25 Wakayama, "Il programma iconografico," 32n34. Bertelli, *Masolino: Gli affreschi*, 39. Roberts, *Masolino da Panicale*, also accepts that Masolino's cycle was inspired by Gentile da Fabriano and Pisanello's work, 141.
26 Wakayama, "Il programma iconografico," 32.
27 Haskell and Penny, *Taste and the Antique*, 308.
28 On the *Spinario* as inspiration for the Salimbeni brothers, see Pogány-Balás, "Problems of Mantegna's Destroyed Fresco," 124n37. On the meaning of the *Spinario*, see "Spinario"; Haskell and Penny, *Taste and the Antique*, 308. Though it is unclear if the *Spinario* was more widely known as a Priapus, if it were so, it may have been a fitting figure to portray someone preparing to be baptized and cleansed of sin.
29 On Mantegna's program more generally, see Sandström, "The Programme for the Decoration."

30 Vasari, *Vite*, 1:490. Volume and page numbers refer to the original 1568 edition and are indicated in Barocchi and Bettarini's modern edition, now available online. As notes Pogány-Balás, "Problems of Mantegna's Destroyed Fresco," 123n14, similar descriptions of Mantegna's fresco can be found in Taja, *Descrizione*, 406, and Chattard, *Nuova descrizione*, 141.
31 Vasari, *Lives*, 1:562. In some cases I have slightly modified de Vere's translation of Vasari.
32 Stowell, "Baptism of Drawing," 312.
33 Vasari, *Lives*, 1:323. "un ignudo che triema tra gl'altri battezzati assiderando di freddo, ... il quale dagli artefici e vecchi e moderni è stato sempre tenuto in riverenza et ammirazione"; Vasari, *Vite*, 1:299.
34 Vasari, *Lives*, 1:323. "per il che da infiniti disegnatori e maestri continuamente fino al dì d'oggi è stata frequentata questa cappella ... esercitandosi e studiando in questa cappella sono divenuti eccellenti e chiari"; Vasari, *Vite*, 1:299.
35 Andrea is named among the devotees to Masaccio's painting; see Vasari, *Lives*, 1:323.
36 Vasari, *Vite*, 2:151.
37 Vasari, *Lives*, 1:825.
38 Geronimus and Waldman, "Children of Mercury," 118–19. See also Salvestrini, "Associazionismo e devozione."
39 Geronimus and Waldman, "Children of Mercury," 120.
40 Geronimus and Waldman, "Children of Mercury," 122. On the Accademia del Disegno's acts of piety, see Barzman, *The Florentine Academy*, particularly ch. 6.
41 Vasari, *Lives*, 2:648–9. Vasari, *Vite*, 3:720.
42 Vasari, *Vite*, 3:725.
43 Vasari, *Lives*, 2:657.
44 See Pogány-Balás, "Problems of Mantegna's Destroyed Fresco," 123n14, citing Tietze-Conrat, *Mantegna*, 22.
45 Vasari, *Vite*, 3:725–6.
46 Vasari, *Lives*, 2:658.
47 Vasari, *Lives*, 1:824. Vasari, *Vite*, 2:150.
48 Rubin, *Seen from Behind*, ch. 6.
49 Vasari, *Lives*, 2:560. Vasari, *Vite*, 3:629.
50 See Rubin, *Seen from Behind*, 107–9.
51 Rubin, *Seen from Behind*, 193.
52 Wolfthal, *In and Out*, 121–7.
53 Mazzi, *Prostitute e lenoni*, 278.
54 On sex work and public baths in Florence, see Mazzi, *Prostitute e lenoni*, 276–80.
55 Rocke, *Forbidden Friendships*, 154; see also Mazzi, *Prostitute e lenoni*, 278–9.

56 Rocke, *Forbidden Friendships*, 166.
57 Rocke, *Forbidden Friendships*, 203.
58 Landucci, *A Florentine Diary*, 222–3. On this event, see also Holmes, *Miraculous Image*, 98–9; Paoletti, *Michelangelo's David*, 188.
59 Tomas, "Did Women Have a Space?" 322.
60 The drawing, ca. 1435–40, is in the collection of the Museum Boijmans Van Beuningen (Rotterdam, Netherlands); accession number: I 240 (PK).
61 Now in the collection of the Sheldon Memorial Art Gallery and Sculpture Garden, University of Nebraska-Lincoln, Lincoln, NE.
62 Jacopo Tintoretto, *Christ Washing His Disciples' Feet*, ca. 1545–55. Now in the collection of the Art Gallery of Ontario, Toronto; object number: 58/51.
63 Spinks, *Early and Medieval Rituals*, pt. 1, ch. 3.
64 Weissman, *Ritual Brotherhood*, 99.
65 Weissman, *Ritual Brotherhood*, 100–1.
66 Weissman, *Ritual Brotherhood*, 101.
67 Weissman, *Ritual Brotherhood*, 103.
68 The widespread nature of sodomy is thoroughly documented by Rocke, *Forbidden Friendships*.
69 See for instance Randolph, *Engaging Symbols*, on Donatello's *David*, particularly.
70 For a broader consideration of this problem, including a fuller bibliography, see Stowell, "Purging the Eye."
71 Salisbury, "The Latin Doctors," 281.
72 Salisbury, "The Latin Doctors," 285.
73 Salisbury, "The Latin Doctors," 285.
74 On the iconography of these scenes, see Roberts, *Masolino*, 140–2, 199–201.
75 Reconstructing the early ritual, see, for instance, Wharton, "Ritual and Reconstructed Meaning."

WORKS CITED

Ambrose, Saint. *The Sacraments: I.* In his *The Theological and Dogmatic Works*. Trans. Roy J. Deferrari. Washington, DC: Catholic University of America Press, 1963, 269–77.

Augustine, Saint. *Confessions*. Trans. Henry Chadwick. Oxford: Oxford University Press, 1998.

Barzman, Karen-edis. *The Florentine Academy and the Early Modern State: The Discipline of Disegno*. Cambridge: Cambridge University Press, 2000.

Bertelli, Carlo. *Masolino: Gli affreschi del Battistero e della Collegiata a Castiglione Olona*. Milan: Skira editore, 1998.

Bossy, John. "Blood and Baptism: Kinship, Community and Christianity in Western Europe from the Fourteenth to the Seventeenth Centuries." In

Derek Baker, ed., *Sanctity and Secularity: The Church and the World*. New York: Harper & Row Publishers, 1973, 129–44.

Chattard, Giovanni Pietro. *Nuova descrizione del Vaticano osia del Palazzo Apostolico di San Pietro*. Vol. 3. Rome: Mainardi, 1767.

Compagni, Dino. *Cronica delle cose occorrenti ne' tempi suoi*. Ed. Gino Luzzatto. Turin: Giulio Einaudi editore, 1968. Online at https://www.liberliber.it/online/autori/autori-c/dino-compagni/.

Coogan, Michael, ed. *The New Oxford Annotated Bible: Augmented Third Edition*. Oxford: Oxford University Press, 2007.

De Clerck, Paul. "Baptism." In Jean-Yves Lacoste, ed., *Encyclopedia of Christian Theology, Volume 1: A–F*. New York: Routledge, 2005, 149–56.

De Marchi, Andrea. "Reconsidering the Traces of Gentile da Fabriano and Pisanello in the Lateran Basilica." In Lex Bosman, Ian P. Haynes, and Paolo Liverani, eds., *The Basilica of Saint John Lateran to 1600*. Cambridge: Cambridge University Press, 2020, 379–99.

Geronimus, Dennis V., and Louis A. Waldman. "Children of Mercury: New Light on the Members of the Florentine Company of St. Luke (c. 1475–1525)." *Mitteilungen des Kunsthistorischen Institutes in Florenz* 47 (2003): 118–58.

Gill, Joseph. *The Council of Florence*. Cambridge: Cambridge University Press, 1959.

Girgensohn, Dieter. "Castiglione, Branda da." In *Dizionario biografico degli Italiani*, 22. Rome: Istituto dell' Enciclopedia Italiana, 1979, *sub voce*. Online at https://www.treccani.it/enciclopedia/branda-da-castiglione_(Dizionario-Biografico).

Haas, Louis. "Il Mio Buono Compare: Choosing Godparents and the Uses of Baptismal Kinship in Renaissance Florence." *Journal of Social History* 29 (1995): 341–56.

Haskell, Francis, and Nicholas Penny. *Taste and the Antique: The Lure of Classical Sculpture, 1500–1900*. New Haven: Yale University Press, 1981.

Holmes, Megan. *The Miraculous Image in Renaissance Florence*. New Haven: Yale University Press, 2013.

Klapisch-Zuber, Christiane. "Parrains et filleuls. Une approche comparée de la France, l'Angleterre et l'Italie médiévales." *Medieval Prosopography* 6 (1985): 51–77.

Landucci, Luca. *A Florentine Diary from 1450 to 1516 by Luca Landucci Continued by an Anonymous Writer till 1542 with Notes by Iodoco del Badia*. Trans. Alice de Rosen Jervis. London: J.M. Dent & Sons, 1927.

Lavin, Marilyn Aronberg. *Piero della Francesca's Baptism of Christ*. New Haven: Yale University Press, 1981.

Mazzi, Maria Serena. *Prostitute e lenoni nella Firenze del Quattrocento*. Milan: Saggiatore, 1991.

Muir, Edward. *Ritual in Early Modern Europe*. 2nd ed. Cambridge: Cambridge University Press, 2005.

Paoletti, John. *Michelangelo's David: Florentine History and Civic Identity*. Cambridge: Cambridge University Press, 2016.

Pogány-Balás, Edith. "Problems of Mantegna's Destroyed Fresco in Rome, Representing the Baptism of Christ." *Acta Historiae Artium. Academiae Scientiarum Hungaricae* 18 (1972): 107–24.

Randolph, Adrian. *Engaging Symbols: Gender, Politics, and Public Art in Fifteenth-Century Florence*. New Haven: Yale University Press, 2002.

Roberts, Perri Lee. *Masolino da Panicale*. Oxford: Clarendon Press, 1993.

Rocke, Michael. *Forbidden Friendships: Homosexuality and Male Culture in Renaissance Florence*. Oxford: Oxford University Press, 1996.

Rubin, Patricia Lee. *Seen from Behind: Perspectives on the Male Body and Renaissance Art*. New Haven: Yale University Press, 2018.

Salisbury, Joyce E. "The Latin Doctors of the Church on Sexuality." *Journal of Medieval History* 12 (1986): 279–89.

Salvestrini, Francesco. "Associazionismo e devozione nella Compagnia di San Luca (1340 ca.– 1563)." In Bert W. Meijer and Luigi Zangheri, eds., *Accademia delle Arti del Disegno: studi, fonti e interpretazioni di 450 anni di storia. Tomo I.* Florence: Leo S. Olschki Editore, 2015, 3–17.

Sandström, Sven. "The Programme for the Decoration of the Belvedere of Innocent VIII." *Konshistorisk tidskrift/Journal of Art History* 29 (1960): 35–75.

Spinks, Bryan D. *Early and Medieval Rituals and Theologies of Baptism: From the New Testament to the Council of Trent*. Aldershot, UK: Ashgate, 2006.

"Spinario." In *The Grove Encyclopedia of Classical Art and Architecture*, ed. Gordon Campell. Oxford: Oxford University Press, 2007, *sub voce*. Online at https://www.oxfordreference.com/view/10.1093/acref/9780195300826.001.0001/acref-9780195300826.

Stowell, Steven. "A Baptism of Drawing: Coming of Age as an Artist in Giorgio Vasari's *Lives*." In Una Roman D'Elia, ed., *Rethinking Renaissance Drawings: Essays in Honour of David McTavish*. Montreal & Kingston: McGill-Queen's University Press, 2015, 107–17.

– "Purging the Eye: Images and the Cure for Lust in Catholic Reformation Italy." In Peter Howard, Nicholas Terpstra, and Riccardo Saccenti, eds., *Renaissance Religions: Modes and Meanings in History*. Turnhout: Brepols, 2021, 207–30.

Taja, D'Agostino. *Descrizione del Palazzo Apostolico Vaticano*. Rome: Niccolò e Marco Pagliarini, 1750.

Tietze-Conrat, Erika. *Mantegna: Paintings, Drawings, Engravings*. London: Phaidon Press, 1955.

Tomas, Natalie. "Did Women Have a Space?" In Roger J. Crum and John T. Paoletti, eds., *Renaissance Florence: A Social History*. Cambridge: Cambridge University Press, 2006, 311–28.

Trexler, Richard C. *Public Life in Renaissance Florence*. New York: Academic Press, 1980.

Vasari, Giorgio. *Vite de' piu eccellenti pittori scultori e architettori, 1550 e 1568.* Florence: Giunti, 1568. Ed. Paola Barocchi and Rosanna Bettarini. Florence S.P.E.S., già Sansoni, 1966–87. Online at https://www.memofonte.it/ricerche/giorgio-vasari/#testi.

– *Lives of the Painters, Sculptors and Architects.* Trans. Gaston du C. de Vere, intro. David Ekserdjian. New York: Everyman's Library, Alfred A. Knopf, 1996.

Wakayama, Eiko M.L. "Il programma iconografico degli affreschi di Masolino nel Battistero di Castiglione Olona." *Arte Lombarda* 50 (1978): 20–32.

Weissman, Ronald F.E. *Ritual Brotherhood in Renaissance Florence.* New York: Academic Press, 1982.

Wharton, Annabel Jane. "Ritual and Reconstructed Meaning: The Neonian Baptistery in Ravenna." *The Art Bulletin* 69 (1987): 358–75.

Wolfthal, Diane. *In and Out of the Marital Bed: Seeing Sex in Renaissance Europe.* New Haven: Yale University Press, 2010.

2 Blasphemous or Beautiful? Leonardo da Vinci's *Saint John the Baptist*: Holy Masculinity and Its Ambiguities ca. 1500

ANNE L. WILLIAMS

Summary: Leonardo da Vinci's sensuous *Saint John the Baptist* (ca. 1513–16) has troubled its modern viewers for centuries, producing a trail of scholarship that attempts to explain its alleged blasphemy, androgyny, or ambiguity by probing Leonardo's sexual life or by claiming that the saint's appearance is irrelevant to its interpretation. In other words, it is assumed that for his period viewer, Leonardo's *Saint John* was understood to be "deviant" with respect to both gender and religious norms. However, period accounts of the painting remark not on blasphemy, but beauty, while depictions of beautiful male saints like John the Evangelist and Sebastian contextualize the painting within a long tradition binding holy masculine beauty and virtue. This article proposes an interpretation of the *Saint John* rooted in Leonardo's engagement with Aristotelian natural philosophy, period conceptions of holy masculinity, and theological discourse, in order to reconstruct the painting's devotional implications for the period viewer.

Leonardo da Vinci's *Saint John the Baptist* (ca. 1513–16; fig. 2.1) confronts the viewer with an intriguing, seductive, and rather enticingly beautiful image of a saint whose vividly well shaped form belies his hermitical life described in the Bible. Walter Pater notes particularly his "delicate brown flesh and woman's hair no one would go out into the wilderness to seek, and whose treacherous smile would have us understand something far beyond the outward gesture or circumstance."[1] The depicted body of Saint John is undeniably sensuous. This has led to modern interpretations that cast the saint as not only androgynous but even blasphemous, while the image's religiosity is overshadowed by a desire to see the saint's beauty as a reflection of Leonardo's alleged

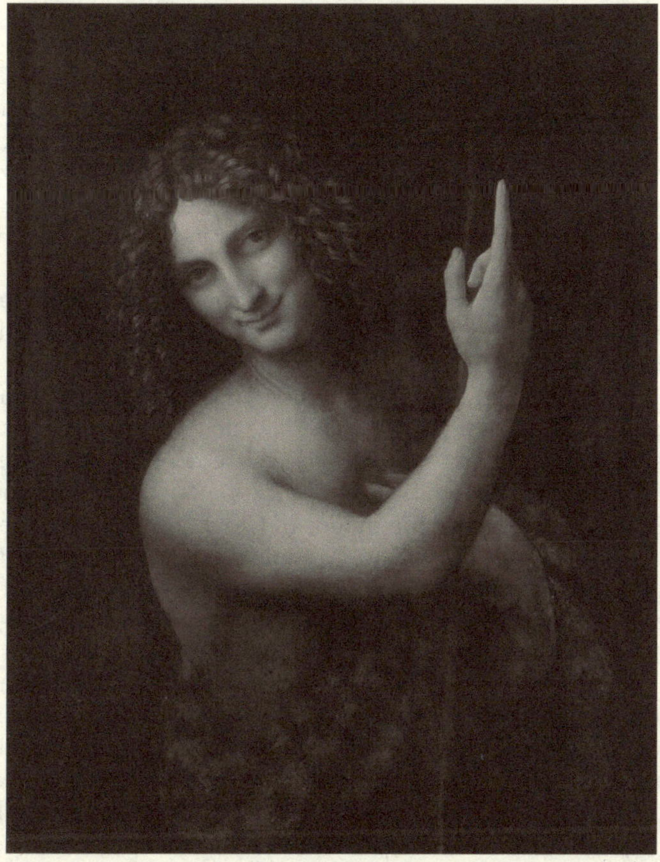

2.1. Leonardo da Vinci, *Saint John the Baptist* (ca. 1513–16). Oil on panel, 69 x 57 cm. Inv. 775, Musée du Louvre, Paris. Photo © RMN-Grand Palais/Art Resource, NY.

homosexuality and weakness for its probable model, Salaì, the painter's assistant. For example, Giuseppe Fornari writes that the painting and Leonardo's related works are filled with "a homoerotic sensuality."[2] Robert Kiely describes the saint as "a soft, coy, effeminate figure smiling with head cocked … His left hand holds up his camelskin in a delicate gesture resembling that of a woman arranging her negligee."[3] As a result, some have suggested that the sensuousness of Saint John's body is inconsequential to its religious interpretation, or have ignored its sacral possibilities entirely.[4] The saint's appearance, as well as its formal relationship to Leonardo's *Bacchus* (1510–15; Musée du Louvre,

Paris), is interpreted as evidence of an artist "ambivalent about sexuality and religion."[5] Yet in focusing on the saint's assumed deviance with respect to gender and religious norms, we overlook the ambiguous nature of period conceptions of ideal, holy masculinity and how Leonardo's Saint John might align with them. This article proposes an interpretation of the painting rooted in late fifteenth- and early sixteenth-century conceptions of beautiful male sanctity – and one that is perhaps more intuitive for an artist whose mind was deeply engaged with Aristotelian scientific tradition.

In Latin and Orthodox Christianity, John the Baptist was understood to be the first saint, although as the precursor to Christ he was likewise a prophet.[6] He therefore functioned simultaneously as a type for Christ and as a likeness of him, a conception aided by the cousins' proximity in age and familial relationship.[7] While we do not know this painting's intended function, patron, or exact date, we do know that the work ended up in the collection of King Francis I after Leonardo brought it to his French workshop at the manor of Cloux in Amboise. The secretary of Cardinal Louis of Aragon, Antonio de' Beatis, observed it there in October of 1517, stating that Leonardo showed the cardinal three pictures, one of which depicted "St. John the Baptist, as a Young Man" and "all of them most perfect."[8] The painting is not noted for its "disturbingly erotic charge,"[9] nor any confounding deviance from norms. The presence of contemporary Italian copies of the painting suggests that it was begun in Italy, possibly in Florence, of which the Baptist was patron saint. The saint's upward-pointing gesture relates closely to that of an earlier sculpture of the Baptist by Gian Francesco Rustici in the Baptistery of Florence, dated 1506–11, which Vasari states was "contrived with the advice of Leonardo."[10]

What is clear is that Leonardo took great care in depicting the luminosity of the saint's skin, the supple curve of the shoulder, the folds in the skin of the neck, the softness of the face, and the gentle curving of the eyes and mouth, all highlighted by different gradations of light in a beautifully nuanced execution of the artist's *chiaroscuro*. Robert Zwijnenberg suggests that the perceived ambiguity of this depiction of John arises from the incompatibility of his hermitical life with his sensuous body, in other words, an opposition between mind, or spirit, and body.[11] However, as has been noted in much recent scholarship, Leonardo's scientific explorations firmly drove his artistic practice; for him, painting was a scientific endeavour.[12] His anatomical illustrations and annotations attest to his fascination with the human reproductive system – the means by which body and spirit conjoined – as well as his espousal of the Hippocratic theory that the soul is directly formative of every characteristic of the body; this conception comes directly from the artist's engagement with Avicenna's *Canon* (1025), following Aristotle. This suggests that the artist would not have entertained such an opposition in the depiction of the body, but particularly an opposition between the beauty of a saint's body and sanctity of his spirit.[13] Paul Barolsky suggests that John's perceived ambiguity is "born of the problematic relation in Leonardo's painting, as in Christianity itself, between the spirit and the flesh, an ambiguity born of Leonardo's audacious and (dare one say it?) flawed attempt to make visible the divine mystery of the spirit in the flesh."[14] Leonardo may not have perceived such an ambiguity, but the question remains whether an early sixteenth-century Catholic mind would.

The beauty of John's fleshly appearance according to a period understanding is substantiated particularly by Protestant critics of the Catholic cult of images, as well as by the painter and critic Giorgio Vasari writing in the mid-sixteenth century. In his *Life of Fra Bartolommeo,* Vasari corroborates the fact that the beauty of a bare male saint certainly did contain the power to incite his viewer to lascivious thoughts. He then recounts a story of a nude Saint Sebastian of such life and great "melting beauty" that it was removed from the church and placed in the chapter house, so as not to incite further sinful thoughts.[15] While Vasari notes the Leonardesque properties of Fra Bartolommeo's work, the "problem" of beautiful, holy masculinity of the kind presented by this Sebastian was not new. The *Expostulatio adversus corruptionem juventutis,* a treatise on the corruption of the youth written by the theologian Jean Gerson in 1402, called for the promulgation of laws against the sale and display of nude and "reprehensible" images.[16] In 1525 the Swiss reformer Huldrych Zwingli (1484–1531) also called attention to the problems associated with possible misuse of beautiful male and female saints. Male saints who were depicted as handsome youths, knights, or nobles posed a particular problem; these typically included Saints Sebastian and John the Evangelist, who were frequently presented, like Leonardo's John the Baptist, as young saints with long hair and a softer visage.[17] Christlike in their martyrdom, young, beautiful, mostly nude Sebastians with long, curly hair proliferated in the churches of fifteenth- and sixteenth-century Italy, exemplified by Perugino's *Saint Sebastian* of ca. 1490 (fig. 2.2).[18] Leonardo's depiction of John the Evangelist at the *Last Supper* (fig. 2.3) in the refectory of Santa Maria delle Grazie, Milan (ca. 1495–8) derives from a long theological tradition that characterizes the disciple as the beloved, beautiful cousin and sometimes mystical bride of Christ (fig. 2.4).[19] According to a widely circulated legend originating in Late Antiquity, John rejected his bride at

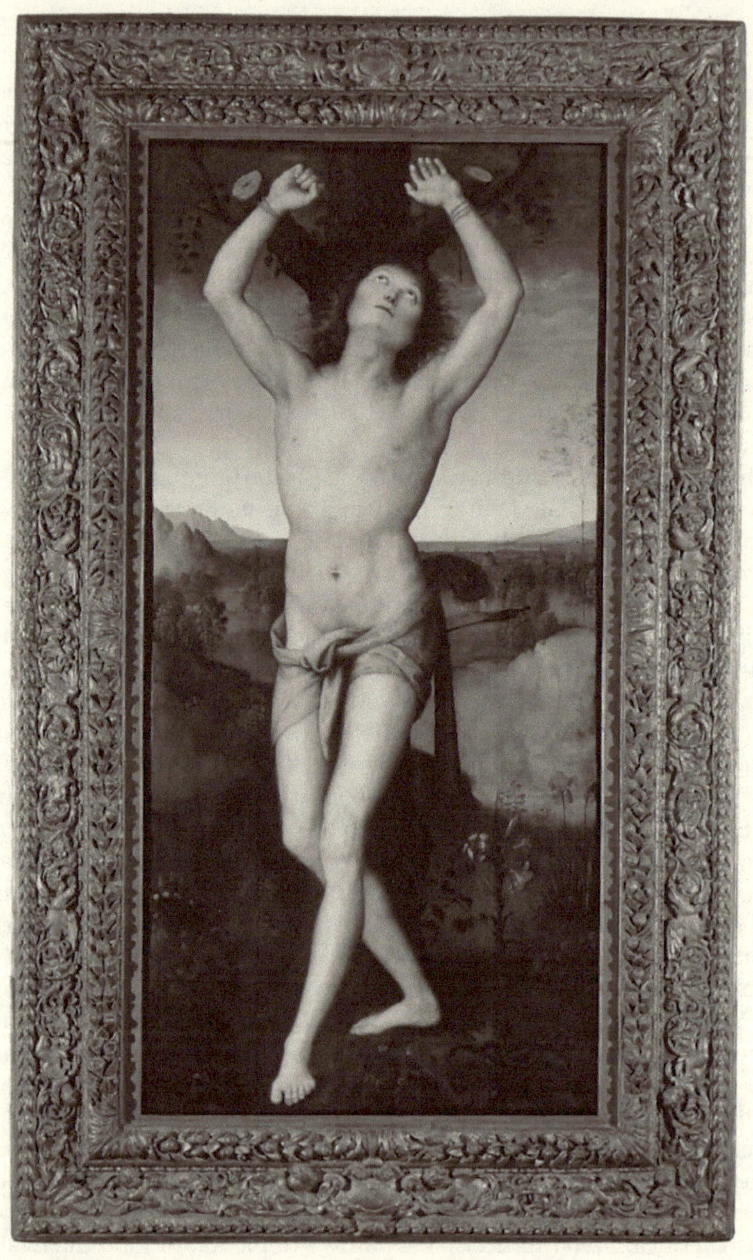

2.2. Perugino, *Saint Sebastian* (ca. 1485). Oil on panel, 174 x 88 cm (excluding frame). Inventory Number NM 2703, Nationalmuseum, Stockholm. Photo: Erik Cornelius /Nationalmuseum. Online. Open access.

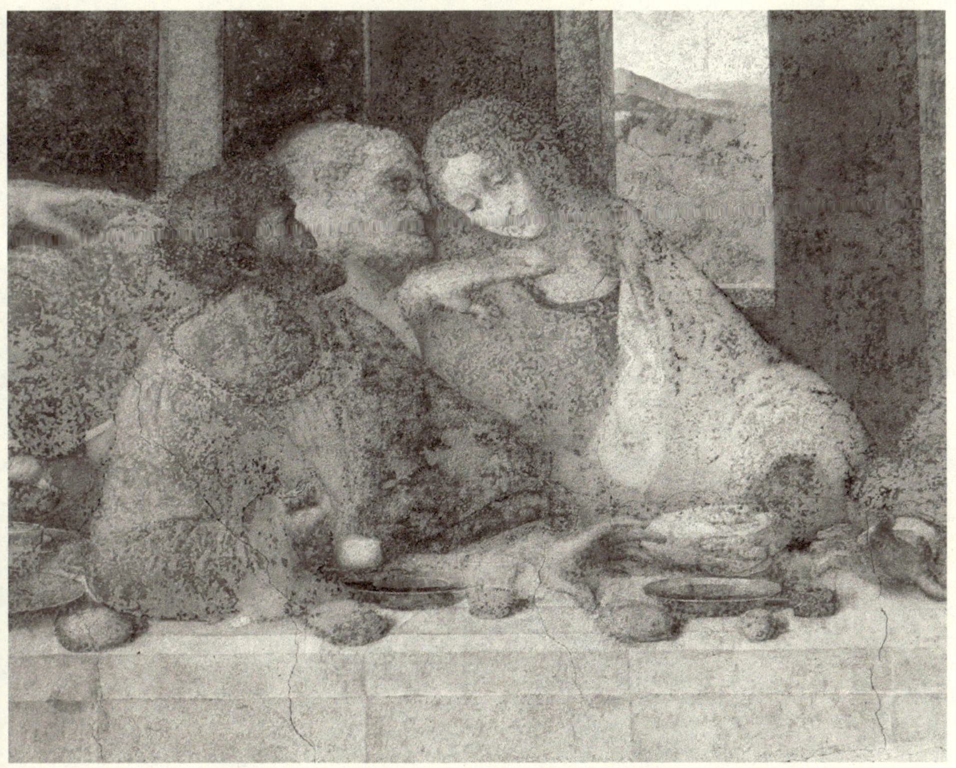

2.3. Leonardo da Vinci, *The Last Supper* (1495–7). Detail of the left side with Saint John. Santa Maria delle Grazie, Milan. Photo © Ghigo G. Roli/Art Resource, NY.

Cana, who was sometimes identified as Mary Magdalene, in favour of his spiritual bridegroom, Christ.[20] As Jeffrey Hamburger indicates, the legend was sufficiently popular by the sixteenth century to warrant denunciation by Counter-Reformation critics. The union is modelled on the Last Supper's final embrace between John and Christ and figured prominently in monastic contexts, where John functioned as the ideal *sponsa Christi* for beholders male and female. John the Baptist's adoption of the Evangelist's beauty as cousin and *sponsa Christi* makes sense not just in the context of both saints' familial relationship with Jesus, but also in their close theològical and iconographical relationship as prophet and evangelist, as proclaimers of Christ's coming in flesh and in Logos, precipitated by the Baptist's words "After me there cometh a man, who is preferred before me: because he was before me" (John

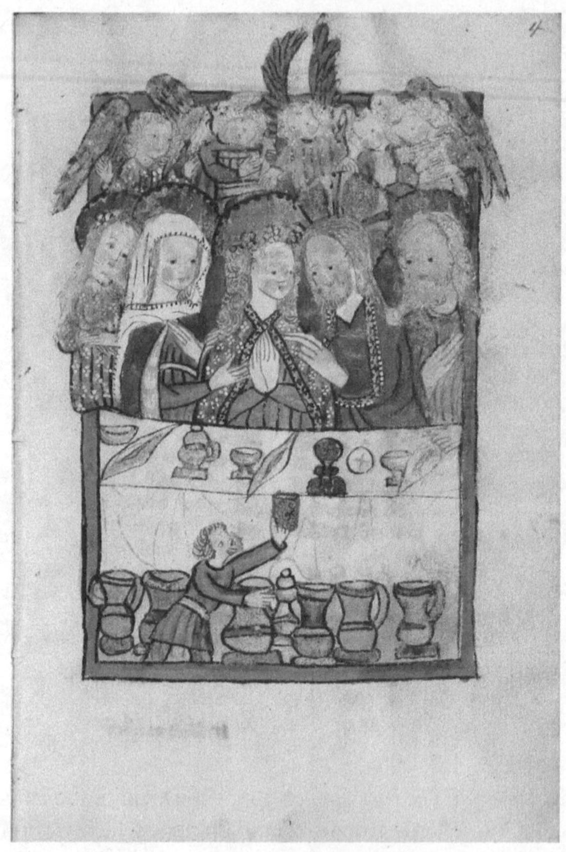

2.4. Marriage of Christ and John the Evangelist at the Marriage of Cana. Libellus for John the Evangelist, Upper Rhine (before 1493). Öffentliche Bibliothek der Universität Basel, MS. A VI 38, fol. 4r. Open access.

1:30). The Lateran Baptistery's pairing of their chapels, flanking a third chapel dedicated to the Cross, also speaks to the saints' theological inseparability.[21]

For the pious Catholic viewer, the beauty of a saint was less a problem than intended to show his goodness. According to the Dominican theologian Thomas Aquinas, inner beauty manifested in external, physical beauty, realized through a correspondence of "clarity" ("claritas") and "good proportion" ("bonae proportiones").[22] Saintly beauty was therefore a physical, external sign of one's spirituality and closeness to God. Rather than being necessarily "womanly," long and curly hair was frequently associated with youthful male nobility, and therefore automatically linked to beauty.[23] While characterizing depictions and descriptions of beautiful male saints and nobles as late as the fifteenth and sixteenth centuries, the tradition dates as early as the Merovingians. In twelfth- and thirteenth-century romances, the ideal beautiful male is often described as a youth having long, curly blond hair and a well-built form; lovers are even described as mirror images of one another in all ways, except for their sex.[24] This concept resonated in fifteenth- and sixteenth-century satirical prints and drawings of "ill-matched couples" by artists including the Housebook Master, Israhel van Meckenem, Urs Graf, and Leonardo himself, in which shrivelled old women are paired with categorically beautiful young men. Leonardo's depiction of a beardless, long-haired, soft-featured John the Baptist aligns with his own conception of these unequally paired youths, evidenced by copies of a drawing he executed in the late 1490s in Milan (fig. 2.5) and indebted in turn to earlier versions of the theme like those of the Housebook Master (1475–80; fig. 2.6).[25] The beauty of Leonardo's saint may therefore be understood as a manifestation of his privileged spiritual and human relationship with God as precursor, prophet, and earthly cousin.

Yet John's sensuality, his carnality, may also speak to his Christlike nature. Images denoting what Leo Steinberg calls the "humanation" of Christ, such as those in which the genitals of the baby or adult Christ are highlighted or alluded to, evoke particularly the sexuality of Christ. This is an aspect that renders him explicitly human and thus sharing in our somatic suffering and pleasure.[26] Richard Rambuss notes that without this acknowledgment of Christ's human sexuality, whether implicitly in text or in image, his unmatched purity and chastity could not be understood as the highest triumph over the challenges posed by the appropriation of earthly flesh.[27] Jesus' own sensual fleshliness and "ambiguous sexuality" come to the fore in the eucharistic body of Rosso Fiorentino's *Dead Christ with Angels* (ca. 1525–6; fig. 2.7), a depiction of a resurrecting Christ marked by a perceived ambivalence between flesh and spirit, as Regina Stefaniak notes, rooted in the "paradoxical historic body of Christ after death and his alternative noncorporeal eucharistic body."[28] As a precursor, proxy, and reflection of Christ incarnate, Saint John's vividly lifelike bodily form and soft, sensuous flesh similarly reflect the forthcoming, fully humanized, and therefore bodily Christ. The early sixteenth-century phenomenon of John's likeness to contemporaneous depictions of Jesus appears as well in Pordenone's *Blessed Giustiniani and Saints* (ca. 1520; fig. 2.8), a conception indebted to the saint's theological affinity to the Saviour as well as to the influence of Michelangelo.

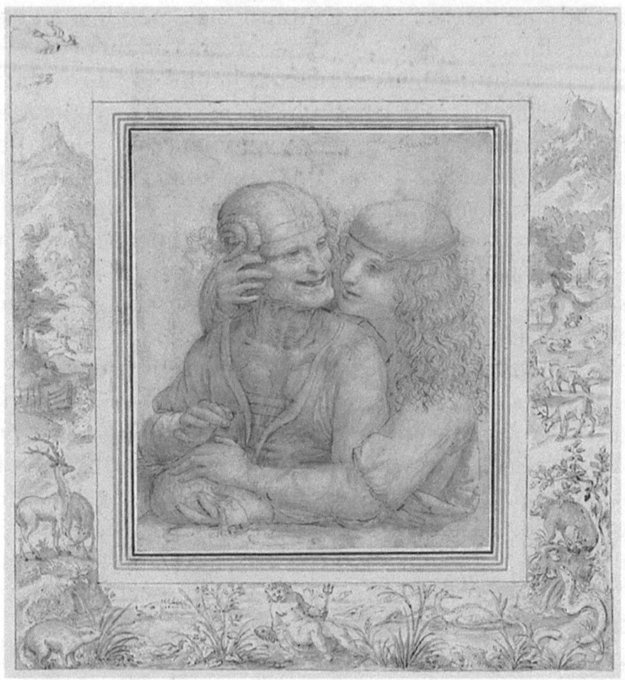

2.5. Jacob Hoefnagel, after Leonardo da Vinci, *Unequal Couple* (1602). Drawing, 31.1 x 29.3 cm. Inventory number 60r, Albertina, Vienna. Photo © Albertina, Vienna. Online. Open access.

John's enticing smile and direct gaze, a seductive invitation when paired with a beautiful bare body, are also endowed with theological meaning. This might distance the saint's visage from such Freudian interpretations as that of the psychoanalyst André Green, who interprets the *Saint John* as a "union of feminine and masculine, perhaps of son and mother … we receive the impression of being not far from the blasphemous."[29] John's smile appears in other depictions of the saint as a baby, as the *Madonna of the Veil* (fig. 2.9) from the School of Raphael. The origin of the smiling friend of Christ lies in theological expositions on the marriage of Christ and Mary, personified as *Ecclesia*, a union derived from that of the *sponsus* and *sponsa* in the Old Testament Song of Songs. According to Origen's mid-third-century Neoplatonic commentary on the Song of Songs, Christ as *sponsus* is the bridegroom, the Word of God; the *sponsa Christi*, the Bride of Christ, is interpreted as *Ecclesia*, metaphorical

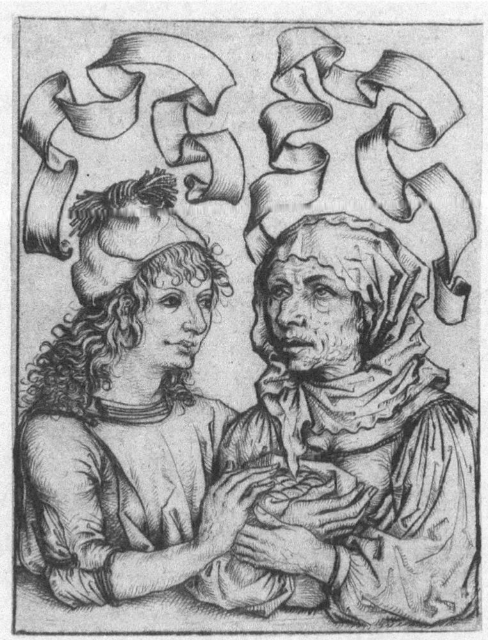

2.6. Master of the Amsterdam Cabinet (Housebook Master), *Unequal Couple* (1475–80). Drypoint, 125 x 98 mm. Object number RP-P-OB-932, Rijksmuseum, Amsterdam. Photo © Rijksmuseum, Amsterdam. Online. Open access.

for the aggregate souls of the believers. Commentaries on the Song of Songs flourished in the Middle Ages and remained popular in sixteenth-century theology and devotion.[30] The Cistercian Bernard of Clairvaux's twelfth-century *Sermons on the Song of Songs* qualify the bride as the Virgin Mary and describe an angelic companion of the bridegroom who turns to the Lord, rejoicing with delight, a passage quoted in the widely read *Meditations on the Life of Christ* (ca. 1300 or 1346–64).[31] John states his role as the friend of the bridegroom in John 3:29: "He that has the bride is the bridegroom: but the friend of the bridegroom, who stands and hears him, rejoices with joy because of the bridegroom's voice. This my joy therefore is fulfilled." This passage inspired the Church Fathers and later theologians to consider the Baptism of Christ as the moment of his marriage to the Church. Christ's naming of John as "angelum meum" (Matthew 11:10) led Bernard of Clairvaux to call him "elect among

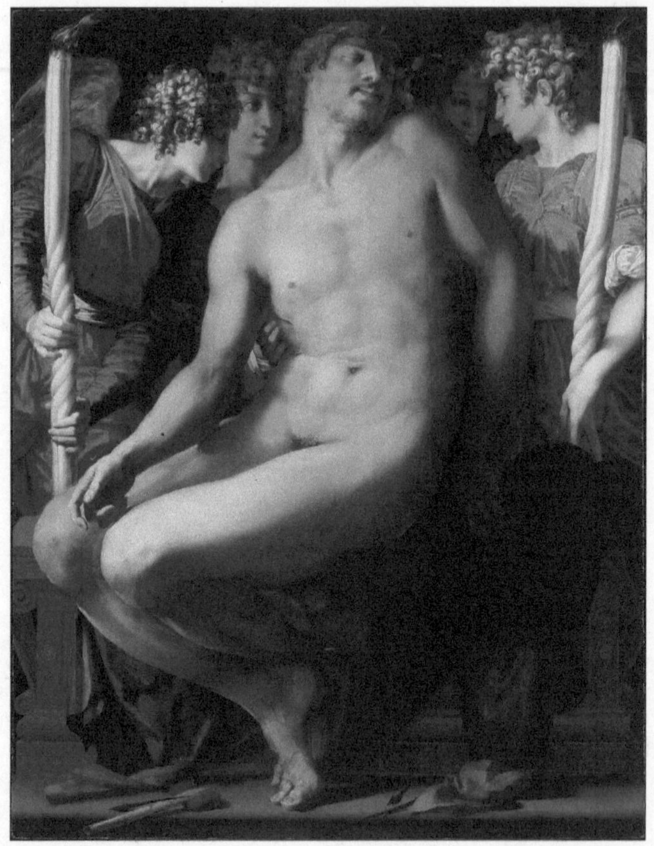

2.7. Rosso Fiorentino, *The Dead Christ with Angels* (ca. 1524–7). Oil on panel, 133.4 x 104.1 cm. Accession number 58.527, Museum of Fine Arts, Boston. Photo © Museum of Fine Arts, Boston.

angels," a title directly quoted in chapter 30 of the *Meditations* and referenced in the popular *Golden Legend* (ca. 1259–66) of Jacobus de Varagine.[32] The joyful smile of John, prophet, friend of the bridegroom, angel, and baptizer of Christ, indicates his role in the mystical marriage of *sponsus* and *sponsa*, with respect to the union of Christ and *Ecclesia*.[33]

As a simultaneous type for and likeness of Christ, the smiling, angelic friend of the bridegroom alludes to the ultimate union sought in mystical commentaries on the Song of Songs, manifested in earlier depictions of John the Evangelist and possibly also in Leonardo's Evangelist in Santa Maria delle Grazie. Cistercian and Franciscan mystical language follows

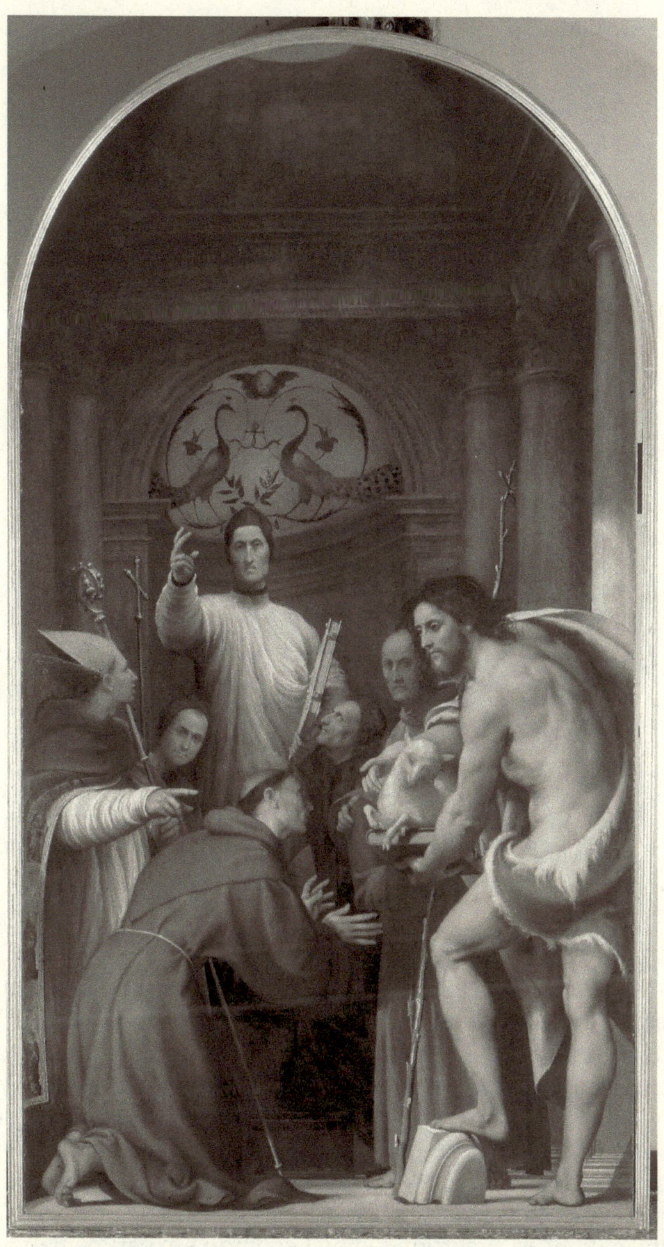

2.8. Giovanni Antonio de' Sacchis, called Pordenone, *The Blessed Lorenzo Giustiniani between Two Monks and Saints Louis of Toulouse, Francis, Bernardino of Siena, and John the Baptist* (ca. 1528–32). Oil on canvas, 420 x 222 cm. Catalogue number 316, Gallerie dell'Accademia, Venice. Photo © Gallerie dell'Accademia, Venice – Archivio fotografico – by concession of the Ministero della Cultura.

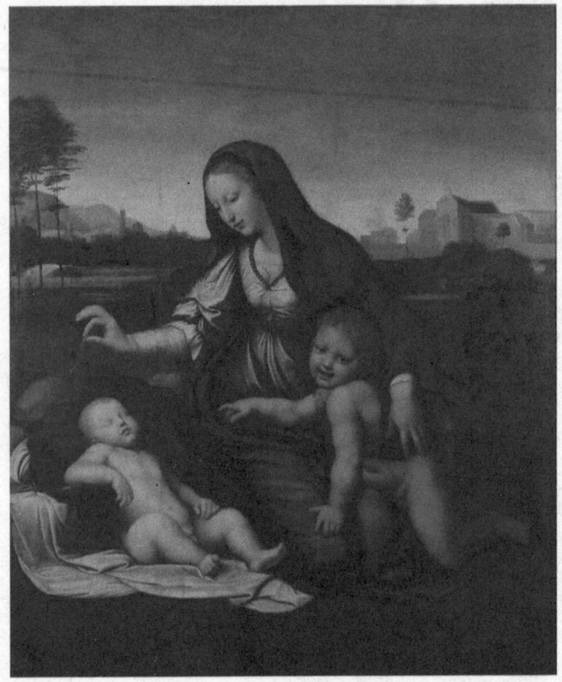

2.9. School of Raphael, *Virgin and Child with Saint John (Madonna of the Veil)* (1483–1520). Oil on wood panel, 132 x 110 cm. Object number y783, Princeton University Art Museum. Photo © Princeton University Art Museum. Online. Open access.

Bernard's explication in adopting the role of the *sponsa* in seeking the kiss of Christ, the *sponsus*. Bernard qualified the *sponsa* as the soul, ever longed for and sought by Christ, the *sponsus*, who was equated with the body. Male and female devotees thus adopted the role of the *sponsa* in awaiting union with the *sponsus*.[34] The "humanation," the carnality, of Christ is therefore centralized, providing a means for humanity to approach divine union with its Saviour – a bridal union employed in the eucharistic theology of Ambrose, Hilary, Chrysostom, and Aquinas.[35] This emphasis on "humanation" is foregrounded by Leonardo's experimentations with an Angel of the Annunciation in a similar pose to that of John the Baptist (fig. 2.10); Vasari notes a finished painting of such an angel by Leonardo in the cabinet of the Florentine Grand Duke Cosimo I, describing "the head of an angel, who is raising one arm in the air, which, coming forward, is foreshortened from the shoulder to the elbow, and with the

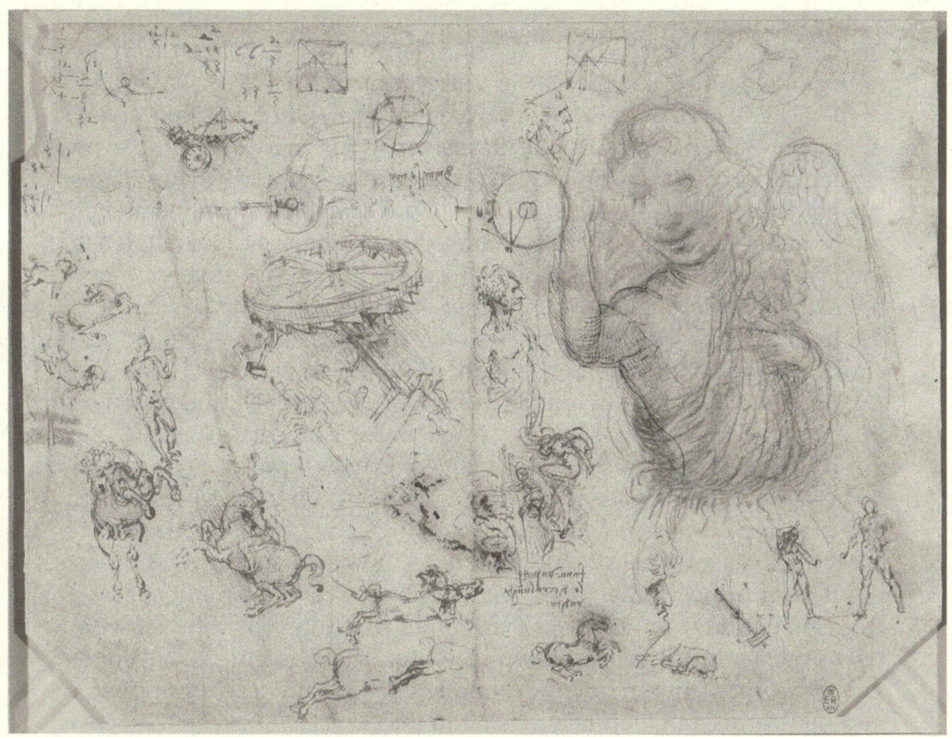

2.10. Leonardo da Vinci and pupil, *Horses and soldiers, mechanics, and the Angel of the Annunciation* (ca. 1503–4). Pen and ink, black chalk, 21.0 x 28.3 cm. RCIN 912328, Royal Collection Trust. Royal Collection Trust/© His Majesty King Charles III 2023.

other he raises the hand to the breast."[36] The original has not been found, but the existence of a number of related drawings suggests there was at least a design for such an angel, seen from the perspective of the Virgin Mary, in Leonardo's workshop. Furthermore, at least three versions by Leonardo's workshop of John the Baptist in the pose of this angel exist. In terms of their roles as messengers announcing the birth of Christ, the relationship between the two makes sense.[37] Yet, the relationship may also run deeper. The smiling, Annunciate angel likewise evokes the mystical marriage of *sponsus* and *sponsa*, Christ and *Ecclesia*, personified as the Virgin, at the moment of the Incarnation. What is depicted at the moment of the Annunciation, typically, is also the moment of Incarnation itself, in which Mary is inseminated by the Holy Spirit. Painters consistently endeavoured to depict this miraculous moment of impregnation, resorting to motifs like that of the tiny nude Christ child flying down from Heaven with a cross on his shoulder, a motif first evident in late medieval Italian art.[38] Leonardo's notes indicate his fascination with the notion of rendering the invisible in visible form, but his extensive studies of medical theory and anatomy perhaps prevented him from conceiving of an abbreviated or unnaturalistic answer, as his concern clearly lay in rendering forms and moments, including conception, as true to life as possible. Leonardo's understanding of impregnation, documented in his drawing of the act of coitus, corresponds primarily to Aristotelian medical theory, which considered conception to be the moment when the soul, the *anima*, given by the father, finds its corresponding body in the mother.[39] For Leonardo, the smiling, Annunciate angel would also evoke the moment of the Incarnation, of the union between Christ and *Ecclesia*, body and soul, word made flesh. In this context, the infamous phallic drawing known as the "Angel Incarnate" or "Angel in the Flesh" (fig. 2.11) makes sense as a subversive play upon the moment of Incarnation, although its attribution to Leonardo himself is contested. The drawing was executed in charcoal on the same blue paper employed for the artist's anatomical studies of 1513, now at Windsor. Written on the back are the words "astrapen," "bronten," and "ceronubolian" – thunder, lightning, and flashes – examples mentioned by Pliny of what only Apelles could represent in painting. These might be linked to Leonardo's contemporaneous experimentations with drawings of wind and rainstorms, but their relationship to the depicted angel on the verso is unclear.[40]

John's formal relationship to the pointing "Angel Incarnate," likely also modelled on the beautiful Salaì, has led some to describe the saint as androgynous.[41] Carlo Pedretti suggests that Leonardo was fascinated by "the idea of having one sex merge into the other – one Platonically complementing the other into a harmonious whole."[42] Leonardo's interpretation of the beautiful body, and that of his followers, the so-called Leonardeschi, in Milan may indeed be attributed to the general influence of Neoplatonic discourse during the Renaissance, like that of Marsilio Ficino's *De amore* (1484) among Milanese courtly circles.[43] Yet, with respect to Leonardo's male saints, what we perceive as "feminine" masculinity is also rooted in an extensive tradition of the beautiful, youthful masculine manifested in earlier depictions of secular nobility and of saints like John the Evangelist, which reveal that a young saint could adopt a beardless, softer visage, even becoming the mystical bride of Christ, while still being perceived as male. The formal affinities of Leonardo's Evangelist in Milan and the Baptist also have much to do with their presentation as youthful cousins of Jesus – two saints who are closest to God made flesh in familial and theological, earthly and spiritual form.

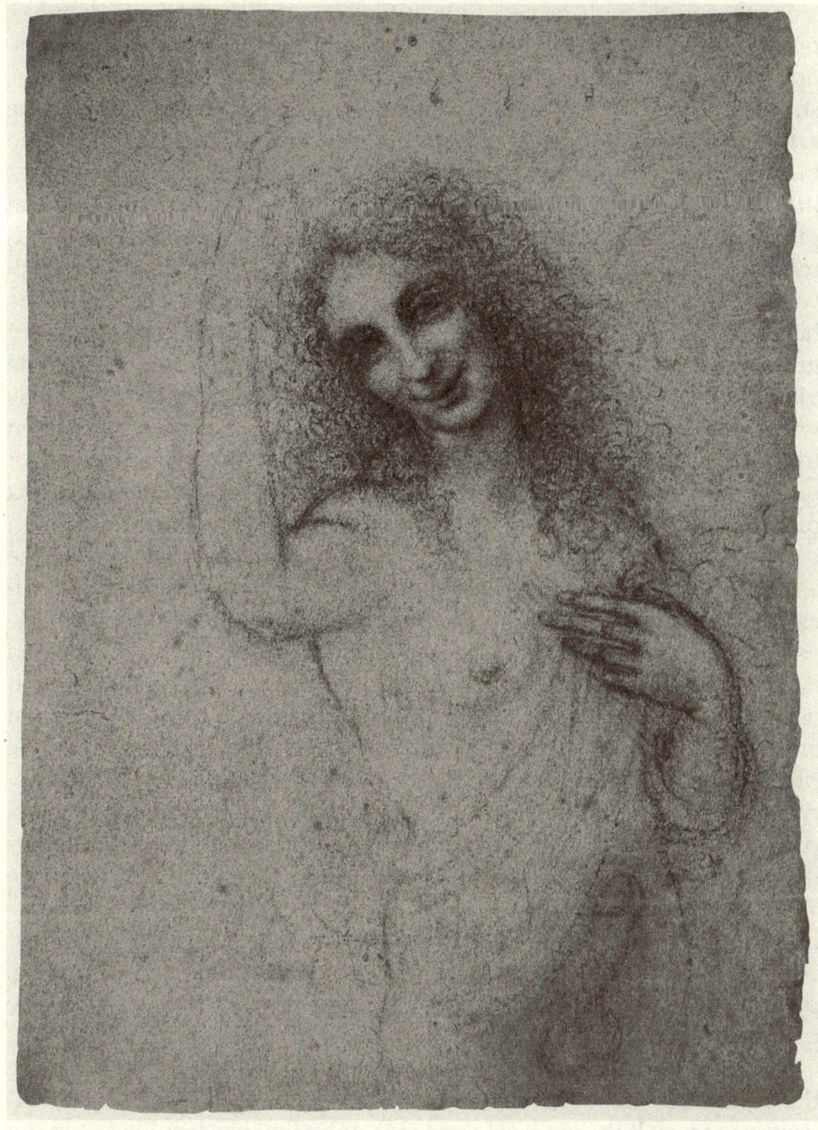

2.11. Leonardo da Vinci (?), *The Angel in the Flesh* (ca. 1510–15). Drawing. Private Collection. Photo © Fine Art Images/Heritage Images.

Furthermore, with respect to beauty, love, and the body, Leonardo's notes reveal his consistent engagement with Aristotelian natural philosophy, far more than the philosophy of contemporary Neoplatonic circles, so it is to this tradition as well that we should look for insight into the artist's conception of gender. Despite some early similarities to Marsilio Ficino's ideas, Leonardo's theories of artistic invention and love are "not in practice developed in a Neoplatonic manner."[44] Aristotelian natural philosophy and medical theory as interpreted by Avicenna certainly admitted the concept of a masculine female or feminine male. Yet, both within and outside of scientific discourse, being feminine or masculine had much to do with one's character, social behaviour, and habits, not just one's genitalia or appearance. Medical treatises acknowledge the viability of "feminine males," grouping men engaging in sexual acts with other men, hermaphrodites, eunuchs, and women dressing as men together under this category.[45] But a soft-featured face or limbs did not qualify as an example of "deviant" masculinity, especially in the context of youth, and the concept of a "feminine" male had much to do with behaviour. What is apparent throughout Aristotelian discourse is the association of passivity and receptivity with the female sex, physiologically and socially.[46] Leonardo's Saint John may adopt a "feminine" role as the object of the viewer's gaze. But *holy* "feminine" masculinity, when it exists, is not perceived as alarming, nor as deviant from maleness, but as a vehicle for spiritual transcendence. According to Donald Weinstein and Rudolph Bell, the thirteenth and fourteenth centuries witnessed the profound rise of male saints that can be termed "androgynous" not because of their sex but because of their virtues of "penitential asceticism, private prayer, mystical communication with the Godhead, and charity," attributes characteristically found in female saints.[47] As Caroline Walker Bynum points out, monks who proclaim their womanlike weakness become Christlike in their humility, and language and images that celebrate the role of Jesus as "mother" evoke life-giving and nurturing, positive qualities.[48] Yet, as Steinberg argues with respect to Renaissance painting, Jesus' "manhood is not thereby diminished."[49]

Far from passive, John's gaze actively engages the viewer, unlike the numerous beautiful wounded Sebastians of fifteenth- and sixteenth-century Italy; yet it is Leonardo's John that has troubled so many modern viewers for its effeminacy. Whether or not John's gaze would have seduced the viewer into a lusty reverie, his gaze, like his beauty, contains devotional implications. Leonardo's notes again provide an insight into the painting's intentions; in his written acclaim for the primacy of painting and for the power of the painter to render the divine, Leonardo writes on the veneration of icons:

> … at the moment of unveiling the great multitude of people who have gathered there immediately throw themselves to the ground, worshipping and praying to the deity, who is represented in the picture … exactly as if this goddess were there as a living presence. This does not happen with any other science or other works of man, and if you claim that this is not due to the power of the painter but to the inherent power of the thing represented, it may be replied that in this case the minds of the men would be satisfied were they to remain in their beds rather than going to wearisome and dangerous places on pilgrimages, as may be continually witnessed. But since such pilgrimages continue to take place, what causes their inessential travels? Certainly you will concede that it is the visual image. All the writings could not do this, by representing so potently the form and spirit of this deity.[50]

This description is marked by the author's fascination with the power and potency of the image as a proxy for the depicted holy person in "form and spirit." The unique frontality and isolation of Leonardo's own saint may have been inspired by the potency of the icons that he contemplates in his notes. John's wall-eyed appearance is notable, and not unlike icons that depict Christ with an unmatched physiognomy reflecting his dual nature as divine and human.[51] The recently rediscovered *Salvator Mundi* attributed to Leonardo (ca. 1500; private collection) reflects this duality through its mismatched portrayal of Christ's eyes and darker shading on the right side of his face. As a proxy for Christ, his prefiguration, as well as his earthly cousin, John's duality mirrors Christ's dual divine and earthly natures. One eye turns towards the cross, in contemplation of and in connection with intangible divinity, while the other engages the earthbound viewer. John's stance is indicative of being caught between two worlds, having just turned towards us. As the last of the prophets, John is the messenger of God, an intermediary between the True Light and man, according to John the Evangelist's Gospel. His mission is only temporary, as an usher of the True Light. He is therefore a transient being, situated between darkness and light, in a role characterized by change.[52] Perhaps the torsion of the saint's body, which Leonardo called "compound," is the artist's attempt to manifest that "otherness" of the transient spiritual.[53] The dark backgrounds of both *Saint John the Baptist* and the *Salvator Mundi* may reflect Leonardo's highly evolved understanding of optics in his later years, associated with his desire to render perspective of shape and form according to the recession of distance as naturalistically as possible. Leonardo's MS D (Paris, Institut de France), probably composed ca. 1508, includes the first challenge by an artist to the physical reality of Alberti's visual pyramid, a group of light rays converging on a single point within the eye. Ultimately, we find Leonardo struggling to reconcile his most advanced and scientifically accurate conception of vision, what he called "prospettiva naturale," and perspective as a geometrical method of constructing space within a picture, "prospettiva accidentale." Leonardo's *Saint John* eliminates the problem of reconciling the two modes of perspective altogether by avoiding any atmospheric or perspectival demonstration of space in the dark, dense background.[54]

The sensuality of this beautiful, bare Saint John has produced a trail of scholarship that attempts to explain the image's alleged ambiguity between spirit and flesh, even its blasphemy, by probing Leonardo's sexual life or by claiming that the saint's appearance is irrelevant to its interpretation. Yet, period conceptions of holy masculinity and Leonardo's notes both suggest that the perception of any ambiguity between spirit and flesh here is a misinterpretation. At least there is no evidence that Leonardo would have understood his saint as anything other than an idealized male saint binding holiness, virtue, and beauty. Indeed, if John's beauty may be attributed to Leonardo's appreciation for the beautiful, young male form, it should also be understood within the context of its theological function, which would certainly encourage the "homoaffective," not just the homoerotic.[55] As the prophet, angelic bridegroom, and image of Jesus, John reflects the unity of human and divine intrinsic to trinitarian conceptions of God in Christ, while embodying theological discourses both spiritual and carnal. Leonardo captures this unity of body and spirit by depicting John in a dual state, mirroring Christ's dual human and divine nature, with one hand and eye towards the cross and Heaven, and a countenance directly engaging the earthly viewer.

NOTES

1 Pater, *The Renaissance*, 118.

2 Fornari, "From the Saint to Bacchus," 151. For similar descriptions, see Pedretti, "Bacchus and Venus," 239; Saslow, *Pictures and Passions*, 89; Aydemir, "The Parting Veil," 133; Clark, *Leonardo da Vinci*, 247; Green, "Angel or Demon?" 159; Gould, *Leonardo*, 125; Douglas, *Leonardo da Vinci*, 104; Heydenreich *Leonardo da Vinci*, 1:56; Stites et al., *The Sublimations of Leonardo da Vinci*, 354, 357–9.

3 Kiely, *Blessed and Beautiful*, 76.

4 Clark, *Leonardo da Vinci*, 246–53.

5 Kiely, *Blessed and Beautiful*, 78. The suggestion that Leonardo was ambivalent about religion is negated by his notes. See Leonardo da Vinci, *Treatise on Painting*, 1:53; Richter, ed., *The Literary Works of Leonardo da Vinci*, 2:101 (no. 837); 2:237 (no. 1134).

6 von Metzsch, *Johannes der Täufer*, 118.
7 Kiely, *Blessed and Beautiful*, 69–70.
8 Quoted in Clark, *Leonardo da Vinci*, 253.
9 Barolsky, "Mysterious Meaning," 14.
10 Vasari, *Lives* (2006), 242; Clark, *Leonardo da Vinci*, 206.
11 Zwijnenberg, "St. John the Baptist and the Essence of Painting," 98.
12 See, for example, Fiorani and Nova, eds., *Leonardo da Vinci and Optics*; Kemp, "'Il Concetto dell'Anima"; Kemp, "Leonardo and the Visual Pyramid"; Lindberg, "Alhazen's Theory of Vision"; Eastwood, "Alhazen, Leonardo, and Late Medieval Speculation"; Richter, ed., *The Literary Works of Leonardo da Vinci*, 1:129–30 (no. 50).
13 Kemp, "'Ogni pittore dipinge sé,'" 314–15; Azzolini, "Exploring Generation."
14 Barolsky, "Mysterious Meaning," 15.
15 Vasari, *Lives* (1912), 4:158.
16 Brown, *Pastor and Laity in the Theology of Jean Gerson*, 241.
17 Egli et al., eds., *Huldreich Zwinglis sämtliche Werke*, 4:145–6; Baxandall, *Limewood Sculptors*, 88–90.
18 For the popularity of Saint Sebastian in Renaissance Italy, see Marshall, "Manipulating the Sacred."
19 According to Christian legend, John the Evangelist, also known as John the Apostle, was the son of Salome, who, again according to legend, was Mary's sister, which would then make John the Evangelist and his older brother James the Great Jesus' cousins, just like John the Baptist. Jones, ed., *Butler's Lives of the Saints*, 12:210.
20 Jansen, *Making of the Magdalen*, 150–1.
21 Hamburger, *St. John the Divine*, 65, 160–2; Hamburger, "Brother, Bride, and *alter Christus*."
22 Thomas Aquinas, *Summa Theologica*, Secunda Secundae Partis, Q.145.2; online.
23 Jaritz, "'Young, Rich and Beautiful,'" 61–5.
24 For example, see *Le Conte de Floire et Blancheflor* (c. 1150). McCaffrey, "Sexual Identity."
25 Stewart, *Unequal Lovers*, 139–41.
26 Steinberg, *Sexuality of Christ*, 11–24.
27 Rambuss, *Closet Devotions*, 63.
28 Stefaniak, "Replicating Mysteries of the Passion," 678–9.
29 Green, "Angel or Demon?" 159. Green is of course inspired by Freud, *Leonardo da Vinci*, 67–8.
30 Stefaniak, "Raphael's *Santa Cecilia*." See also Mews, "Intoxication and the Song of Songs."
31 Attributed to the anonymous "Pseudo-Bonaventure," the manuscript was likely compiled in Tuscany for a nun of the Poor Clares, possibly by the Franciscan preacher Johannes de Caulibus. Recent work dates it between

1346 and 1364. See McNamer, "Further Evidence"; McNamer, "Origins of the *Meditationes vitae Christi*"; McNamer, *Affective Meditation*, 86–8.
32 Ragusa and Green, eds., *Meditations on the Life of Christ*, 183; Varagine, *The Golden Legend*, 1:333–4.
33 Lavin, "The Joy of the Bridegroom's Friend," 194–200.
34 Muir, "Bride or Bridegroom?"; Lochrie, "Mystical Acts, Queer Tendencies," 180–2; Holsinger, "The Color of Salvation," 159.
35 Ambrose, *De sacramentis* 2.5, PL 16:447; Hilary, *Homilia ad Mattheum* 9:14–15, PL 9:963; Chrysostom, *Homilia ad Ioannem* 46, PG 59:260–1; Thomas Aquinas, *Summa Theologica*, Tertia Partis, Q.79.3; online.
36 Vasari, *Lives* (2006), 233.
37 Clark, *Leonardo da Vinci*, 250.
38 Robb, "Iconography of the Annunciation."
39 Windsor, RL 19097v, ca. 1493; Kemp, "'Il Concetto dell'Anima.'"
40 Zwijnenberg, "St. John the Baptist and the Essence of Painting," 110.
41 Zwijnenberg, "'Ogni pittore dipinge sé,'" 61.
42 Pedretti, "The 'Angel in the Flesh,'" 35.
43 Corry, "Alluring Beauty," 579.
44 Kemp, "Ogni pittore dipinge sé,'" 316; Pedretti, *Leonardo da Vinci on Painting*, 53.
45 Cadden, *Meanings of Sex Difference*, 202–9.
46 Simons, *Sex of Men in Premodern Europe*, 129–31.
47 Weinstein and Bell, *Saints and Society*, 237.
48 Bynum, *Jesus as Mother*, 110–69.
49 Steinberg, *Sexuality of Christ*, 366.
50 Urb 2v–3v, quoted in Leonardo, *Leonardo on Painting*, 20.
51 Schönborn, *God's Human Face*, 154.
52 Bouvrande, "Entre ombre et lumière," 268.
53 Urb. 107r, quoted in Kemp, *Leonardo da Vinci*, 341.
54 Kemp, "Leonardo and the Visual Pyramid," 147.
55 For this concept, see Murray, "Masculinizing Religious Life," 32. See also Holsinger, "The Color of Salvation," 163 and McGuire, *The Difficult Saint*, 32–3.

WORKS CITED

Printed Sources

Ambrose. *De sacramentis*. In J.-P. Migne, ed., *Patrologia Latina*, vol. 16. Paris: J.-P. Migne, 1880, 417–64.

Aydemir, Murat. "The Parting Veil: Jacques Lacan and the 'Angel in the Flesh.'" In Carlo Pedretti, ed., *Leonardo da Vinci: L' "Angelo incarnato" e Salai*. Perugia: Cartei & Bianchi, 2009, 130–40.

Azzolini, Monica. "Exploring Generation: A Context to Leonardo's Anatomies of the Female and Male Body." In Alessandro Nova and Domenico Laurenza, eds., *Leonardo da Vinci's Anatomical World: Language, Context and "Disegno"*. Venice: Marsilio, 2011, 79–98.

Barolsky, Paul. "The Mysterious Meaning of Leonardo's 'Saint John the Baptist.'" *Source: Notes in the History of Art* 8.3 (1989): 11–15.

Baxandall, Michael. *The Limewood Sculptors of Renaissance Germany*. New Haven: Yale University Press, 1982.

Bouvrande, Isabelle. "Entre ombre et lumière: le *Saint Jean-Baptiste* de Léonard de Vinci." In Christian Trottmann and Anca Vasiliu, eds., *Du visible à l'intelligible: Lumière et ténèbres de l'Antiquité à la Renaissance*. Paris: Honoré Champion Éditeur, 2004, 265–79.

Brown, D. Catherine. *Pastor and Laity in the Theology of Jean Gerson*. Cambridge: Cambridge University Press, 1987.

Bynum, Caroline Walker. *Jesus as Mother: Studies in the Spirituality of the High Middle Ages*. Berkeley: University of California Press, 1984.

Cadden, Joan. *Meanings of Sex Difference in the Middle Ages: Medicine, Science, and Culture*. Cambridge: Cambridge University Press, 1995.

Chrysostom, John. *Homilia ad Ioannem*. In J.-P. Migne, ed., *Patrologia Graeca*, vol. 59. Paris: J.-P. Migne, 1862, 23–482.

Clark, Kenneth. *Leonardo da Vinci: An Account of His Development as an Artist*. Cambridge: Cambridge University Press, 1939; reprint, London: Penguin Books, 1993.

Corry, Maya. "The Alluring Beauty of a Leonardesque Ideal: Masculinity and Spirituality in Renaissance Milan." *Gender & History* 25.3 (2013): 565–89.

Cullum, P.H., and Katherine J. Lewis, eds. *Holiness and Masculinity in the Middle Ages*. Toronto: University of Toronto Press, 2004.

Douglas, R. Langton. *Leonardo da Vinci: His Life and Pictures*. Chicago: University of Chicago Press, 1944.

Eastwood, Bruce. "Alhazen, Leonardo, and Late Medieval Speculation on the Inversion of Images in the Eye." *An International Review of the History of Science and Technology from the Thirteenth Century* 43.5 (1986): 413–46.

Egli, Emil, et al., eds. *Huldreich Zwinglis sämtliche Werke*. 12 vols. Munich: Kraus-Reprint, 1981.

Fiorani, Francesca, and Alessandro Nova, eds. *Leonardo da Vinci and Optics: Theory and Pictorial Practice*. Venice: Marsilio, 2013.

Fornari, Giuseppe. "From the Saint to Bacchus." In Carlo Pedretti, ed., *Leonardo da Vinci: L' "Angelo incarnato" e Salai*. Perugia: Cartei & Bianchi, 2009, 148–55.

Freud, Sigmund. *Leonardo da Vinci and a Memory of His Childhood*. Trans. Alan Tyson. New York: W.W. Norton and Company, 1964.

Gould, Cecil. *Leonardo: The Artist and the Non-Artist*. Boston: New York Graphic Society, 1975.

Green, André. "Angel or Demon?" In Carlo Pedretti, ed., *Leonardo da Vinci: L' "Angelo incarnato" e Salai*. Perugia: Cartei & Bianchi, 2009, 156–68.

Hamburger, Jeffrey F. "Brother, Bride, and *alter Christus*: The Virginal Body of John the Evangelist in Medieval Art, Theology, and Literature." In Ursula Peters, ed., *Text und Kultur: Mittelalterliche Literatur 1150–1450*. Stuttgart: Metzler, 2001, 296–328.

– *St. John the Divine: The Deified Evangelist in Medieval Art and Theology*. Berkeley: University of California Press, 2002.

Heydenreich, Ludwig H. *Leonardo da Vinci*. Trans. Dora Jane Janson. 2 vols. New York: Macmillan, 1954.

Hilary. *Homilia ad Mattheum*. In J.-P. Migne, ed., *Patrologia Latina*, vol. 9. Paris: J.-P. Migne, 1844, 917–1078.

Holsinger, Bruce. "The Color of Salvation: Desire, Death, and the Second Crusade in Bernard of Clairvaux's *Sermons on the Song of Songs*." In David Townsend and Andrew Taylor, eds., *The Tongue of the Fathers*. Philadelphia: University of Pennsylvania Press, 1998, 156–86.

Jansen, Katherine Ludwig. *The Making of the Magdalen: Preaching and Popular Devotion in the Late Middle Ages*. Princeton: Princeton University Press, 2000.

Jaritz, Gerhard. "'Young, Rich and Beautiful': The Visualization of Male Beauty in the Late Middle Ages." In Balázs Nagy and Marcell Sebök, eds., *The Man of Many Devices, Who Wandered Full Many Ways: Festschrift in Honor of János M. Bak*. Budapest: Central European University Press, 1999, 61–77.

Jones, Kathleen, ed. *Butler's Lives of the Saints: New Full Edition*. Vol. 12. Collegeville, MN: Liturgical Press, 2000.

Kemp, Martin. "'Il Concetto dell'Anima' in Leonardo's Early Skull Studies." *Journal of the Warburg and Courtauld Institutes* 34 (1971): 115–34.

– "Leonardo and the Visual Pyramid." *Journal of the Warburg and Courtauld Institutes* 40 (1977): 128–49.

– *Leonardo da Vinci: The Marvellous Works of Nature and Man*. Cambridge, MA: Harvard University Press, 1981.

– "'Ogni pittore dipinge sé': A Neoplatonic Echo in Leonardo's Art Theory?" In Cecil H. Clough, ed., *Cultural Aspects of the Italian Renaissance: Essays in Honour of Paul Oskar Kristeller*. Manchester: Manchester University Press, 1976, 311–23.

Kiely, Robert. *Blessed and Beautiful: Picturing the Saints*. New Haven: Yale University Press, 2010.

Lavin, Marilyn Aronberg. "The Joy of the Bridegroom's Friend: Smiling Faces in Fra Filippo, Raphael, and Leonardo." In Moshe Barasch and Lucy Freeman Sandler, eds., *Art the Ape of Nature: Studies in Honor of H.W. Janson*. New York: Harry N. Abrams, 1981, 193–210.

Leonardo da Vinci. *Leonardo on Painting: An Anthology of Writings by Leonardo da Vinci with a Selection of Documents Relating to His Career as an Artist*. Ed. and trans. Martin Kemp and Margaret Walker. New Haven: Yale University Press, 1989.

– *Treatise on Painting*. Trans. A. Philip McMahon. 2 vols. Princeton: Princeton University Press, 1956.

Lindberg, David C. "Alhazen's Theory of Vision and Its Reception in the West." *Isis* 58.3 (1967): 321–41.

Lochrie, Karma. "Mystical Acts, Queer Tendencies." In Karma Lochrie, Peggy McCracken, and James A. Schultz, eds., *Constructing Medieval Sexuality*. Minneapolis: University of Minnesota Press, 1997, 180–200.

Marshall, Louise. "Manipulating the Sacred: Image and Plague in Renaissance Italy." *Renaissance Quarterly* 47.3 (1994): 485–532.

McCaffrey, Philip. "Sexual Identity in *Floire et Blancheflor* and *Amie et Amile*." In Karen J. Taylor, ed., *Gender Transgressions: Crossing the Normative Barrier in Old French Literature*. New York: Garland Publishing, 1998, 129–32.

McGuire, Brian Patrick. *The Difficult Saint: Bernard of Clairvaux and His Tradition*. Kalamazoo, MI: Cistercian, 1991.

McNamer, Sarah. *Affective Meditation and the Invention of Medieval Compassion*. Philadelphia: University of Pennsylvania Press, 2010.

– "Further Evidence for the Date of the Pseudo-Bonaventuran *Meditationes vitae Christi*." *Franciscan Studies* 50 (1990): 235–61.

– "The Origins of the *Meditationes vitae Christi*." *Speculum* 8 (2009): 905–55.

Metzsch, Friedrich-August von. *Johannes der Täufer: Seine Geschichte und seine Darstellung in der Kunst*. Munich: Callway, 1989.

Mews, Constant J. "Intoxication and the Song of Songs: Bernard of Clairvaux and the Rediscovery of Origen in the Twelfth Century." In Naama Cohen Hanegbi and Piroska Nagy, eds., *Pleasure in the Middle Ages*. Turnhout: Brepols, 2018, 329–52.

Muir, Carolyn Diskant. "Bride or Bridegroom? Masculine Identity in Mystic Marriages." In P.H. Cullum and Katherine J. Lewis, eds., *Holiness and Masculinity in the Middle Ages*. Toronto: University of Toronto Press, 2004, 58–78.

Murray, Jacqueline. "Masculinizing Religious Life: Sexual Prowess, the Battle for Chastity and Monastic Identity." In P.H. Cullum and Katherine J. Lewis, eds., *Holiness and Masculinity in the Middle Ages*. Toronto: University of Toronto Press, 2004, 24–42.

Pater, Walter. *The Renaissance*. Chicago: Academy, 1977.

Pedretti, Carlo. "Bacchus and Venus." In Carlo Pedretti, ed., *Leonardo da Vinci: L' "Angelo incarnato" e Salai*. Perugia: Cartei & Bianchi, 2009, 236–57.

– *Leonardo da Vinci on Painting: A Lost Book (Libro A)*. Berkeley: University of California Press, 1964.

– "The 'Angel in the Flesh.'" *Achademia Leonardi Vinci* 4 (1991): 34–48.

Pedretti, Carlo, ed. *Leonardo da Vinci: L' "Angelo incarnato:" e Salai*. Perugia: Cartei & Bianchi, 2009.

Ragusa, Isa, and Rosalie B. Green, eds. *Meditations on the Life of Christ: An Illustrated Manuscript of the Fourteenth Century*. Princeton: Princeton University Press, 1961.

Rambuss, Richard. *Closet Devotions*. Durham, NC: Duke University Press, 1998.
Richter, Jean Paul, ed. *The Literary Works of Leonardo da Vinci*. 2 vols. London: Phaidon, 1970.
Robb, David M. "The Iconography of the Annunciation in the Fourteenth and Fifteenth Centuries." *The Art Bulletin* 18.3 (1936): 489–526.
Saslow, James M. *Pictures and Passions: A History of Homosexuality in the Visual Arts*. New York: Penguin Books, 1999.
Schönborn, Christoph. *God's Human Face: The Christ-Icon*. Trans. Lothar Krauth. San Francisco: Ignatius Press, 1994.
Simons, Patricia. *The Sex of Men in Premodern Europe: A Cultural History*. Cambridge: Cambridge University Press, 2011.
Stefaniak, Regina. "Raphael's *Santa Cecilia*: A Fine and Private Vision of Virginity." *Art History* 14 (1991): 345–71.
– "Replicating Mysteries of the Passion: Rosso's *Dead Christ with Angels*." *Renaissance Quarterly* 45.4 (1992): 677–738.
Steinberg, Leo. *The Sexuality of Christ in Renaissance Art and in Modern Oblivion*. 2nd ed. Chicago: University of Chicago Press, 1996.
Stewart, Alison. *Unequal Lovers: A Study of Unequal Couples in Northern Art*. New York: Abaris Books, 1977.
Stites, Raymond S., et al. *The Sublimations of Leonardo da Vinci*. Washington, DC: Smithsonian Institution Press, 1970.
Varagine, Jacobus de. *The Golden Legend: Readings on the Saints*. Trans. William Granger Ryan. 2 vols. Princeton: Princeton University Press, 1995.
Vasari, Giorgio. *The Lives of the Most Excellent Painters, Sculptors, and Architects*. Ed. Philip Jacks, trans. Gaston du C. de Vere. New York: Modern Library, 2006.
– *Lives of the Most Eminent Painters, Sculptors, and Architects*. Trans. Gaston du C. de Vere. 10 vols. London: Macmillan, 1912.
Weinstein, Donald, and Rudolph M. Bell. *Saints and Society: The Two Worlds of Western Christendom*. Chicago: University of Chicago Press, 2010.
Zwijnenberg, Robert. "'Ogni pittore dipinge sé': On Leonardo da Vinci's *Saint John the Baptist*." In Florike Egmond and Robert Zwijnenberg, eds., *Bodily Extremities: Preoccupations with the Human Body in Early Modern European Culture*. Burlington, VT: Ashgate, 2003, 48–67.
– "St. John the Baptist and the Essence of Painting." In Claire Farago, ed., *Leonardo da Vinci and the Ethics of Style*. Manchester: Manchester University Press, 2008, 97–118.

Electronic Source

Thomas Aquinas. *Summa Theologica*. Online at https://www.newadvent.org/summa/4079.htm.

3 Sharing a Bed with Dominic: Celibacy and Masculinity in the Cult of Saint Vincent Ferrer

LAURA ACKERMAN SMOLLER

Summary: In a *vita* of the Dominican preacher Vincent Ferrer (1350–1419, canonized 1455), Pietro Ranzano described a curious incident. One night, while Vincent was sleeping in his cell, Saint Dominic appeared to him, asked to share the friar's bed, and spent the night praising the younger man. This episode highlighted Vincent's spiritual worth, just like his visions of the Virgin Mary and Christ, also catalogued in Ranzano's *vita*. Unlike these others, however, Dominic's apparition seems to have caused Ranzano and subsequent hagiographers some degree of anxiety over its erotic overtones. Tracking this discomfort through close readings of several *vitae*, this chapter situates their authors' squeamishness in several intersecting trends in the fifteenth and sixteenth centuries: questions about clerical masculinity, increasing prosecutions of sodomites, and worries about the presence of sodomy among monks and friars. Furthermore, hagiographers' differing treatments of the potentially eroticized saintly body reveal the way in which attitudes about sodomy and masculinity varied across time and space.

In a *vita* of the Dominican preacher Vincent Ferrer (1350–1419), composed shortly after his 1455 canonization, a Sicilian Dominican humanist named Pietro Ranzano described a rather curious incident in the famous preacher's life. One night, while Vincent was sleeping in his cell, Saint Dominic appeared to him, asked to share the friar's bed, and spent the night praising the younger man and exhorting Vincent to keep up his good work. Meanwhile, Vincent's brothers, awakened by the sound of talking, spied through the cracks in the wall to see Vincent conversing with a venerable friar, bathed in a heavenly light. Pressing him, the next morning, to reveal who his nocturnal visitor was, Vincent's brothers at last succeeded in prying the truth out of him, but he swore them to secrecy.[1] (Presumably, they waited until after Vincent's death to tell their story.) This small episode was an evident marker of Vincent's spiritual worth, just like his visions of the Virgin Mary and of Christ, standing alongside Saints Francis and Dominic, also catalogued in Ranzano's *vita*.[2] Unlike these other visions, however, Dominic's apparition to Vincent seems to have caused Ranzano and subsequent hagiographers some degree of anxiety, a discomfort that can be tracked through a close reading of their *vitae*. As these authors confronted the intersection of sanctity and the eroticized male body, their squeamishness in narrating this episode reflected several trends in the fifteenth and sixteenth centuries: questions about clerical masculinity, increasing prosecutions of sodomites, and worries about the presence of sodomy specifically among monks and friars. Furthermore, examination of differences among hagiographers in treating the apparition points to the way in which attitudes about sodomy and masculinity could vary across time and space.

Christian authors have long recognized the tensions between the demands of a religious life and cultural expectations surrounding masculinity. Hence, early Christian martyrs in the arena were recast as spiritual athletes gaining the palm of victory; lives of the desert fathers portray them heroically battling onslaughts from demons. Still, celibacy, whether the monk's vow of chastity or the required chastity of the post-Gregorian reform secular clergy, posed a particular challenge to clerical masculinity. One marker of manliness, after all, was the fathering of children, a process in which, as Aristotelian scholastics taught, the man represented the active supplier of "seed," and the woman a mere passive vessel or receptacle – a hierarchy enshrined in the only approved position for coitus, with the man on top. Celibate clerics, who neither fought nor begot offspring, were not performing masculinity via its most obvious markers. In answer, from the time of the Church Fathers, the struggle to maintain one's chastity was presented in military language, with monks and clerics, fortified by spiritual armour, manfully fighting to resist and repel fleshly (or demonic) temptations.[3] The potentially fallible, eroticized male body, thus, was the crucial foil to the cleric's heroic virtue.

Assaults on one's chastity could come in a number of forms. For the secular clergy and mendicant friars who went out into the world to preach, contact with women was framed as a sure source of such temptation. The *Augustinian Rule*, which also served as the rule for the Order of Preachers, acknowledged this likelihood in a series of strictures urging friars to avoid, if possible, the presence or even sight of women and exhorting brothers to admonish any of their number whom they believed to be trapped in the snares of lust.[4] For similar reasons, presumably, the primitive constitutions of the Dominican Order quite simply forbade women's entry into the friars' cloister or private chapel.[5] In the case of enclosed monks, living amongst their spiritual brothers, or of mendicant friars when they were safely in their all-male houses, however, fleshly temptation was not absent, but, it was presumed, would manifest itself in one of three ways: demonic assaults, masturbation, or sex with other friars.[6] The latter two of these dangers received tacit acknowledgment in the *Rule of Saint Benedict*, where the twenty-second chapter, "How the monks are to sleep" ("Quomodo dormiant monachi"), enjoins:

> Each one should sleep in his own bed ... A candle should burn in that room continually until morning. They should sleep clothed, girded with belts or cords ... Younger brothers should not have beds next to one another.[7]

This set of commands is the last of a series of prescriptive chapters detailing how monks are to live and worship; what follows immediately is a set of eight chapters devoted to the correction of brothers who display faults, as if such misbehaviours flowed logically from the dangers lurking in the dormitory.

By the later Middle Ages, the anxieties inherent in the Benedictine Rule's regulations about monks' sleeping arrangements were amplified by the increased persecution of "sodomites" in western Europe.[8] Evidence from fifteenth- through seventeenth-century sources, for example, suggests that monks were often presumed to be guilty of sodomy; the monastic bed was again the locus of sexual temptation and sin. One mid-fifteenth-century English episcopal visitation, for example, turned up the complaint that "brother John Alforde is wont to have youths lying with him of a night in his bed in the dorter."[9] As one Spanish proverb put it, "Save us God from friar by night, soldier by day, and pimp in the whorehouse."[10] In Alan Stewart's pithy summation, "sodomy [was] literally *embedded* within the [monastic] institution."[11]

But sodomy was not just a violation of the monk's or cleric's chastity; it could also pose a threat to his masculinity. While the term "sodomy" encompassed a wide range of nonprocreative sexual behaviours, moralists and civic and ecclesiastical authorities became most exercised about anal intercourse among men, in part because the partner who was penetrated was enacting a feminine, passive role.[12] Such an interpretation could find reinforcement in the frequently observed Mediterranean pattern in which mature men sought teenage boys as their sexual partners.[13] Moralists, from the fifteenth-century Italian preacher Bernardino of Siena to prosecutors at the sixteenth-century High Courts in Seville and Granada, frequently denounced the passive partner as having invited the other man's advances by dressing or acting in an effeminate manner.[14] When monks' or friars' sexual temptations were framed in terms of sodomy – particularly when temptation came in the form of an older man's sexual advances – it became more difficult to present chastity in manly terms, however heroically the importuned friar might resist. That a woman should feel attraction to a handsome young friar did not raise questions about his masculinity, but if he should arouse the erotic gaze of another man, particularly an older one, it was quite a different story.

Viewed through the intersecting lenses of sodomy, celibacy, and masculinity, then, the squeamishness with which hagiographers approached Dominic's nighttime apparition in Vincent's cell makes more sense. This anxiety is perhaps most pronounced in the earliest surviving narration of the tale, Pietro Ranzano's 1455–6 *Life of Vincent* (*Vita Vincentii*). Every detail of Ranzano's presentation suggests his discomfort with this episode, which he cannot ignore, however, because of the great honour shown to Vincent by Dominic's apparition. First, one has the sense that Ranzano genuinely did not know where to put this story, which he presents as a stand-alone, "one other thing" addition at the end of the second book of the *vita* (the book treating the labours of the adult Vincent). Certainly, his introduction to the story is odd. He begins by saying:

> In the last place in this book, this one thing is to be said, which is a marvellous testimony and manifest index of [Vincent's] virginity, as well as of many other virtues of his.[15]

Now, the heart of Ranzano's tale was Dominic's explaining to Vincent the "many things" that made Vincent "similar to [Dominic]": that they were both members of the Order of Preachers, that they both were "preacher[s] of Evangelical doctrine" sent by Christ, and that they were both marked with the virtue of virginity.[16] Given the order in which Dominic enumerates Vincent's several virtues, it is strange that Ranzano in his preface to the tale mentions only the third of these traits: virginity. This fact is even more puzzling when one realizes that Ranzano had already treated Vincent's chastity at some length in book 1 of his *vita*, in which he detailed six incidents in which the friar was tempted by demons and lustful women to break his vow of chastity.[17] If this story were really "a marvellous testimony and manifest index"[18] of Vincent's virginity, why not include it with the other tales in book 1?

And why was this story a "manifest index" of Vincent's virginity anyway? The only plausible answer is that Ranzano had to have been thinking about Dominic's offer to get into bed with Vincent. Sharing a bed need not, of course, have sexual connotations, but it could, a fact apparently acknowledged by the injunction in the Benedictine Rule cited above. Ranzano, who had attended university in Florence in 1440–1, would have been attuned to such nuances, given Florence's reputation as a hotbed of sodomites and the city's Office of the Night, created to deal specifically with sodomy in 1432.[19] Ranzano must have been aware of the awkwardness of that part of his tale, a scenario made even more uncomfortable because it seemingly replicated the well-known pattern in which an older man or teacher sought out a younger man as his sexual partner.[20] Whereas the tales of sexual temptation in Ranzano's book 1 allowed him to present Vincent manfully and heroically defending his virginity, the story of Dominic's request to lie down next to Vincent threatened to undercut that work by presenting a situation in which the younger friar stood in the place of the effeminate, passive partner in a potential sodomitical relationship.

What is more, by framing the story as a manifestation of Vincent's virginity, Ranzano almost seems to embrace rather than play down the *frisson* of sodomy hovering at the edges of the tale. Indeed, Ranzano lards his narration with details that seemingly invite an eroticized reading of the night's events. After all, he might easily have omitted the part about Dominic seeking to share Vincent's bed, but chose not to. When Ranzano described the Virgin's appearance to Vincent in book 1, for example, he simply reported that "The Blessed Virgin appeared to him, visibly, with a great light,"[21] with no further location specified. And, as I have argued previously, Ranzano certainly had no trouble elsewhere in his *vita* in manipulating his sources or in taking a loose approach to the facts when it suited his rhetorical or hagiographical purposes.[22] Additionally, Ranzano appears to play up the sexual connotations of "going to bed" with someone by his very choice of words: Dominic asks Vincent to make a place for him in his "lectulus" (literally, "little bed"), a word that in classical, patristic, and medieval Latin could carry connotations of a bed in which one had sex, as opposed to the simple "lectus" ("bed") of the Benedictine Rule, such as the bed shared by the lovers in the Song of Songs 1:15: "Our bed is flourishing" ("lectulus noster floridus").[23] The humanist Ranzano, with whom Lorenzo Valla traded Latin translations, could not have been unaware of the nuances of this word.[24] In fact, it is the very same word that Ranzano puts in the mouth of one of Vincent's would-be seducers in book 1, who demands that "we sleep in this *lectulo* together tonight," promising Vincent not to deny him any pleasure of her body that he might desire.[25] Furthermore, Ranzano had earlier specified that Vincent "slept on a pallet of rushes or husks or straw, or on a humble sack filled with wool," not a "lectus" or a "lectulus."[26]

Ranzano's vocabulary in the Dominic story thus appears to be deliberately provocative. Moreover, he repeats the same word when Vincent, refusing Dominic's offer, asks "And whence comes such an honour to me ... that a citizen of heaven ... should wish to rest in my most vile *lectulo*?"[27] Although Ranzano is coy about whether Dominic actually prevailed and did get into bed with Vincent, his description of Vincent's brothers leering through the cracks has something of the voyeuristic in it. (And it is difficult to imagine that the two men would have spent the remainder of the night standing.)

But why would the hagiographer stress rather than omit such a potentially embarrassing detail? One can posit here three possible explanations for Ranzano's awkward narration. The first is that he wished to draw a parallel between Vincent Ferrer and the Dominican saint Peter Martyr, about whom it was related that he had been punished by his prior after fellow friars reported hearing female voices in Peter's cell one night. As it turned out, the voices were not those of women with whom Peter was enjoying a dalliance, but rather those of heavenly virgins, who had come to visit Peter in recognition of his sanctity and virginity. Given Ranzano's framing of his tale specifically in terms of Vincent's virginity, this explanation could be plausible.[28] A second possibility is that, by implicitly inviting the reader to think back to his earlier stories of women's attempts to seduce his hero, Ranzano was making an oblique swipe at the rival Franciscan Order's newest saint, Bernardino of Siena. Canonized only five years before Vincent, Bernardino was reported to have been twice propositioned by lecherous older men as a young man (a situation for which in later sermons he would often blame the victim).[29]

The third option is that the incident appeared in Ranzano's sources, and/or that it was well enough known among Dominican friars (now some thirty-five years after Vincent's death) that Ranzano could not alter its crucial elements, such as Dominic's request to share Vincent's bed. Support for this latter possibility is suggested by two details that emerge – and become almost canonical – in later hagiography: first, that the apparition had occurred in the Catalan town of Cervera and, second, that among the friars who, peering through the cracks, witnessed this incident was a follower of Vincent by the name of Pedro de Moya (Petrus Muya). The story's Catalan setting was first revealed by a Dominican chronicler in Bologna named Girolamo Albertucci de' Borselli in a life of Vincent that formed part of his *Cronica magistrorum generalium Ordinis fratrum praedicatorum* (*Chronicle of the Masters General of the Dominican Order*), composed in 1493–6.[30] Albertucci de' Borselli's biography of Vincent was largely based on Ranzano's *vita*, although he also drew upon the life of the saint embedded in the *Chronicle* of Archbishop Antoninus of Florence for some of Vincent's miracles.[31] But in neither of those sources would Albertucci de' Borselli have found the detail that Dominic had appeared to Vincent in the convent in Cervera (which was, incidentally, dedicated to Saint Peter Martyr); in fact Antoninus omits the episode altogether.[32]

It is, however, possible that Albertucci de' Borselli discovered the tale's setting in the records of Vincent's canonization inquests. The bull of Vincent's canonization (issued in 1458) had specified that copies of the canonization inquests were to be deposited in the Dominican church of Santa Maria Sopra Minerva in Rome.[33] Antoninus of Florence evidently had access to those inquests and made clear reference to them in his *vita* of Vincent.[34] Unfortunately, Dominic's visit to Vincent's cell appears nowhere in the three surviving canonization inquests. We know from the canonization bull, however, that there was a fourth inquest, held in Avignon, of which all traces are now lost, presumably a casualty of the 1527 sack of Rome.[35] Perhaps Pedro de Moya, who is known to have preached Lenten cycles in Cervera in 1421 and 1438,[36] testified at the Avignon inquest and there related the story of Vincent and Dominic told by Ranzano. While Albertucci de' Borselli spent most of his career in his native Bologna, he did preach a series of Lenten sermons at Santa Maria Sopra Minerva in 1495 (around the time he is thought to have been composing his chronicle).[37] While in Rome, he may have found irresistible the opportunity to examine Vincent's canonization inquests at the Minerva, and thus conceivably he discovered in the Avignon inquest the story of Dominic's apparition, complete with its location in Cervera.

But why would Pedro de Moya have included such a potentially compromising detail in his testimony about a hoped-for saint? Borrowing Christian Berco's concept of "local sexual economies," we can posit that the Catalan Pedro de Moya did not share in Ranzano's anxieties about sodomy.[38] Indeed, Federico Garza Carvajal has argued that the expulsion of the Moors in 1492 marked the turning point in Spanish attitudes about sodomy, with a new harshness enshrined in a royal *Pragmática* issued in 1497 condemning sodomy as a crime and an offence against God.[39] Further, prosecutions of sodomites did not take place in the crown of Aragon until a 1524 papal brief granted the Inquisition there jurisdiction over such cases, and began in earnest only several decades later, in the second half of the sixteenth century.[40] And, as Berco notes, even in the sixteenth and seventeenth centuries, male same-sex relations in Aragon were evidently regarded as so commonplace as not to be treated with great alarm.[41] So the Catalan Pedro de Moya, spying the two saints chatting in Vincent's bed sometime in the first or second decade of the fifteenth century, might not have immediately thought of an illicit sexual relationship and, more importantly, would not have worried that someone hearing his tale would jump to a similar conclusion if he included that element in stories he told about the saintly friar.

Albertucci de' Borselli's reaction to this tale may also have been conditioned by the situation in his native Bologna. True, as Trevor Deane has demonstrated, there were sodomy prosecutions in Bologna in the fifteenth century, but their numbers were nowhere near the hundreds of cases seen in Venice or the thousands seen in Florence in the same century, and Bolognese sodomy trials clustered in only a few years during the fifteenth century. The last such cluster had been in 1473–4, two decades before Albertucci de' Borselli penned his *Chronicle*.[42] Thus, sodomy may not have been on the chronicler's mind as he thought of Vincent and Dominic sharing a bed. He certainly evinces none of Ranzano's awkwardness in framing the tale. Albertucci de' Borselli's Vincent lies sleeping in a (more humble) "stratus," a word with none of the sexual connotations of Ranzano's "lectulus," and the very word used by Peter the Deacon for "bed" in his commentary on the *Rule of Saint Benedict*.[43] (And perhaps we may posit that Albertucci de' Borselli here repeated the vocabulary of Pedro de Moya's account in the canonization inquest.) Further, and perhaps not coincidentally, Albertucci de' Borselli is the only pre-eighteenth-century author of a life of Vincent to specify that Vincent and Dominic did in fact have their extended chat in Vincent's bed, as Dominic, "settling (collocans) himself next to [Vincent], spoke with him for a long time."[44] Unlike Ranzano, who appears to be uncomfortable with aspects of the story that he nevertheless feels he cannot suppress, Albertucci de' Borselli evinces no such squeamishness.

If Albertucci de' Borselli provided the Catalan location of Dominic's nighttime sojourn in Vincent's cell, it was another Bolognese humanist hagiographer, Giovanni Antonio Flamini, who brought forth the name of Pedro de Moya as a witness to the two saints' colloquy. Flamini provided a life of Vincent for Leandro Alberti's *De viris illustribus ordinis praedicatorum* (*Concerning the Illustrious Men of the Order of Preachers*), published in Bologna in 1517.[45] In this *vita*, which drew heavily upon both Ranzano and Albertucci de' Borselli as sources, Flamini related the episode of Dominic and Vincent very much as Ranzano had, complete with the use of the word "lectulus" for "bed" (although Flamini altered other of Ranzano's word choices, for example, substituting the classicizing "divus" for "beatus" or "sanctus"). His framing of the tale removed Ranzano's puzzling emphasis on Vincent's virginity, as Flamini specified simply that this moment represented a "chief index" of the way in which Vincent defined "the summit of virtues."[46] Flamini did not hide Dominic's request to share Vincent's bed, but he also did nothing to point to – or to excuse – the story's sexual connotations. Flamini's supplying of the name of Pedro de Moya, absent in both of his sources, suggests that the story of Dominic appearing to Vincent had a circulation apart from Ranzano's or Albertucci de' Borselli's *vita*. In fact, one can suppose that this episode was an especially cherished tale in Flamini's and Albertucci de' Borselli's Bologna, the site of Dominic's own splendid tomb.

The tale also featured in two late sixteenth-century vernacular lives composed by Dominican friars from Vincent's native Valencia, Vicente Justinian Antist (1575) and Francisco Diago (1600), *vitae* that are noteworthy for their attention to detail and critical source analysis.[47] Both authors' reactions to this now well known incident may have been shaped by the "local sexual economy," as prosecutions of sodomites by the Aragonese Inquisition had ramped up, beginning in the 1560s.[48] Thus, both authors, while they highlighted the tale's veracity by specifying its location and the name of its witness Pedro Moya, also played down any possible sexual innuendo in the event. Removing Ranzano's awkward lead-in to the story, for example, Antist now situated the tale in the midst of a chapter devoted to "the things that the saint did for Catalonia" ("De las cosas que el Santo hizo por Cataluña"), just after a similar chapter devoted to Perpignan and before one on Toulouse.[49] Francisco Diago similarly made note of Dominic's apparition in a chapter highlighting the saint's activities in Catalonia, specifically dating the occurrence to the year 1416, but he reserved the full narration of the story for his second book, on Vincent's disciples and followers, effectively removing it from his biography of the saint.[50] Both authors replaced Ranzano's "lectulus" with something more penitential and seemly; their Vincent reposed upon a "poor bed" ("pobre cama"), which evidently consisted of nothing more than a few *tablas* or boards.[51] Antist presented the episode not as a manifestation of Vincent's virginity but rather as "the occasion to treat of the great resemblance between Saint Vincent and the father Saint Dominic."[52] For Diago, the incident was a testament to the worthiness of Vincent's follower Pedro de Moya, who had "merited to enjoy and be witness to a signal mercy that the Lord granted to his master [Vincent]."[53] In a climate where the Aragonese Inquisition was trying sodomites in increasing numbers, and in which clerics in particular were suspected of the sin, Antist and Diago, while beholden to their sources, appear to have sought to mitigate any chance that this episode might invite speculations about sodomy among Dominican friars or sniggering comparisons of their Vincent to the passive (effeminate) recipient of an older man's sexual advances.

Conclusion

This brief survey of some key *vitae* of Vincent Ferrer composed between the time of his 1455 canonization and the end of the sixteenth century reveals a variety of strategies amongst hagiographers in dealing with the uncomfortable possibility that Saints Dominic and Vincent spent a blissful night in bed together, and the equally uncomfortable implication that Vincent – in this tale – took the place not of the manly saint heroically battling for his chastity, but rather of the desirable youth whose effeminate traits had turned the head of an older male predator. The differences among their various accounts of this potentially erotic episode reflect attitudes about sodomy and masculinity that fluctuated across time and place in the early modern Mediterranean world. The story must have appeared harmless enough to its original teller, Pedro de Moya, that he had no problem in describing the older man sharing the younger friar's bed. Pietro Ranzano's account, by contrast, suggests the willingness of one in the know to play up a well-known story's sexual connotations in order, awkwardly, to refocus his reader's gaze upon Vincent's virginity (and his manly struggles against demonic and feminine temptation). For Girolamo Albertucci de' Borselli and Giovanni Antonio Flamini, writing in a city less marked by the fear of sodomy, the tale appears to have represented a singularly well witnessed moment linking the new Dominican saint to the order's founder, whose remains graced their own Bologna. And, as the Aragonese Inquisition's investigations of sodomy heated up in the post-Tridentine years, the Valencians Justinian Vicente Antist and Francisco Diago both worked to minimize any chance that their readers might fixate upon the saint's bed – or on Dominic's desire to share it.

Scholars sometimes point to the eighteenth century as marking a new era in the understanding of sodomy in early modern Europe, one in which moralists began to view sodomy as "an external sign of an interior disorder" and the sodomite as "one who had 'abandoned himself'" and was thereby a libertine, a "threat to the state."[54] Perhaps it was with such thoughts in mind that the Italian Dominican Antonino Teoli penned the version of the tale included in his 1735 life of Vincent Ferrer, a narration that presents a manly Vincent and a chummy Dominic settling down for a night of homosocial bonding. To do so, Teoli transforms Pietro Ranzano's awkward "lectulus" into a site of "heroic mortification" ("eroica mortificazione") of the flesh, describing the bed as no more than a few "planks, which had scarcely anything in common with a bed other than the name," and which, far from serving as a place of "repose," served rather "to afflict limbs worn out from the toils of his voyages."[55] And, rather than ask to repose in Vincent's bed with him, Teoli's Dominic simply scoops up the younger friar, now prostrate at his feet, and "sets him to sit with him on that little bed," in which position they spend the rest of the night, chatting "familiarly."[56] Finally Teoli, unlike previous hagiographers, has at last placed this incident in what seems the most logical setting for it: a series of chapters describing Vincent's visions. Dominic's apparition thus confirms a portrait of a manly (but celibate) saint, strenuously pursuing his preaching duties, heroically punishing his flesh, and receiving visits from the citizens of heaven as a reward for his efforts. The liberties Teoli takes in de-eroticizing his sources – all scrupulously cited in his footnotes – demonstrate perhaps more forcefully than any of my other examples the ways in which the story of Dominic and Vincent's bed forced hagiographers to confront intersecting but ever varied discourses about celibacy, sodomy, and masculinity in early modern Europe.

NOTES

1 Ranzano, *Vita Vincentii*, 2.4.23, 497–8; online. Here and elsewhere references to this work provide book, chapter, and paragraph numbers, as well as the page numbers from the *Acta Sanctorum* database. On Ranzano's *Vita*, and the cult of Vincent Ferrer in general, see Smoller, *The Saint and the Chopped-Up Baby*. I briefly treat the episode of Dominic's apparition to Vincent in Smoller, "Dominicans and Demons," 1031–4.

2 Ranzano, *Vita Vincentii*, 1.3.15, 488, and 2.1.4, 491.

3 See, e.g., Brakke, *Demons and the Making of the Monk*; Murray, "Masculinizing Religious Life," 27–30, 36–7; Weissenberg, "Generations of Men," esp. 674; Karras, "Thomas Aquinas's Chastity Belt"; Thibodeaux, *The Manly Priest*, esp. 32–40; Arnold, "Labour of Continence"; Smoller, "Dominicans and Demons," 1024–31. Sarah Salih cites (via James Brundage) the example of thirteenth-century Parisian prostitutes who, when clerics shunned their advances, shouted at them, "Sodomites!" Salih, "Sexual Identities," 119.

4 Augustine, *Regula Sancti Augustini*, ch. 4 ("De custodia castitatis et fraterna correctione"), online.

5 Creytens, "Les Constitutions," dist. 2, ch. 1 ("De domibus cocedendis"), 48, making an exception for Good Friday ("Parasceve") and for the consecration of a church.

6 Or in the form of intercourse forced upon young boys (child oblates, pupils, or boys otherwise working at the monastery), as Dyan Elliott has forcefully argued in her poignant new *The Corrupter of Boys*. That danger of masturbation perhaps is inherent a brief remark in a life of Vincent Ferrer by the Florentine canon Francesco Castiglione: "It is said that the blessed Vincent during thirty years never saw the flesh of his body or even his feet other than his hands, [for], he said, such was a very great incitement to lust"; *Vita Vincentii abbreviata*, sign. a2r: "Diciturque beatus Vincentius triginta annis numquam carnem sui corporis ne pedes quidem praeter ipsas manus proprias conspexisse. Hoc enim asserebat esse maximum hominibus ad libidinem incitamentum."

7 "Singuli per singula lecta dormiant"; *Rule of St. Benedict*, ch. 22, 96–7. Also cited in Elliott, *Fallen Bodies*, 31. A Carolingian commentary on the *Rule* specified that this injunction was designed to prevent sodomy between monks; Elliott, *The Corrupter of Boys*, 45–6.

8 See, e.g., Boswell, *Christianity, Social Tolerance*, 269–332; Jordan, *Invention of Sodomy*; Cadden, *Nothing Natural*, 188–202; Rocke, *Forbidden Friendships*; Berco, *Sexual Hierarchies*, 78–83; Puff, *Sodomy*, 17–30; Kuefler, "Homoeroticism," 1262–4; Karras, "Regulation of 'Sodomy.'"

9 Quoted in Salih, "Sexual Identities," 124. See also Trexler, *Sex and Conquest*, 49; Elliott, *The Corrupter of Boys*, 147–70.

10 Sebastián de Orozco, quoted and translated in Berco, "Social Control," 345. According to Christian Berco's research, sixteenth-century clerics (both regular and secular clergy) were denounced for sodomy in Valencia in numbers strikingly disproportionate to their representation in the population at large, yet received relatively lenient sentences for their lapses; Berco, "Social Control," 334–9, 345, 349–50. See also Carrasco, *Inquisición y represión sexual*, 174–87.

11 Quoted in Salih, "Sexual Identities," 123–4.

12 E.g., Rocke, *Forbidden Friendships*, 13; Berco, "Producing Patriarchy," 357–8; Berco, *Sexual Hierarchies*, 23–35; Cadden, *Nothing Natural*, 106–38; Elliott, *The Corrupter of Boys*, 48.

13 E.g. Rocke, *Forbidden Friendships*, 12; Berco, "Social Control," 353; Berco, *Sexual Hierarchies*, 9, 39–40, 48–55; and, drawing parallels to the contemporary sexual abuse scandal in the Catholic Church, Elliott, *The Corrupter of Boys*, 4.

14 Mormando, *The Preacher's Demons*, 130, 133–5; Berco, *Sexual Hierarchies*, 34–5; Garza Carvajal, *Butterflies Will Burn*, 65–71; Davidson, "Sodomy," 67.

Berco argues, in fact, that in the crown of Aragon, a man who penetrated another man was still viewed as manly, with the act being viewed as an assault on the passive partner's masculinity. Berco, "Producing Patriarchy," 358–60.

15 "Ultimo hujus libri loco illud unum dicendum est, quod est tam virginitatis quam multarum aliarum virtutum ejus testimonium mirabile ac manifestum indicium, quod non solum a seculi hujus hominibus, sed etiam a caelestibus civibus venerabatur"; Ranzano, *Vita Vincentii*, 2.4.23, 497.

16 "volo te scire, quod multa sunt, quae te mihi similem efficiunt, propter quae non immerito dignus es, ut mecum uno in loco quiescas"; "Euangelicae doctrinae praedicator[es]"; Ranzano, *Vita Vincentii*, 2.4.23, 498. In fact, Dominic informed Vincent, there was only one respect in which Dominic would be placed above Vincent: that he himself had founded the Order of Preachers of which they were both members.

17 Ranzano, *Vita Vincentii*, 1.3.14 [=13]–18, 487–90. See Smoller, "Dominicans and Demons," 1024–31.

18 "testimonium mirabile ac manifestum indicium "; Ranzano, *Vita Vincentii*, 2.4.23, 497.

19 Rocke, *Forbidden Friendships*, is the classic study of same-sex activities and the prosecution of sodomy in Florence. For Ranzano's biography, including his ties with important fifteenth-century humanists, see Smoller, *The Saint and the Chopped-Up Baby*, 122–5, and the references therein.

20 Moralists like Bernardino of Siena, who had preached a series of Lenten sermons against sodomy in Florence in 1424 and 1425, often blamed the younger man for attracting the older sodomite by his fashionable clothes or painted face. Rocke, *Forbidden Friendships*, 36; Mormando, *The Preacher's Demons*, 130. See also n. 14, above.

21 "ei beata Virgo cum luce magna visibiliter apparuit"; Ranzano, *Vita Vincentii*, 1.3.15, 488.

22 Smoller, *The Saint and the Chopped-Up Baby*, 139–50; Smoller, "From Authentic Miracles," 783–7; Smoller, "From 'Real Life,'" 44–8.

23 Blaise, ed., *Dictionnaire, sub vocibus* "lectus," "lectulus"; Latham et al., eds., *Dictionary, sub vocibus* "lectus," "lectulus"; Forcellini et al., eds., *Lexicon, sub vocibus* "lectus," "lectulus"; Gaffiot, ed., *Dictionnaire, sub vocibus* "lectus," "lectulus"; Lewis and Short, eds., *Latin Dictionary, sub vocibus* "lectus," "lectulus." Although Gaffiot and Blaise both include a bed for having sex as a possible meaning for "lectus," most tellingly, in both Forcellini's and Lewis and Short's dictionaries, if "lectus" is to connotate the marital bed, it is modified by the adjective "genialis" or "adversus." For other examples drawn from mystical writings in which the narrowness of the bed pointed to (symbolic) sexual intimacy, see Hamburger, *The Visual and the Visionary*, 386, 389–90, 394.

24 For Ranzano's closeness to Valla, see Smoller, *The Saint and the Chopped-Up Baby*, 123–4.

25 "Nunc autem a nemine hominum visa, huc ingressa sum, & necessarium est ut in hoc lectulo simul hac nocte dormiamus: & ex hoc nunc tibi promitto, quod quoties de meo corpore voluptatem capere volueris, ad hoc, consimili modo & quo nunc feci, me conferam"; Ranzano, *Vita Vincentii*, 1.3.17, 489.

26 "Super culcitras non dormiant fratres nostri, nisi forte stramen vel aliquid tale super quod dormiant, habere non possint. Super stramina, laneos et saccones dormire licebit"; Ranzano, *Vita Vincentii*, 2.2.9, 493. Ranzano's description is reminiscent of language in the Constitutions of the Dominican Order. Creytens, "Les Constitutions," dist. 1, ch. 9 ("De lectis"), 36.

27 "Et unde mihi, o Pater sanctissime, tantum honoris advenit, ut tantus vir, caelestis civis, ad me venire; & mecum qui mortalis sum, velit in vilissimo lectulo meo quiescere?"; Ranzano, *Vita Vincentii*, 2.4.23, 497.

28 See Smoller, "Dominicans and Demons," 1026. Unfortunately, the earliest known written version of this Peter Martyr story is in the life of the saint composed by Saint Antoninus of Florence at around the same time Ranzano was writing his own *vita*. As Prudlo notes (*The Martyred Inquisitor*, 28), Antoninus was drawing in part upon a sermon preached by the Dominican Leonardus de Utino in 1446. Unless Ranzano happened to have heard the same sermon that may have been Antoninus's source, it seems unlikely that he knew the tale.

29 See Smoller "Dominicans and Demons," 1027–8, 1031–4; Smoller, "From 'Real Life' to Saint's Life," 38–9, 47–9; Smoller, *The Saint and the Chopped-Up Baby*, 37–8. Dominic's apparition, perhaps not coincidentally, immediately follows a tale in which Vincent prophesies Bernardino's future greatness in *vitae* written by Albertucci de' Borselli (largely based on Ranzano) and Flamini, both discussed below.

30 Albertucci de' Borselli, *Cronica magistrorum generalium Ordinis fratrum praedicatorum*, BUB, MS. 1999, fol. 155r–160v. The tale appears on fol. 159v. On Albertucci de' Borselli and for the date of composition of this work, see Damian-Grint, "Albertucci de' Borselli" and Rabotti, "Albertucci de' Borselli."

31 Smoller, *The Saint and the Chopped-Up Baby*, 185–6. Interestingly, a life composed sometime after 1467 in the Dominican convent of Chioggia omits Dominic's nighttime visit to Vincent's cell, but inserts a new (or sanitized?) apparition by Dominic, in which he commands the younger friar to go forth and preach the imminent Last Judgment: *Vita monacho clugiensi*, WBSA, MS. 27, fols. 23v–24r. This injunction was, according to Vincent himself, part of Vincent's Avignon vision of Christ with Saints Dominic and Francis; the Chioggia friar omits this detail in describing the vision in Avignon (fol. 14r). On the Avignon vision, see Smoller, *The Saint and the Chopped-Up Baby*, 6, 133, 141–2; Daileader, *Saint Vincent Ferrer*, 36–8.

32 Antoninus, *Chronicon*, vol. 3, pt. 3, title 23, ch. 8, fols. CCVIIv–CCXr. On Antoninus's life of Vincent Ferrer, see Smoller, *The Saint and the Chopped-Up Baby*, 136–8, 175–9. For Cervera's Dominican convent, see Beseran i Ramon, "El convent." A vernacular life largely based on Antoninus's by Miquel Peres, writing in 1510 in Valencia, also lacks this tale: Peres, *La vida*.

33 Pius II, *Rationi congruit*, 149.

34 Smoller, *The Saint and the Chopped-Up Baby*, 174.

35 For details, Smoller, *The Saint and the Chopped-Up Baby*, 59–60.

36 Miró i Baldrich, "Predicadors," 170–1.

37 Rabotti, "Albertucci de' Borselli," online.

38 Berco, "Social Control," 331, 342, 348.

39 According to Garza Carvajal, sodomy was "one of the most horrendous and scandalous crimes to preoccupy the monarchy in sixteenth- and seventeenth-century Spain." Garza Carvajal, *Butterflies Will Burn*, 39.

40 Berco, "Producing Patriarchy," 356; Carrasco, *Inquisición y represión sexual*, 66–76. Further, according to Garza Carvajal, effeminacy "did not constitute the predominant discourse associated with sodomy prosecutions during the early modern period in the peninsula." Garza Carvajal, *Butterflies will Burn*, 71.

41 Berco, "Producing Patriarchy," 363: "the widespread culture of penetrative virility allowed many men to seek sexual gratification with other males with surprising indifference to the possibility of punishment." See also Berco, "Social Control," 313; Deane, "Sodomy," 430.

42 Deane, "Sodomy," 430–1.

43 Petrus Diaconus, *Disciplina casinensis*, cols. 1136–7; online. The succeeding injunctions make it clear that the concern is with the possibility of intimate sexual relationships: "Nullus cum altero dormiat in uno stratu. Nullus manum alterius teneat. Sive ambulaverint, vel sederint, vel steterint, uno cubitu distent ab altero." "Stratus," from "sterno/sternere" (to spread, scatter, or lay out), has the connotation of any place prepared for one to lie down: Forcellini et al., eds, *Lexicon*, *sub voce* "stratus."

44 "B Dominicus iuxta se collocans multa cum eo locutus est"; Albertucci de' Borselli, BUB, MS. 1999, fol. 159v.

45 Flamini, *Vita Divi Vincentii*, fols. 156v–174v. On Flamini, see Smoller, *The Saint and the Chopped-Up Baby*, 188–90.

46 Flamini, *Vita Divi Vincentii*, fol. 171r: "Verum ad quantum uirtutum cumulum iam deuenisset ex iis quae retulimus abunde patuit: Sed illud quoque quod huiusce rei praecipuum est indicium silentio praetereundum non est."

47 Antist, "La vida e historia"; Diago, *Historia de la vida*. See Smoller, *The Saint and the Chopped-Up Baby*, 234–45.

48 Carrasco, *Inquisición y represión sexual*, 66–76. Berco, "Social Control and Its Limits," 334.

49 Antist, "La vida e historia," pt. 1, ch. 27, 201 (title), 204–5 (the episode in Cervera).

50 Diago, *Historia de la vida*, bk. 1, ch. 32, 360; and bk 2, ch. 4, 522–4.

51 Antist, "La vida e historia," 204: "Durmiendo San Vicente en su pobre cama … [Santo Domingo] quería reposar con él en las mesmas tablas o cama donde sant Vicente estaba." Diago, *Historia de la vida*, 522: "[Santo Domingo] queria reposar con el en las mismas tablas." Both Antist ("La vida e historia," 204) and Diago (*Historia de la vida*, 523) have Vincent express amazement that the senior friar should wish to "reposar conmigo" ("rest with me," not "share my bed with me"). Dominic uses the same word ("reposar") when he tells Vincent he is worthy "to rest/reside in Heaven with me" ("digno de reposar en el cielo conmigo": Antist, "La vida e historia," 205; "reposar comigo en el cielo": Diago, *Historia de la vida*, 523).

52 "Ofresíasele ahora ocasión de tratar la gran semejanza que hubo entre San Vicente y el padre Santo Domingo"; Antist, "La vida e historia," 205.

53 "[Fray Pedro Moya] mericio gozar, y ser testigo de vna señalada merced que el señor hizo a su maestro en la villa de Ceruera del principado de Cathaluña"; Diago, *Historia de la vida*, 522.

54 Garza Carvajal, *Butterflies Will Burn*, 71–2, quoting works by Rafael Carrasco and by F. Vázquez García and A. Morena Mengíbar.

55 "S. Vincenzo coricato su certi banchi, che di letto appena altro aveano, che il solo nome, non sò se debba dirmi per riposare, o per affliggere le membra stanche dalle fatiche de' viaggi. Vedea Iddio [Dominic] questa eroica mortificazione"; Teoli, *Storia della vita*, bk. 2, tr. 1, ch. 12 (D'altre Visioni, ch'ebbe S. Vincenzo), 327.

56 Teoli, *Storia della vita*, 328: "Sbalzò incontanente Vincenzo a terra, prostrandosi a piè del Santo Patriarca, per riverentemente baciarglieli. Ma gli fu vietato quell'atto d'ossequio, e sollevato da terra, posesi il Santo Padre con esso lui a sedere su quel letticciuolo, ed ivi tragli altri celesti discorsi, co' quali passarono familiarmente tutta quella notte." That the two are sitting on the planks ("tavole") is repeated when Teoli describes the other friars witnessing the conversation ("veddero ambedue sedere sulle tavole di quel letticciuolo").

WORKS CITED

Manuscript Sources

Bologna. Biblioteca Universitaria (BUB)
MS. 1999. Albertucci de' Borselli. *Cronica magistrorum generalium Ordinis fratrum praedicatorum*.
Walberberg. Bibliothek St. Albert (WBSA)
MS. 27 (Hill Monastic Manuscript Library 35238).

Printed Sources

Antist, Vicente Justiniano. "La vida e historia del apostólico predicador Sant Vicente Ferrer, Valenciano, de la Orden de Santo Domingo." In José de Garganta, OP, and Vicente Forcada, OP, eds., *Biografía y escritos de San Vicente Ferrer*. Madrid: Biblioteca de Autores Cristiano, 1956, 94–334.

Antoninus Florentinus, Saint. *Chronicon seu opus historiarum*. 3 vols. Nuremberg: Koberger, 1484.

Arnold, John H. "The Labour of Continence: Masculinity and Clerical Virginity." In Anke Bernau et al., eds., *Medieval Virginities*. Toronto: University of Toronto Press, 2003, 102–18.

Benedict of Nursia, Saint. *The Rule of St. Benedict*. Ed. and trans. Bruce L. Venarde. Dumbarton Oaks Medieval Library. Cambridge, MA, and London: Harvard University Press, 2011.

Berco, Christian. "Producing Patriarchy: Male Sodomy and Gender in Early Modern Spain." *Journal of the History of Sexuality* 17.3 (2008): 351–76.

– *Sexual Hierarchies, Public Status: Men, Sodomy, and Society in Spain's Golden Age*. Toronto: University of Toronto Press, 2007.

– "Social Control and Its Limits: Sodomy, Local Sexual Economies, and Inquisitors during Spain's Golden Age." *Sixteenth Century Journal* 36.2 (2005): 331–58.

Beseran i Ramon, Pere. "El convent de Sant Domènec de Cervera." In Antoni Pladevall, ed., *L'art gòtic a Catalunya. Arquitectura I. Catedrals, monestirs i altres edificis religiosos, 1*. Barcelona: Enciclopèdia Catalana, 2002, 224–5.

Boswell, John. *Christianity, Social Tolerance, and Homosexuality: Gay People in Western Europe from the Beginning of the Christian Era to the Fourteenth Century*. Chicago: University of Chicago Press, 1980.

Brakke, David. *Demons and the Making of the Monk: Spiritual Combat in Early Christianity*. Cambridge, MA: Harvard University Press, 2006.

Cadden, Joan. *Nothing Natural Is Shameful: Sodomy and Science in Late Medieval Europe*. Philadelphia: University of Pennsylvania Press, 2013.

Carrasco, Rafael. *Inquisición y represión sexual en Valencia: Historia de los sodomitas (1565–1785)*. Barcelona: Laertes S.A. de Ediciones, 1985.

Castiglione, Francesco. *Vita Beati Vincentii abbreviata*. In Vincent Ferrer, *Sermones Sancti Vincentii fratris ordinis predicatorum de tempore. Pars hyemalis*. Venice: Jacobus Pentius de Leuco, for Lazarus de Soardis, 1496, sign. a1v–a5r.

Creytens, R. "Les Constitutions des Frères Prêcheurs dans la rédaction de s. Raymond de Peñafort (1241)." *Archivum fratrum praedicatorum* 18 (1948): 5–68.

Daileader, Philip. *Saint Vincent Ferrer, His World and Life: Religion and Society in Late Medieval Europe*. The New Middle Ages. New York: Palgrave Macmillan, 2016.

Damian-Grint, Peter. "Albertucci de' Borselli, Girolamo." In Graeme Dunphy, ed., *Encyclopedia of the Medieval Chronicle*. Leiden: Brill, 2010, 1:25–6.

Davidson, N.S. "Sodomy in Early Modern Venice." In Tom Betteridge, ed., *Sodomy in Early Modern Europe*. Studies in Early Modern European History. Manchester and New York: Manchester University Press, 2002, 65–93.

Deane, Trevor. "Sodomy in Renaissance Bologna." *Renaissance Studies* 31.3 (2016): 426–43.

Diago, Francisco. *Historia de la vida, milagros, muerte y discípulos del bienaventurado predicador apostólico valenciano S. Vicente Ferrer*. Barcelona: Gabriel Graells y Giraldo Dotil, 1600; facsimile, Valencia: Paris-Valencia SL, 2001.

Elliott, Dyan. *The Corrupter of Boys: Sodomy, Scandal, and the Medieval Clergy*. The Middle Ages Series. Philadelphia: University of Pennsylvania Press, 2020.

– *Fallen Bodies: Pollution, Sexuality, and Demonology in the Middle Ages*. The Middle Ages Series. Philadelphia: University of Pennsylvania Press, 1999.

Flamini, Giovanni Antonio. *Divi Vincentii Valentini Ordinis Praedicatorum vita*. In Leandro Alberti, ed., *De viris illustribus ordinis praedicatorum libri sex*. Bologna: Hieronymus Plato, 1517, fols. 156v–174v.

Garza Carvajal, Federico. *Butterflies Will Burn: Prosecuting Sodomites in Early Modern Spain and Mexico*. Austin: University of Texas Press, 2003.

Hamburger, Jeffrey F. *The Visual and the Visionary: Art and Female Spirituality in Late Medieval Germany*. New York: Zone Books, 1998.

Jordan, Mark D. *The Invention of Sodomy in Christian Theology*. Chicago: University of Chicago Press, 1997.

Karras, Ruth Mazo. "The Regulation of 'Sodomy' in the Latin East and West." *Speculum* 95.4 (2020): 969–86.

– "Thomas Aquinas's Chastity Belt: Clerical Masculinity in Medieval Europe." In Lisa M. Bitel and Felice Lifshitz, eds., *Gender and Christianity in Medieval Europe: New Perspectives*. Philadelphia: University of Pennsylvania Press, 2008, 52–67.

Kuefler, Mathew. "Homoeroticism in Antiquity and the Middle Ages: Acts, Identities, Cultures." *AHR* Reappraisal. *American Historical Review* 123.4 (2018): 1246–66.

Miró i Baldrich, Ramon. "Predicadors a Cervera (segles XV–XVIII)." *Miscel·lània Cerverina* 19 (2009): 165–221.

Mormando, Franco. *The Preacher's Demons: Bernardino of Siena and the Social Underworld of Early Renaissance Italy*. Chicago: University of Chicago Press, 1999.

Murray, Jacqueline. "Masculinizing Religious Life: Sexual Prowess, the Battle for Chastity and Monastic Identity." In P.H. Cullum and Katherine J. Lewis, eds., *Holiness and Masculinity in the Middle Ages*. Cardiff: University of Wales Press, 2004, 24–42.

Pius II. *Rationi congruit*. In Francisco Gaude, ed., *Bullarum diplomatum et privilegiorum sanctorum romanorum pontificum, Taurinensis editio*, vol. 5. Turin: Seb. Franco et Henrico Dalmazzo, 1860, 144–9.

Prudlo, Donald. *The Martyred Inquisitor: The Life and Cult of Peter of Verona (†1252)*. Church, Faith and Culture in the Medieval West. Aldershot, UK, and Burlington, VT: Ashgate, 2008.
Puff, Helmut. *Sodomy in Reformation Germany and Switzerland, 1400–1600*. Chicago: University of Chicago Press, 2003.
Rocke, Michael. *Forbidden Friendships: Homosexuality and Male Culture in Renaissance Florence*. Oxford: Oxford University Press, 1996.
Salih, Sarah. "Sexual Identities: A Medieval Perspective." In Tom Betteridge, ed., *Sodomy in Early Modern Europe*. Studies in Early Modern European History. Manchester: Manchester University Press, 2002, 112–30.
Smoller, Laura Ackerman. "Dominicans and Demons: Possession, Temptation, and Reform in the Cult of Vincent Ferrer." *Speculum* 93.4 (2018): 1010–47.
– "From Authentic Miracles to a Rhetoric of Authenticity: Examples from the Canonization and Cult of St. Vincent Ferrer." *Church History* 80.4 (2011): 773–97.
– "From 'Real Life' to Saint's Life: Biography and Hagiography in the *Vitae* of Bernardino of Siena and Vincent Ferrer." In Samantha Kahn Herrick, ed., *Hagiography and the History of Latin Christendom, 500–1500*. Leiden: Brill, 2020, 33–51.
– *The Saint and the Chopped-Up Baby: The Cult of Vincent Ferrer in Medieval and Early Modern Europe*. Ithaca: Cornell University Press, 2014.
Teoli, Antonio, OP. *Storia della vita, e del culto di S. Vincenzo Ferrerio dell'Ordine de' Predicatori*. Rome: Giovanni Battista de Caporali, 1735.
Thibodeaux, Jennifer. *The Manly Priest: Clerical Celibacy, Masculinity, and Reform in England and Normandy, 1066–1300*. The Middle Ages Series. Philadelphia: University of Pennsylvania Press, 2015.
Trexler, Richard C. *Sex and Conquest: Gendered Violence, Political Order and the European Conquest of the Americas*. Ithaca: Cornell University Press, 1995.
Weissenberg, Marita von. "Generations of Men and Masculinity in Two Late-Medieval Biographies of Saints." In Raffaella Sarti, ed., *Men at Home*, special issue of *Gender & History* 27.3 (2015): 669–83.

Electronic Sources

Augustine of Hippo, Saint. *Regula Sancti Augustini*. Online at https://www.thelatinlibrary.com/augustine/reg.shtml.
Blaise, Albert, ed. *Dictionnaire latin-français des auteurs chrétiens*, rev. Paul Tombeur. In Database of Latin Dictionaries (DLD). Online at http://www.brepolis.net.
Forcellini, Aeg., et al., eds. *Lexicon totius latinitatis cum appendicibus*. In Database of Latin Dictionaries (DLD). Online at http://www.brepolis.net.
Gaffiot, Félix, ed. *Dictionnaire latin-français*. In Database of Latin Dictionaries (DLD). Online at http://www.brepolis.net.

Latham, R.E., et al., eds. *Dictionary of Medieval Latin from British Sources.* In Database of Latin Dictionaries (DLD). Online at http://www.brepolis.net.

Lewis, Charlton T., and Charles Short, eds. *A Latin Dictionary.* In Database of Latin Dictionaries (DLD). Online at http://www.brepolis.net.

Peres, Miquel. *La vida de sant Vicent Ferrer*, ed. Carme Arronis I Lloopis. Valenciana prosa. Biblioteca. Online at http://tintadellamp.ua.es/biblioteca/santvicentfitxa.htm.

Petrus Diaconus. *Disciplina casinensis.* In *Patrologia Latina: The Full-Text Database*, vol. 173, cols. 1133–8. Online at http://gateway.proquest.com.ezp.lib.rochester.edu/openurl?url_ver=Z39.88-2004&res_dat=xri:pld-us&rft_dat=xri:pld:ft:all:Z300114782.

Rabotti, Giuseppe. "Albertucci de' Borselli, Girolamo." In *Dizionario biografico degli italiani*, vol. 1. Rome: Istituto della Enciclopedia italiana, 1960, *sub voce*. Online at https://www.treccani.it/enciclopedia/albertucci-de-borselli-girolamo_(Dizionario-Biografico)/.

Ranzano, Pietro. *Vita Vincentii.* In *Acta Sanctorum: The Full-Text Database.* Aprilis, vol. 1, 482–512. Online at http://gateway.proquest.com.ezp.lib.rochester.edu/openurl?url_ver=Z39.88-2004&res_dat=xri:acta-us&rft_dat=xri:acta:ft:all:Z400053868.

4 The Body of Christ: Suffering and Desire in Gianfrancesco Pico della Mirandola's *De Venere et Cupidine Expellendis*

MARCO PIANA

Summary: The article analyses the role of Christ's wounded body as a source of sexual purification in the poem *De Venere et Cupidine expellendis* (1513) by Gianfrancesco Pico della Mirandola (1469–1533). In the text, the Savonarolan humanist proposes meditation on the battered and gory body of Christ as a remedy against the snares of carnal Venus and unsanctioned love. According to him, the vision of a suffering Christ, combined with various forms of physical self-punishment, is the best way to counteract the lures of bodily desire represented by Venus' sensual ideal. Comparing the representation of Christ in *De Venere et Cupidine expellendis* with that of earlier poems and other contemporary sources, this article shows how the messianic body permeates Pico's spiritual poetry, framing its languid and suffering model of masculinity as a weapon against profane forms of carnal desire.

De Venere et Cupidine Expellendis: *Plot, History, and Legacy*

Gianfrancesco Pico della Mirandola (1469–1533), one of the most important Savonarolan thinkers of the Italian Renaissance, composed the poem *De Venere et Cupidine expellendis* (On banishing Venus and Cupid) during a time of dire need.[1] In 1512, having been banished from his lands for the second time, he visited Pope Julius II (r. 1503–13) in Rome to beseech his help in reconquering the counties he had lost to his brothers. During those long days, waiting between his hearings, Pico had the opportunity to wander through the pontiff's statue garden, the Cortile del Belvedere, and reflect on the presence of pagan and lascivious deities in the very heart of Catholicism. Their presence, abhorrent to his eyes, prompted Pico to compose the poem and publish it in 1513 in Rome and Strasbourg. Strongly inspired by Neoplatonic philosophy and Dominican devotion, *De Venere* is a poem in Latin hexameters that deals with the treacherous influence of earthly beauty and love in both ancient and modern times, and the spiritual and practical ways to resist its lures. Because of the complexity and intricacy of the themes here addressed, it is best to start with a summary.

The poem begins with an invocation to the Virgin Mary to banish the figures of Venus and Amor (vv. 1–8), and continues with a short synopsis of how, according to Plato's *Symposium* and other ancient mythological traditions, the two gods were born (vv. 9–26). The third section is dedicated to the reinterpretation of several love myths found in Ovid's *Metamorphoses* and other classical works. Here, Pico mentions the tales of Apollo and Daphne, Endymion and Selene, Orpheus and Eurydice, Pirithous and Persephone, and the many transformations of Zeus (vv. 27–49). After that, he briefly explains the reasons why beauty and love affect the human spirit (vv. 53–7) and exhorts his young readers to ascend to the heavens with the help of the Virgin Mary, and not flock to the temptations of the Neoplatonic Venus and her divinely imparted frenzy (vv. 58–70). Then, he describes the causes and the nefarious effects of Venus and Cupid's influence, a magnetic force that brings men to brief and painful moments of lust (vv. 71–105).

In the next section, we find a series of metaphors describing the lustful thirst caused by Venus and Cupid (vv. 106–23) and another section of exempla based on classical sources. This time, instead of gods, Pico thoughtfully focuses on the human victims of erotic frenzy: Agamemnon, Diomede, the Maenads, Acteon, Sappho, Dido, Thisbe, and many others (vv. 124–38). The second tier of exempla is dedicated to myths of bestial transformation and human reincarnation, and ends with an open accusation of Hermotimus, allegedly one of Pythagoras' earlier incarnations (vv. 139–75). Verses 175–96 are an exhortation to youths to flee the languid poison of "false Babylon" (i.e., Rome) and its temples crawling with monsters. Pico suggests that divine law is the remedy against such creatures (vv. 197–202). After that, he dedicates several verses to the necessity of choosing the proper wife (vv. 203–23) and the fundamental importance of chastity before marriage. Pico then explains the benefits of a strong will against the guilty pleasures provided by Venus: eye contact must be prevented, seductive whispers shunned (vv. 224–49); otherwise, one can become a slave to Venus and Cupid. Verses 250–75 are dedicated to the infernal tortures inflicted upon the slaves of beauty and love after their brief moment of pleasure. After this short parenthesis, Pico returns to his personal selection of *remedia amoris*, among which we find the sight of rotting corpses, the cold embrace of snow, and self-mutilation (vv. 276–302). In a nutshell: Celestial Venus and all of Plato's "lofty ghosts" must be avoided at all costs because our love must be directed to the figure of the crucified Christ, the saviour of humanity, and to God's eternal rewards (vv. 303–23).

Little is known about the influence that the poem had on early modern readership. As far as we are able to understand from the sources available today, the work was published – together with a letter to Pico's friend Lilio Gregorio Giraldi (1479–1552) and two hymns dedicated to Saint Lawrence and Saint Gimignano – for the first time in 1513 by Giacomo Mazzocchi.[2] A second edition, edited by Johann Schott,[3] appeared the same year in Strasbourg in a collection dedicated to the theme of love. Here, Pico's poem precedes Baptista Mantuanus' elegiac carmen *In amorem* and a Latin translation of Lucian's poem *In cupidinem*. Lilio Giraldi, addressee of the 1512 letter contained in the first editions of the *De Venere*, includes a short but heartfelt reference to Pico's poem in his *De Poetis nostrorum temporum dialogi duo* (1545).[4] After this honourable mention, the poem seems to disappear from the pages of sixteenth-century collections and chronicles discovered so far. A later edition was included in the 1608 collection *Delitiae CC Italorum poetarum huius superiorique aevi illustrium*, edited by Jan Gruter (1560–1627), testifying to its circulation in the early seventeenth century.[5] The 1712 collection *Carmina illustrium poetarum Italorum*, edited by Joannes Cajetanus Tartinius, is proof of the poem's survival well into the eighteenth century.

Although the scarcity of contemporary and later sources on the *De Venere et Cupidine expellendis* indicates a relative lack of interest in the poem, the text had significant relevance in scholarly publications during the second half of the twentieth century.[6] This was due especially to Ernst Gombrich, who decided to include the text as a primary source for his article "Hypnerotomachiana."[7] Although Gombrich concentrated his efforts on the letter to Giraldi, considering Pico's poem "little more than a pastiche of the conventional themes of Platonic love and the *remedia amoris* known from Lucretius and Ovid, culminating in a devout exhortation to Christian chastity,"[8] the importance of Pico's work as a text source became progressively manifest.[9] Pico's letter quickly converted into an essential early witness to Julius II's Cortile del Belvedere, thus appearing in more and more scholarly works dedicated to the statue garden. Well aware of Pico's contribution to the subject, Hans Henrik Brummer quoted the letter to Giraldi in his often-cited thesis *The Statue Court in the Vatican Belvedere* (1970).[10] After him, Pico's work has been mentioned by a large variety of scholars, among them Leonard Barkan (1993), Francesco Tateo (1998), Sofia Maffei (1999), Regina Stefaniak (2000), Stephen J. Campbell (2004), Jill Burke (2006), Brian Curran, Robert H.F. Carver (2007), Patricia Simons, Katherine M. Bentz, and Matteo Soranzo (2015).[11] Notwithstanding the widely recognized importance of the *De Venere et Cupidine expellendis* as a text source for art and philosophy historians, few academics ventured into an analysis of the poem itself, with the notable exception of Luis Marques (2013), who provided the first modern translation and analysis of the poem.[12]

Meditating on the Body

One of the most interesting aspects of Pico's *De Venere et Cupidine expellendis* is the imperfect mirroring between its beginning and ending sections. The first verses of the poem are a heartfelt invocation to the Virgin Mary that she might cast away Venus and "those winged brothers [the two Cupids] whom mad antiquity forged / as foolish gods."[13] The poem's invocation provides a convenient dichotomy between two female entities as carriers of divine and mundane values. Pico's parallel between Venus and the Virgin Mary not only presents a perfect symbolic response to the newly discovered Neoplatonic idea of a twofold Venus, but also mirrors his mentor Girolamo Savonarola's well-known poetic allegory between the original Church of Rome and the corruption of Babylon.[14]

Notwithstanding this perfect symmetry between the figure of Venus and that of the Virgin Mary – a symmetry that Pico employed with success in his previous poetic collection, *Hymni heroici tres* (1507)[15] – the author evokes a different image in the last section of the poem, that of the dying Christ on the Cross. In a passage that recalls the gruesome imagery of Christ's Passion, the poem culminates in the graphic evocation of the blood and wounds of the crucified Christ as powerful instruments to keep bodily desire at bay:

> Love him [Christ] back as you look at his hair
> filthy with dust, and that forehead crowned
> with prickly thorns: with a nod it illuminates the entire Heaven,
> with a nod it would have made the Devil in chain tremble.
> Look at the body drenched in dark blood,
> the wounded side, the stretched-out arms and the hands
> and feet transfixed by nails; look at the many wounds
> with their gushing flow of sacred blood.[16]

This visual ending section, so explicit compared to the lofty initial invocation to the Virgin Mary, opens the floor to many questions. Why, instead of going full circle and closing the poem with the Virgin Mary's triumph over Venus (as the author did in his *Hymni heroici tres*), did Pico decide to linger on a detailed and gruesome description of Jesus' suffering body? To properly understand this passage, we argue, one must first understand the importance of the body of Christ in Pico's spiritual practices against the lures of worldly lust.

Pico's gruesome meditation on the wounded body of Christ is not an isolated case in late medieval and early modern Italy – quite the opposite. The presence of the battered and bloody corpse of Jesus crucified is almost a constant in late medieval forms of meditative prayer, especially in mendicant orders. A prime example of this trend can be found in the writings of Dominican Archbishop Antoninus of Florence (1389–1459). In his 1454 treatise *Opera a ben vivere*, for example, the Dominican theologian urges his readers, while in church or in their room, to kneel before a crucifix and imagine the suffering body of Christ with the eyes of their mind. According to Antoninus' advice, believers should focus their attention on the wounded and bleeding body of Christ. His description of the crucified Jesus is as gruesome as it is detailed:

> First with the crown of thorns, pressed against his head, towards his brain; then the eyes, full of tears, blood, and sweat; then the nose, full of mucus, tears, and blood; the beard, similarly full of saliva, blood, and bile, being full of spit and being all messy; then his face, all darkened, spat on, and livid through the blows of the whips, and bloodied all over. And in reverence of all these things, say a *Paternoster* with an *Ave Maria*.[17]

A similar image can be found in the work of Antoninus' successor to San Marco's priory in Florence: Pico's own mentor, Girolamo Savonarola (1452–1498). Echoing Antoninus' gruesome meditation on the body of Christ, in his Sermon 44 on Amos and Zacharias the leader of the *piagnoni* describes the crucifixion in similar, ghastly, detail:

> As He offered this sacrifice, they put Him on the Cross. They took that holy hand and began to strike it with a hammer and to pierce it and pass through it with nails and to fasten it to the wood; then they took the other hand, and with the same cruelty they fixed it to the wood. Likewise, they pierced the holy feet with nails such that blood poured forth abundantly from every part, and the whole body was stretched on the Cross.[18]

In line with numerous late medieval and early modern iconographical renditions of the *Christus patiens*, these two passages show how the visualization of the body of Christ was a crucial part of late medieval Dominican devotion in Florence and beyond. Gianfrancesco Pico, a diehard follower of Girolamo Savonarola and an ally to the Dominican order's most radical fringes, was deeply influenced by these devotional practices, as his poetic and theological corpus shows.

Christ's suffering body is present in several of Pico's poetic compositions. Together with the ending of *De Venere et Cupidine expellendis*, another notable example of Pico's meditation on Christ's Passion can be found in his 1507 hymn, *Staurostichon*.[19] In the poem, dedicated to Holy Roman Emperor Maximilian I (1459–1519) and discerning the recent rain of bloody crosses in German lands, Pico interprets the event as a miraculous reminder of the Passion – a reminder built around a harrowing description of the suffering Christ.

> A punishment in just blood is required, tortures are demanded,
> as a spectacle for the savage crowd
> They nailed the limbs of the salvific king on the Cross.
> Innocent blood is poured from the whole body,
> copiously the notorious stream of water flowed, mixed with blood,
> By which the ancient crime from the first origin of the world
> Is washed away; the youthful, expiatory offering for original sin.
> Certainly stricken down for love of the human race,
> Cruel nails, laughter, and harsh whiplashes,
> Spitting, slaps, tearing of the beard, and a dire, rough crown
> Bristling with thorns he suffered, determined to chase away death
> by a death on the Cross. O Christ, what kind of clemency
> forced you to suffer death, to rescue from death
> the most ungrateful mortals and their hardened hearts?[20]

In his recent article dedicated to the *Hymni heroici tres*, Matteo Soranzo successfully demonstrated how Pico's poetic reflections, in line with other medieval and early modern forms of prayer and devotion, must be read not only as literary works but also and most importantly as spiritual exercises.[21] Therefore, according to this point of view, in Pico's poetical works the contemplation of Christ's body is much more than a mere trope – it is an active spiritual and visual meditation on the Crucified. For this very reason, Pico's use of the body of Christ, and not the image of the Virgin, at the end of his *De Venere et Cupidine expellendis* must be read as a deliberate choice to guide the reader into a voyage of spiritual purification. This path, beginning with the heavenly blessing of the Virgin Mary, must end – just like any Way of Sorrows – at the feet of the dying Christ.

A Mind of Iron

In his poems, as in his philosophical and theological treatises, Gianfrancesco Pico saw the use of holy images as an instrument to counteract the influence of impure and demonic thoughts. According to

Pico, since the soul governs the senses through the imagination, battles against the affliction of sensual imagery require a spiritual cure by training one's mind towards Christian imagery only.[22] In order to help his fellow Christians in their battle against the sensual body of Venus, in his *De Venere et Cupidine expellendis* Pico provides a theoretical and practical guide to eliminating the human thirst for mundane love, guiding them towards the glory of the Crucified.

According to Pico, the nuptial bed and marriage with a humble wife are undoubtedly the best option. However, there are ways in which even bachelors can keep their chastity and aspire to godly love, that is, with cold water, hard iron, and constant contemplation of chaste images and thoughts, away from any form of impure thinking.[23] According to him, physical fetishes can be of help (he mentions a small cross in his pocket as a useful weapon against Venus' spells).[24] However, only the most rigid training of one's body and mind can genuinely keep demonic temptations at bay. As Pico states later in his poem:

> A mind of iron, untainted by the guilt of Venus,
> is a sword, young men: it turns the languid wing [of Amor]
> into nothing; it breaks the bow and the flying arrows
> and extinguishes the burning flame and the blaze of Erycina,
> dispersing them into pure breeze.[25]

According to Pico's poem, in the battle between *caritas* and *cupiditas*, "it is right to avoid the nets of lustful love / and convert intellect and senses somewhere else,"[26] training one's imagination to a holy life, unencumbered by worldly desires. For Pico, imagination is a necessary but imperfect channel of communication between the soul and the body. As such, it is a powerful instrument that can either save or condemn people to eternal suffering. According to Pico's earlier treatise, *De imaginatione*, in fact, "all the good, universally, but also all the bad, can be derived from the imagination."[27]

In the same text, Pico also stated: "He who strives to dominate phantasy, persists in that dignity in which he has created and placed, and by which he is continually urged to direct the eye of the mind towards God."[28] In this sense, Pico's reflection on the body of Christ derives from his desire to educate his readers' imagination to resist the temptations found in the sensual body of Venus and to turn their imagination towards the only real source of blessings, Jesus Christ. The introductory letter to the Roman edition of *De Venere et Cupidine expellendis* provides further proof of this reasoning. In it, Pico underlines that the poem's objective is to free the minds of those ensnared by the spell of Venus and Cupid, a spell that turns them into mindless animals:

> And so, while I consider that I am placed amongst these very animals accustomed to the grove of Venus and Cupid, I wrote these verses on how to chase out Venus herself and Cupid. Chasing them out, I say, certainly not from the grove – how such a thing could be accomplished by me? – but from the souls of the wild beasts.[29]

These fundamental pieces of information allow us to read the final section of the poem with new eyes. According to Pico's letter, therefore, his *De Venere et Cupidine expellendis* is not just a poetic attack against the presence of pagan gods in the Vatican, but is also meant to be a practical guide on how to resist the enticements of *voluptas* and *cupiditas* through contemplation of Christ's Passion.

Spiritual Cleansing in Three Easy Steps

As we have stated before, Pico's meditation on the body of Christ is the closing act of the path to enlightenment contained in his *De Venere et Cupidine expellendis*. This is because, the importance of visualizing Christ's gruesome corpse notwithstanding, to Pico – we argue – envisioning the Crucified must be conceived as the apex of a series of physical and spiritual exercises to train one's body and mind in (as the title of the poem suggests) the banishing of Venus and Cupid from the soul.[30] For this reason, in the second part of his *De Venere et Cupidine expellendis*, Pico suggests a series of spiritual exercises divided into three stages: a meditation on death, the act of self-discipline, and the tuning of one's mind's eye towards the image of the Crucified. Since we have already outlined the third stage of this spiritual process in the previous sections, we will now focus on the first two steps. The first involves the idea of interiorizing life's brevity and the prospect of eternal salvation (or damnation). Under the ubiquitous image of the dying Christ, the believer must concentrate on life's brevity and the imminence of death:

> May misery be transformed into a lovely sight for your eyes:
> then it will become the substitute of a healthy medicine
> when it will wear the aged wrinkles of old age.
> For certainly the illnesses and discomforts of a wretched life
> increase up to the point when you see as putrid corpses
> consumed by decay, what a moment before the rose together with
> the white privet adorned, and captivated miserable lovers.

> And so the value of my poem consists in reminding of terrible
> death, who cuts down the joys of life with her terrible scythe.[31]

Like his mentor Savonarola before him, Pico understood the great potential of death and disease imagery for instilling a perception of ruin and decay in his brethren.[32] In order to counteract Venus' sensual image, therefore, believers must first picture the body they sexually desire withering, dying, and putrefying before their eyes. This exercise follows an essential part of ascetic disciplines created to perfect the character by cultivating detachment and other virtues and turning the attention towards the immortality of the soul and the afterlife. For Pico, the image of death, pain, and decay exemplified by the Passion is bound to trigger the reader's desire to seek that which does not wither or decay, that is, the resurrected Christ.

Pico's second step is more hands-on and describes the physical exercises that the believer should undertake to clean their spirit from Venus' sensual desires. Following the teachings included in his *De amore divino*,[33] *De Venere et Cupidine expellendis* encourages its readers to follow the examples of the saints who inflicted terrible agonies on their bodies in order to purify their souls:

> Consider the example of those
> who whipped dirty Venus with torment,
> stone and often with a hardened bed,
> and remember him who, they say, defeated Venus' heats
> throwing himself in the snow, uncovering the new seeds
> of the Devil's fraud. And he who avoiding blind Amor's
> darts and those worries tied up with thorns deep inside
> the hollow heart, the gifts of fierce Erycina,
> lacerated his body on sharp thorns.
> And may those come to mind who despised false Cupid's
> bows, while they throw their bodies on the naked
> ground and bear the fasting of their ravenous stomach.[34]

This section of the poem hints at the late medieval and early modern practices of self-discipline adopted by many religious orders of the time. The episode of the snow, for example, hints at the temptation of Francis of Assisi contained in Jacobus de Varagine's *Golden Legend*,[35] thus establishing a direct link between the poem and medieval Franciscan tradition. Another good example of the practices mentioned in the poem can be found in texts describing the life stories of friars and nuns of the Dominican order. In her hagiographic stories of the nuns of the Dominican convent of Unterlinden, the fourteenth-century Dominican nun Sister Catherine von Gebersweiler describes such practices in detail:

> At the end of matins and compline, the sisters remained together in the choir and prayed until they received a sign, upon which they began the most rapturous forms of worship. Some tormented themselves with genuflections while praising the power of God. Others, consumed with the fire of divine love, could not hold back their tears, which were accompanied by rapturous crying voices. They did not move from the spot until they glowed with fresh grace and found the one "whom his soul loveth." (Canticles 1.6.) Finally, others tortured their flesh by maltreating it daily in the most violent fashion, some with blows from rods, others with whips equipped with three or four knotted straps, others with iron chains, and still others by means of scourges arrayed with thorns. At Advent and during the whole of Lent, the sisters would make their way after matins into the main hall or some other place devoted to their purpose. There they abused their bodies in the most acute fashion with all manner of scourging instruments until their blood flowed, so that the sound of the blows of the whip rang through the entire convent and rose more sweetly than any other melody to the ears of the Lord. For God takes pleasure in these exercises of humility and worship and does not fail to hear the groaning of those who are filled with penance. Some of them, inflamed with divine fire, would spend the entire night in deepest prayer and nonetheless take part in early Mass with as much devotion as the rest. Still others, even if they were weak and brittle, did not withdraw after matins, but remained sunken in prayer without stirring. Their cravings were not in vain, for they were filled to the point of overflow by the drops of grace that flowed over them. To those who came closer to God in all these ways, their hearts were illuminated, their thoughts became pure, their sentiments burned, their conscience was cleared, and their spirits were raised toward God.[36]

Just like the first and third stages of his personal Way of Sorrows, Pico's second step towards spiritual purification against Venus is linked to his deep Dominican devotion. Pico's strategy against the lures of the pagan goddess of love is not merely a generic form of penance, but a very specific routine common in the mendicant orders of the time, and more importantly, among the *piagnoni*. Self-mortification in imitation of Christ's Passion, in fact, was an important aspect of Savonarola's spiritual teachings.[37] In showing a way to escape Venus through Jesus, we argue, Pico meant to accompany the reader towards a Dominican – and more specifically Savonarolan – spiritual experience: an open invitation to join the ranks of the *piagnoni*.

Conclusion

In light of late medieval and early modern Dominican and Savonarolan devotion, Gianfrancesco Pico's *De Venere et Cupidine expellendis* combines visions of death, disease, and decay with physical acts of self-punishment, including starvation, self-injury, and other instruments of discipline such as sleeping on the ground or, more simply, on a hard bed. These sanctioned devotional practices, combined with the realignment of one's inner eye with the divine, all culminate in the third step: the image of Christ's body crucified. In Pico's eye, reminiscent of Savonarola's spiritual theology and poetry,[38] the suffering and death of God's son is the highest example of authentic beauty and love and is thus the best instrument to banish the malevolent influence of Venus and Cupid. Jesus' languid body, hanging on the Cross, reminds the believer that love must not be directed towards transitory things but to the one who sacrificed his mortal body to bestow on humanity eternal happiness.[39]

In resonance with late medieval and early modern Dominican devotion, Gianfrancesco Pico's spiritual practices found in his *De Venere et Cupidine expellendis* are exercises of meditation, self-humiliation, and discipline, consumed with the blessing of the Virgin Mary and under the vigilant presence of the crucified body of Christ. However, is the figure of Christ here employed just as an anti-erotic device to quell the readers' desire? Is the sacred male body used merely as a simple counter-spell to unholy female eroticism? We believe that the answer is more complex than that. In Pico's poem, the image of the naked goddess of the Cortile del Belvedere is indeed "exorcised" through the image of a naked and suffering Christ: the unholy feminine against the holy masculine, unholy desire versus holy desire, sensuality against suffering. However, how is this holy desire articulated? Is the suffering of one's flesh in front of the blood-drenched, ecstatic, dying body of Christ an anti-erotic alternative to carnal thoughts (or acts) in front of the unveiled body of Venus? In this case, we argue, the line between Eros and Thanatos is much more blurred than one might initially think. In line with the flagellant narratives of the time, Pico's solution against the carnal desires for Venus is yet another bodily desire, which rejects any sinful thought of self-gratification in front of Venus to indulge in the sanctioned pleasures of self-mortification under the watchful eye of the Crucified. In Pico's verses, unholy urges are replaced with holy longings, and the life-giving womanly body of Venus gives way to the dying manly body of Christ as the ultimate object of desire.

NOTES

1 If not otherwise specified, all translations are mine. For a short biography of Gianfrancesco Pico della Mirandola, see Piana, "Pico della Mirandola, Gianfrancesco." For a longer discussion of Gianfrancesco's life, see Schmitt, *Gianfrancesco Pico della Mirandola*, 11–31.
2 Pico della Mirandola, *De Venere & Cupidine expellendis carmen*. For further details on the *editio princeps* of this work, see Quaquarelli and Zanardi, *Pichiana*, 265–6. For information on Giacomo Mazzocchi, a learned bookseller, printer, and noted antiquarian active in papal Rome in 1505–27, see Rhodes, "Further Notes."
3 An important book publisher active between 1500 and 1544. See Koerner, *The Moment of Self-Portraiture*, 214.
4 Giraldi and Grant, *Modern Poets*, 34: "[Gianfrancesco Pico] composed a poem about expelling and driving out Venus and Cupid, and such was his great fondness for me that he sent me a copy of this. He was the first to reintroduce hymns written in dactylic hexameters after they had fallen into disuse for many centuries, and he certainly alone found the way to hold pagan learning up for display." For further information on Giraldi and his relationship with Pico, see Pettinelli, "Roma, ponte tra antico e moderno."
5 Gruter, *Delitiae*, 205–6.
6 The earliest reference to Pico's *De Venere* in the twentieth century is most probably an article written by Guido Manacorda in 1908. See Manacorda, "Notizie."
7 Gombrich, "Hypnerotomachiana," 120–4.
8 Gombrich, "Hypnerotomachiana," 123.
9 Gombrich used Pico's *De Venere et Cupidine expellendis* again in 1991, comparing Gianfrancesco Pico's take on sixteenth-century Rome to that of Ulrich von Hutten (1488–1523), German scholar, poet, satirist, and reformer; see Gombrich, "Archaeologists or Pharisees," 255.
10 Brummer, *The Statue Court in the Vatican Belvedere*, 273–4.
11 See Barkan, "The Beholder's Tale," 143–4; Tateo, "I due Pico"; Settis et al., *Laocoonte, fama e stile*, 174; Stefaniak, "Raphael's *Madonna di Foligno*," 175; Campbell, *The Cabinet of Eros*, 89; Burke, "Sex and Spirituality in 1500s Rome," 488; Curran, *The Egyptian Renaissance*, 171–2; Carver, *The Protean Ass*, 252–3; Simons, "The Crone, the Witch, and the Library," 277; Bentz, "Ancient Idols," 420. See also Soranzo, "Un'identità religiosa," 54–5.
12 Marques, "L'attacco."
13 Pico della Mirandola, *De Venere & Cupidine Expellendis Carmen*, vv. 1–8: "Idalios ignes caecique Cupidinis arma / Atque Dionaeos procul ablegare furores / Fert animus. Da, casta parens, Iessaea propago, / Da, virgo, aeternum virgo, quae sola furentum / Nequitiam sacro praestas

compescere partu, / Da, praecor, et Veneres et quos malesana uetustas / Aligeros finxit dementia numina fratres / Exturbare, nouo longe et dispellere cantu" ("The Idalean flames blind Cupid's weapons, / and Dione's frenzies – these do the soul seek / to banish. Grant me, chaste mother, offspring of Jesse, / virgin, eternally virgin, you who alone, with the sacred birth, / restrained the sacrilege of fools; / now grant me, I beg you, to chase twofold Venus away / and those winged brothers whom mad antiquity forged / as foolish gods; grant me to cast them out with this new song").

14 A first attempted dichotomy between two female entities as carriers of divine and mundane values can be found in one of Savonarola's poem, "De ruina ecclesiae" (1475). In the poem, the Church is depicted as the earthly spouse of the Virgin Mary, a "pious mother" abandoned by her people, and stripped down to her sober and spiritual vestments. This woman brings Savonarola to witness the entrance of a "haughty woman" into the gardens of Rome. See Savonarola, *A Guide to Righteous Living*, 68: "– My lady, – said I, then – if you don't mind, / My soul would gladly weep along with you. / What power is this that takes your kingdom from you? / What haughty person so disturbs your peace? / She answered with a sigh – One false, / and haughty prostitute, Babylon. – / And I: – By God, Lady, / If one could only break those mighty wings – And she: – A mortal tongue / Can not, nor may, nor could it raise a weapon. / Weep and be silent, this seems the best to me."

15 Pico della Mirandola, *Ioannis Francisci Pici Mirandulani Principis: Concordiaeque Comitis Hymni heroici tres*, hymn II, vv. 44–189.

16 "Hunc redama aspiciens [*adspiciens*] foedatos puluere crines / Atque coronatam dumis pungentibus illam, / Fronte[m] illam, nutu totum quae illustrat Olympum, / Quaeque catenatum nutu tremefecerit Orcum. / Hunc redama aspiciens [*adspiciens*] foedatos puluere crines / Atque coronatam dumis pungentibus illam, / Fronte[m] illam, nutu totum quae illustrat Olympum, / Quaeque catenatum nutu tremefecerit Orcum. / Aspice [*Adspice*] purpureo madefactum sanguine corpus, / Disiectumque latus, distentaque brachia, clauis / Transfixasque manus, plantasque; sacrique cruoris / Aspice [*Adspice*] multiplices undanti flumine riuos"; Pico della Mirandola, *De Venere & Cupidine expellendis carmen*, vv. 310–17.

17 Cited in Zaru, *Art and Observance in Renaissance Venice*, 73–4: "Quando avete udito messa o innanzi, o volete in chiesa o volete in camera vostra, inginnochiatevi; davanti ad un Crucifisso, e cogli occhi della mente, più che con quelli, del corpo, considerate la faccia sua. Prima alla corona delle spine, fittigliele in testa, insino al celabro; poi gli occhi, pieni di lacrime e di sangue e di sudore; poi lo naso, pieno di mocci e di lacrime e di sangue; la barba, similmente piena di bava e di sangue e di fiele, essendo tutta sputacchiata a spelazzata; poi la faccia, tutta oscurata, e sputacchiata, e

livida per le percosse della gotate e della canna, e tutta sanguinosa. E a reverenza di tutte queste cose, direte un paternostro con l'avemaria."

18 Savonarola, *Selected Writings*, 31. A modern edition of the original text can be found in Savonarola, *Prediche sopra Amos e Zaccaria*, 284: "E offerendo quello sacrificio e' lo messono in su la croce. E presono quella mano santa e col martello incominciarono a percuoterla e forare e passare col chiodo e attaccarla al legno; e dipoi presono l'altra mano e con la medesima crudeltà la confissono al legno; e ancora li santi piedi con li chiovi passarono acerbamente, per modo che da ogni parte usciva el sangue in abbondanzia, e tutto il corpo era disteso in su la croce."

19 See Piana, "Written in Blood," 85–102. See also Lucioli, "Poesia e profezia."

20 "Supplicium petitur iusto de sanguine, poenae / Poscuntur, saeuae condunt spectacula plebi / Membra salutiferi transfixo stipite regis. / Funditur innocuus toto de corpore sanguis, / Ubertim celebris mixto fluit unda cruore: / Qua scelus antiquum primaque ab origine mundi / Eluitur, patriae primaeua piacula noxae. / Scilicet humani generis perculsus amore / Crudeles clauos, risus, atque aspera flagra, / Sputa, alapas, barbae uulsus, diramque coronam / Sentibus horrentem subiit, mortemque fugare / Morte Crucis uoluit. Quae te clementia Christe / Ingratos nimium mortales, ferrea corda, / ut morte eriperes, mortem perferre coegit?"; Pico della Mirandola, *Staurostichon*, vv. 91–104.

21 Soranzo, "Un'identità religiosa," 70–2.

22 Pico della Mirandola, *On the Imagination*, 45. See also Moreschini, *Rinascimento Cristiano*, 48–9.

23 Pico della Mirandola, *De Venere & Cupidine expellendis*, vv. 223–31: "If you are willing to spend your life as bachelors, / constantly extinguish the flames with chaste springwater / and drown Venus in a freezing sea, / lying open towards the North Wind of the always frozen Hibernia: / if they fly repeatedly over the mind and the eyes, and if they want / to pour a silent venom with evil flames into the heart, / the winged brothers, crowd of flying children, / as the vicious flock scatters in the air with smooth wings, / you must cut off the wings with hard iron at once" ("Caelibe si uultis uitam traducere lecto / Continuo castis restinguite fontibus ignes / Et venerem [veneres] gelido, venerem [veneres] submergite ponto. / Qua patet ad Boream semper glacialis Hiberniae [Hyberne] / Pervolitent mentem atque oculos, facibusque malignis / Si instillare uelint tacitum in praecordia virus / Aligeri fratres, puerorum turba uolantum, / Vos subito ut leuibus difflauerit aera pennis, / Turba nocens duro pennas praecidite ferro").

24 See Piana, "Inter animalia," 61.

25 "Ferrea mens nulli Veneris obnoxia culpae, / Ensis adest Iuuenes quo mollis in aera penna / Dissecta [*Dessecta*] est: quo neruus agens uolucresque sagittae / Diffractae rutilaeque faces Erycinaque lampas / Extincta, in

liquidas resolutaque protinus auras"; Pico della Mirandola, *De Venere & Cupidine expellendis carmen*, vv. 232–6.

26 "Nam fugitare decet lasciui retia amoris, / Atque alio mentem atque alio conuertere sensus"; Pico della Mirandola, *De Venere & Cupidine expellendis carmen*, vv. 250–1.

27 Pico della Mirandola, *On the Imagination*, 43.

28 Pico della Mirandola, *On the Imagination*, 44–5.

29 "Haec itaque inter animalia Venereo Cupidineoque nemori assueta cum me positum existimarem. De ipsa venere et cupidine expellendis carmina istaec faciebam / expellendis inquam non sane extra lucum: qui enim a me parari id posset operis? Sed ab animis ferarum"; Pico della Mirandola, *De Venere & Cupidine expellendis carmen*. Letter to Lilius Giraldi.

30 On Pico's theories on the magical influence of Venus and Cupid, see Piana, "Inter animalia," 58–62.

31 "Ante oculos etiam macies uersetur amicam / in faciem succo tum successura salubri / cum senium rugas secum portarit aniles. / Quod certe et morbi miseraeque incommoda vitae / Ingeminant foeda ut confecta cadauera tabe / Nunc spectes, albo quae iam rosa mista [*mixta*] ligustro / Punicea exornans miseros captabat amantes. / Hinc operae pretium est mortis meminisse tremendae / terribili excindit quae vitae gaudia falce. / Sic mors flagrantes compescet [*conpescit*] frigida curas / tempore non certo et certo rapidissima cursu"; Pico della Mirandola, *De Venere & Cupidine expellendis carmen*, vv. 278–87.

32 See Assonitis, "Fra Girolamo Savonarola and the Aesthetics of Pollution," 148.

33 Moreschini, *Rinascimento cristiano*, 52.

34 "Exempla virorum / accedant Venerem immundam qui uerbere [*verbere*] torto / et silice et rigido domuerunt saepe cubili / Quique niuem insiliens Veneris superasse calores / Dicitur occurat, retegens noua semina fraudis / Infernae. Nec non qui caeci spicula amoris / Quique illas quondam sub inani pectore curas / Consertas spinis, Erycinae munera saeuae / Deludens se se in spinas destrusit acutas. / Et qui fallacis tempsere Cupidinis arcus / obrepant menti: dum nudae corpora terrae / collidunt, avidique ferunt ieiunia uentris"; Pico della Mirandola, *De Venere & Cupidine expellendis carmen*, vv. 291–302.

35 Jacobus de Varagine, *Golden Legend*, ch. 149, online: "And when the devil saw that he might not prevail against him, he tempted him by grievous temptation of the flesh, and when this holy servant of God felt that, he despoiled him of his clothes and beat himself right hard with a hard cord, saying: Thus, brother ass, it behoveth thee to remain and to be beaten. And when the temptation departed not, he went out and plunged himself in the snow all naked, and made seven great balls of snow and purposed to have taken them into his body and said: This greatest is thy wife, and of these four, two be thy daughters, and two thy sons, and the other twain, that one thy chamberer,

and that other thy varlet or yeoman; haste thee and clothe them, for they all die for cold, and if thy business that thou hast about them grieve thee sore, then serve our Lord perfectly. And anon the devil departed from them all confused, and St. Francis returned again into his cell glorifying God."

36 Ancelet-Hustache, "Les 'Vitae sororum' d'Unterlinden," as cited in Largier, *In Praise of the Whip*, 36.

37 See Viladesau, *The Triumph of the Cross*, 29–43.

38 See Savonarola's "Song of Praise to the Crucifix" in Savonarola, *A Guide to Righteous Living*, 76–7.

39 Moreschini, *Rinascimento cristiano*, 51.

WORKS CITED

Printed Sources

Assonitis, Alessio. "Fra Girolamo Savonarola and the Aesthetics of Pollution in Fifteenth-Century Rome." In Mark Bradley and Kenneth R. Stow, eds., *Rome, Pollution, and Propriety: Dirt, Disease, and Hygiene in the Eternal City from Antiquity to Modernity*. Cambridge: Cambridge University Press, 2012, 139–52.

Barkan, Leonard. "The Beholder's Tale: Ancient Sculpture, Renaissance Narratives." *Representations* 44 (1993): 133–66.

Bentz, Katherine M. "Ancient Idols, Lascivious Statues, and Sixteenth-Century Viewers in Roman Gardens." In Marice E. Rose and Alison C. Poe, eds., *Receptions of Antiquity, Constructions of Gender in European Art, 1300–1600*. Boston: Brill, 2015, 418–19.

Bottari, Giovanni Gaetano. *Carmina illustrium poetarum Italorum*. Florence: Tartini & Franchi, 1719.

Brummer, Hans Henrik. *The Statue Court in the Vatican Belvedere*. Stockholm: Almqvist & Wiksell, 1970.

Burke, Jill. "Sex and Spirituality in 1500s Rome: Sebastiano Del Piombo's Martyrdom of Saint Agatha." *The Art Bulletin* 88.3 (2006): 482–95.

Campbell, Stephen J. *The Cabinet of Eros: Renaissance Mythological Painting and the Studiolo of Isabella d'Este*. New Haven: Yale University Press, 2004.

Carver, Robert H.F. *The Protean Ass: The Metamorphoses of Apuleius from Antiquity to the Renaissance*. Oxford: Oxford University Press, 2007.

Curran, Brian A. *The Egyptian Renaissance: The Afterlife of Ancient Egypt in Early Modern Italy*. Chicago: University of Chicago Press, 2007.

Giraldi, Lilio Gregorio. *Modern Poets*. Ed. and trans. John N. Grant. Cambridge, MA: Harvard University Press, 2011.

Gombrich, Ernst H. "Archaeologists or Pharisees? Reflections on a Painting by Maarten Van Heemskerck." *Journal of the Warburg and Courtauld Institutes* 54 (1991): 253–6.

– "Hypnerotomachiana." *Journal of the Warburg and the Courtauld Institutes* 14 (1951): 120–5.

Gruter, Jan, ed. *Delitiae CC Italorum poetarum huius superiorisque aevi illustrium*. Frankfurt: Jonas Rosa, 1608.

Koerner, Joseph L. *The Moment of Self-Portraiture in German Renaissance Art*. Chicago: University of Chicago Press, 1993.

Largier, Niklaus. *In Praise of the Whip*. Ed. and trans. Graham Harman. New York: Zone Books, 2007.

Lucioli, Francesco. "Poesia e profezia nello Staurostichon di Giovan Francesco Pico della Mirandola." *Archivio italiano per la storia della pietà* 25 (2012): 275–301.

Manacorda, Guido. "Notizie intorno alle fonti di alcuni motivi satirici ed alla loro diffusione durante il Rinascimento." *Romanische Forschungen* 22.3 (1908): 733–60.

Marques, Luiz. "L'attacco di Giovanni Francesco Pico della Mirandola alla 'Venus felix' e alla Stanza della Segnatura." *FIGURA Studi sull'immagine nella tradizione classica* 1 (2013): 363–436.

Moreschini, Claudio. *Rinascimento cristiano: Innovazioni e riforma religiosa nell'Italia del quindicesimo e sedicesimo secolo*. Rome: Edizioni di Storia e Letteratura, 2017.

Pettinelli, Rosa Alhaique. "Roma, ponte tra antico e moderno per due umanisti ferraresi: Lilio Gregorio Giraldi e Celio Calcagnini." In Silvia Danesi Squarzina, ed., *Roma, centro ideale della cultura dell'antico nei secoli XV e XVI: da Martino V al sacco di Roma, 1417–1527*. Milan: Electa, 1989, 365–70.

Piana, Marco. "'Inter animalia Venereo Cupidineoque nemori assueta': Il Cortile del Belvedere in due lettere di Gianfrancesco Pico della Mirandola." *Studi Rinascimentali* 18 (2020): 53–64.

– "Written in Blood: Blood Devotion in Gianfrancesco Pico's Staurostichon." *Renaissance and Reformation* 42.4 (2020): 85–102.

Pico della Mirandola, Gianfrancesco. *Illustrissimi ac doctissimi Principis Jo. Francisci Pici Mirandulae […] De Venere & Cupidine expellendis carmen; Item eiusdem Laurentius & Geminianus Hymni*. Rome: Iacobus Mazochius, 1513.

– *Ioannis Francisci Mirandulae Dn. De expellendis Venere & Cupidine carmen heroicu[m]; Eiusdem hymnus de Diuo Laurentio. Baptistae Mantuani elegia in Amorem; eiusdem in Venerem heroicu[m]. In Cupidinem nociuum carmen Luciani*. Strasbourg: Ioannes Schottus, 1513.

– *Ioannis Francisci Pici Mirandulani Principis: Concordiaeque Comitis Hymni heroici tres ad Sanctissimam Trinitatem: ad Christum: et ad Virginem Mariam*. Milan: Alessandro Minuziano, 1507.

– *On the Imagination*. Ed. and trans. Harry Caplan. New Haven: Yale University Press, 1930.

– *Staurostichon*. In Pico della Mirandola, *Opera omnia*. Ed. Luigi Firpo. 2 vols. Turin: La Bottega d'Erasmo, 1972, 2:355–65.

Quaquarelli, Leonardo, and Rita Zanardi. *Pichiana: Bibliografia delle edizioni e degli studi*. Florence: L.S. Olschki, 2005.

Rhodes, Dennis E. "Further Notes on the Publisher Giacomo Mazzocchi." *Papers of the British School at Rome* 40 (1972): 239–42.

Savonarola, Girolamo. *A Guide to Righteous Living and Other Works*. Ed. and trans. Konrad Eisenbichler. Renaissance and Reformation Texts in Translation 10. Toronto: Centre for Reformation and Renaissance Studies, 2003.

– *Prediche sopra Amos e Zaccaria*. Ed. Paolo Ghiglieri. Rome: Angelo Belardetti, 1972.

– *Selected Writings of Girolamo Savonarola: Religion and Politics, 1490–1498*. Ed. and trans. Donald Beebe et al. New Haven: Yale University Press, 2008.

Schmitt, Charles B. *Gianfrancesco Pico della Mirandola (1469–1533) and His Critique of Aristotle*. The Hague: Martinus Nijhoff, 1967.

Settis, Salvatore, et al. *Laocoonte, fama e stile*. Rome: Donzelli, 1999.

Simons, Patricia. "The Crone, the Witch, and the Library: The Intersection of Classical Fantasy with Christian Vice during the Italian Renaissance." In Marice E. Rose and Alison C. Poe, eds., *Receptions of Antiquity, Constructions of Gender in European Art, 1300–1600*. Boston: Brill, 2015, 264–304.

Soranzo, Matteo. "Un'identità religiosa nel primo Cinquecento." *Italian Studies* 70.1 (2015): 53–75.

Stefaniak, Regina. "Raphael's *Madonna di Foligno*: Vergine Bella." *Konsthistorisk tidskrift/Journal of Art History* 69.3–4 (2000): 169–95.

Tateo, Francesco. "I due Pico e la tematica d'amore nel Cinquecento." In Patrizia Castelli, ed., *Giovanni e Gianfrancesco Pico. L'opera e la fortuna di due studenti ferraresi*. Florence: Leo S. Olschki, 1998, 313–24.

Viladesau, Richard. *The Triumph of the Cross: The Passion of Christ in Theology and the Arts, from the Renaissance to the Counter-Reformation*. Oxford: Oxford University Press, 2008.

Zaru, Denise. *Art and Observance in Renaissance Venice: The Dominicans and Their Artists (1391–ca. 1545)*. Trans. Sarah Melker. Rome: Viella, 2014.

Electronic Sources

Jacobus de Varagine. *Golden Legend*. Trans. William Caxton. Online at https://www.christianiconography.info/goldenLegend/francis.htm (accessed 26 January 2021).

Piana, Marco. "Pico della Mirandola, Gianfrancesco." In Marco Sgarbi, ed., *Encyclopedia of Renaissance Philosophy*. Online at https://doi.org/10.1007/978-3-319-02848-4_743-1 (accessed 26 January 2021).

PART TWO

Women and Men: Masculinity, Effeminacy, and Desire

5 *A Dio Zerbini a Dio, a Dio Narcisi*: Satirizing Effeminacy in Margherita Costa's Florentine Works (1638–1641)

SARA E. DÍAZ

Summary: This article investigates an effeminate masculine type found in several works by the seventeenth-century author and performer Margherita Costa (ca. 1610–after 1657). It focuses on foppish paramours, or *zerbini,* who are derisively compared to Ganymede and Narcissus in ways that reveal the fault lines between transgressive effeminacy and heteronormative masculinity. Too young and financially disenfranchised to command authority, these male figures are mocked for their feminine clothing, mannerisms, and vanities, and sharply rebuked by the women they attempt to woo. Proceeding chronologically, the article surveys parodic references to these dandies in four of the volumes Costa published during her years in grand ducal Florence, namely, *La chitarra* (The Guitar, 1638), *Lo stipo* (The Cabinet, 1639), *Lettere amorose* (Love Letters, 1639), and *Li buffoni* (The Buffoons, 1641). It demonstrates how Costa's *zerbini* are closely linked to the Medicean courtly milieu and reflect contemporary tastes for epic literature, comic performances, and Baroque entertainments. As it ultimately argues, Costa's efforts to police fragile masculinity in her Florentine publications constitute just one of her many bids to assert her literary authority, in this case, at the expense of a disempowered male.

Margherita Costa was the most successful secular female writer of her day. Having achieved a degree of fame and notoriety as a young *virtuosa* in her native Rome, she translated her musical talents into invitations to perform on the stages and salons of Europe's leading courts.[1] Her singing career was matched by her accomplishments on the page. Over the course of nearly twenty-five years she published fourteen volumes including a history, comedy, horse ballet, hagiographic poem, operatic libretto, letter collection, and several books of poetry.[2] She showed off her dexterity with genre, tone, and content in these publications, particularly in lyric collections where she moved from the laudatory to the satirical. And, unlike the demure *petrarchiste* of the previous century, Costa showed no compunction in attaching her name to works filled with ribald wordplay and parodic caricatures of familiar courtly figures. Nothing was off limits for this resourceful artist – not even her own reputation as a woman of letters.

There is much to be said about Costa's contradictory approach to gender in her expansive corpus of printed works. As a woman competing for patronage in the male-dominated field of letters, her own sex was at the forefront of her mind. Her dedications, thick with the rhetoric of false modesty, draw attention to the wondrous, even monstrous singularity of her status as female author. In her *canzonieri*, she defends her right to write as a woman in one autobiographical lyric, only to reverse course and swear off her poetic births in the next. Meanwhile, several of her compositions feature the voices of ladies who reject the limitations placed on them by society, while others satirize female foibles using some of the same misogynist tropes found in contemporary male-authored literature. Though the subject of women in Costa's oeuvre certainly warrants further investigation, this article will look at the construction of a marginal form of masculinity in her comic production. To do so, it will focus on men who display pejorative markers of femininity in the volumes Costa published during her years under the aegis of the Medici grand dukes in Florence (c. 1628–44). Central to this investigation will be two key questions: Why would a woman writing at a time hostile to her gender repeatedly target an effeminate man in her publications? And how does an unflattering characterization of these men as womanish advance the cause of a female author? With these questions in the foreground, the pages that follow explore the understudied subject of effeminacy in this early modern author's satirical interludes.

Today, Margherita Costa is enjoying a renaissance of her own, due in part to new scholarship that situates her work within the trajectory of female authorship in Italy. One of the foremost critics to rescue her from oblivion is Virginia Cox, who, in her landmark study, draws attention to the singularity of Costa's many accomplishments at a time when opportunities for women writers were otherwise on the decline.[3] As she observes, Costa flourished in an era that increasingly prized "the daring, the exuberant, and the irregular, both as its subject matter and style," thanks to her skilful self-fashioning as an eccentric voice.[4] Picking up on this thread, Jessica Goethals tracks Costa's repeated efforts to project a uniquely "bizarre" female identity that would appeal to her patrons, especially in her burlesque compositions.[5] According to

Goethals, "Costa's plurality – in genre, register, and content – made her especially adept at using literary and theatrical play as a way of crafting her multifaceted authorial persona."[6] Other recent inquiries focus on the interplay of gender and authorship in her individual works. Marina di Maro, for example, has identified a proto-feminist current in Costa's *Violino*, seeing in it a defence of female independence in both the public and the amorous spheres.[7] Meanwhile, Meredith Ray dedicates several pages of her investigation of women's epistolary collections to Costa's *Lettere amorose*.[8] Central to her discussion of Costa's "hermaphroditic" style – her ability to ventriloquize both male and female voices – is a letter exchange between a Lovely Lady ("Bella donna") and an effeminate *zerbino*. The almost theatrical contrast between the two, notes Ray, serves to mark the limits of socially acceptable gender displays.[9] The present article builds upon Ray's insights by expanding our investigation to contemporary works by Costa that police transgressive masculinity through the parodic figure of the *zerbino*.

While studies that frame Margherita Costa's life and works in relation to female authorship are beginning to trickle in, the topic of effeminacy in early modern Europe has long attracted experts from a variety of disciplines.[10] For scholars of the Italian Renaissance, research on the gendering of elite men often leads to Baldassare Castiglione's critique of the effeminate courtier in the *Libro del cortegiano*.[11] Fashion historians, not surprisingly, have taken a keen interest in the dialogue's "sartorial signifiers of effeminacy."[12] As their works variously demonstrate, early modern conduct manuals like Castiglione's *Cortegiano* or Giovanni Della Casa's *Galateo* frequently present vestimentary excess as a source of masculine anxiety. Castiglione's arguments against effeminacy have also been studied in relation to court culture and, in particular, the emasculating presence of the courtly lady.[13] Gerry Milligan's work on this front has been especially illuminating.[14] Building off of earlier studies that see the feminization of the courtier as a sort of contagion brought on by his proximity and subordination to female members of the court, Milligan demonstrates that "women are an integral and powerful discursive force in the bolstering and policing of a pragmatic masculinity."[15] Both men and women participate in the culture of surveillance, he argues, using the mechanisms of gender shaming to bring about political change. Keeping Milligan's insights on the gendered culture of surveillance in the Italian courts in mind, this article will explore what happens when these shaming mechanisms are employed, not by a male insider like Castiglione, but rather by a woman.

Before proceeding, we should pause to ask who, or what, was a *zerbino*? In contemporary Italian, the term *zerbino* translates as doormat, both literally and figuratively. When applied to a person, it can refer to a servile flatterer, or bootlicker. Early modern readers of *Orlando furioso* would have recognized Zerbino instead as one of Ariosto's famed paladins. Here, he was a young Scottish prince and the lover of the Saracen Isabella, in whose arms he ultimately died. At the same time, his name was synonymous with a class of young, handsome, and well-dressed gallants dedicated to the service of women.[16] However, though always characterized as beautiful, the *zerbino*'s physical charms and attention to his appearance were seen to border dangerously close to the feminine. For example, in a play performed a decade prior to Costa's arrival in Florence, *La Fiera*, Michelangelo Buonarroti the Younger likened the "delights of the *zerbino*" to women's cosmetic and sartorial displays.[17] Perfumes, lotions, soaps, and delicate gloves and shoes are cited as the special pleasures of this soft and indolent class of man. At the same time, he enjoyed a second life in the *commedia dell'arte*, where he inhabited the less than heroic role of a preening *capitano*. As an etching by Jacques Callot shows (fig. 5.1), the *zerbino* of the *commedia* would have been a masked character sporting a plume in his hat and a sword by his side – details not coincidentally alluded to in Costa's send-ups of the boastful fop. He therefore had a place in both high and low culture – in the romance of Ariosto's meandering epic and the improvised comedy of professional actors. And while Costa was not the first to have her fun with the comically amorous *zerbino*, her repeated efforts to mock him across genres and volumes raise questions about his special appeal for this author.

Costa's recurring interest in this masculine character is closely bound to her time in Florence. She moved from Rome to the grand ducal court some time after 1628, perhaps to perform as part of the festivities for Margherita de' Medici's wedding to Odoardo Farnese.[18] Her new home was one that favoured all manner of Baroque spectacles. In addition to the operas, concerts, comedies, tragedies, dances, and equestrian ballets that were regularly performed on the city's many stages, the Medici also delighted in grotesque and bizarre forms of occasional entertainment.[19] Tournaments, plays, and races featuring dwarf and disabled performers were popular during Carnival and feast days and were even documented by some of the leading artists of the time, as seen in a print of a dwarf spectacle by Stefano della Bella (fig. 5.2). It was a Baroque court, driven by a desire for the marvellous, the novel, and the grotesque – tastes that Costa proved more than capable of satisfying.

The years between 1628 and 1644 at the Medici court were Costa's most productive, resulting in nine of her fourteen published volumes. Explicit references to *zerbini* are found in several of her Florentine works, beginning with *La Chitarra* (1638).[20] It is here that we observe

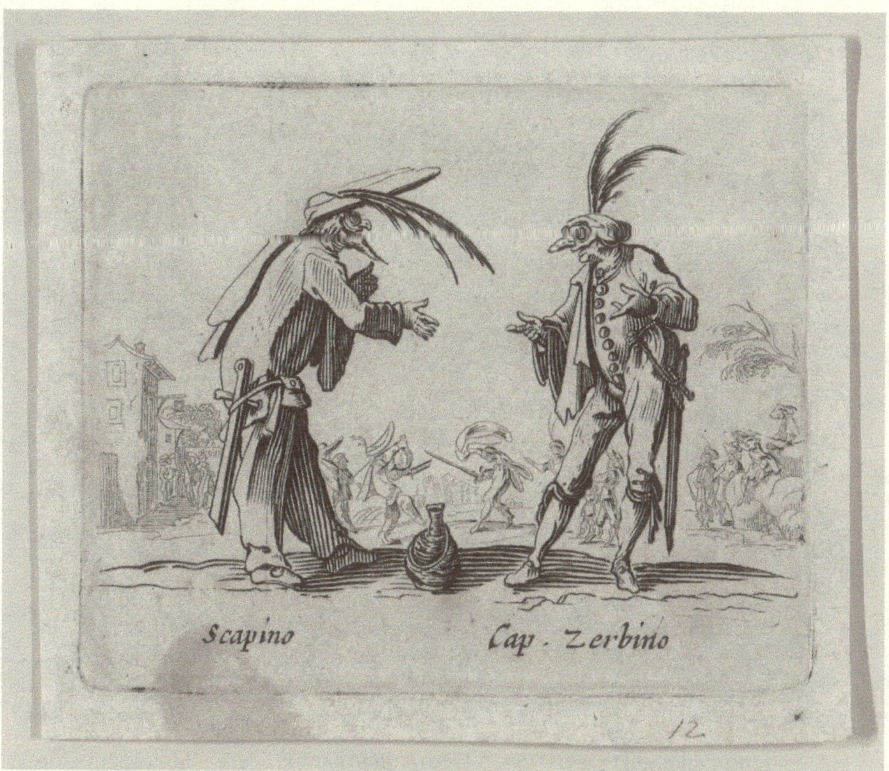

5.1. Jacques Callot (1592–1635), *Scapino and Cap. Zerbino. Balli di Sfessania* series, ca. 1622. Washington, National Gallery of Art, Rosenwald Collection. NGA.org open access image.

some of her first attempts to insert herself into Medicean court culture by policing masculinity through the medium of print.

The *Chitarra* is a substantial 584-page *canzoniere* largely devoted to amorous themes. It is the first book-length publication to have unquestionably been authored by Costa, and introduces many of the subjects and stylistics that are found in her subsequent volumes.[21] The collection opens with laudatory poems in praise of the Medici and their associates, but then shifts to a number of playful lyrics, including *canzonette* and *scherzi*, that signal the light-hearted tone of her verse. Octaves, sonnets, and idylls give voice to the highs and lows of romantic intrigues, concluding with an autobiographical *capitolo scherzoso* defending Costa's right, as a woman, to write.[22] Barely masking her pride under

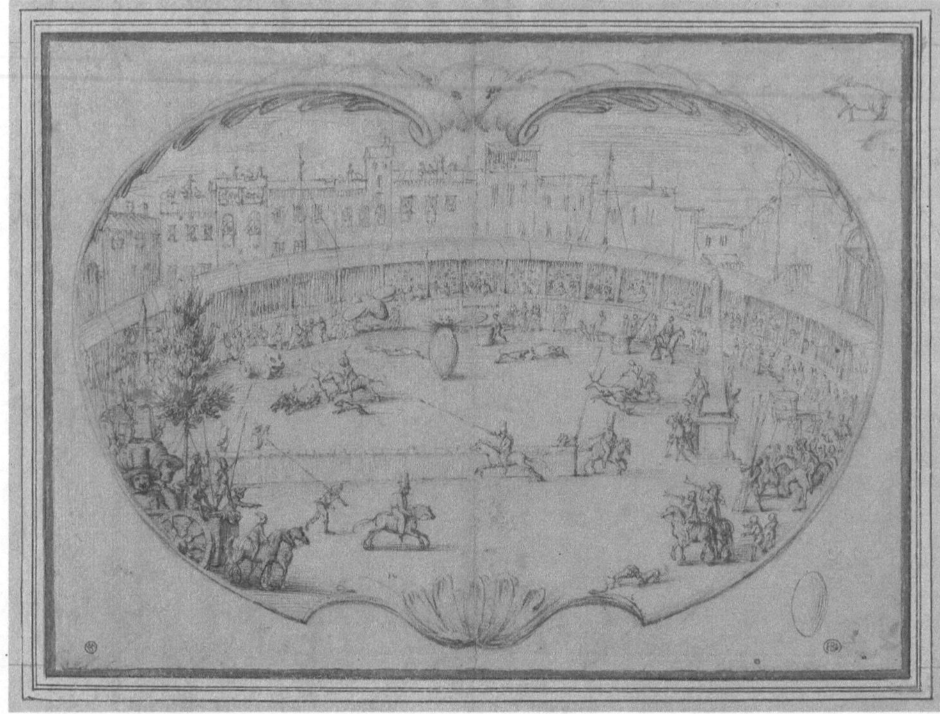

5.2. Stefano della Bella (1610–1664), *Dwarfs' Tournament*. Paris, Bibliothèque de l'École des Beaux-Arts.

a veil of false modesty, Costa touts her ability to have assumed in the preceding pages a variety of real and imagined personas:

> I sang of true and false cases of love,
> I mixed affection with disdain, and anger,
> I made up hearts, both deceptive and sincere:
> I sought to conceal one under another name,
> and by a thousand metamorphoses I proved,
> that the art of love is not joy:
> Here I praised, there obscured another's merits,
> not to put them down, but simply in jest;
> And when I spoke ill, it was always a joke …[23]

Costa uses her gender to excuse her unpolished verse and draw attention to the singularity of her literary accomplishments. While she acknowledges that delicate matters of the heart are the proper purview of female authors like herself, she nonetheless brings the volume to a close on a defiant, satirical note.[24] She presents herself as both a fabulist and a truth teller, using her pen to critique contemporary mores, especially in matters of love. But among the many types of lovers addressed in her work, none receives as thorough of a dressing-down as the dandy – a vulnerable class of men with a history of attracting the derisive laughter of the Medici court.

Most relevant to this study, the *Chitarra* contains a three-part exchange between pretty-boys (*Begli'imbusti*), court dwarfs (*Caramogi*), and women (*Donne*), each consisting of a prose letter and a lyric in the same voice.[25] The two classes of suitors engage in a debate over their superiority in the arena of love. Their verbal contest is judged by ladies who pronounce both groups of men to be utterly undesirable. Interestingly, the opening *Caramogi* text is attributed to Andrea Salvadori (1591–1634), while the responses from the dandies and adjudicating women are instead the identified as Costa's. The attribution is not coincidental – Salvadori was the Medici's leading poet and author of the libretto for *La Flora*, the opera composed for Margherita de' Medici's marriage in 1628, in which Costa may have performed during her first days in Florence.[26] Salvadori is also known to have published a pamphlet on *Caramogi* to commemorate a costumed *palio*, or race, staged between dwarfs and dandies in Florence in 1629.[27] But while Salvadori's name is clearly advertised on the page as the author of the *Caramogi* text and is even highlighted by a decorative border not found elsewhere in the *Chitarra* (fig. 5.3), Costa appears to have repurposed his original pamphlet for her volume, rewriting the male parts and adding a response from the female voices.[28] We thus observe Costa's first efforts to capitalize on the reputation of a Medici favourite with a humorous theme designed to appeal to the court's taste for human exotica.

Turning now to the *Caramogi*'s opening sally, we see court dwarfs attack with insults that immediately strike at their handsome rivals' outward appearances:

> If you think, oh you fine dandies, that beauty consists of a smooth cheek, a well-styled hairdo, a craning of the neck, a strutting of your body around like a peacock, you are in grave error. Beauty is not that easily defined. And even if a fitting definition does exist, certainly it is just the one that long ago was written on the pages of Love: *Beauty is in the eye of the beholder*.[29]

Using an aphorism lifted from Salvadori's original pamphlet, "Bello è quel che piace," Costa enters into the debate over the subjective nature of male beauty.[30] According to the *Caramogi*, the *Belgi'imbusti* are

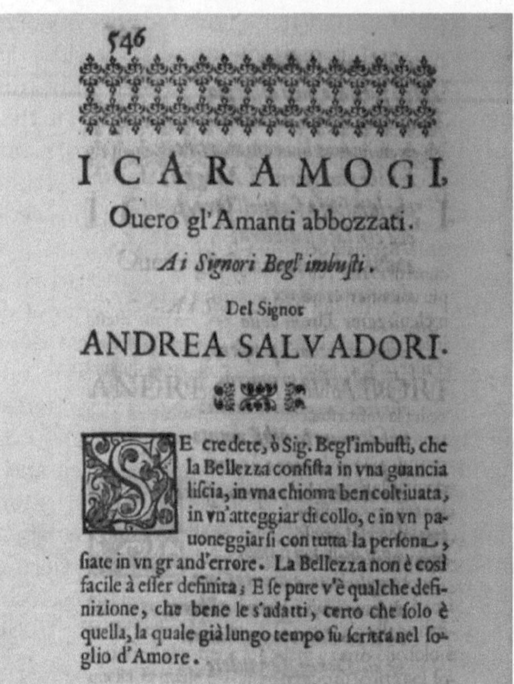
546

I CARAMOGI.

Ouero gl'Amanti abbozzati.

Ai Signori Begl'imbusti.

Del Signor

ANDREA SALVADORI.

SE credete, ò Sig. Begl'imbusti, che la Bellezza consista in vna guancia liscia, in vna chioma ben coltiuata, in vn'atteggiar di collo, e in vn pauoneggiarsi con tutta la persona, siate in vn grand'errore. La Bellezza non è così facile à esser definita; E se pure v'è qualche definizione, che bene le s'adatti, certo che solo è quella, la quale già lungo tempo fu scritta nel foglio d'Amore.

5.3 Margherita Costa, *La chitarra, canzoniere amoroso.* [Frankfurt: Daniel Wastch], 1638, 546. The British Library. Accessible via open access Google Books.

mistaken in believing that the masculine ideal consists in a manicured appearance. The result is abnormally feminine. The gallants' comeliness is then defined as a deformity in the prose that follows: they are vain and vapid "mostri dell'Affrica" – African monsters with women's faces and animals' bodies.[31] The *Begli'imbusti* are thus hybrid anomalies likened to a gendered and racialized Other, marginalized for transgressing against contemporary norms for restrained masculinity.

The *Caramogi* expand upon the *Begli'imbusti*'s defects in their ensuing octaves. Unlike their antagonists, the dwarfs take pride in *not* indulging in such foppish pastimes as biting their gloves, ripping up handkerchiefs, or parading up and down the streets with a sword by their side. Intertextual allusions to Ariosto's *Orlando furioso* and Pulci's *Morgante maggiore* abound: the *Caramogi* boast of their superiority over the paladins Rinaldo and Tancredi; they claim to courteously serve all women, even ones as ugly as the witch Gabrina; they recall the wisdom of the queen of the Lombards, who famously chose a dwarf lover for herself in canto 38 of the *Furioso*.[32] They also dismiss their foppish rivals as Narcissuses and Ganymedes ("Tratevi in disparate, o voi Narcisi; / Disgombrate le Piazze, o Ganimedi").[33] When the women finally respond, they criticize the *Begli'imbusti*'s effeminate vanity, stupidity, verbosity, youth, and lack of money. They also pick up on the *Caramogi*'s earlier line of attack by calling the dandies "deformed Ganymedes" and "vain Narcissuses," criticizing their beauty as an affront to their feminine sex.[34] Thus in the *Chitarra* these dapper dons are repeatedly characterized as gendered anomalies – men whose cultivated good looks and affectations blur the lines between masculine and feminine identity. And while they are not explicitly referred to by name, the twin allusions to Narcissus and Ganymede within a critique of effeminacy establish a solid link between the *Begli'imbusti* of the *Chitarra* and the *zerbini* of Costa's subsequent publications.

References to Narcissus and Ganymede were hardly new in the literatures of early modern Europe. They could trace their roots back to classical mythology and belonged to the shared patrimony of humanistic culture. Long before Freud coined "narcissism" as a clinical term in the study of the human psyche, early moderns pointed to Narcissus when criticizing men overly concerned with their own beauty. Not only was the narcissistic man's self-love solipsistic, it was considered unmanly. His vanity was associated with an overindulgence in elaborate clothing and cosmetics that was potentially effeminizing. However, it is important to note that Costa's readers would not necessarily have conflated effeminacy with homosexuality. On the contrary, the early modern Narcissus was guilty of an immoderate devotion to the opposite sex. Tommaso Garzoni (1549–89), writing about the ways of lovers in his *La piazza universal*, mocked some of the courtship rituals of young men by likening them to the mythological pretty-boy:

> These naughty men never have anything to say other than the names of Laura, Vittoria, Colombina, Flaminia, and Isabella. They never speak of anything aside from their beauty; they praise only their grace; they speak only of their merits; they compare them to the Helens, Lucretias, and Cleopatras; they resemble the Venuses, Cloris, and Galateas; and with every word manage to favour the manners, courtesies, and sweetness that come out of these celestial divas, for whom they walk all day dressed like nymph-like Narcissuses, with a flower behind their ear, with a rose in their hand, with their little perfumed gloves, with their finely attired legs, with a studied stride, and gallant words.[35]

Garzoni's Narcissus is emphatically heterosexual. He is consumed by the Isabellas and Colombinas of the *commedia* stage – women who in his mind resemble the great goddesses and divas of Antiquity. He adopts a number of showy fashions and affectations to catch their eye. The result is a gendered performance defined by excess: displays that go far beyond the prescribed limits of decorous masculinity.

Ganymede was similarly linked to gender nonconformity, particularly at the court. As the cup-bearer to Zeus from classical mythology, he was commonly associated with homoerotic subordination.[36] Though most often seen as an emblem for same-sex desire, another variation of the Renaissance Ganymede was excessively attracted to women. Much like Narcissus, he was accused of the kind of fashion crimes that resulted from trying too hard to impress others, both male and female. Pietro Aretino (1492–1556), for example, complained against Ganymedes with purple cheeks ("Ganimedi con le guance d'ostro") in his courtly satire, *Lamento de uno cortigiano*.[37] Giovanni Della Casa (1503–1556) advised the ideal gentleman of his *Galateo* to be attentive to current trends, but to avoid overly elegant attire such as "Ganymede's hose" ("le calze di Ganimede").[38] Writers on courtly decorum thus associated the two mythological figures with sartorial and cosmetic fulsomeness – visible transgressions against good taste and heteronormative masculinity.

Narcissus and Ganymede are twice more linked to unmanly displays in Costa's *Lo stipo* (1639). This time, however, the effeminate object of ridicule is identified by name: Zerbino. Much like her *Chitarra* of the previous year, the *Stipo* is a collection of lyrics ranging from lofty poems of praise in the beginning of the volume to lighthearted verse towards its end. It concludes with another autobiographical piece in Costa's voice cursing her poetic creations and vowing (falsely) never to write again.[39] Adulatory lyrics addressed to the Medici and the era's leading academicians give way to a series of poems lampooning figures such as the "Repentant Courtier," the "Repentant Gambler," and the "Woman Who Bemoans Her Wasted Beauty."[40] Among these satirical compositions is long piece in *ottava rima* entitled *Il Zerbino ravveduto*, or the "Repentant Zerbino."[41] Here, the down-on-his-luck Zerbino looks back at how he squandered his youth and money on expensive fashions. Now old and impoverished, he longs for the days when he could conquer hearts by showing off his richly adorned body and martial bravura:

No longer is time spent on the balconies
Looking down as troops of *zerbini*
In expensive scarves and fine plumes
Hit the Saracen with a spear;

And in full stockings and golden spurs,
Wound by striking with a little curtsy;
...
No longer does the proud gaze turn
Filled with pride over so many prey,
Ganymede's arrow no longer shoots,
Nor does the flowering faith of Narcissus.[42]

Zerbino made a spectacle of his body. He showed off for a crowd of observers, perhaps in a festive joust like the one documented by Andrea Salvadori and Stefano della Bella (fig. 5.4), eager to attract their desirous gaze. His spears, spurs, and swords – remnants from his days as one of the *Furioso*'s paladins and the *commedia dell'arte*'s boastful soldiers – are comically ineffectual in the hands of this primped-up paramour. No longer a comely Ganymede or Narcissus, he now serves as a cautionary tale for men who place too much value on their superficial powers of attraction.

The "Reformed Zerbino" relays additional details concerning the habits of this effeminate class of men. He confesses to have used sighs, tears, clothing, perfumes, and cosmetics to attract a lover. He warns his readers not to trust the outward beauty of a *zerbino*'s blond curls, alabaster breast, ivory visage, and ruby lips. Stripped of all of his romantic pretensions, he now sees the exchange of human affections in cold economic terms. The former gallant has learned the real worth of his fleeting charms, and bids the reader a final adieu with another allusion to the two mythological Romeos:

Goodbye Zerbini goodbye, goodbye Narcissuses!
I am done with you Ganymedes, and to you I cede
The work of wooing among sweet laughter.
Too late I am aware of my foolish error.
Go on, enjoy the beautiful ladies and their lovely visages.
As for me, I no longer believe more beauty to be beautiful,
I prize only gold's lovely splendour,
For if you have no gold, you cannot follow *Amor*.[43]

Money emerges as a central theme in this lyric. After spending his youth trying to trade on his looks, this *zerbino* comes to the late realization that the price of love is beyond his means. His surplus beauty is of little value to him now that it has faded. In this sense, the "Repentant Zerbino" recalls the "Repentant Courtier" and the "Woman Who Bemoans Her Wasted Beauty" of *Lo stipo*, who also lament their fashion faux pas and insolvency. The servile courtier regrets spending his money on fine

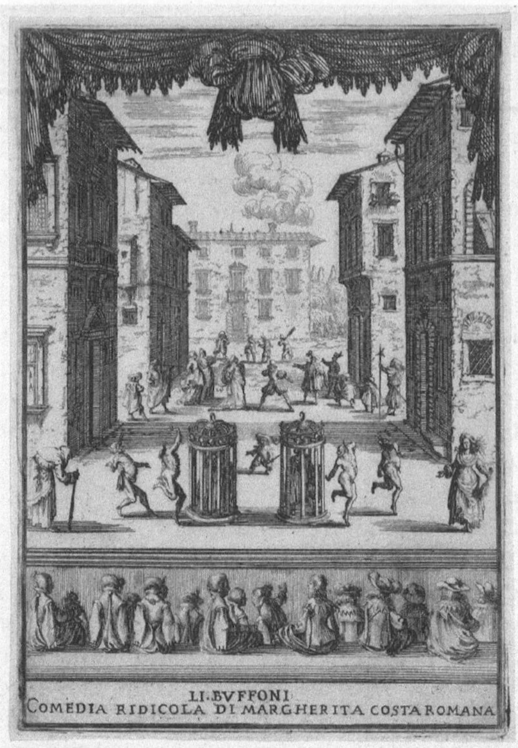

5.4 Stefano della Bella, frontispiece to Margherita Costa's *Li buffoni* (Florence, 1641). Courtesy of the Metropolitan Museum of Art. Bequest of Phyllis Massar, 2011. Part of the Met's Open Access program.

clothes, trying to fit in and transcend his station, only to find himself put in his place by the rigid class hierarchies at court.[44] The former beauty recalls the thousand little tricks she used to enhance her appearance – her whitened face, cinnabar lips, dyed golden locks, and latest fashions – inevitably to lose out to the passing of time. The *zerbino* might therefore be seen as a type of the effeminate courtier, drawing from criticism of female consumption and male servility to form a hybrid figure that transgresses both masculine and feminine gender norms.

Financial subordination is just one of the themes that re-emerges in the Zerbino exchanges of the *Lettere amorose*. Originally published the same year as *Lo stipo* in 1639, Costa's epistolary collection proved to be her most successful work, enjoying several reprints during her lifetime.[45] In it, both male and female voices initiate and reciprocate with prose letters and short lyrics on the subject of love. Much as we saw in her earlier Florentine works, in this volume the parodic compositions are again reserved for the tail end of the volume. The first half features exchanges between generic *amanti* and their *belle donne*, while the rest is reserved for dwarf, hunchbacked, syphilitic, maimed, mangy, mute, cross-eyed, and noseless lovers, to name but a few. Save for one brief, disparaging reference to a *cavaliere* as an impertinent *zerbino* in the earlier portion of the text, it is in the latter section populated by comically embodied lovers where we find the most pronounced references to men identified as *zerbini*.[46]

The *Lettere amorose* contains two *zerbino* sequences, each consisting of four letter exchanges between a dandy and a beautiful woman. The first sequence is initiated by a female voice ("Bella donna ad un Zerbino"), while the second begins with a male ("Zerbino a vaga donna"), possibly the same *zerbino* rejected by the woman in the preceding sequence.[47] As the opening letter from the "Bella donna" series makes clear, the *zerbino*'s attempts to attract the lady fail because of his cosmetic, sartorial, and verbal transgressions:

> If you could wrap up my opinions with your cloak, wipe away my tears with your ripped clothes, work my farm with your ornate collars, and gallantly attract me with your fineries, then it could be possible that I, convinced by your wiles, wounded by your affectations, and forced into love by your silliness, might give myself to you. But I find your lure to be so odious, your venery so tedious, and the vanity of your opinion so scornful that I hate your polished beauty, abhor your gilded face, and turn red in the face at your feminine zeal. If I were to accept your love I would have to call myself a lady lover of a lady ...[48]

His silly mannerisms and flirtations are over the top. His studied beauty is unmanly. His use of make-up and other frilly fashions is effeminizing and makes her see him more as a female lover than as a male. Through a series of mixed metaphors involving ships, bells, gourds, and vases, the female voice then insinuates that he lacks any sense, or worse, the most distinguishing external feature of a biologically sexed male.[49] An acrostic further emasculates the would-be lover by calling him a hermaphrodite. And, as her closing lyric emphasizes, his womanly affectations do not charm this lady:

> Ripping off a glove and a kerchief with your teeth,
> Breaking your shoes on your high heels,
> Smearing your cheeks with rouge,

And making little curls in your hair
Does not please me.
Nor do I sigh and pine for
A lock held up with a tonic of jasmine.
I want a man for a lover, not a Zerbino.[50]

His response is understandably defensive. He writes that he is mortified to discover the true character of this woman, who, though undeniably beautiful, is nonetheless worthless, slovenly, and lazy. He answers with an acrostic of his own, spelling out that she is a half-wit. He also reintroduces a familiar point of contention into their exchange, namely, their age disparity. The *zerbino* is in the flower of his youth, looking to spread his "seed" in a mature "field," and proud that his beauty distinguishes him from "bearded and silvered lovers."[51] She responds again to his missive, this time addressing him as Mr. Ganymede and Narcissus.[52] More humorous details regarding his flamboyant mannerisms are reported, including biting his lip and stamping his foot, raising his eyes to the sky and sighing, writhing while on horseback, dancing, and exaggerated curtsying. His lack of money, perhaps a function of his youth, is cited as another reason for his lack of manly appeal. Having suffered enough abuse, the *zerbino* finally brings their correspondence to a close by vowing to seek another woman who will "pay for [his] beauty in cash."[53]

The following sequence featuring a *zerbino*'s overtures to another *vaga donna* build upon some of the themes from the previous letters while introducing new comic elements. In brief, this *zerbino* begins their correspondence by describing himself as a phoenix aflame with love, burned and reborn a thousand times over.[54] Predictably, his maudlin efforts to project the signs of elite masculinity come off as comically effeminate. Her response again takes aim at his youth, false flatteries, and affectations. Rather than accept his comparison to a mythological phoenix, she mockingly dismisses him as a featherless bat, a tattling crow, and a "backwoods Narcissus."[55] For all of his gallant pretensions, the *zerbino* repeatedly fails to attract her with his charms or convince her of the sincerity of his affections:

You might say
That you are like a hawk,
Since you grab at everything;
Moreover, your rose
Without a prick is thorny;
Thus I disdain the wings of your love,
Since a *zerbino* is the death of women.[56]

In the arena of love, the lady has the power to accept or reject her suitor's amorous overtures. She exerts control over their debate by focusing on his many gender transgressions, relegating him to a subaltern position as the object of her scorn. Couched in humour, these staged *contrasti* between weak male and strong female types use satire to keep flashy expressions of non-normative masculinity in check.

An oblique reference to effeminate Narcissus or Ganymede types can also be found in Costa's last Florentine work, *Li buffoni* (1641).[57] The play is the first scripted comedy published by a woman in Italy and features a host of figures drawn from the Medici's Florentine entourage.[58] Male characters such as Baldassarre, Tedeschino, Meo, and Masino take their names from the foreigners, dwarfs, and buffoons who provided occasional forms of entertainment to Grand Duke Ferdinando II and his brothers. In this mirror inversion of the court, servants play the part of princes, paramours, and politicos. A buffoon named Tedeschino attempts to climb the social ladder by wooing the princess Marmotta, only to find himself severely castigated at the play's end for his audacity. The buffoon Tedeschino also gets roped into cross-dressing, as one might expect in an early modern comedy. While this bombastic character does take evident pleasure in his feminine appearance, the subject of effeminacy is first satirized in the prologue of the play. Here, Ganymede and Narcissus are once more dragged into an invective against several classes of impoverished and disempowered men.

The prologue of the *Buffoni* has no expository value. It communicates little to the reader about the play's setting, plot, or characters. Instead, its primary function is to champion the merits of contemporary buffoonery over Graeco-Roman comedy. Interestingly, Costa inserts a satire of various masculine types at the Medici court within this debate over comic styles. As the curtain rises, an old crone identified as Ancient Comedy starts the performance by railing against the adulterers, moochers, gamblers, misers, swindlers, soldiers, and finally, courtiers in attendance (fig. 5.4). Among the men she singles out for their faults are lovers who are always feigning to be on the brink of death for love:

> Another guy plays the Narcissus or the Ganymede
> and a thousand times a day dies and is reborn,
> his love always thrown in a state of doubt.
> He is heavy with sleep and light in the brains,
> but even more than in brains he is light in the purse.[59]

Ancient Comedy describes Narcissus and Ganymede types as sleepy, penniless dimwits. Costa does not explicitly take aim at male fashions or cosmetics, but the references to Narcissus, Ganymede, and the laughably hyperbolic language of love make it clear that her contemporaries would have understood this to be an allusion to effeminate men. It is important to note, however, that Costa's critique of effeminacy takes place outside the topsy-turvy fiction of the play. Ancient Comedy addresses her remarks to the audience – both the original spectators and its subsequent readers. She strikes directly at Costa's peers – courtly men subject to the gender norms of the Medicean patriarchy. Costa can thus be seen to leverage the rhetoric of gender shaming to her advantage, using this metatheatrical moment to police marginal types while demonstrating her command of the specialized language of courtly satire.

Several common elements emerge from the four works surveyed above. Costa repeatedly draws a connection between youth, finances, and effeminacy. The young lover's decadent spending on clothing and cosmetics is the cause of his ruin and goes against contemporary ideals for sober, decorous, and mature masculinity. He shows no restraint, especially when it comes to the opposite sex. Foolish extravagance, not sexual orientation, is the mark of his effeminacy. As a result, his exaggerated displays draw attention to the anomaly of masculine identity. Indeed, the dwarfs and dandies of the *Chitarra* are both presented as aesthetic extremes, each diverging from an implicit masculine ideal. And in the series of publications that followed, Costa consistently presents the gallant's studied beauty as a non-normative construct that threatens the comfortable limits of prevailing gender binaries. But beyond these efforts to affirm hegemonic masculinity by mocking a conspicuously vulnerable type, Costa also used these humorous figures to gain a foothold at the Medicean court.

Costa's rhetorical use of effeminacy might be seen as a defensive strategy designed to buttress her position as a female author through a scapegoated male. Seicento women of letters were subject to scrutiny and insinuation, often finding themselves pushed into an authorial position of "perpetual self-defense."[60] Indeed, Costa's lyrics at times betray her frustrations with the misogynist distrust of her critics.[61] Beyond the page, however, Costa could claim authorial distance from the faults attributed to her gender by shifting those misogynous tropes onto a disempowered *zerbino*. After all, the *zerbino*'s comic efforts to attract and be attractive to the female sex would have made him an easy target for our author. However, it must be acknowledged that it is hard to uncouple Costa's effeminate subjects from their underlying misogyny, or from the assumption that qualities identified as feminine are defects, especially, but not exclusively, when attributed to a man. Indeed,

Costa reproduces several misogynist tropes in her mockery of the *zerbino*'s frivolous, foolish, and ultimately womanly ways, particularly in her condemnation of cosmetics. The context, however, is important. Costa operated within the confines of the Florentine court. Her parodies of the preening paramour echo critiques of effeminacy found in male-authored courtly literature and, as we saw in the *Chitarra* and in the *Buffoni*, allude to some of the comic spectacles held in grand-ducal Florence. Most importantly, the *zerbino* was considered funny, and this presented an opportunity for Costa to distinguish herself through humour. More than just defending her gender, then, Costa's *zerbino* lyrics showcase her command of one of the many forms of comic discourse that were then favoured by her Medicean hosts, just as she said she would in her first Florentine lyric collection:

> Here I praised, there obscured another's merits,
> not to put them down, but simply in jest;
> And when I spoke ill, it was always a joke ...[62]

NOTES

1 The principal biographical studies of Margherita Costa include Bianchi, "Una cortigiana rimatrice del Seicento"; Capucci, "Costa, Margherita"; and Costa-Zalessow, "Margherita Costa" and "Margherita Costa Ronaca." See also the introductions to the two modern editions of her scripted comedy: *Li buffoni*, 234–359 and *The Buffoons*, 1–72.

2 Costa also published several pamphlets in praise of the Medici, and penned a manuscript entitled *Le sette giornate*. For more on the latter, see Goethals, "The Bizarre Muse."

3 According to Cox, women seeking to publish in the Seicento could no longer count on the patrons, philogyny, or ennobling aesthetics enjoyed by women writers of the preceding century. For more on the backlash against female authors in Seicento Italy, see Cox, *Women's Writing*, 166–227.

4 Cox, *Women's Writing*, 209.

5 Goethals, "The Bizarre Muse," 72.

6 Goethals, "The Bizarre Muse," 52.

7 Di Maro, "*Il Violino* di Margherita Costa," 43–56. Costa-Zalessow attributes an anonymous poem of 1672 to Costa based on stylistic elements and feminist themes also found in her *Chitarra*. Costa-Zalessow, "Una poesia femminista del 1672," 79–85.

8 Ray, *Writing Gender*, 179–80.

9 Ray, *Writing Gender*, 182.

10 Some recent literature on effeminate masculinity in and beyond early modern Italy includes DiGangi, *Sexual Types*, 91–121; Richards, "'A wanton trade of living'?"; and several essays in Milligan and Tylus, *The Poetics of Masculinity in Early Modern Italy and Spain*.

11 For a review of the criticism on gender, masculinity, and effeminacy in the *Cortegiano*, see Milligan's indispensable article, "The Politics of Effeminacy."

12 Currie, *Fashion and Masculinity in Renaissance Florence*, 119. Other studies that broach the social significance of masculine attire in the *Cortegiano* include Milligan, "Aesthetics, Dress, and Militant Masculinity in the *Courtier*," 141–59; and Paulicelli, "Fashion, Gender and Cultural Anxiety in Italian Baroque Literature," 35–46 and *Writing Fashion in Early Modern Italy*.

13 For a recent work that looks at the interrelationship between women and effeminate men at the court from the perspective of anti-courtly satire, see Ugolini, *The Court and Its Critics*, 51–7.

14 In addition to his aforementioned works on the subject, see Milligan, "Masculinity and Machiavelli."

15 Milligan, "The Politics of Effeminacy," 348.

16 One of Costa's immediate contemporaries and secretary of the Accademia della Crusca, Carlo Dati, provided the following definition that identifies the *zerbino* both with the *Furioso* and more generally with men inclined to love: "*Fare il Zerbino*, vale fare l'attillato, il bello, 'l galante, e che mostrasi inclinato agli amori. È venuto questo nome da Zerbino, di coi il Cantor Ferrarese ne fa il carattere: *Bello era, ed a ciascun così parea; / Ma di molto egli ancor più si tenea*"; Dati, *Lepidezze di spiriti bizzarri*, 44.

17 "Perch'ancor giovanetto, / Non ebbi sin allora espresso cura / Ne' domestici affari, / Vivendo in ozio delicato e mole, / Mio gusto e mio diletto fu dar opra / Agli odori, a i profumi, all'ambre, agli olj, / Pasticchi, saponetti, delicate / Conce di guanti, e di scarpíni adorni, / Delizie di zerbín, pregj da dame"; Buonarroti il Giovane, *La Fiera*, 481. Buonarroti's play was originally staged on 11 February 1619.

18 Bianchi, "Una cortigiana rimatrice," 10–11.

19 For more on the Medici court and their entertainments, see Introduction to *The Buffoons*, 26–35; or Goethals, "The Patronage Politics of Equestrian Ballet."

20 While the *Chitarra* is said to have been printed in Frankfurt and both the *Stipo* and the *Lettere amorose* bear Venetian imprints, all three are most likely clandestine Florentine publications.

21 The first book published under Costa's name in Florence was a history of Grand Duke Ferdinando II's 1627–8 travels to Germany based largely on the expedition notes of his secretary, Guerrini: *Istoria del viaggio d'Alemagna del serenissimo Gran Duca di Toscana Ferdinando Secondo. Il violino* (not

discussed here) was published the same year as the *Chitarra*, and under the same false imprint. Both volumes are dedicated to Ferdinando II, though the *Chitarra*'s dedicatory letter is dated to 15 April 1638, while the *Violino*'s dates to 24 June 1638, making the *Chitarra* the earlier of the two by a matter of months.

22 "Capitolo scherzoso dell'Autora, per quegli, che potessino tacciare le sue rime di troppo vestite d'Amorosi affetti, o vero, in altro" ("Playful *Capitolo* by the Author, for those who Would Silence Her Verse for Being Overly Dressed in Amorous Conceits, or for Some Other Reason"); Costa, *Chitarra*, 567–73.

23 "Cantai casi in amor mendaci, e veri, / mischiai gl'affetti con gli sdegni, e l'ire, fingei cor simulate, e cor sinceri; / Cercai sotto altro nome altrui coprire, / e in mille metamorfosi provai, / che l'arte dell'amar non è gioire: / Hor lodai gl'altrui pregi, hor gl'oscurai, / non per biasmar Altrui, ma sol per gioco; / e di chi dissi mal, sempre burlai"; Costa, *Chitarra*, 571. Unless otherwise indicated, all translations are mine. I have modernized the accents, punctuation, and capitalizations, and removed the pseudo-etymological *h* in the Italian transcriptions of Costa's texts.

24 "E con più chiari, e più mordaci detti / farò sentir con strepitoso suono / negli segreti miei gl'altrui difetti: / Abbiate dunque a gl' error miei perdono, / e come donna, compatite al meno / della forza d'amore l'ardente sprono"; Costa, *Chitarra*, 573.

25 Costa, *Chitarra*, 546–66. Though not discussed in this article, the *Chitarra* contains additional references to *zerbini* in a satirical sonnet entitled "Scherzo di Bella Donna per due Donne troppo fastose"; Costa, *Chitarra*, 442.

26 Salvadori, *La Flora*, 1628.

27 Salvadori, "Caramogi. Palio e mascherata faceta." An anonymous response from the *Begl'imbusti* also survives in pamphlet form: *Risposta de Begli'imbusti a Caramogi. Palio, e mascherata: Fatta in Firenze il dì 28. D'agosto 1629.*

28 The decorative band appears twice, once on top of the page of the *Caramogi*'s prose letter and again before the accompanying lyric. *Chitarra*, 246 and 248. Aside from the lyric response from the *Begli'imbusti* (555), all of the texts in the *Caramogi/Begl'imbusti* sequence begin with a decorative initial letter not found elsewhere in *La chitarra*. These printed embellishments, along with the sequence's proximity to the authorial *capitolo scherzoso* at the end of the volume, suggest that both author and printer wanted to showcase this series of exchanges and their connection to the famed poet Salvadori.

29 "Se credete, ò Signori Begl'imbusti, che la bellezza consista in una guancia liscia, in una chioma ben coltivata, in un'atteggiar di collo, e in un pavoneggiarsi con tutta la persona, siete in un grand'errore. La bellezza non è così facile à esser definita; e se pure v'è qualche definizione, che bene le

s'adatti, certo che solo è quella, la quale già lungo tempo fu scritta nel foglio d'Amore. *Bello è quel che piace*."; Costa, *Chitarra*, 546.

30 For more on Costa's references to Salvadori's pamphlet in the *Caramogi/Begl'imbusti* sequence, see Robarts, "Challenging Male Authored Poetry," 214–15.

31 Costa, *Chitarra*, 547.

32 Costa, *Chitarra*, 548–9, 551. These connections to Ariosto's and Pulci's texts, and their relationship to grotesque court performances featuring dwarf entertainers, are explored in Robarts, "Challenging Male Authored Poetry," 208–17.

33 Costa, *Chitarra*, 548.

34 "À voi diciamo difformi Ganimedi, che se la natura vi fù così avara di quello, che ad ogn'altro è liberale, pensate quello che vi faremo noi, ch'avare siamo ad ogn'uno. Dichiamo poi a' voi Narcisi, che non solo ci rassembrate quei mostri d'Africa, ma in tutto, e per tutto animalacci inrazionali"; Costa, *Chitarra*, 561.

35 "Non hanno i cattivelli mai altro in bocca, che i nomi di Laura, di Vittoria, di Colombina, di Flamminia, d'Isabella; non parlano d'altro, che delle loro bellezze; non essaltano altro che la loro gratia; non favellano d'altro, che de'meriti loro; l'antepongono all'Helene, alle Lucretie, alle Cleopatre, l'assomigliano alle Veneri, alle Clori, alle Galathee; & ogni parola riesce in favorire le maniere, le cortesie, le dolcezze, che spunta fuori da coteste loro celesti Dive, per le quali caminano tutto il giorno vestiti come ninfati Narcisi, col fiore nell'orecchia, con la rosa in mano, co'i suoi guantetti profumati, con la gamba attilata, col passo artificioso, col motto galantine"; Garzoni, *La piazza universale di tutte le professioni del mondo*, 715.

36 For an art historical perspective on the subject, see Saslow, *Ganymede in the Renaissance*.

37 Aretino, *Lamento de uno cortigiano*, 57.

38 Della Casa, *Galateo*, 59.

39 Costa, *Lo stipo*, 288–304.

40 Costa, *Stipo*, 222–42; 259–66; 178–93.

41 Costa, *Stipo*, 194–207. For more on this "aging toy boy" in *Lo stipo*, see Cox, *Women's Writing*, 214.

42 "Non si spende più il tempo sù i balconi / Rimirando in gran schiera ogni Zerbino / Con ricche ciarpe, e lindi pennacchioni / Colpir colpo di lancia al Saracino; / E 'n calza intiera, e dorati speroni / Ferir colpendo con un scorcio inchino; / … Non si rivolge più l'altero sguardo / D'alterigia ripien di tante prede, / Nè più di Ganimede scocca il dardo, / O di Narcisco la fiorita fede"; Costa, *Stipo*, 201–2.

43 "A Dio Zerbini a Dio, a Dio Narcisi? / Ganimedi io vi lascio, e con voi cedo / L'opre del zerbinar tra dolci risi, / E del mio sciocco error tardi

m'avvedo; / Godete pur le belle, e i vaghi visi, / Ch'io per me più beltà bella non credo, / Ma sol dell'oro stimo il bel splendore, / E chi l'oro non hà, non segue Amore"; Costa, *Stipo*, 207.

44 Costa, *Stipo*, 223.

45 Costa, *Lettere amorose*. Large portions of Costa's *Lettere* were also anthologized alongside works by male libertine authors in *Scelta di lettere amorose* (1656).

46 Costa, *Lettere*, 59. For more on comic embodiment in this volume, see Díaz, "Exceptional Bodies and Ludic Lovers."

47 Costa, *Lettere*, 255–65; 265–73.

48 "Se con le vostre ciarpe si acciarpassero i miei pensieri, con gli stracciati vestiti si risanassero i miei squarci, con i lavorati collari si lavorassero i miei poderi, e con le vostre gale mi riducereste galante, potrebbe essere, che dai vostri scorci convinta, dalle vostre smorfie ferita, e dalla vostra melesaggine oppressa ad amarvi mi dessi. Ma sì odioso mi è il vostro zimbello, sì annoio il vostro zimbellare, e sì a sdegno la vanità della vostra opinione, che odio la vostra coltivata bellezza, abborrisco il vostro inorpellato volto, e m'arrossisco del vostro feminil talento. Né d'altro mi darei nome, se al vostro amore m'apprendessi, che di donna di donna amante"; Costa, *Lettere*, 255–6.

49 Costa, *Lettere*, 256.

50 "Stracciar coi denti il guanto, e 'l fazzoletto, / Romper le scarpe sopra i calcagnini, / Imbraitarsi le gote di rossetto, / E far nella chioma i ricciolini / A me non piaccion, né men del ciuffetto / Alzato col licor dei gelsomini / Non mi fanno gettar sospiri, e pianti, / Che non Zerbini in me godo gli amanti"; Costa, *Lettere*, 257.

51 "Ma di nostra beltà portiamo i vanti / Più de' barbuti, e inargentati amanti"; Costa, *Lettere*, 261.

52 Costa, *Lettere*, 261.

53 Costa, *Lettere*, 265.

54 Costa, *Lettere*, 265.

55 Costa, *Lettere*, 271.

56 "Simile allo sparviero / Chiamar voi vi potete, / S'ogni cosa prendete; / E più la vostra rosa / Senza spine è spinosa; / Onde del vostro amore disprezzo l'ale, / Ch'il zerbin delle donne è l'ospidale"; Costa, *Lettere*, 273.

57 In addition to the reference to Ganymede and Narcissus to be discussed below, there is a passing allusion to a *zerbino* later in the play (II.ii.28), which I omit from our discussion owing to space constraints.

58 Indispensable for any understanding of the characters in the *Buffoni* and their relationship to actual personages at the Medici court is Megale, "La commedia decifrata."

59 "Ed altri fa il Narciso, e 'l Ganimede, / E mille volte il dì more, e rinasce; / Sempre il suo amore in dubbio stato inforsa; / Di sonno è carco, e di cervel

leggero, / Ma più che di cervel, lieve è di borsa"; Costa, *Li buffoni*, Prologue, 32–6. Text and translation from *The Buffoons*, 84–5.

60 Cox, *Women's Writing*, 211.

61 For example, see the poem "Elissa infelice" in Costa, *La selva di cipressi*, 229–56.

62 "Hor lodai gl'altrui pregi, hor gl'oscurai, / non per biasmar Altrui, ma sol per gioco; / e di chi dissi mal, sempre burlai"; Costa, *Chitarra*, 571.

WORKS CITED

Printed Sources

Aretino, Pietro. *Lamento de uno cortigiano già favorito in palazzo, et hora in grandissima calamità*. In *Operette politiche e satiriche*, vol. 2. Ed. Marco Faini. Rome: Salerno editrice, 2012, 51–60.

Bianchi, Dante. "Una cortigiana rimatrice del Seicento: Margherita Costa." *Rassegna critica della letteratura italiana* 29 (1924): 1–31 and 187–203; and 30 (1925): 158–211.

Buonarroti il Giovane, Michelangelo. *La Fiera commedia, e La Tancia di Michelangelo Buonarroti il giovane*, vol. 1. Florence: Felice Le Monnier, 1860.

Capucci, Martino. "Costa, Margherita." In *Dizionario biografico degli italiani*, vol. 30. Rome: Istituto della Enciclopedia italiana, 1984, *sub voce*. Online at https://www.treccani.it/enciclopedia/margherita-costa_%28Dizionario-Biografico%29/.

Costa, Margherita. *Il violino*. [Frankfurt: Daniel Wastch], 1638.

– *Istoria del viaggio d'Alemagna del serenissimo Gran Duca di Toscana Ferdinando Secondo*. Venice: n.p., n.d. [after 1632?].

– *La chitarra, canzoniere amoroso*. [Frankfurt: Daniel Wastch], 1638.

– *La selva di cipressi, opera lugubre*. Florence: Massi e Landi, 1640.

– *Lettere amorose*. Venice: n.p., 1639. Reprints: Venice: Li Turini, 1643; Venice: Turrini, 1651; Venice: Giacomo Turini, 1674.

– *Li buffoni, commedia ridicola*. Florence: Massi e Landi, 1641.

– *Li buffoni*. In Siro Ferrone, ed., *Commedie dell'arte*. 2 vols. Milan: Mursia, 1985–6, 2:234–359.

– *Lo stipo*. Venice: n.p., 1639.

– *The Buffoons, A Ridiculous Comedy*. Ed. and trans. Sara Díaz and Jessica Goethals. The Other Voice in Early Modern Europe. Toronto: Iter Press; Tempe: Arizona Center for Medieval and Renaissance Studies, 2018.

Costa-Zalessow, Natalia. "Margherita Costa." In Albert N. Mancini and Glenn Palen Pierce, eds., *Seventeenth Century Italian Poets and Dramatists*. Detroit: Gale Cengage Learning, 2008, 113–18.

– "Una poesia femminista del 1672 anonima e dimenticata, da attribuire a Margherita Costa." *Esperienze letterarie* 35.4 (2010): 79–85.

– "Margherita Costa Ronaca (1600c.–1657c)." In Natalia Costa-Zalessow, ed., *Scrittrici italiane dal XIII al XX secolo: Testi e critica*. Ravenna: Longo, 1982, 146–52.

Cox, Virginia. *Women's Writing in Italy, 1400–1650*. Baltimore: Johns Hopkins University Press, 2008.

Currie, Elizabeth. *Fashion and Masculinity in Renaissance Florence*. London: Bloomsbury Academic, 2017.

Dati, Carlo. *Lepidezze di spiriti bizzarri e curiosi avvenimenti raccolti e descritti da Carlo Dati*. Florence: Magheri, 1829.

Della Casa, Giovanni. *Galateo, overo de' costume*. Ed. Emanuela Scarpa. Modena: Franco Cosimo Panini Editore, 1990.

Díaz, Sara E. "Exceptional Bodies and Ludic Lovers: Humor, Disability, and the Grotesque in Margherita Costa's *Lettere amorose* (1639)." *Early Modern Women: An Interdisciplinary Journal* 16.2 (2022): 265–88.

DiGangi, Mario. *Sexual Types: Embodiment, Agency, and Dramatic Character from Shakespeare to Shirley*. Philadelphia: University of Pennsylvania Press, 2011.

Di Maro, Maria. "*Il Violino* di Margherita Costa: prime indagini." In Salvatore Bartolotta and Mercedes Tomo-Ortiz, eds., *Escritoras italianas inéditas en la querella de las mujeres: traducciones en otros idiomas, perspectivas y balances*, vol. 2. Madrid: UNED editorial, 2019, 43–56.

Garzoni, Tommaso. *La piazza universale di tutte le professioni del mondo*. Venice: Gio. Battista Somascho, 1586.

Goethals, Jessica. "The Bizarre Muse: The Literary Persona of Margherita Costa." *Early Modern Women: An Interdisciplinary Journal* 12.1 (2017): 48–72.

– "The Patronage Politics of Equestrian Ballet: Allegory, Allusion, and Satire in the Courts of Seventeenth Century Italy and France." *Renaissance Quarterly* 70.4 (2017): 1397–1448.

Kaborycha, Lisa. *A Corresponding Renaissance: Letters Written by Italian Women, 1375–1650*. Oxford: Oxford University Press, 2016.

Megale, Teresa. "La commedia decifrata: Metamorfosi e rispecchiamenti in *Li buffoni* di Margherita Costa." *Il Castello di Elsinore* 2 (1988): 64–76.

Milligan, Gerry. "Aesthetics, Dress, and Militant Masculinity in the *Courtier*." In Jacqueline Murray and Nicholas Terpstra, eds., *Sex, Gender and Sexuality in Renaissance Italy*. London: Routledge, 2019, 141–59.

– "Masculinity and Machiavelli: How a Prince Should Avoid Effeminacy, Perform Manliness, and Be Wary of the Author." In Patricia Vilches and Gerald Seamon, eds., *Seeking Real Truths: Multidisciplinary Perspectives on Machiavelli*. Leiden: Brill, 2007, 149–72.

– "The Politics of Effeminacy in *Il cortegiano*." *Italica* 83.3–4 (2006): 345–66.

Milligan, Gerry, and Jane Tylus, eds. *The Poetics of Masculinity in Early Modern Italy and Spain*. Essays and Studies 22. Toronto: Centre for Reformation and Renaissance Studies, 2010.

Paulicelli, Eugenia. "Fashion, Gender and Cultural Anxiety in Italian Baroque Literature." *Romance Notes* 50.1 (2010): 35–46.
– *Writing Fashion in Early Modern Italy*. Burlington, VT: Ashgate, 2014.
Ray, Meredith. *Writing Gender in Women's Letter Collections of the Italian Renaissance*. Toronto: University of Toronto Press, 2009.
Richards, Jennifer. "'A wanton trade of living'? Rhetoric, Effeminacy, and the Early Modern Courtier." *Criticism* 42.2 (2000): 185–206.
Risposta de' Begl'imbusti a Caramogi. Palio, e mascherata: Fatta in Firenze il dì 28. d'agosto 1629. Florence: Pietro Cecconcelli, 1629.
Robarts, Julie Louise. "Challenging Male Authored Poetry: Margherita Costa's Marinist Lyrics (1638–1639)." PhD dissertation, University of Melbourne, 2019.
Salvadori, Andrea. "Caramogi. Palio e mascherata faceta fatta in Firenze il di 6 agosto 1629." In *Le poesie del Sig. Andrea Salvadori fra le quali contengonsi unite insieme tutte quelle, che furono divisamente impresse in diverse stampe vivente l'autore, e l'altre non più divulgate. Parte Prima*. Rome: Michele Ercole, 1668.
Salvadori, Andrea. *La Flora*. Florence: Pietro Cecconcelli, 1628.
Saslow, James. *Ganymede in the Renaissance: Homosexuality in Art and Society*. New Haven: Yale University Press, 1986.
Scelta di lettere amorose di Ferrante Pallavicino, Luca Asserino, Margarita Costa romana, Gerolamo Parabosco e d'altri più eruditi scrittori italiani. Con una raccolta di rime amorose. Venice: Giacomo Bortoli, 1656.
Ugolini, Paola. *The Court and Its Critics: Anti-Court Sentiments in Early Modern Italy*. Toronto: University of Toronto Press, 2020.

An important addition to the critical bibliography on Margherita Costa was published shortly before this article went to press:

Goethals, Jessica. *Margherita Costa, Diva of the Baroque Court*. Toronto: University of Toronto Press, 2023.

6 Masculine-Feminine Dichotomy in the Sixteenth Century: Mythological *Donna con Donna* Images from Fontainebleau and Northern Italy

TARA WHITE

Summary: Sixteenth-century Italians used the term *donna con donna* to refer to sexual acts between women. Judith Butler's theory of gender performance, when considered beside early modern concepts of gender and sex, helps us understand how female figures in many Italianate *donna con donna* images assert a masculine-feminine dichotomy through their positions, skin tones, and body types. This article analyses Pierre Milan's engraving of *Jupiter in the Guise of Diana Seducing Callisto* (1543–5), Master GK's etching of a *Satyr Surprising Four Bathing Nymphs* (1550), a detail of two nymphs in Parmigianino's Diana and Actaeon fresco cycle (1523–4), and a maiolica dish by the Fontana family workshop showing *Diana and Her Nymphs Bathing* (1560–70). By considering these works in light of contemporary literary descriptions of *donna con donna* encounters, this article argues that artists and writers employed recognizable conventions to maintain this masculine-feminine dichotomy. In doing so, they upheld the idea that women who took an active role in sex with other women were masculine.

This article addresses portrayals of masculine traits in female figures who take the active role in depictions of *donna con donna* encounters, or sexual interactions between women. Focusing on sixteenth-century mythological *donna con donna* images, it analyses four scenes from Fontainebleau and northern Italy in particular. Two are prints after designs by Italian artists working in Fontainebleau, the first showing Jupiter in the guise of Diana seducing Callisto (fig. 6.1), and the second a satyr spying on nymphs bathing (fig. 6.2). The other two, both by northern Italian artists, portray Diana and her nymphs, one in a small frescoed room by Parmigianino (figs. 6.3–6.6) and the other on a maiolica dish (fig. 6.7). These examples are chosen because they

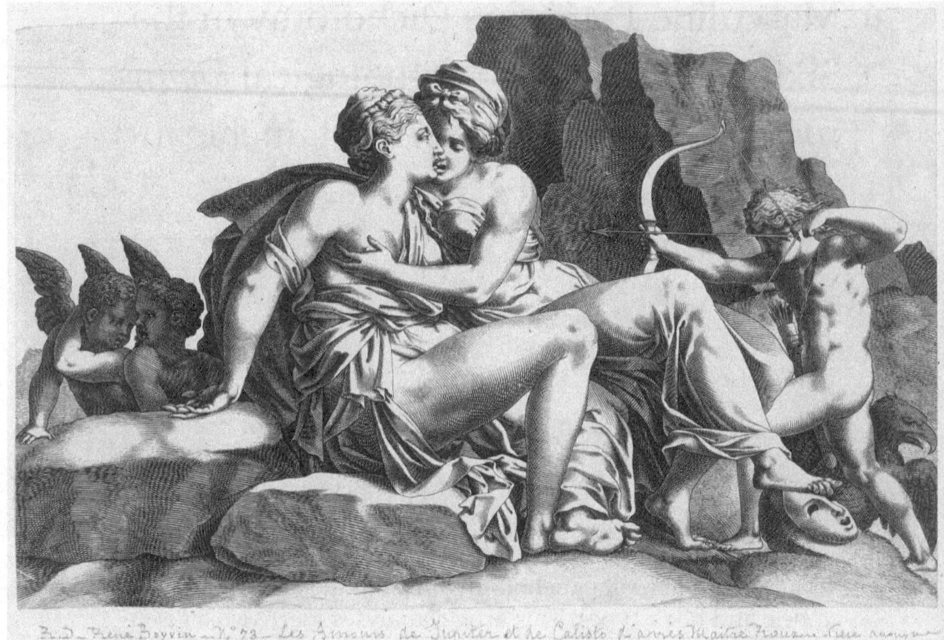

6.1. Pierre Milan (after Primaticcio), *Jupiter and Callisto* (1537–40). The Metropolitan Museum of Art, New York. Public domain.

each show a particular way in which the artist conveyed masculine-feminine difference, rendering it visible across artistic mediums throughout the sixteenth century. Because the original compositions of all four were made by Italian artists, the Italian term *donna con donna* is used throughout this article to highlight connotations of sexual intimacy between women in the early modern mindset. Notably, the term *donna con donna* was used not only by Italians but also by the French historian Pierre de Bourdeille, seigneur de Brantôme, who stated that the practice came to France from Italy.[1] Rather than positing how women who engaged in sex with one another actually behaved or appeared, this article addresses how male artists and writers associated masculine attributes with such women. As we will see, the fact that sixteenth-century *donna con donna* fantasies typically included a relatively masculine, active participant and a relatively feminine, passive one demonstrates that in the early modern mindset taking an active sexual role was inseparable from masculinity.

Parts of my argument are informed by the work of other scholars who have studied early modern portrayals of sexual interaction between

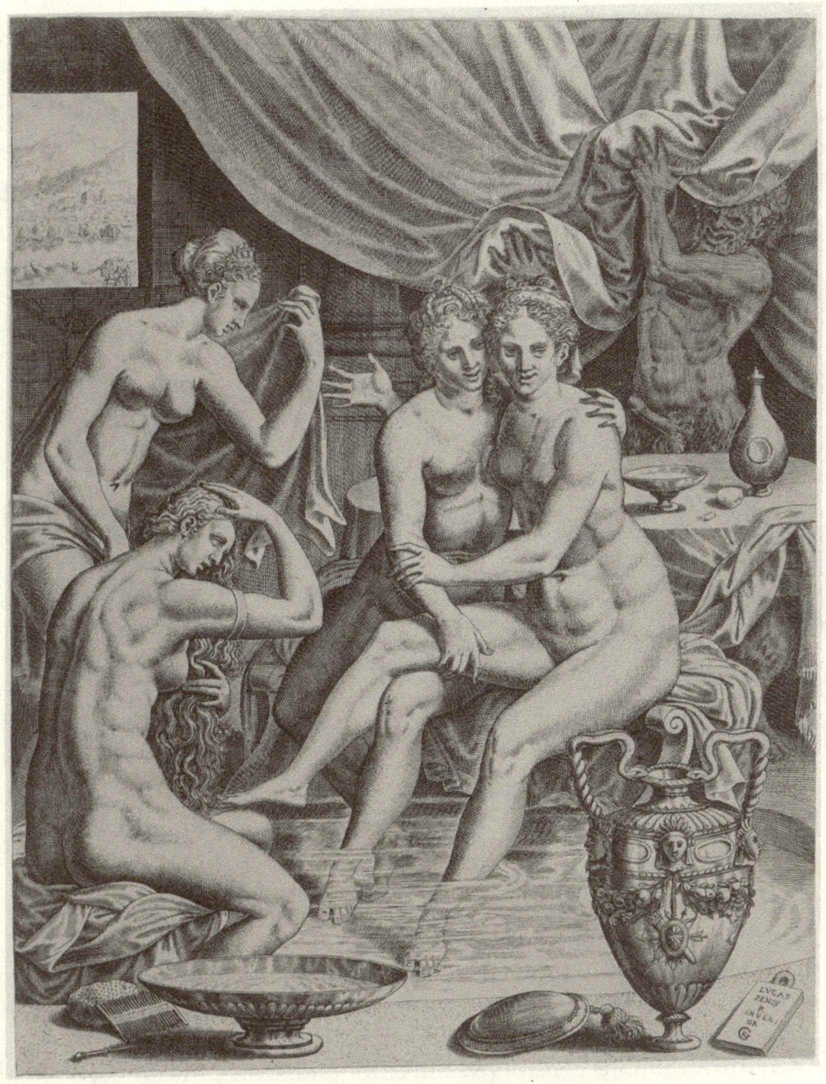

6.2. Master GK (after Luca Penni), *A Satyr Surprising Four Bathing Nymphs* (ca. 1550). Princeton University Art Museum, Princeton. Public domain.

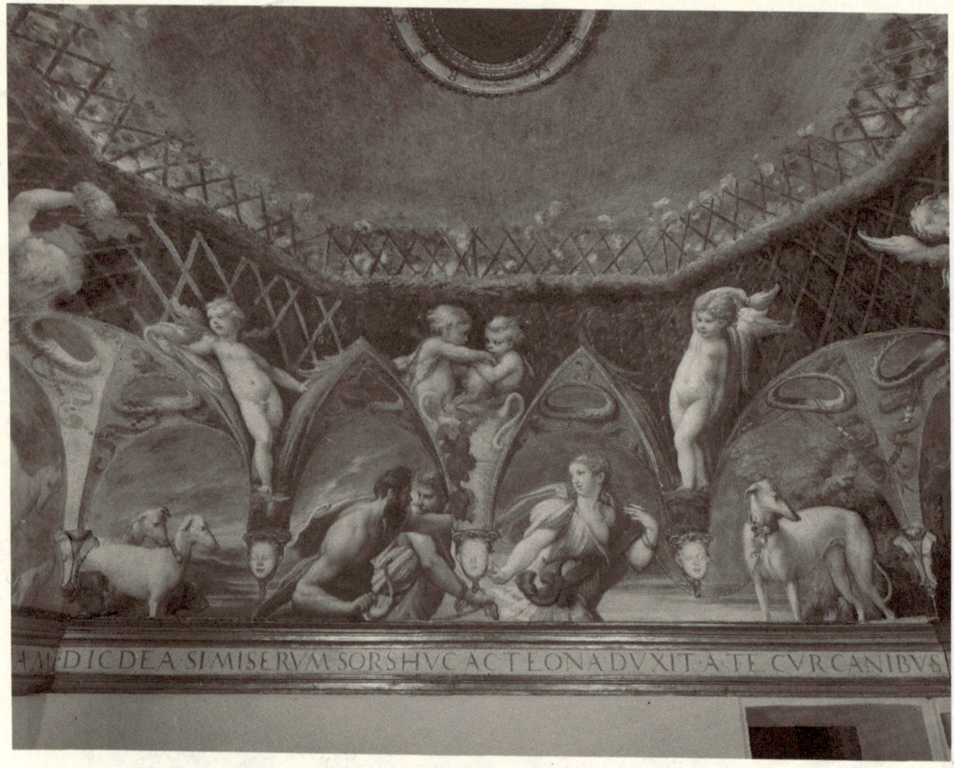

6.3. Parmigianino, *Story of Diana and Actaeon* (northern lunettes) (1523–4). Rocca Sanvitale, Fontanellato (Parma). Photo credit: Scala/Art Resource, New York.

women. Patricia Simons has written the most extensively on Italian images that depict what was known as *donna con donna*. She builds upon the historian Judith Brown's argument that the phallocentric view of sex in early modern Europe caused a relative lack of concern over sex between women compared to sex between men.[2] In a pioneering 1994 article, Simons considered fifteenth- and sixteenth-century Italian images of Diana bathing with her nymphs to argue that sex between women was nearly unimaginable and therefore typically "invisible" in the early modern imagination even when in plain sight.[3] According to Simons, the widespread disbelief in the possibility of women having sex with one another allowed them to engage in such acts without violating chastity. In her view, images of women and nymphs caressing each other sensually represent the reality of *donna con donna* that took place in female-only spaces.[4] Both Simons and Brown point out, however, that

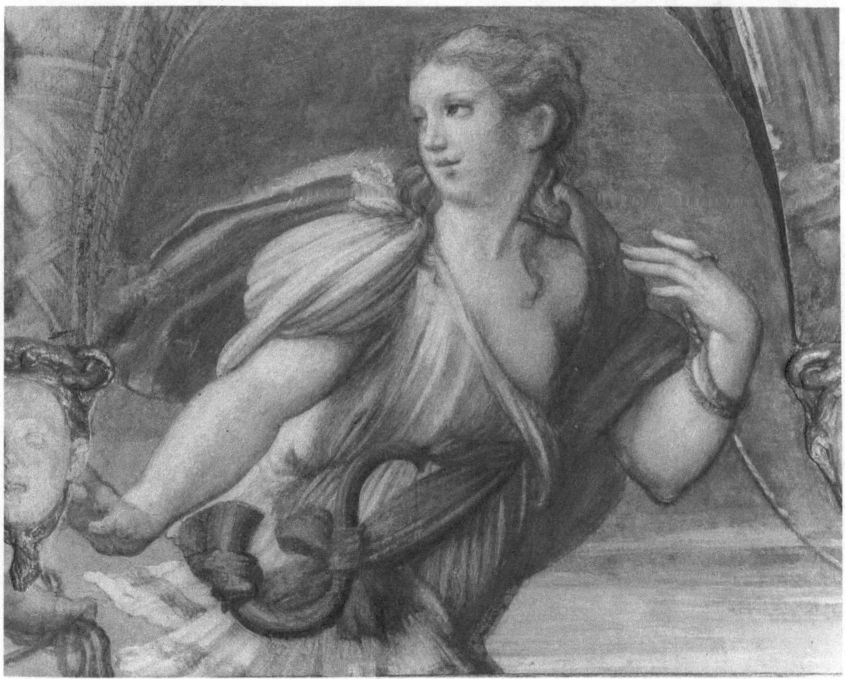

6.4. Detail of fig. 6.3 showing lunette with Actaeon in human form. Photo credit: Ghigo G. Roli/Art Resource, New York.

lawmakers typically considered sexual acts between females more morally transgressive and more worthy of punishment by death if they involved penetration with a material instrument.[5] Though this distinction was not shared by all authorities, it nevertheless highlights the early modern association of sexual penetration with the role of men.

While most scholars across disciplines uphold Brown's and Simons' foundational idea of the early modern semi-inconceivability of sex between women, some have added even more nuance to the discussion. Valerie Traub argues that early modern Europeans had a cultural awareness of not only physical intimacy but also sexual desire and amorous love between women.[6] She analyses sixteenth- and seventeenth-century English poems, plays, prints from medical treatises, and images of women embracing or kissing to show that homoeroticism between women was visible and that sex between women was considered possible. Traub uses Judith Butler's theory of gender as performance to analyse the extent to which women who engaged in sexual activity with one

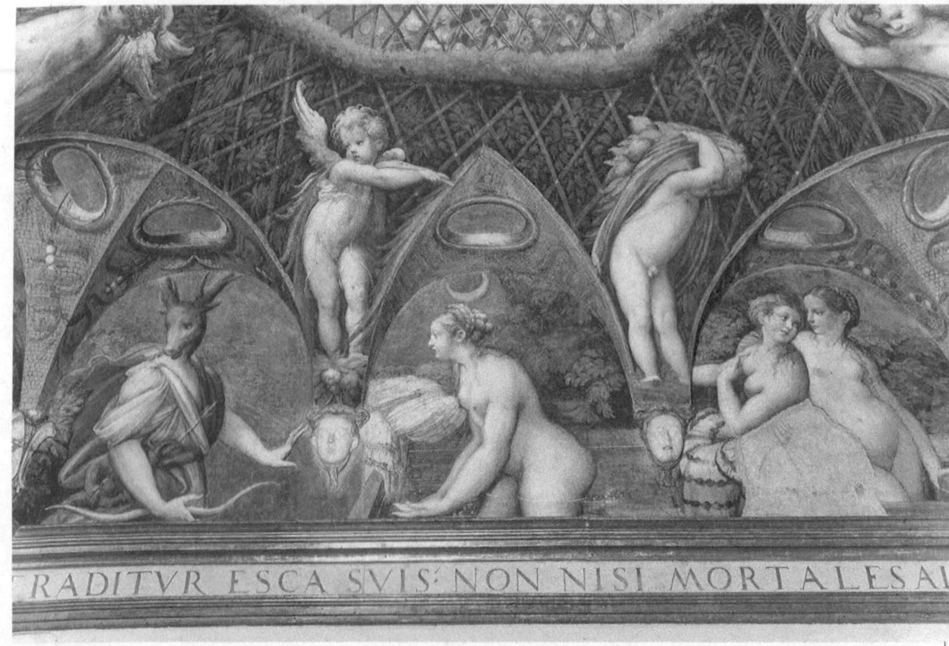

6.5. Parmigianino, *Story of Diana and Actaeon* (east lunettes) (1523–4). Rocca Sanvitale, Fontanellato (Parma). Photo credit: Ghigo G. Roli/Art Resource, New York.

another conformed to or threatened gender boundaries, arguing that until the end of the sixteenth century, amorous love between traditionally feminine women could exist within the roles of chastity while sex acts involving women taking masculine roles could not.[7] Her argument that women's relationships were considered chaste as long as they did not involve displays of masculinity highlights the early modern categorization of the active sexual role as masculine behaviour. While Traub uses Butler's idea of gender performance in a social context, she does not apply Butler's theories to visual representations of *donna con donna* encounters.

This article compliments Traub's work by bringing her discussion to a new geographical area. It aims to fill a gap in the topic of sixteenth-century masculinity as well as the study of *donna con donna* images by considering the images in context with both modern and early modern perspectives on gender. In doing so, it points out a previously overlooked pattern: the depiction of a masculine-feminine dichotomy between figures in mythological *donna con donna* scenes in

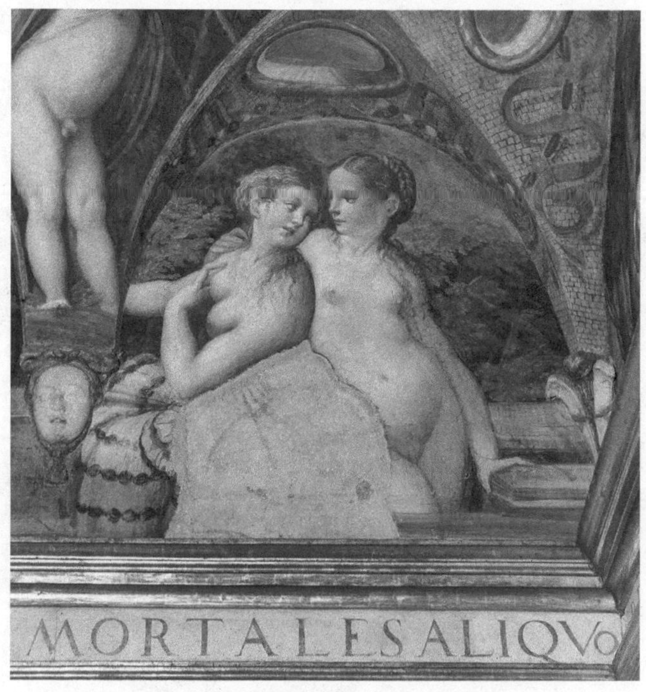

6.6. Detail of fig. 6.5 showing lunette with nymphs. Photo credit: Ghigo G. Roli/Art Resource, New York.

sixteenth-century Italy and France. Drawing on elements of Traub's analysis, the article challenges the idea of the perceived impossibility of sex between women. Instead, it argues that early modern literature and images from Italy and France point to the perceived incomprehensibility of a completely *feminine* sexual experience even when both sexual partners are women. Indeed, the early modern association of masculinity with taking an active sexual role often rendered images of physical intimacy between women asexual *unless* they included at least one relatively masculine participant. As we will see, the consistent tendency to depict a masculine-feminine difference between figures in *donna con donna* images and texts of this period points to an attempt to make the sexual nature of their intimacy recognizable.

Judith Butler's theory of gender as performance, seen in the context of early modern concepts of masculinity and femininity, helps us understand how many figures in *donna con donna* images assert a masculine-feminine dichotomy through their poses, skin tones, and body types. In *Gender Trouble*, Butler argues that gender is constituted through

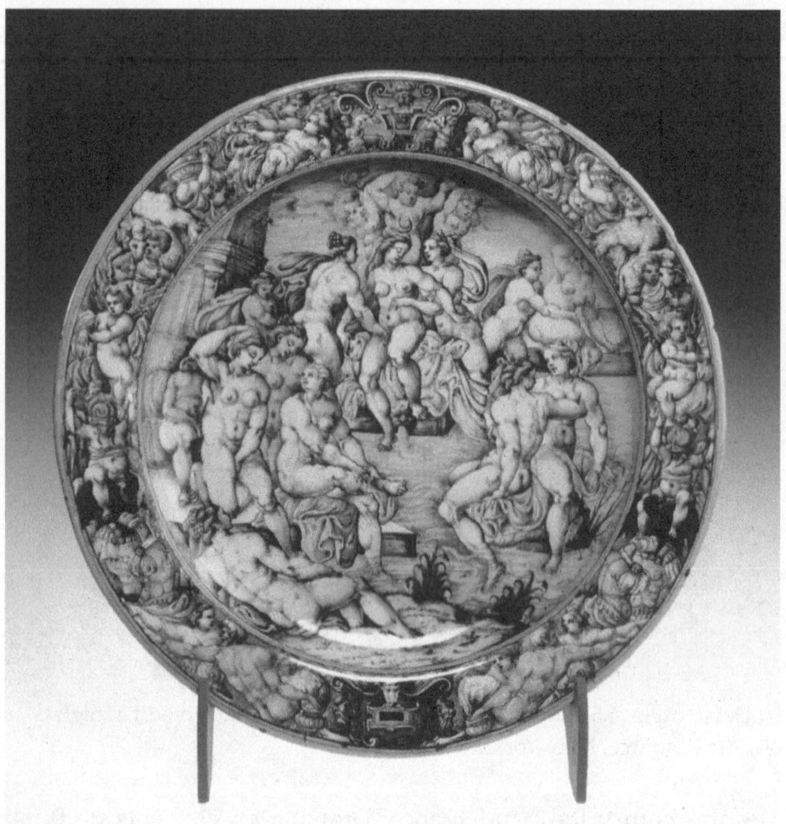

6.7. Fontana Family Workshop, *Dish with Diana and Her Nymphs Bathing* (ca. 1560–70). The Walters Art Museum, Baltimore. Public domain.

the repeated performance of distinguishing acts that solidify historically and culturally specific ideas of what makes a person a man or woman. This concept differs from the notion of sex, which categorizes individuals as male, female, or intersex depending on genitalia, chromosomes, and other physical attributes. However, Butler points out that gender and sex are linked because the categorization of bodies into sexes only seems natural because of the gendered meanings assigned to body parts. Similarly, as this article will demonstrate, early modern ideas of masculinity and femininity posited that certain physical characteristics lead to gender-specific action. Therefore, it uses the terms "masculine" and "feminine" to categorize early modern signifiers of both gender *and* sex.

To provide a broader cultural context and demonstrate that the concept of masculine-feminine dichotomy extended to French and Italian literature, this article's first section addresses three period texts: the Italian epic poem *Orlando furioso* by Ludovico Ariosto (1474–1533), the account of the travels of French geographer Nicolas de Nicolay (1517–1583) in Turkey, and *Lives of Fair and Gallant Ladies* by the French author Brantôme (1540–1614). Each author describes *donna con donna* encounters in relation to masculinity, comparing the bodies or actions of women to those of the eroticized male. The following sections will explore this phenomenon as manifested in the four aforementioned visual examples of *donna con donna* encounters. As the examples will show, because masculinity and the active sexual role were so linked to one another in the early modern mindset, both images and literature had to assert a masculine presence within erotic scenes between women in order to make the sexual nature of the encounters clear.

Donna con Donna *in Sixteenth-Century Italian and French Literature*

Most sixteenth-century writers who described *donna con donna* encounters compared them to attraction or sex between men and women. One example is found in Ludovico Ariosto's *Orlando furioso*, an immensely popular and influential Italian epic poem published in its complete form in 1532. In canto 25, Ricciardetto tells the story of the Spanish Saracen princess Fiordispina, who falls in love with Ricciardetto's twin, a female warrior named Bradamante.[8] Fiordispina is attracted to Bradamante by "la faccia, e le viril fattezze" (her "face and manly features") and initially mistakes her for a man.[9] However, after Bradamante tells Fiordispina that she is a woman, Fiordispina's passion towards her remains. Though Fiordispina's desire is one-sided, the women are nevertheless an example of masculine-feminine difference within a representation of female homoeroticism. By referencing Bradamante's "viril fattezze," Ricciardetto implies that his sister's facial features appear masculine. The word "fattezze" typically refers to features of the face, rather than attire or accoutrements.[10] Ricciardetto's description of Bradamante's masculine facial features, which seems incongruous with descriptions of her feminine beauty throughout the majority of the *Furioso*, suggests that Ariosto used the idea of perceived masculinity to make Fiordispina's attraction to a woman believable.[11] Regardless of her attraction to Bradamante, Fiordispina's desire goes unsatisfied until Ricciardetto takes his twin sister's place at Fiordispina's castle, convincing the princess that he is Bradamante. When Ricciardetto reveals his body to Fiordispina, the fact that the person she thinks is

Bradamante has a penis makes her so overjoyed that she wonders if she is dreaming.[12] While Ariosto's narrative uses a male character to assert the idea that sexual satisfaction without the phallus itself is impossible, he nonetheless makes Fiordispina's attraction to Bradamante seem logical to an early modern audience by describing Bradamante as having a masculine appearance. Sixteenth-century readers would have understood that Bradamante's masculine facial features, suit of armour, and shorn hair initially suggested to Fiordispina that Bradamante was male and therefore capable of penetrative sexual action, even though it is her brother who ultimately fills the sexual role.[13]

In an account of his travels to Turkey, published in 1585 as *The Navigations, Peregrinations and Voyages*, Nicholas de Nicolay compares women engaging in *donna con donna* sexual acts to men. According to Nicolay, Turkish women enjoyed the public baths because these spaces gave them freedom from being locked up due to the "jealousy of their husbands."[14] The women supposedly found the baths attractive because bathing kept them healthy and cleansed for religious purposes, but especially because they could display their "lascivious voluptuousness" in these spaces.[15] Nicolay states that the women who pursue other women at the baths are full of "feminine wantonness."[16] However, he also writes that they feel burning passion for other women "as if it were with men." This statement can have one of two implications: that the feminine, wanton women fall in love with other women as they would typically fall in love with men, *or* that these women behave like men by pursuing other women. Either way, Nicolay inserts a masculine presence within sexual encounters between women by likening their desires and behaviours to lustful and amorous interactions between men and women.

In *Vies des dames galantes*, or *Lives of Fair and Gallant Ladies*, written around 1584, Brantôme similarly compares women who take the active role in *donna con donna* encounters to men and he states that sex between women is merely a less satisfying imitation of sex between a man and a woman.[17] Brantôme provides anecdotes of the licentious activities of sixteenth-century women. In a section that addresses the question of whether women who have sex with other women can make their husbands cuckolds, Brantôme describes several examples of women's sexual relationships with one another as well as their husbands' reactions to them. He states that the most common names for such women in early modern Europe were the Greek-derived word *tribades* and Latin-derived word *fricatrices*.[18] Both terms come from root words that mean "to rub" and refer to a specific *donna con donna* act in which a woman rubs her genitals against those of another woman. By emphasizing women's sexual action (as opposed to passivity), the words *tribades* and *fricatrices* therefore relate them to the masculine role in sex, as men were expected to take the active lead in sexual encounters with women.[19] According to Brantôme, women who use "obscure lascivious and monstrous instruments" to behave like men in sex by penetrating a partner likely possess more positive masculine attributes, such as courage and valour, than other women.[20] He also asserts that sexual relationships between women are an "apprenticeship to come to that one with great men."[21] Using Sappho, "the Mistress" of them all as an example, Brantôme emphasizes that women commonly abandon their *donna con donna* practices to pursue men when the opportunity arises.[22] Arguing that sex between women is ultimately unsatisfying, Brantôme concludes that *donna con donna* sexual intimacy cannot make husbands cuckolds.[23] Although Brantôme's text was first published posthumously in 1665, the fact that it records court gossip suggests that it likely reflects ideas that were diffuse during the late sixteenth century among the higher echelons of French society.

In these texts, Ariosto, Nicolay, and Brantôme all compare one or both partners in *donna con donna* encounters to men. Although the texts address human subjects rather than mythological ones, they nonetheless describe fantasies. In the *Orlando furioso,* not only does Fiordispina's lust for Bradamante take place within an epic poem, but it is told through the perspective of Bradamante's twin brother rather than that of the women themselves. Nicolay describes sexual activity between women within an "exotic" culture. Brantôme relays court gossip to readers who may not otherwise have had access to court rumours about the lascivious activities of women. Because the aforementioned texts and the mythological images addressed in this article all approach fantasies of lustful interactions between women, it is no wonder that they show similar ways of making sense of *donna con donna* encounters. As the visual evidence will demonstrate, early modern artists imagined a masculine presence within *donna con donna* scenes similar to those found in sixteenth-century literature.

The Masculine-Feminine Dichotomy: Pose at the Fontainebleau Baths

Pierre Milan's engraving of *Jupiter and Callisto* (1537–40; fig. 6.1) provides an ideal starting point because the two title figures show the intentionality of the masculine-feminine dichotomy. As we will see, Jupiter's female disguise necessitates the communication of masculinity through pose in order to make him recognizable. Early modern versions of the Callisto story vary, but the most well known was from Ovid's *Metamorphoses*. In

Ovid's retelling, Callisto, whose name is derived from the Greek word *calliste*, meaning "the very beautiful one," is Diana's favourite nymph.[24] Jupiter attempts to fool Callisto into having sex with him by disguising himself as Diana. The seduction part of the story, which is depicted in Milan's print, begins as a *donna con donna* encounter (at least from Callisto's perspective, as she believes that she is interacting with Diana). Jupiter kisses Callisto passionately and the two go on talking, implying that kissing is a welcome expression of affection between Diana and her nymphs.[25] However, Jupiter then forces himself on Callisto, and Diana later banishes Callisto from her company after discovering her pregnancy.

Milan's print records a fresco by Francesco Primaticcio, a Bolognese artist who trained in Mantua.[26] Primaticcio's fresco was located in a lunette on the south wall of the cold bath area of the Fontainebleau palace's Appartement des Bains, the public baths that were built around 1534 and torn down in 1697.[27] Other scenes from the Callisto story filled the surrounding lunettes in the cold bath area.[28] Commissioned by King Francis I (r. 1515–47), the bathing complex included seven rooms dedicated to lounging, grooming, and hot and cold bathing.[29] It was a rarity in a time that witnessed closures of such facilities on a large scale, partially because of outbreaks of plague and syphilis.[30] Francis I had a taste for the sensual imagery that became popular during his rule and employed Italian artists like Primaticcio as the main designers to decorate his palace interior accordingly.[31]

In Milan's sexually charged engraving after Primaticcio, *putti* and a cupid flank Jupiter and Callisto, who sit in a rocky setting as Jupiter kisses Callisto and cups her breast. One who is familiar with the Callisto myth can easily identify Jupiter as the figure in the back because his pose is more sharply angled than Callisto's. His left arm and right leg flex at nearly ninety-degree angles while Callisto's exposed arm makes a relaxed, fluid movement. Reaching behind her back, Callisto bends her right arm slightly at the elbow and twists it so her fingers point away from her body as the back of her hand rests on top of a rock. Her right shoulder shrugs and her back curves as her neck cranes. Period texts on social etiquette, such as Baldassare Castiglione's extremely popular *Book of the Courtier*, which was first published in 1528 and circulated throughout Europe in multiple translations, reveal that such flowing, languid movements were considered feminine, while sturdiness was thought to be masculine.[32] Even Callisto's twisting drapery alludes to her fluid unsteadiness, a quality that Jupiter's drapery lacks even though he is dressed as Diana.

Jupiter pivots at the waist to lean in with closed eyes and parted lips towards Callisto to initiate a kiss. He is relatively covered, with only his feet, ankles, one shoulder, and one arm visible to the viewer. Contrastingly, Callisto's drapery leaves her chest exposed. A thin piece of fabric drops halfway down the bicep of Callisto's otherwise bare right arm, implying that Jupiter is undressing her. While Jupiter's initiation of the sexual encounter is in line with the story, it also highlights his masculinity, as conventional gender roles upheld the idea that men should be active while women should be passive except when rejecting sexual advances.[33] Jupiter's slightly higher position over Callisto also gives him away, as it was typical in early modern images for men to be shown physically above women. Though for the sake of brevity this article cannot discuss in depth the poses of figures in every image, each *donna con donna* scene it addresses represents a similar contrast between an active masculine figure initiating a sexual act above and behind a passive feminine figure whose body is more on display for the viewer.

Adaptations of Recognizable Compositions: An Engraving from Fontainebleau

The mid-sixteenth-century Fontainebleau School engraving attributed to "Master GK" after Luca Penni entitled *A Satyr Surprising Four Bathing Nymphs* depicts nymphs in the act of *donna con donna* (fig. 6.2).[34] Penni was a Florentine painter and printmaker who came to Fontainebleau by 1537.[35] Becoming the head of printmaking for Francis I after 1545, he signed his works as "Luca Penni Roman" to highlight his associations with Raphael's workshop in Rome.[36] He trained with Raphael, and his older brother, Francesco Penni, was the heir of Raphael's studio along with Giulio Romano.[37]

Several versions of Penni's print exist, and another engraving by Jean Mignon depicting a larger gathering of women at a bath was likely truest to Penni's original composition, since Mignon was known to follow Penni's designs exactly (fig. 6.8).[38] However, because the subject of this article is mythological *donna con donna* imagery, only Master GK's version will be analysed in depth. In Master GK's engraving, four nymphs gather around a shallow bath. On the left, one nymph stands, bending down and holding her drapery loosely around her body as if preparing to drop her covering and wade into the water. In front of her, another nymph sits and combs her long, wavy hair with her fingers. In the centre of the composition, two additional nymphs embrace, entwine their legs, and face forward as if looking directly at the viewer. The nymph on the right raises her open palm from behind the other figure's back as if reacting to the surprise of being caught by the viewer during an act of debauchery with her partner. In the background of the scene, to the right, a satyr with

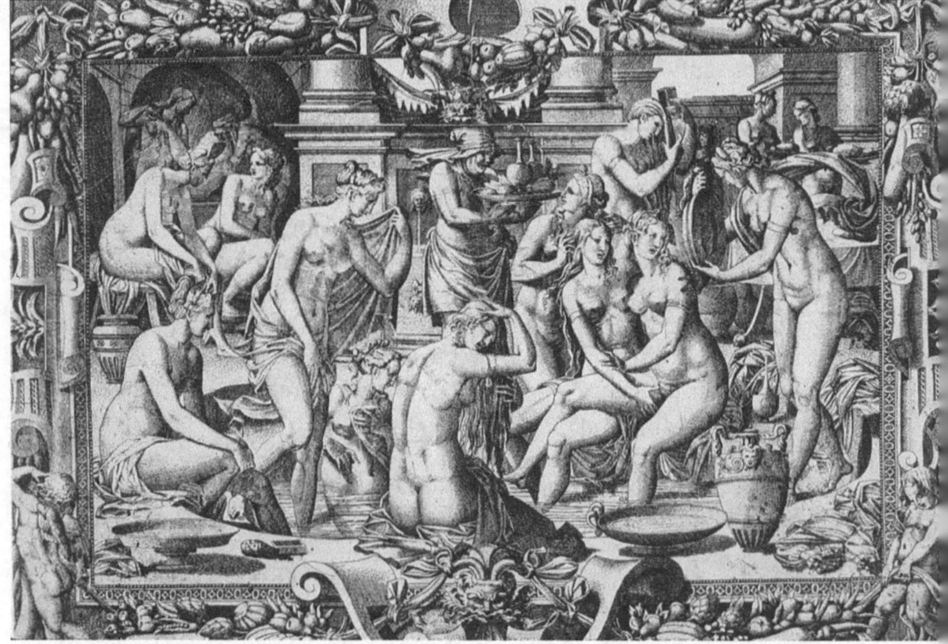

6.8. Jean Mignon (after Luca Penni), *Women Bathing* (1547–50). Bibliothèque Nationale de France, Paris. Public domain.

a prominent erection emerges from the shadows, lifting a curtain to spy on the nymphs. The satyr serves as a voyeuristic masculine presence that, in addition to the masculine-feminine difference between the nymphs themselves, makes the nature of the scene unambiguously sexual.

As the front nymph swings her leg over the back nymph's thigh, the pair recall the frontal nudity and slung legs commonly found in high-end erotic prints throughout Europe.[39] Compositions depicting a figure slinging a leg over one or both legs of a sexual companion appear slightly before 1520, but the motif was fully developed in the late 1520s and 1530s by artists in Raphael's circle.[40] In Italy, the woman is typically portrayed with her leg slung over the man's, as seen repeatedly in the sexually explicit *Loves of the Gods* print series of circa 1527 by Giovanni Jacopo Caraglio (fig. 6.9).[41] *Venus and Mars with Cupid*, painted around 1550 by Bernardino Lanino (an Italian artist mainly active in Milan) also suggests sexual interaction through entwined legs (fig. 6.10). In *Lot and His Daughters*, painted by an anonymous Fontainebleau artist around the same time, Lot's legs are in a similar position to those of the nymph

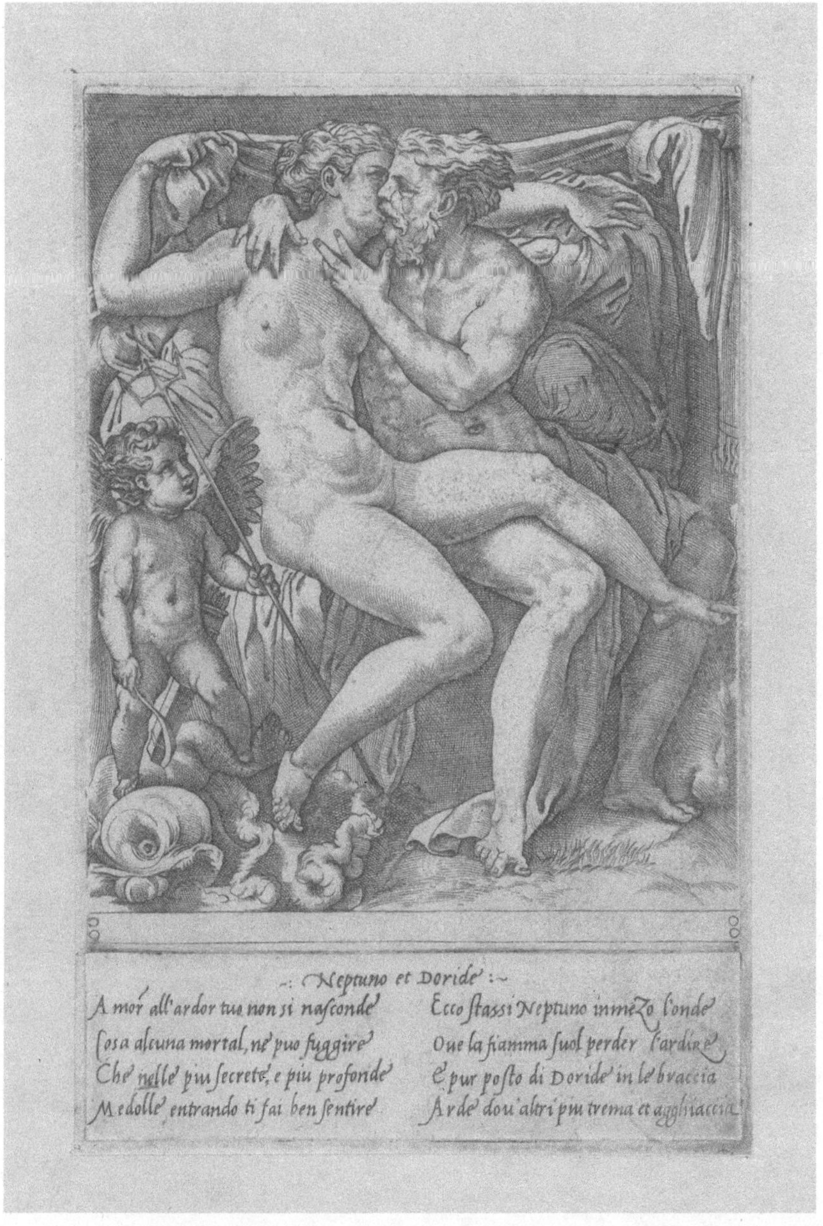

6.9. Giovanni Jacopo Caraglio (after Perino del Vaga), *Neptune and Doride* from the *Loves of the Gods* (1515–65). Rijksmuseum, Amsterdam. Public domain.

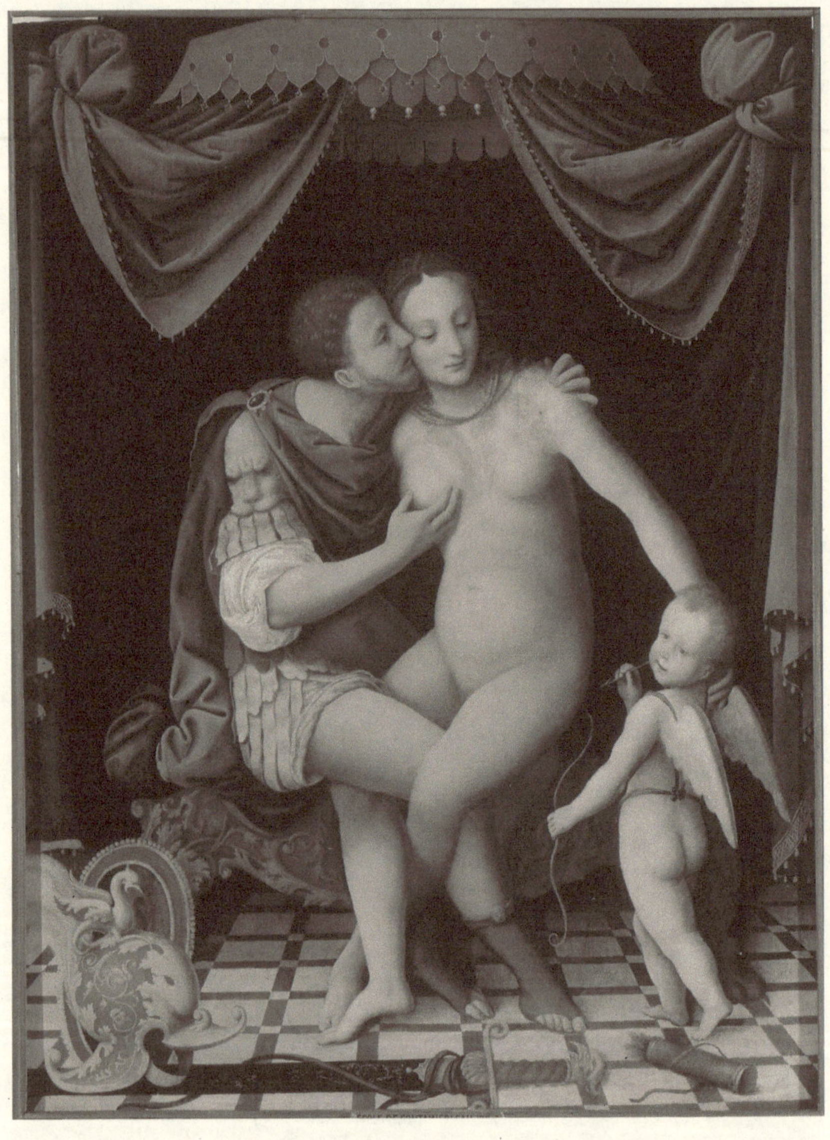

6.10. Attributed to Bernardino Lanino, *Venus and Mars with Cupid* (ca. 1550). Musée du Petit Palais, Paris. Public domain.

in the centre of Master GK's print who caresses the thigh of the nymph in front of her. The figures' crossing arms, along with the fact that Lot's daughter bends her knees with one leg higher than the other, makes the painting even more compositionally similar to the *Satyr Surprising Four Bathing Nymphs*. These three examples demonstrate how the nymphs in Master GK's print after Lucca Penni entwine their limbs in a way typical of figures in male-female sexual scenes. By placing the rear nymph in a position typical of males and the front nymph in a position typical of females, the composition makes the sexual nature of the nymphs' encounter clear by portraying a masculine-feminine difference.

Skin Tone and Humoral Theory: Parmigianino's Fresco Cycle at Fontanellato

Parmigianino uses skin tone variation to communicate levels of femininity and masculinity in his *Story of Diana and Actaeon* in the lunettes, spandrels, and ceiling of Paola Gonzaga's *camerino* at the Rocca Sanvitale (figs. 6.3–6.6). Completed in 1523–4, the fresco cycle portrays a story from Ovid's *Metamorphoses* in which the hunter Actaeon stumbles upon Diana and her nymphs bathing. Because he sees Diana nude, Diana turns Actaeon into a stag, and his own hunting dogs then chase and kill him. It is unclear whether the cycle was commissioned by Paola Gonzaga herself, her husband Giangaleazzo Sanvitale, or both. Parmigianino completed the frescoes three or four years after Paola arrived at Fontanellato.[42] Paola became an active participant in Sanvitale court life. As the daughter of Ludovico Gonzaga, lord of Sabbionetta (near Mantua), she was already educated in letters, music, and embroidery.[43] Paola hosted court functions and cultural gatherings at her new home, as was appropriate for women of her social station.[44] Contemplation of the *camerino*'s decoration may have been part of these entertainments as well as a way of impressing important guests.

Small and rectangular, the *camerino* is located on the ground floor close to the northwestern corner tower of the moat-enclosed Rocca Sanvitale.[45] Scholars are unsure of the room's original purpose. Some suggest it was a boudoir, while others believe it was a *stufetta* or washroom.[46] Katherine McIver argues that it was a shrine made after the death of one of Paola's children.[47] Whatever the intended function, the room's obscure location and its accessibility by only one door down a long corridor off the kitchen suggest that it was a private space.[48] Fitting for a hidden room because of its theme of secrecy, the subject of the fresco cycle is due in part to the location of the castle at Fontanellato, a name derived from *Fontana Lata*, which means "secret fountain" or "hidden source," referencing Diana's secret bathing place.[49]

In Parmigianino's fresco cycle, Actaeon approaches from the north lunettes in human form (figs. 6.3–6.4). On the east side of the room, he has the head of a stag, indicating that Diana has begun his transformation by splashing him from the centre lunette (fig. 6.5). Actaeon appears significantly feminine, owing to his soft facial features and languid pose (figs. 6.3–6.5). Because of this, some scholars interpret the scene on the north wall as hunters chasing a nymph. Mary Vaccaro identifies the figure in the centre-right lunette on the north vault as a female hunter even though she acknowledges that the word "acteona," which appears directly underneath this figure, is likely a literary joke suggesting the feminization of Actaeon.[50] However, this literary jest, along with the identical drapery and accoutrements worn by Actaeon with the head of a stag (fig. 6.5) and the "female hunter" (fig. 6.4), indicates that both figures are indeed Actaeon. Both wear white drapery tied around one shoulder, red-orange drapery over the other, and a green horn on their hip. Patricia Zalamea points out that Actaeon's feminine appearance may be due to the gender-bending implications of his role as the object of the hunt. Transformed into a stag, Actaeon is placed in the woman's role within allegories of the hunt as a metaphor for love. In such allegories, the hunter represents the man/lover, while the deer represents the woman/beloved.[51] On the south wall, Actaeon in the form of a stag is attacked by dogs.

In the lunette to the right of Diana, two nymphs gaze intimately into each other's eyes while remaining indifferent to or unknowing of Actaeon's presence (fig. 6.6). Because of the restoration carried out in 1964–6, which involved removing overpainting from the fresco cycle, a section of the left nymph is missing from her waist down.[52] Although, throughout the cycle, the nymphs, Diana, and Actaeon all share similar skin tones on their bodies, the face of the back nymph, whose hair is wrapped in a braid, appears much redder than the faces of Diana and the front nymph. This difference in facial skin tone may be tied to the long Western tradition, found even in ancient Egyptian painting, of depicting men with darker skin than women. In early modern Europe, the visual convention was due in part to the ideal of women staying inside the home and men venturing outdoors, therefore allowing elite women to avoid the sun and retain fair skin tones.[53] The difference in skin colour also relates to the widely accepted humoral theory that stated that men's bodies are hot and dry while women's bodies are cold and wet.[54] According to Aristotelian and Galenic anatomy and physiology, which partially informed early modern European understandings of medicine, complexion was an indication of the temperature and level of moisture inside the body.[55]

Humoral theory upheld the idea that women were almost always colder than men, but women's temperatures became warmer when experiencing love or lust.[56] In the sixteenth-century European mindset, sudden motion or sexual excitement could cause an abnormal amount of heat in women, which in the most extreme cases could push their vaginas outside their bodies to form penises.[57] By the seventeenth century, women who had sex with other women were often described as having prolapsed vaginas or enlarged clitorises with which they could penetrate their partners.[58] Even without referencing such genital differences, Brantôme's discourse on *tribades* speaks to the perception that women who initiate sex with other women are internally masculine. Brantôme quotes an ancient text by Lucian that describes a woman's recollection of her sexual encounter with another woman who kissed her passionately "like men do," saying that although she does not have a "virile member," she has the heart, affection, and all other attributes associated with virility.[59] Likewise, though the two nymphs in Parmigianino's fresco cycle appear to have the same external sex characteristics, the back figure's ruddier skin tone in her face may indicate bodily warmth that leads her to initiate the sexual encounter, a role typically expected of males.

The inclusion of a nymph with a darker, redder skin tone taking the active, masculine role in a *donna con donna* encounter appears in the following century in many scenes from across Europe, suggesting that this becomes a recognizable convention. For example, in Joachim Anthonisz Wtewael's *Diana and Actaeon* (1608), the nymphs in the bottom right corner differ drastically in their skin tones. While other figures in this scene differ in skin tone as well, the extreme contrast between the only two figures engaging in sexual intimacy is hardly coincidental. The back figure who reaches for her partner's genitals shares the skin tone of Actaeon (the only man in the scene), while the front figure shares the skin tone of Diana (who was especially associated with cold, wet humours due to her connection to the moon).[60] In Peter Paul Rubens' *Jupiter and Callisto* (1613), we see a similar contrast between the masculine Jupiter and feminine Callisto. While these images are much later than Parmigianino's fresco cycle, the difference between the nymphs in Parmigianino's fresco may be an earlier, more subtle example of the same pictorial convention. At the very least, within the context of physical affection between nymphs, the excessive redness in the back nymph's face implies lustful excitement through blushing. This makes the erotic nature of the nymphs' encounter more apparent and therefore brings attention to the back nymph's masculine role in initiating the sensual embrace.

Masculine and Feminine Body Types: A Maiolica Dish

A large maiolica (tin-glazed earthenware) dish made between 1560 and 1570 by the Fontana family workshop depicts Diana and her nymphs engaging in *donna con donna* intimacy in a watery setting, likely an outdoor bath. The image conveys masculinity through the nymphs' body proportions (fig. 6.7). Guido Durantino, who adopted the name Fontana, founded his studio in Urbino around 1528.[61] He employed his sons Nicolo, Camillo, and Orazio Fontana, as well as his grandson, Flaminio Fontana.[62] With great commercial success, the family produced high-quality *istoriato* (narrative wares) and white-ground grotesque wares.[63] Maiolicaware like this dish was typically displayed by noble families for their guests during social events. Because they were less expensive and appeared more rustic than gold, silver, or pewter, sixteenth-century maiolica vessels were considered most suitable for use in suburban villas.[64] According to some scholars, maiolicaware was usually kept on a credenza and was not meant for actual use.[65] Jacqueline Musacchio, however, argues that the vessels were likely used for dining on special occasions.[66] Maiolica dishes were typically about twenty-seven centimetres in diameter, an appropriate size for individual portions of food.[67] The fact that the dish with Diana bathing measures about forty-three centimetres in diameter suggests that it was used as a serving platter. The dish was meant to enhance the luxurious ambiance in an entertainment setting revolving around food. Some wealthy families, like the Gonzaga rulers of Mantua, dined on maiolica vessels personalized for the villa where they were used.[68] The sensual nature of the imagery on many of these vessels is therefore fitting, as the pleasurable atmosphere of elite dining settings was sometimes enhanced with sexually explicit decorations, often couched in mythological narratives.[69]

On this dish, Diana's nymphs chase after one another, grabbing and caressing each other's bodies in a way that recalls Nicolay's account of women expressing their lascivious wantonness at the baths. Diana appears at the top centre of the composition, where she lowers her head in feminine modesty as the nymphs flanking her caress her body.[70] The nymph on the left faces away from the viewer and with her right arm reaches out to touch Diana's genitals. While this figure may be washing Diana, the placement of her hand between Diana's thighs is sexually evocative. The fact that Diana's body is clearly visible while the nymphs to either side of her are partially obscured from view plays into the masculine-feminine dichotomy. This is because the body parts visible on Diana, namely her breasts and plump thighs, were understood as feminine in an early modern mindset.[71] For example, sixteenth-century French erotic poems described the ideal woman as having breasts like small balls of ivory and rounded but firm, thick, thighs.[72] Because the nymphs to either side of Diana have their breasts hidden from view by their positions, they lack the signifier of femininity that Diana displays. While all of the figures on the dish are particularly muscular, the fact that the nymph touching Diana's genitals turns her back to the viewer ensures that her muscular back, shoulder, and arm are her most visible body parts. By simultaneously obscuring her physical attributes associated with female bodies and highlighting those associated with male bodies, this figure appears relatively masculine, especially when compared to Diana.

Details in the top right and bottom right of the dish's central composition show similar masculine-feminine differences in body type between other nymphs. In the top right, a nymph chases and grabs another around her waist in a way that evokes pastoral scenes of men or satyrs rushing after female nymphs. The fleeing nymph has noticeably plumper thighs than the nymph pursuing her. On the bottom right, a seated nymph pivots at the waist to embrace her companion, who responds by turning to face her. The seated nymph twists her body in a way that emphasizes her broad shoulders, creating the illusion of top-heavy proportions similar to those of early modern male figures. According to humoral theory, the heat in men's bodies naturally moved upward, giving them large chests and shoulders, while the coldness in women sank downward, making them heavier in the lower parts of their bodies.[73] By contrasting proportions recognized as masculine with those understood as feminine in the early modern perspective, the artist employs elements familiar from male-female sexual pursuit to help the viewer recognize unfamiliar sexual interactions between females. The masculine proportions of some nymphs suggest the possibility of taking an active sexual role that was typically associated with males.

Conclusion

By applying Judith Butler's theory of gender as performance in combination with early modern European perspectives on gender, this article has shown that masculinity and femininity can be visually communicated in sixteenth-century mythological *donna con donna* scenes through sharply angled versus more fluid poses, revealing or hiding body parts associated with the female sex, positions similar to male-female sexual positions, and dark reddish skin tones compared to pale skin tones. Through the case studies of Pierre Milan's print after Primaticcio's fresco of Jupiter and Callisto, Master GK's print after Luca Penni depicting a satyr spying on bathing nymphs, Parmigianino's fresco cycle of the Diana and Actaeon story at the Rocca Sanvitale, and a historiated dish by the Fontana Family Workshop depicting Diana bathing with her nymphs, we can see that artists in Fontainebleau and northern Italy consistently asserted a masculine-feminine dichotomy in *donna con donna* scenes. This dichotomy suggests that early modern individuals imagined sex between women as involving at least one masculine participant, thereby implying that taking an active sexual role was considered inseparable from masculinity, even when both sexual partners were women.

NOTES

1 Brantôme, *Vies des dames galantes*, in *Memoires*, 230. "en nostre France, telles femmes sont assez communes, & si dit on pourtant, qu'il n'y a pas long-temps qu'elles s'en sont mestées, mesme que la façon en a esté portée d'Italie par une Dame de qualité, que je ne nommeray point."

2 For a consideration of European attitudes toward sex between women throughout the early modern period, as well as the case study of Benedetta Carlini, see Brown, *Immodest Acts*, especially 4–20, 117–21. For a more recent analysis of the case of Benedetta Carlini, see Simons, "'Bodily Things' and Brides of Christ."

3 Simons, "Lesbian (In)Visibility."

4 For additional information on early modern attitudes toward *donna con donna* encounters in spaces where women were secluded, see Simons, "Images of Bathing Women."

5 Simons, "Lesbian (In)Visibility," 86–7; Brown, *Immodest Acts*, 12–13.

6 See Traub, *Renaissance of Lesbianism*, especially 7, 13.

7 See Traub, *Renaissance of Lesbianism*, especially 182, 193–7, 230–1. For an additional consideration of the perceived possibility of love and sex between women in early modern Europe, see ch. 5 of Ferguson, *Queer (Re)Readings in the French Renaissance*, 245–91.

8 Ariosto, *Orlando furioso*, 25.26.1–25.70.8.

9 "E quando ritrovo la mia sirocchia tutta coperta d'arme eccetto il viso, c'havea la spada in luogo di conocchia, le fu vedere un Cavalliero aviso. La faccia, e le viril fattezze adocchia tanto, che se ne sente il cor conquiso"; Ariosto, *Orlando furioso*, 25.28.1–6.

10 For an additional translation, see DeCoste, *Hopeless Love*, 82–3. DeCoste translates "la facia e le virile fattezze" as "face and manly build," suggesting that Bradamante has a masculine body rather than a masculine face.

11 For a consideration of how Bradamante represents a feminine ideal while simultaneously challenging gender roles, see Mac Carthy, *Women and the Making of Poetry*, 137–9 and 146–8.

12 "Fa Dio (disse ella), se son sogni questi, ch'io dorma sempre, e mai piu non mi desti"; Ariosto, *Orlando furioso*, 25.67.7–8.

13 Ariosto, *Orlando furioso*, 25.26.5. Ricciardetto explains that Bradamante had cut her hair short to treat a head wound before Fiordispina found her, saying "Fu di scorciarsi astretta i lunghi crini."

14 De Nicolay, *The nauigations*, 60.

15 De Nicolay, *The nauigations*, 60.

16 "[the women] sometimes become so fervently in love the one of the other as if it were with men, in such sort that perceiving some maid, or woman, of excellent beauty they will not cease until they have found means to bath with [her], & to handle & grope them everywhere at their pleasures, so full they are of luxuriousness and feminine wantonness"; De Nicolay, *The nauigations*, 60.

17 Brantôme, *Vies des dames galantes*, 226–43. For the original French passages, see notes 18 and 20–3.

18 "ainsi que dit Lucian, que telles femmes sont les femmes de Lesbos, qui ne veulent pas souffrir les hommes mesmes; & telles femmes qui aiment cet exercice, ne veulent souffrir les hommes, mais s'adonnent à d'autres femmes, ainsi que les hommes mesmes: elles s'appellent Tribades, mot Grec, dérivé, ainsi que j'ay appris des Grecs, de τρίβω τρίβειν qui est autant à dire, que *fricare*, frayer, ou friquer, ou s'entrefrotter; & Tribades se disent *fricatrices* en François fricatrices, ou qui font la fricarelle en mestier de *Donne con Donne*, comme l'on l'a trouvé ainsi aujourd'huy"; Brantôme, *Vies des dames galantes*, 228.

19 Nelson, "Leonardo e la reinvenzione della figura femminile," 16. For an additional consideration of how taking an active role in sex was associated with masculinity while the passive sexual role was thought to be feminine even within the context of same-sex male relationships, see Rocke, *Forbidden Friendships*.

20 "Le bon compagnon Lucian en fait un chapitre, & dit, ainsi que les femmes viennent naturellement à conjoindre comme les hommes, conjoignant des instruments lascifs obscurs & monstrueux, faits d'une forme sterile, & ce nom, qui rarement s'entend dire de ces fricarelles, vaque librement par tout; & qu'il faille que le sexe feminin soit Filenes, qui faisoit faction de certaines amours hommasses; toutes soit il adjouste, qu'il est bien meilleur qu'une femme soit adonée à une libidineuse affection de faire le mâle, que n'est à l'homme de s'effeminer, tant il se monstre peu courageux & noble; la femme donc selon cela, qui contrefait aussi l'homme peut avoir réputation d'être plus valeureuse & courageuse qu'une autre; ainsi que j'en ay connu aucunes tant pour le corps que pour l'ame"; Brantôme, *Vies des dames galantes*, 228–9. For an additional consideration of early modern men admiring women who express amorous love towards other women, see Eisenbichler, *The Sword and the Pen*, 101–63.

21 "ce petit exercice, a ce que j'ay ouy dire, n'est qu'un apprentissage pour venir à celuy des grand hommes"; Brantôme, *Vies des dames galantes*, 232.

22 "Que j'en ay veu de ces Lesbiennes, qui pour toutes leurs fricarelles & entre-frottements, n'en laissent d'aller aux hommes; mesme Sappho, qui en a esté la Maîtresse, ne se mit elle pas à aymer son grand amy Faon; aprés lequel elle mouroit; car enfin, comme j'ay ouy raconter à plusieurs Dames, il n'y a que les hommes; & que de tout ce qu'elles prennent avec les autres femmes, ne sont que des tiroüers, pour s'aller paistre de gorges chaudes avec les hommes; & ces fricarelles ne leur servent qu'à faute des hommes; que si elles les trouvent à propos, & sans scandales, lairroient bien leurs compagnes, pour aller à eux, & leur fauter au collet"; Brantôme, *Vies des dames galantes*, 233.

23 "je n'en aye point veu qui ne fussent tres aises que leurs femmes s'amourachastent de leurs compagnes, & qu'ils voudraient qu'elles ne fussent jamais plus adulteres qu'en cette façon; comme de vray telle cohabitation est bien differente de celle d'avec les hommes; & quoy que die Martial, ils n'en sont pas Cocus pour cela, ce n'est pas texte d'Evangile que celuy d'un Poete fol"; Brantôme, *Vies des dames galantes*, 239–40.

24 Croizat-Glazer, "Fashioning Femininity," 115.

25 Ovid, *Metamorphoses*, 88–97.

26 Knecht, *French Renaissance Court*, 175.

27 Croizat-Glazer, "Fashioning Femininity," 108–9.

28 Croizat-Glazer, "Fashioning Femininity," 111.

29 Croizat-Glazer, "Fashioning Femininity," 109.

30 Matthews-Grieco, "The Body, Appearance and Sexuality," 46.

31 For more on Francis I's taste for sensual imagery as well as his history of employing Italian artists, see Knecht, *French Renaissance Court* and Zerner, *Renaissance Art in France*.

32 Castiglione, *Book of the Courtier*, 27.

33 Nelson, "Leonardo e la reinvenzione della figura femminile," 16.

34 Though the Princeton University Art Museum does not provide a specific date for this print, it is likely that it was printed (or at least designed) roughly around the same time as the identical ca. 1550 version in the Bibliothèque Nationale de France in Paris.

35 Boorsch et al., *Master Drawings from the Yale University Art Gallery*, 60.

36 Zerner, *Renaissance Art in France*, 143.

37 Zerner, *Renaissance Art in France*, 142.

38 Zerner, *Renaissance Art in France*, 143.

39 Matthews-Grieco, "Satyrs and Sausages," 27–8.

40 Steinberg, "Michelangelo's Florentine Pietà," 343–4.

41 Steinberg, "Michelangelo's Florentine Pietà," 343.

42 McIver, *Women, Art, and Architecture*, 35.

43 McIver, *Women, Art, and Architecture*, 36.

44 McIver, *Women, Art, and Architecture*, 36–7.

45 Vaccaro, "Reconsidering Parmigianino's Camerino," 178.

46 McIver, *Women, Art, and Architecture*, 125.
47 McIver, "Love, Death, and Mourning."
48 McIver, *Women, Art, and Architecture*, 125.
49 Franklin, *Art of Parmigianino*, 8.
50 Vaccaro, "Reconsidering Parmigianino's Camerino," 180.
51 Zalamea, "Subject to Diana," 218–19.
52 For more on the restoration history of Parmigianino's fresco cycle, see Bandini et al., "Parmigianino a Fontanellato."
53 Filipczak, *Hot Dry Men, Cold Wet Women*, 8.
54 Simons, *Sex of Men*, 13, 27.
55 Gage, "Complexion and Palette," 399.
56 Filipczak, *Hot Dry Men, Cold Wet Women*, 17, 73–4, 131.
57 Traub, *Renaissance of Lesbianism*, 45–6.
58 Donoghue, "Imagined More Than Women," 199. For more information on the seventeenth-century association of *tribades* with enlarged clitorises resulting from an abundance of heat in women's bodies, see Long, *Hermaphrodites in Renaissance Europe*, 92.
59 "En un autre endroit Lucian introduit deux Dames, devisantes de cet amour; & une demande à l'autre, si une telle avoit esté amoureuse d'elle, & si elle avoit couché avec elle, & ce qu'elle luy avoit fait; l'autre luy respondit librement. premièrement elle me baisa ainsi que font les hommes, non pas seulement en joignant les levres, mais en ouvrant aussi la bouche, cela s'entend en pigeonne, la langue en bouche: & encor qu'elle n'eust point le membre viril, & qu'elle fust semblable à nous autres, si est-ce qu'elle disoit avoir le cœur, l'affection & tout le reste viril ..."; Brantôme, *Vies des dames galantes*, 229.
60 Filipczak, *Hot Dry Men, Cold Wet Women*, 25.
61 Watson, "Fontana family," online.
62 Watson, "Fontana family," online.
63 Watson, "Fontana family," online.
64 Vitela, "Dining in the Gonzaga Suburban Palaces," 105.
65 Simons, "Cultural Context of Maiolica," 15.
66 Musacchio, *Marvels of Maiolica*, 29.
67 Vitela, "Inscriptions and the Dynamic Reception of Renaissance Maiolica," 169.
68 Vitela, "Dining in the Gonzaga Suburban Palaces," 103.
69 For an example of sexual imagery in banquet settings, see scholarship on the Cupid and Psyche Room at the Palazzo Te such as Furlotti, "Eros and Imagery," 44–55.
70 For a consideration of the ideal conventions used to portray feminine modesty in female figures, particularly in the art of Leonardo, see Nelson, "Leonardo e la reinvenzione della figura femminile," especially 16.

71 For more on how large, round thighs were understood as characteristic of women's bodies in the early modern mindset, see Berriot-Salvadore, *Un Corps, un destin*, 23.

72 For an analysis of sixteenth-century French erotic poems describing ideal as well as undesirable body parts of women, see Croizat-Glazer, "Fashioning Femininity," 25–41.

73 Filipczak, *Hot Dry Men, Cold Wet Women*, 125.

WORKS CITED

Printed Sources

Ariosto, Ludovico. *Orlando furioso di M. Ludovico Ariosto novissimamente alla sua integrità ridotto et di varie figure ornato*. Venetia: Niccolò Bascarini, 1543.

Bandini, Fabrizio, Cristina Danti, Lucia Fornari Schianchi, Maria Rosa Lanfranchi, and Luisa Viola. "Parmigianino a Fontanellato. Il restauro delle 'Storie di Diana e Atteone.'" *OPD Restauro* 12 (2000): 13–47.

Berriot-Salvadore, Evelyne. *Un Corps, un destin: la femme dans la medicine de la Renaissance*. Paris: Éditions Honoré Champion, 1993.

Boorsch, Suzanne, John Marciari, Nicole Bensoussan, Margaret E. Hadley, Elizabeth Hodermarsky, Rena Hoisington, Jan Leja, and Edgar Munhall. *Master Drawings from the Yale University Art Gallery*. Ed. Suzanne Boorsch and John Marciari. New Haven: Yale University Art Gallery, 2006.

Brantôme, Pierre de Bourdeille. *Memoires de Messire Pierre de Bourdeille, Seigneur de Brantome: contenant les vies de dames galantes de son temps*. Leyde: Chez Jean Sambix le Jeune, 1699.

Brown, Judith C. *Immodest Acts: The Life of a Lesbian Nun in Renaissance Italy*. New York: Oxford University Press, 1986.

Butler, Judith. *Gender Trouble: Feminism and the Subversion of Identity*. New York: Routledge, 1990.

Castiglione, Baldassare. *The Book of the Courtier*. Ed. Daniel Javitch. New York: W.W. Norton & Company, 2002.

Croizat-Glazer, Yassana. "Fashioning Femininity: Beauty, Royalty and the Rhetoric of Gender at Fontainebleau (1528–1547)." PhD dissertation, New York University, 2008.

DeCoste, Mary-Michelle. *Hopeless Love: Boiardo, Ariosto, and Narratives of Queer Female Desire*. Toronto: University of Toronto Press, 2009.

De Nicolay, Nicolas. *The nauigations, peregrinations and voyages, made into Turkie by Nicholas Nicholay Daulphinois, Lord of Arfeuile, chamberlaine and geographer ordinarie to the King of Fraunce*. Trans. Thomas Washington the Younger. London: Thomas Dawson, 1585.

Donoghue, Emma. "Imagined More Than Women: Lesbians as Hermaphrodites, 1671–1766." *Women's History Review* 2.2 (1993): 199–216.

Eisenbichler, Konrad. *The Sword and the Pen: Women, Politics, and Poetry in Sixteenth-Century Siena*. Notre Dame: University of Notre Dame Press, 2012.

Ferguson, Gary. *Queer (Re)Readings in the French Renaissance: Homosexuality, Gender, Culture*. Burlington, VT: Ashgate Publishing Company, 2008.

Filipczak, Zirka Z. *Hot Dry Men, Cold Wet Women: The Theory of Humors in Western European Art, 1575–1700*. New York: American Federation of Arts, 1997.

Franklin, David. *The Art of Parmigianino*. New Haven: Yale University Press, 2003.

Furlotti, Barbara. "Eros and Imagery at the Court of Federico II Gonzaga." In Barbara Furlotti, Guido Rebecchini, and Linda Wolk-Simon, eds., *Giulio Romano: Art and Desire*. Milan: Mondadori Electa, 2019, 44–55.

Gage, Frances. "Complexion and Palette in Giulio Mancini's Theory of Beauty and His Critique of Caravaggio." In Maurizio Calvesi and Alessandro Zuccari, eds., *Da Caravaggio ai Caravaggeschi*. Rome: CAM Editrice, 2009, 391–423.

Knecht, Robert J. *The French Renaissance Court, 1483–1589*. New Haven: Yale University Press, 2008.

Long, Kathleen P. *Hermaphrodites in Renaissance Europe*. Burlington, VT: Ashgate Publishing Company, 2006.

Mac Carthy, Ita. *Women and the Making of Poetry in Ariosto's Orlando Furioso*. Leicester: Troubador, 2007.

Matthews-Grieco, Sara F. "The Body, Appearance and Sexuality." In Natalie Zemon Davis and Arlette Farge, eds., *A History of Women in the West*, vol. 3, *Renaissance and Enlightenment Paradoxes*. Cambridge, MA: Harvard University Press, 1993, 46–84.

– "Satyrs and Sausages: Erotic Strategies and the Print Market in Cinquecento Italy." In Sara Matthews-Grieco, ed., *Erotic Cultures of Renaissance Italy*. Burlington, VT: Ashgate Publishing Company, 2010, 19–60.

McIver, Katherine A. "Love, Death, and Mourning: Paola Gonzaga's Camerino at Fontanellato." *Artibus et Historiae* 18.36 (1997): 101–8.

– *Women, Art, and Architecture in Northern Italy, 1520–1580: Negotiating Power*. Aldershot, UK: Ashgate Publishing Company, 2006.

Musacchio, Jacqueline Marie. *Marvels of Maiolica: Italian Renaissance Ceramics from the Corcoran Gallery of Art Collection*. Charlestown: Bunker Hill Publishing, 2004.

Nelson, Jonathan Katz. "Leonardo e la reinvenzione della figura femminile: Leda, Lisa e Maria." *XLVI lettura vinciana 22 aprile 2006*. Florence: Giunti, 2006.

Ovid. *Metamorphoses*. Trans. Northrop Frye and Frank Justus Miller. London: Heinemann, 1921.

Rocke, Michael. *Forbidden Friendships: Homosexuality and Male Culture in Renaissance Florence*. Oxford: Oxford University Press, 1996.

Simons, Patricia. "'Bodily Things' and Brides of Christ: The Case of the Early Seventeenth- Century 'Lesbian Nun' Benedetta Carlini." In Jacqueline Murray and Nicholas Terpstra, eds., *Sex, Gender and Sexuality in Renaissance Italy*. London: Routledge, 2019, 97–124.

– "The Cultural Context of Maiolica in Renaissance Italy." *Bulletin of the Detroit Institute of Arts* 87.1–4 (2013): 14–19.

– "Images of Bathing Women in Early Modern Europe and Turkey." In Jaynie Anderson, ed., *Crossing Cultures: Conflict, Migration and Convergence: The Proceedings of the 32nd International Congress in the History of Art*. Carlton: Miegunyah Press, 2009, 267–71.

– "Lesbian (In)Visibility in Italian Renaissance Culture: Diana and Other Cases of *donna con donna*." *Journal of Homosexuality* 27.1 (1994): 81–122.

– *The Sex of Men in Premodern Europe: A Cultural History*. Cambridge: Cambridge University Press, 2011.

Steinberg, Leo. "Michelangelo's Florentine Pietà: The Missing Leg." *The Art Bulletin* 50.4 (1968): 343–53.

Traub, Valerie. *The Renaissance of Lesbianism in Early Modern England*. Cambridge: Cambridge University Press, 2002.

Vaccaro, Mary. "Reconsidering Parmigianino's Camerino for Paola Gonzaga at Fontanellato." In Giancarla Periti, ed., *Drawing Relationships in Northern Italian Renaissance Art: Patronage and Theories of Invention*. Burlington, VT: Ashgate Publishing Company, 2004, 177–97.

Vitela, Lisa Boutin. "Dining in the Gonzaga Suburban Palaces: The Use and Reception of Istoriato Maiolica." *Predella Journal of Visual Arts* 33 (2013): 103–18.

– "Inscriptions and the Dynamic Reception of Renaissance Maiolica." *Word & Image* 30.2 (2014), 168–76.

Zalamea, Patricia. "Subject to Diana: Picturing Desire in French Renaissance Courtly Aesthetics." PhD dissertation, Rutgers University, 2007.

Zerner, Henri. *Renaissance Art in France: The Invention of Classicism*. Paris: Flammarion, 2003.

Electronic Source

Watson, Wendy M. "Fontana family (i)." *Grove Art Online*. 2003. Online at https://doi.org/10.1093/gao/9781884446054.article.T028829.

PART THREE

Knowledge and Emotions: Forbidden and Required

7 Wounded Histories on the Stages of Old and New Worlds: Vivaldi's *Motezuma* and the Cries of Conquest

KATE DRISCOLL

Summary: This article considers the representations of masculinity, emotion, and the performance of loss in Baroque opera. The genre or episode emphasized herein is the lament envoiced by male political figures who challenge the symbolic order that associates expressions of plaintive vocabulary with women. On stage, the gesture of male lamentation complicates traditional structures of subordination both between the sexes and between rival patriarchal systems, constructed and reconstructed as part of colonial historiography. Such is the case in Antonio Vivaldi and Alvise (Luigi) Giusti's *Motezuma* (1733), where the shifting landscapes of centralized and compromised powers renegotiate the legacies of European heroism in encounters with "New World" populations. At times on top and at times stripped nearly bare, the opera's Spanish and Aztec men oscillate between superior and submissive subject positions. *Motezuma*'s duelling spectacles of manhood outline the opera's critiques of history-making, which finds its voice in men's lament that sings the personal for the sake of the political.

"And, for you, the history of America is neither great nor respectable?"[1] A critique of opera's twinned hands in history- and world-making, these words are issued by an unnamed Mexican nobleman (El Amo), the protagonist of Alejo Carpentier's work of magical realism, *Concierto barroco* (1974). Set in 1709, the novel traces the adventures of a travelling "New World" nobleman and his Afro-Cuban servant, Filomeno, who arrive in Venice at the time of the "Old World" premiere of Antonio Vivaldi's opera *Motezuma*, an occasion that did not take place historically until 14 November 1733 at the Teatro Sant'Angelo. During his Italian holiday, the

Mexican "master" encounters Vivaldi and other famed Baroque composers, Handel and Scarlatti among them, in front of whom he dons the clothing and accessories of Moctezuma II (ca. 1466–1520), whose Aztec empire fell to the Spanish crown during the Conquest of Mexico (1519–21). Carpentier's Vivaldi appears as enchanted by El Amo's embodied rehearsal of Moctezuma's life as the touring pair do by the Venetian lagoon's seemingly infinite carnal delights. A night of storytelling and cross-cultural conviviality inspires the composer to see in Moctezuma's defeat thematic material fit for the stage, a "good theme for an opera" ("buen asunto para una ópera").[2] At *Motezuma*'s premiere, however, the Mexican spectator is left shocked, rather than flattered. Alarmed by the opera's distorted anachronisms, concocted love stories, and audacious praise for the Spanish slaughterer Hernán Cortés (1485–1547) – whose Italianate name in the opera is Fernando – El Amo criticizes the composer's embroidered licence towards Indigenous history. The nobleman aims his outrage precisely at the opera's softened portrait of lyric violence and tyranny, a failure (according to him) in cultural translation. El Amo departs Venice at the end of the novel to return home with an enlivened appreciation for the land and legacy from which he comes – a heritage that, as he witnessed on the Italian stage, has been harmfully misunderstood on the other side of the world.

What is rehearsed in Carpentier's novel is the interpretive work that underscores transnational opera in performance, however real or imagined. The fictional debate posited in *Concierto barroco* between Old and New World approaches to global history resonates in critical reflections on Eurocentrism's project to "sanitiz[e] Western history while patronizing and even demonizing the non-West."[3] The relationality of power and the power of relationality, which lie at the core of the making and unmaking of history, are as potent in Carpentier's novel as they are in Vivaldi's opera. In both cases, idealized versions of history – the chronicles of champions who are awarded representation as such – are challenged by figures who resist double colonization at the discursive and performative levels. The pages that follow seek to place such resistance in conversation with critical and theoretical inquiries drawn from early modern historiography, literary history, musicology, and masculinity studies. The choice to root these questions in a case study from the Baroque operatic repertoire is informed by the genre's critical interaction with the reception, production, and circulation of colonial histories, of which *Motezuma* is just one of many examples.

Vivaldi's opera locates in its protagonist's expressions of political-territorial loss a challenge to the symbolic order that associates plaintive vocabulary and its performance for live audiences with women.

On stage, the gesture of male lamentation complicates classical and early modern structures of subordination both between the sexes and between rival patriarchal systems. The implication in Plato's *Laws*, at least, is that the ritual of lament yields contagious forms of feminine excess that, when experienced by an ordinary citizen, can dangerously derange and misguide him. On the early modern stage, the female lament oscillated between ardent expression and cautious self-censure, and thus conveyed "new social meaning" for female audiences: "as a much loved image of womanhood, [the lament] encouraged young women to emulate its heroine's delicate balance of passion and piteousness, speech and silence, agency and submission."[4] In *Motezuma*, the shifting landscapes of centralized and compromised powers (e.g., territorial, religious, gendered, and moral) evolve through the juxtaposition of brutal warfare, attempted suicide, ritual sacrifice, and triumphal procession. These episodes and the responses recorded to them renegotiate the legacies of European male heroism and its place in "New World" historiography, obscuring the very notion of cultural superiority as it reflects less in the colonizers' conquest of the Aztec empire than in the fictional invention of its leader's survival. By exposing the circulating precarities of religiopolitical dominance and exploitation, *Motezuma*'s laments recast Spain's very triumph as Mexico's resounding resistance.

The reflexive relationship traced here between the lament and revisionist historiography maps onto a similarly reflexive relationship between power and masculinity. To what extent do the political messages about historical and heroic legacies in *Motezuma* depend on matters of content and means of communication? To answer this question, a methodological cue must be taken from feminist musicology's study of the lament as a vehicle of "undoing" for female characters, who vocally protest undesirable (at times even fatal) consequences in love and betrayal, and thus claim agency even as victims. That figures who lament ultimately dissolve is fundamental for performance itself to take place, since, as Catherine Clément claimed, "opera concerns women. No, there is no feminist version; no, there is no liberation. Quite the contrary: they suffer, they cry, they die."[5] Though Clément's argument can hardly apply to all women across the comprehensive span of the operatic repertoire, the correlation between pathetic expression and the threat of lethal elimination is pertinent to the narrative of resistance conveyed in *Motezuma*. Akin to Carpentier's Mexican nobleman, the figures who lament history in Vivaldi's opera are those who seemingly lack control over its transmission and reproduction. Thinking through history as the space which occupies loss – following Michel de Certeau – the lament's narrative potential is to reimagine circumstance and thus instrumentalize alternative historiography. Here, there lies power. Here, there lies new voice.

The opera, with a libretto by Alvise (Luigi) Giusti, unfolds as an ambiguous spectacle of power and authority, tasked with grappling with a difficult, but not so distant past. The *argomento* of Giusti's libretto announces that the work is based on the Spanish playwright and historian Antonio de Solís' royal chronicle, *Historia de la conquista de México* (Madrid, 1684), which was translated into Italian and sponsored by Florence's Accademia della Crusca in 1699.[6] De Solís' *Historia* is only one example of the kind of published patriotism for the royal crown that demonstrated an "implacable partiality for the Spanish side,"[7] and which gained increasing visibility among international readers both during and after the nation's colonial campaigns.[8] Although the librettist purports to represent the figure of Cortés as a "most valiant" ("valorosissimo") leader in prudence and courage, a contradiction surfaces in *Motezuma*'s sympathetic portrait of the demise of an empire at the hands of a "monstrous" tyrant (a charge made against the conquistador in act 1, scene 16). Despite Giusti's own claim, there extends a potential for an alternative interpretation of the place of valour, prudence, and courage in the opera.[9] At times on top and at times stripped nearly bare, Vivaldi's men oscillate between superior and submissive subject positions. This redistribution of political weight and its influence reflects in the opera's representation of masculinity as a "position *always contestable*."[10] The three acts of *Motezuma*'s duelling spectacles of manhood – enactments of the "sociology of masculinity" constituted as a "political order" – critique not only gendered hierarchies but also constructed histories.[11] This occurs most acutely and audibly through the mouthpiece of the afflicted male. The opera's laments envoice the personal for the sake of the political in such a way as to anticipate the collective consciousness of twentieth-century feminism.[12] For what concerns the opera's depiction of political collectivities, it is worth noting that there are many more individual Aztec than Spanish figures: Motezuma is joined by his wife Mitrena, their daughter Teutile, and the loyal general Asprano, while Fernando and his brother Ramiro – whose wedding to Teutile at the conclusion of the opera fictionally and temporarily establishes peace between the two sides – are the named envoys of the Spanish empire. The other figures in the opera (e.g., the chorus, enslaved Mexicans, and warring soldiers) are not individuated.

Venice's engagement with New World encounters evolved as part of a "geographic imagination," through which image- and text-based channels of representation created ways for writers, cartographers, and cosmographers to see themselves reflected in their American counterparts. Such reflexive practices were enhanced with visual clarity in the Venetian *isolarii* that "emphasiz[ed] Tenochtitlan as the most significant city in the New World," not least because of the topographical similarities between the two canal-matrixed cities.[13] Within and beyond Venice, the fruits and labours of globalization that resulted from transoceanic maritime explorations enhanced the sense of "group identity" across cultures in "an era of rapidly accelerating cultural transformation."[14] In the centuries leading up to Vivaldi's *Motezuma* and its suggestive rewriting of global historiography, poetic narratives about encounters with American populations filled the pages of Italian Baroque epic fiction, notably by poets employed at courts with favourable attitudes towards the Spanish, such as Tommaso Stigliani.[15] David Quint's conclusion that "the indispensable condition for a politics of expansion and conquest" lies at the heart of the epic project resonates with some cases of Baroque opera's intervention as a cultural mediator of colonial memory.[16] The increasingly audiovisual representation of sociopolitical orders that both separated and united early modern communities on the Baroque stage appealed particularly to international theatre-going audiences. Vivaldi's *Motezuma* – if not the first ever opera to stage encounters in the New World, a topic trodden upon lightly after the "unsuccessful" attempt by Pietro Ottoboni and Bernardo Pasquini, *Il Colombo, overo l'India scoperta* (1690) – was the first full-scale musical-theatrical production based on the events of the Conquest of Mexico.[17] Henry Purcell's unfinished semi-opera *The Indian Queen* (1695) recounts earlier (and no doubt imaginary) parts of Moctezuma II's life, prior to the arrival of Cortés' armies. Contemporary anxieties regarding Spain's expanded presence on the Italian peninsula in the early 1730s, in tandem with Venice's "imperial decline" and diminishing command of parts of the Mediterranean, likely informed the sympathetic representation of conquered peoples in performance.[18]

Before turning to a close reading of the libretto, some further notes regarding methodology are required. What runs as a current throughout this research is a commitment to take quite seriously the epistemological and imaginative work that opera conducts in the historical production and circulation of information about the globe and its inhabitants. This commitment, to be clear, recognizes the many caveats and reasons for caution inherent in any style of listening that would insist too firmly and too narrowly upon opera's capacity – and perhaps, too, its willingness – to encapsulate history. In seeking to join interdisciplinary dialogues about how the early modern world came to know and recognize itself, the analysis that evolves here follows the lead of multicultural opera historians, who have set into motion methods for contextualizing this art form within transhistorical and transnational sociopolitical discourses that "[think] through the interrelations of the dialectic of Self and Other."[19] Similar analysis of the "diplomatic functions of theatrical entertainment" in early modern European politics informs the greater arguments herein.[20] Political scientists, too, have adopted a "historical-political approach" to looking at opera through the lens of political ideology and its manifestation in the public sphere.[21] Thus this article reads opera as an instrument of political diplomacy, which serves as much to entertain audiences as it does to culturally mediate the information to which it exposes them. The decision to align Vivaldi's opera within the theoretical contours of gender and sexuality studies serves not only to offer a humble contribution to the polyphony of perspectives in this present volume, but to illustrate how the overlapping concerns of the personal and the political are as resonant today as they were centuries ago.

Engendering Lament: The Songs That Warriors Sing

The constellation of masculinities arranged in the *opera seria Motezuma* is shaped by the genre's conventional depiction of competing political orders, whereby figures both male and female debate the legitimacy and effectiveness of one's ability to rule. The "reiteration of social hierarchies whose implications were nothing short of cosmological" takes centre stage in this genre, which simultaneously outlines and obfuscates the divisions between authorial and submissive figures.[22] As the birthplace of public opera in the seventeenth century, Venice's cultural identity wove its origins – mythological and triumphant – into "verisimilar" discursive and performative fabrics.[23] If we consider the city's unique political structure – a republican oligarchy governed by an elected doge and representatives in a Senate – the depiction of supreme male authoritarianism, as noted by Wendy Heller, would have been met with critically distanced eyes, for there was no direct parallel between the monarchal figures represented on stage and the group of officials charged with the joint task of governing the city. Yet, the image of centralized (often jeopardized) control in the body of a single male ruler promised not only heightened drama and raised stakes in plots of suspense and deception, but also economic boosts in the form of increased ticket sales and smoother operational efficiency, since productions were often recycled from one Carnival season to the next.[24]

But what of Vivaldi's *Motezuma*? The librettist Giusti looked beyond La Serenissima's republican political system for subject matter that would embody gripping theatrical entertainment. For all that appeared foreign among audiences attending its 1733 premiere, the opera's most compelling moments were conveyed via familiar means. The lyrical interventions and sympathetic laments issued by Motezuma and other Aztec figures offer tones of contemplation that were essential to the success of Baroque opera and were most frequently sung by women. It is through the mode of lament that *Motezuma* – which takes its name not from the idol of conquest, but from the victim of colonization – underscores the symbolic order that associates Spain with invasive tyranny and Mexico with tragic vulnerability. While later eighteenth-century operatic adaptations of the Aztec-Spanish struggle would draw greater attention to "the Montezuma conundrum,"[25] or the question of how to represent the heroic non-Christian male before public (and not royal) audiences, the laments by non-Europeans in Vivaldi and Giusti's work take hold of audiences' sympathies.

Often an opera's dramatic apex, when the envoiced pathos of struggle opposes a plot that has harmed its speaker, laments intone the possibility of a counter-narrative – a fiction of alternative happenstance that looks upon certain fates with kinder eyes. *Motezuma*'s laments conduct imaginative work, much like how epic poetry's curse of the "nonnarratable" – "an alternative history of resistance" circumscribed within a hero's narrative victory – disturbs the genre's many gestures towards closure by seeking to reverse the fates of vanquished figures. Though epic poetry's convenient dovetailing of fiction and history often favours its protagonist's future, the antagonist's curse and cries for reversal "[call] the idea of ending into question … the words of [the] curse echo on, a threat that all is not over."[26] Accounting for the potential for a counter-narrative to surface in the language and pathos of loss, particularly in performance, it is worth approaching our analysis of lament in *Motezuma* with some critical questions in mind: thinking alongside critics of queer studies, if the patriarchy exists as "a structure of masculine bonds," how might we consider the dynamics between men that lead to scenes of lamentation?[27] When men's actions make other men cry in the "coupling … romance of words and music," what political stakes are at play that solidify or unsettle positions of authority, dominance, and submission?[28] To what degree has the modern stigmatization of men lamenting constituted a fiction of misappropriation, one that has long overlooked how community-building emotions, such as sorrow and grief, have been shared publicly, privately, and historically between the sexes?

Let us begin with the libretto's opening. The voice of the lament is that which speaks first in *Motezuma*. As the curtains rise, revealed is the "Laguna del Messico"[29] – the physical borderland between the

Aztec imperial palace and the Spanish military camps. Rather than depict the first meeting between the Indigenous population and the *conquistadores*, Giusti's libretto begins from a critical perspective. Gazing out over the horrors of war "with dagger in hand" ("con spada alla mano"), Motezuma recoils at his bitter defeat, accounting for the doubled sense of loss, as it has injured both the personal and collective body:

> Son vinto eterni Dèi! Tutto in un giorno
> lo splendor de' miei fasti, e l'alta Gloria
> del valor Messican cade svenata. (1.1.9)
>
> (I am conquered, eternal gods! All in one day
> the splendour of my riches, the lofty glory
> of Mexican valour falls blood dry.)

Motezuma's first self-identification is that of a conquered subject ("Son vinto"). The opera's representation of the distraught emperor consumed by melancholy resembles elements of his character represented in Solís' *Historia* and the visual-discursive scenes of Moctezuma II's weeping illustrated in Book XII of the Florentine Codex, where the descriptions of fright born from conquest indicate that "when the leader suffered his people suffered too."[30] In performance, Motezuma embodies the "alternative masculinity" with which Catherine Bates has associated male authors of Renaissance lyric "recuperative narratives."[31] The Aztec's wielding of lament as a recuperative strategy is at play each time he assesses the harm his empire has suffered and the potential for vendetta to which he and his armies may aspire. If abjection is the process of disgust and repulsion – à la Kristeva – then lament acts as Motezuma's instrument of repair and resistance.

The "politics of lack" that surface in Motezuma's vocalized grief complicate the gendered distinctions evidenced in psychoanalytic readings of early modern mourning and melancholia.[32] The ritual of expressing loss demonstrated by Motezuma's first words contrasts with his wife Mitrena's unfaltering pledge to challenge Spanish authority. The Aztec matriarch reserves any commentary about the Europeans' actions for when she appears in the immediate audience of her enemies' troops, indicating an insistence on perceivable listening that will mark her character's will throughout. While Motezuma directs his words to a nostalgic past, a splintered present, and an uncertain future, Mitrena emphasizes the necessity to focus on the here and now. Her first words in the opera criticize Motezuma's exaggerated self-reflexivity and lack of bravery, spurring him back into action with questions that doubt his ability to lead:

Olà che fai?
Ove da te lontano
trovar speri pietà?
…
Modera, amato sposo,
questi eccessi funesti.
Respiraremo un giorno,
se costante sarai.
…
Habbiam sudditi, ed armi. Armata anch'io
farò l'ultime prove
d'esperienza, e valor … Ma ti confondi?
Il coraggio dov'è? (1.1.9–10)

(Come on, what'are you doing?
Where do you hope
to find mercy alone, far away?
…
Temper, beloved spouse,
these fatal excesses.
We will breathe one day,
if constant you will be.
…
We have subjects and weapons. Armed even I
will demonstrate
experience and fortitude … But are you confused?
Where is your courage?)

The Aztec queen protests her husband's submission to a vocabulary of utter defeat. Rather than saturating her prospects with the memory of things past and the fear of what is to come, Mitrena's debut on stage manifests a rhetorical prowess that enunciates self-confidence and collective restraint. As the words "armed even I will demonstrate experience and fortitude" suggest, Mitrena's command of speech resonates in her command of warfare. The image of the "woman on top" embodied in her presence on stage carries almost comical, though no less serious, implications later in the first act. In scene 13, the queen refuses the Spaniards' mechanical impulse to treat her politely simply because she is a woman. Though she has crossed enemy lines, Mitrena assumes dominant authority: "Where I command and rule, I give honour, I do not receive it" ("Ove io comando, e impero, / dò l'onor, no 'l ricevo"; 1.13.21). Cowering to the side, crouched in hiding from Fernando's view, Motezuma whispers affirmation to the audience that, indeed, his wife is correct ("E questo è vero!").

The question of audience is essential for contextualizing to and for whom laments are sung in this opera. As the previous citations demonstrated, the desire to dialogue while lamenting is not shared equally between Motezuma and Mitrena. While the Aztec emperor spends the majority of the first part of the opera avoiding confrontation with Fernando and his men, Mitrena accredits a higher value in having the Spanish hear directly what she has to say. The political valences of the queen's laments emerge translucent when they appear in the form of a critique. The Aztec queen reproaches her enemies' cruelty for placing Motezuma in chains, condemning not only the violence ordered by Fernando's authority but also his subjects' passive willingness to observe it. The libretto directs her words solely "to the Spaniards" ("ai spagnoli"):

E voi potete
a sì barbaro Duce
senza timor, soldati,
e servir e ubbidir
...
Questa, ingrati, è virtù? Questi i costumi,
che dalla Spagna vostra, e dall'Europa
al nostro Mondo oppresso,
a confusion di chi resiste a voi,
portate e seminate illustri Eroi? (1.14.24)

(And, soldiers, you can,
without fear,
both serve and obey
a leader so barbaric.
...
Ungrateful ones, is this virtue? Are these the customs
that, from your Spain and your Europe
to our oppressed world,
to the confusion of those who resist you,
you bring and seed illustrious heroes?)

What is of note in the lines above is Mitrena's entreaty to a specific group of listeners. The deferred reference to "illustrious heroes" in

Mitrena's song submerges the image of Spain's military missionaries under the repressive consequences they leave in their wake. Throughout the opera, the word "barbaro" is used far more frequently to label the behaviours of the Europeans than those of the Aztecs, anticipating the representation of "exoticism *à l'envers*"[33] that will emerge with greater detail in the 1755 opera *Montezuma*, with music by Carl Heinrich Graun and a libretto by Frederick the Great. Mitrena's reproof of Spanish and European footprints in lands where their arrival is unwelcome will echo once again in her stinging debate with Fernando in act 2, an episode treated in more precise detail below. Even if, immediately after these lyrics, Fernando halts Mitrena's voice – "No more" ("Non più") he demands – her call for sympathy with the "oppressed world" of the afflicted, together with her husband's fractured hope for Mexico's future, chart an affective course of grieved disappointment that lasts throughout the opera, leading to the final cry for revisionist historiography uttered by the final Aztec to sing alone on stage.

Theorizing Loss: Constructions of Masculinities in Performance

It is worth repeating that *Motezuma* transcends the gendered presumptions that map the expression of loss exclusively onto the female body. As we saw in the examples from act 1, characters both male and female search for the language of restorative critique for reasons both individual and collective. Speakers of lament are, by definition, figures of affliction in pursuit of a rubric fit to describe disappointment, a factor of the human condition that does not uniquely depend on gendered ideologies or identities. Indeed, the male and female figures of *Motezuma* have more traits in common than divide them. Using feminist critical vocabulary to study the opera's men and masculinities allows for continuities to surface in "the enactment of gendered subjectivity" across a variety of different subjects.[34] Judith Butler's fundamental lessons on gender as a culturally presupposed performance resonate in Stephen Greenblatt's sociological readings of early modern men as composite, self-fashioning spectacles. For what concerns the emotional vectors of masculinity and its social composition, Kalle Berggren's idea of "sticky masculinities" illustrates how male subject positions are erected and exchanged in layering (sometimes contradicting) discourses. "This is always a contested, variable, and uncertain process," Berggren claims, "but one in which the repeated enactment of masculinity tends to be sticky and naturalize."[35] The compositional structure of masculinities built from a culmination of cultural and affective forces – processes of acquiring, overturning, and intermixing – offers a compelling lens through which to trace further the relational contours of the lament in opera. As the characters in *Motezuma* confirm, operatic laments envoice discontent, regardless of gender. Rather than sound as a discourse rooted in alienation, the lament hinges on a politics of relationality. Expressed otherwise, the lament yearns for an audience; it "observes struggle and registers the failure of the desired world without wanting to break with the conditions of that struggle."[36] The relational, gravitational pull of the lament turns on a set of conditions that gives shape to why and for whom laments are spoken or, in the case of opera, sung. The question of boundaries informs not only the content about which the lament speaks but also the bridge – the voice – across which it reaches audiences. As Rebecca Comay eloquently considers it, "the expression of loss is bound to the loss of expression."[37]

The hypothesis subtending this analysis – namely, that laments in *Motezuma* give voice to the historically non-narratable by improvising hope for defeated male rulers – is more broadly informed by the history of influences that have sought to keep men from narrating lament, perhaps even experiencing it at all. Even though examples of men's lament widely populate both the literary and musicodramatic repertoires from antiquity to the early modern era and beyond, the fantasy of men's historical abstinence from sentimental self-reflexivity has continued to gain traction because of the oppressive, inappropriately obtuse slogan that suggests "real men don't cry." In its critical reception, the first two words of this principle have been identifiably problematic, leading to an expanded body of criticism on the non-existence of "real" men, in that there is nothing transcendent, "invariable, inherent or flatly definitive" in the social and cultural production of any gender.[38] On the level of affect, the myth and pressures of hypermasculinization and its drive to drain men of their emotional reactions have been historically numerous: the Enlightenment's alignment of civility and rationality, capitalism's carnivorous approach to market competition, the visions of buff muscled bodies that stretch the edges of the silver screen, and the illusions of geopolitical dominance via the mass production of weapons are only some examples among many. Such phenomena have been persistent in their attempt to bar men from contemplating and openly demonstrating complex emotions. This toxic trajectory has far more layers and contradictions than can be recalled here, but the conviction that "real men don't cry" reveals an "act" of manhood – a behavioural mode "aimed at claiming privilege, eliciting deference, and resisting exploitation" – with contours outside the lines of historical and artistic fact.[39]

What early modern literary, performance, and social histories reveal is that, prior to the mirage of the fearless, tearless man, premodern masculinities developed within and because of scenes of public mourning and intimate weeping. The classical model of Odysseus struggling to return home, which provided the subject matter for an opera by Monteverdi, is replete with episodes of sorrow in which the wandering hero longs for community and grieves his fallen comrades. Books of early modern lyric and epic poetry are filled with moments of regret and anguish, as abject male characters wail at the bitter conditions of isolation, hostility, and exile. These examples and others like them reveal how, for many premodern men, the signs of masculinity evolved within the broader condition of being human, at times in direct imitation of their female counterparts. As Marjorie Curry Woods has shown, women's "emotions permeated and sometimes dominated the [medieval] classroom experience,"[40] whereby schoolboys learning the art of writing took their pedagogical cue from classical Dido. This style of modelling the male voice upon that of a woman recalls Ovid's ventriloquizing the female voice in the *Heroides* and its many later re-elaborations in sixteenth-century poetry and madrigals. If, today, masculinity has been conceptualized as an "invisible" power, in that, "ubiquitous in positions of power everywhere, men are invisible to themselves," men's lament serves as an audible testament to the power to resist not only the conditions to which some men feel subject, but the factors that have since sought to silence them.[41] Such formulations of men's sonic agency and its relationship to other forms of authority provided dynamic ground upon which the European performing arts could revisit and retell the continent's colonial past, inspired in broad step by Enlightenment reworkings of ideas surrounding heroism and tyranny.

Envoicing History: The Lament as Conquest Reimagined

If it is said that "history has been written by the victors," by what means do we come to know the vanquished? The single case study of *Motezuma* is not enough to provide a comprehensive answer to this question, but the opera does have nuanced messages to convey about the very art of history-making. While some Baroque operas staged the feats of mythological heroes, some composers – Vivaldi among them – adapted knights' tales from the epic fictions by Ariosto and Tasso. In the beginning of the eighteenth century, the aesthetic palettes for historical operas increased as more librettists and drama theorists defended *opera seria* as a moralizing, edifying instrument that could "encourag[e] [the spectator] to identify with the heroes in their humanity."[42] Central to this question of identifying with operatic men is the issue of power. *Motezuma*'s duelling leaders each raise questions concerning political impotence in the form of waning authority. As the substitute body for a higher male power – three, if he represents not only the emperor but both the Christian God and a demigod among the Aztecs – the surrogate Cortés wields the imperial authority of Emperor Charles V, at times frighteningly enough to make Motezuma avoid speaking with him. Even as the Aztec warrior recognizes his impending defeat, Motezuma's wavering defiance against Fernando and his army through his actions and song rises and falls throughout the opera, manifesting the incompatibility of silent subordination and histrionic grief. Moreover, the opera's experiments with gender roles make it difficult to pin voices and bodies as categorically male or female, not least because of Mitrena's dominating presence as a military commander of a canoe armada and a skilled rhetorician tactfully rehearsed in Enlightenment critique. Each act's attempt to thread gendered behaviour as either masculine or feminine unravels a consistently contradicting tapestry of gender identities and performance subjectivities.

A spectator interested in addressing this fluidity via the lens of the Baroque castrato tradition might pose a different set of questions about the opera's portrayal of gender roles than those treated here. As per the genre's casting traditions, the heroic figure Fernando was played by the Italian castrato-soprano Francesco Bilanzoni, while the German baritone Massimiliano Miller performed the role of Motezuma. The understanding in these pages of matters of pitch and perceived masculinity in Baroque opera follows the analysis of Susan McClary, who has emphasized the virility that castrati embodied in their primary roles as "romantic idols" who sing in a high tessitura, and whose intense adoration by audience members is a trait in common with pop music icons today. Rather than being identified with their perceived "damaged manhood," these singers had an allure that allowed them to play convincingly "heroes and lovers, powerful in battle and irresistible in romantic engagements with women."[43] Audiences' "insatiable appetite"[44] for high voices persisted from the sixteenth-century performances in Ferrara by the court's *concerto delle donne* through the seventeenth- and eighteenth-century operatic productions that starred castrato singers in leading roles, whether as Cortés, Xerxes, Caesar, Jason, or Nero. The "strong resonance … understood as relative loudness and intensity"[45] with which the castrato sang was certainly not perceived as similar to a woman's voice. The castrato's "piercing" vocal quality enabled his sound to "penetrat[e] the accompaniment" and "ris[e] above all instruments."[46] What is of note in *Motezuma* is that the lower voice of the Aztec king is granted superior access to expressive vocabulary, despite the tradition that more frequently relegated "the expressive domain … to higher voices."[47] That Motezuma's emotional range extends beyond the boundaries of the baritone voice's tessitura is a testament to the opera's more pressing interest in rewriting a narrative of conquest than in convincing audiences of its fictional matrimonial conclusion.

Since the conditions for *Motezuma*'s 1733 premiere permitted women to perform on the Venetian stage – unlike in the papal states, from whose theatrical productions actresses were banned – female singers were permitted to play all the female characters. The role of Fernando's fictional brother Ramiro was played *en travesti* by the mezzo-soprano Angiola Zanuchi, who continued in the longstanding tradition of gender-bending actresses made visible already in the sixteenth century by *commedia dell'arte* troupes. Mitrena, the woman of action who most forcefully resists Spanish colonization at the discursive and military levels, was played by Vivaldi's protégée, the mezzo-soprano Anna Girò, who had collaborated with the composer in over a dozen of his premieres. The favour for his student with which Vivaldi approached the writing of Mitrena's part no doubt contributes to the sharp contrasts listeners observe between her character and the two opposing military leaders.

The emotional penetrability reflected in Motezuma's laments, which occur more frequently when he does not appear alongside Fernando on stage, contrasts with Mitrena's willingness to offer up critique only when she is in the direct company of her oppressors. As witnessed in the passages cited above, Mitrena's desire for her audience's attention demands that those whom she criticizes listen carefully to what she has to say. Throughout the opera, Mitrena's Enlightenment-style idioms celebrate reason's conquest over the passions, as when she calms her daughter with the words "in a strong heart reason triumphs" ("in petto forte, / trionfa la ragion"; 1.3.12). An exemplar and champion of justice, and the most rhetorically savvy character in the opera, the Aztec queen condemns the barbaric customs and lack of civility displayed by European male tyrants. Through her, the voice of civilization acts as a mouthpiece of critique against the means by which Western civilization forced itself upon non-Westerners.

Upon learning that her family has been detained by the foreign army, Mitrena steers a rescue team towards the Spanish quarters, where she arranges to meet privately with Fernando. The Aztec empress's tactful diplomacy shines in act 2, scene 4, in which she delivers a biting anti-Spanish, anti-colonial invective, the longest of any character in the opera. Recalling the charges of brutality issued by Bartolomé de las Casas is his *Brevísima relación de la destrucción de las Indias* (Seville, 1552) – whose printing in Venice was "received with overwhelming enthusiasm"[48] – Mitrena's complaints cut directly to the chase: Fernando and his men are not welcome and are asked to leave her nation in peace. While earlier in the opera Fernando had silenced Mitrena from sowing further doubt in the minds of his Spanish subjects, in act 2 he must wait his turn to speak. Mitrena appears most like a woman of the theatre when she imbues her preface with dramatic suspense: "Fernando, the great moment between us approaches. Hear me again" ("Fernando, il gran momento / s'avicina fra noi. Sentimi ancora"; 2.4.31). Thinly feigning flattery and gratitude for Fernando's benevolent awakening of the Mexicans from their "blindness," Mitrena sings to Cortés the words that he might, in a different context, have always wanted to hear:

Vivea fra l'ombre ancora
di natia cecità, fuori del Mondo,
ignobile, negletta,
questa vasta Region. Fra mille errori
di culto, e di costume
ogni mente sommersa oltre misura
il metodo passava
d'una civil, e regular coltura.
Per secoli sì lunghi
furo i popoli miei cotanto idioti
ch'anche propri tesor gl'erano ignoti. (2.4.32)

(This vast, base, neglected
region lying outside the world
still lived among the shadows
of native blindness.
Submerged among a thousand errors
of cult and custom,
every mind
overlooked the method of a
civil and acceptable culture.
For centuries so long,
my people were such fools
that even their own treasures were unknown to them.)

Mitrena's simulated appreciation for the "salvific" intervention of heaven's *seminume* (demigod) Fernando is nothing short of a rhetorical seduction enacted to ensnare her colonizer within her contradicting words. Recognizing the patronizing tones in Mitrena's word-painting praise, Fernando attempts to interrupt her, only to be held subject to an unfamiliar form of rhetorical torture: listening. In order to catalogue the list of crimes with which Mitrena charges him – among which are the breaking of "every law and a hundred acts of violence" ("veggo infranta ogni legge, e sento usarmi / cento violenze"; 2.4.33) – the queen silences the Spaniard's attempts to speak with the words, "Suffer still a little longer, I'm almost done" ("Soffri ancora un momento, ho già compito"; 2.4.33). If Spanish conquest is achieved with steel and bloodshed, Mitrena opts for words and wit.

From here, Mitrena launches into a lesson about the consequences that befall those who would inflict injury upon others: "From such a fortunate event, you lose all your respect. There remains no shadow of mercy, nor of virtue" ("Da un sì felice effetto / perdi tutto il rispetto. Ombra non resta / di pietà, di virtù"; 2.4.33–4). By translating Fernando's victory as that which will deprive him of respect among others, Mitrena points to the long horizon of historical memory. Undoubtedly her mother's daughter, Teutile, a despondent presence in the opera who waits patiently and most ardently for its happy ending, similarly directs her eyes towards history when she confronts the betrayal of her beloved Ramiro in the words:

> Calpesta, ingrato,
> i Numi, i Templi, e ogni ragion sconvolta,
> l'eccidio universal vanta una volta. (2.11.42)
>
> (Trample, ungrateful one,
> our gods and our temples, and once every reason
> is overturned, boast of your universal massacre.)

The queen's teachings about how histories are made resound in her repeated attempts to hush her student-captor, "Listen to me and be silent" ("M'ascolta e taci"; 2.4.32), words that leave little room for Fernando's arrogance to defend himself as a "minister and not a tyrant" ("Ministro e non Tiranno"; 2.4.34). When he is allowed to speak, Fernando's alternative and much-abbreviated account of what took place – "I came to your dominion, I won, I fought" ("Giunsi ne' Regni tuoi, vinsi, pugnai"; 2.4.34) – forges an unstable parallel with the language of legal justification used by such classical conquerors as Julius Caesar, echoes of whose "veni, vidi, vici" ("I came, I saw, I conquered") may be heard coursing throughout Fernando's defence. The fact, however, that the Spanish captain imagines having won before having fought ("vinsi" and only later "pugnai") speaks to his distorted perception of the sequence of military history and thus his anachronistic place within it.

When their competing narratives fail to resolve, Mitrena calls for Fernando to depart her land, lest he choose to compete with her in mortal combat. Aroused by the prospects of yet another victory – "I never refuse occasions for glory" ("io non rifiuto mai / l'occasioni di Gloria"; 2.4.35) – Fernando eagerly agrees. Motezuma overhears his wife's lessons in heroism and its fate in posterity, and regains the courage to confront his oppressor. The Aztec king challenges the Spaniard to a duel under the unique condition that Fernando remove his armour and appear equally vulnerable in their battle:

> Disarma, o vile,
> tu il petto ancor. In singolar cimento
> vieni, se puoi, ch'allor con armi pari
> misurarem i sitibondi acciari. (2.5.35)
>
> (Disarm, o vile one,
> your chest some more. In single combat
> come, if you can, so that we may
> measure our bloodthirsty steel with equal arms.)

Militarily stripped of its "imagery of dominance," Fernando's now puncturable body mirrors the figural virginity embodied by Motezuma and the appeal of his untouched "terra nova."[49] Each man's now equally exposed body reflects in the symbolic illustrations of the New World that assigned feminine characteristics to the American continent. In the *Allegory of America* (ca. 1600; fig. 7.1) by Jan van der Straet (better known as Stradanus) that was included in the print series *Nova reperta*, Amerigo Vespucci is depicted during his first encounter with America, a sexualized, nearly naked young woman, who reclines before the European explorer and observes the emblems of strength and virility (e.g., the staff and the sword) that flank his figure. Stradanus' conflation of the vulnerable body with the vulnerable earth reflects in the full-length portrait of Moctezuma II, the historical figure, drawn by the Venetian nun Isabella Piccini (fig. 7.2). Giusti would have enjoyed access to this portrait, for it appeared in the 1699 Italian translation of Solís' *Historia*. Piccini's portrait displays a decoratively exposed Moctezuma, whose tall and erect posture nearly defies the edges of the image's frame. This representation of the Mexican leader sharply contrasts with her depiction of Cortés, whose limbs are covered and protected by layers of impenetrable armour.

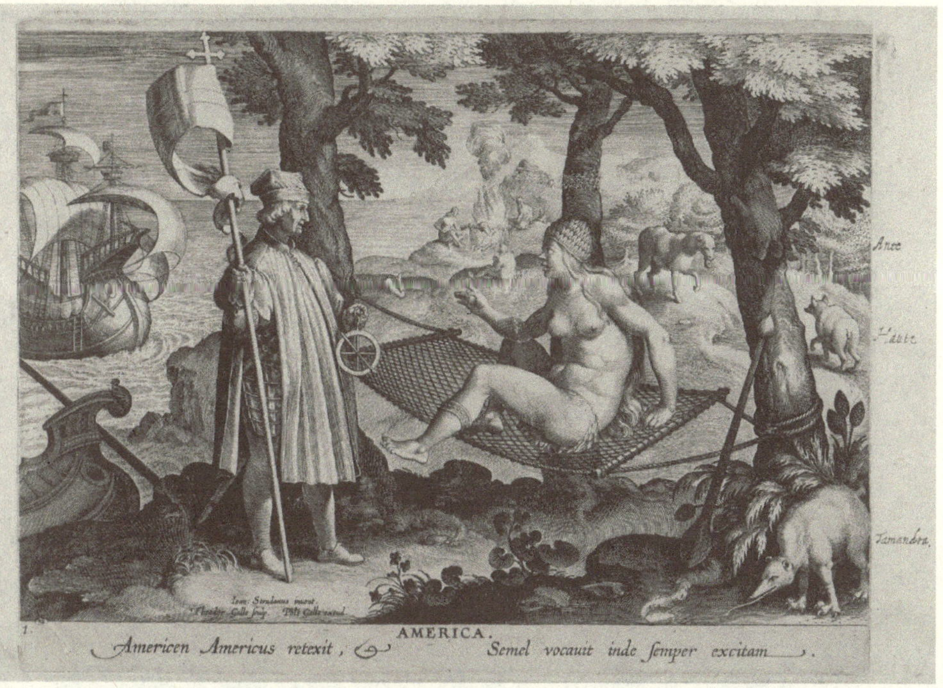

7.1. Jan van der Straet, *Allegory of America* (ca. 1600). From *Nova reperta*. Antwerp: Philips Galle, ca. 1600. The Metropolitan Museum of Art, Harris Brisbane Dick Fund. Accession Number 34.30(2). Public domain.

As a war cry before they begin, the duelling combatants sing in unison, "To battle, to battle! My sword, disdain, and honour await you" ("A battaglia, a battaglia! T'aspetta / il mio brando, lo sdegno, l'onor"; 2.5.36), indicating that the painful promise of penetration lies only moments away. Erotic hints of bellicose desire surface in Motezuma's anticipation of the pleasure he seeks to take inside his opponent: "I will satisfy my vendetta in your blood, o traitor" ("Sazierò la mia vendetta / nel tuo sangue, o traditor"; 2.5.36). The warriors' lyrics weave in and out of one another in the rhymes "orgoglio" ("pride") and "cordoglio" ("sorrow"), just after Mitrena's voice is brought into harmony, transforming the scene from a duet to a trio. The three voices unite in the utterance "cruel" ("crudel") yet use it to describe three distinct phenomena. While Motezuma wails hopelessly against "cruel fate" ("sorte crudel"), Mitrena understands the events to be more historically precise in her lament against the "cruel day" ("giorno crudel"). The misalignment

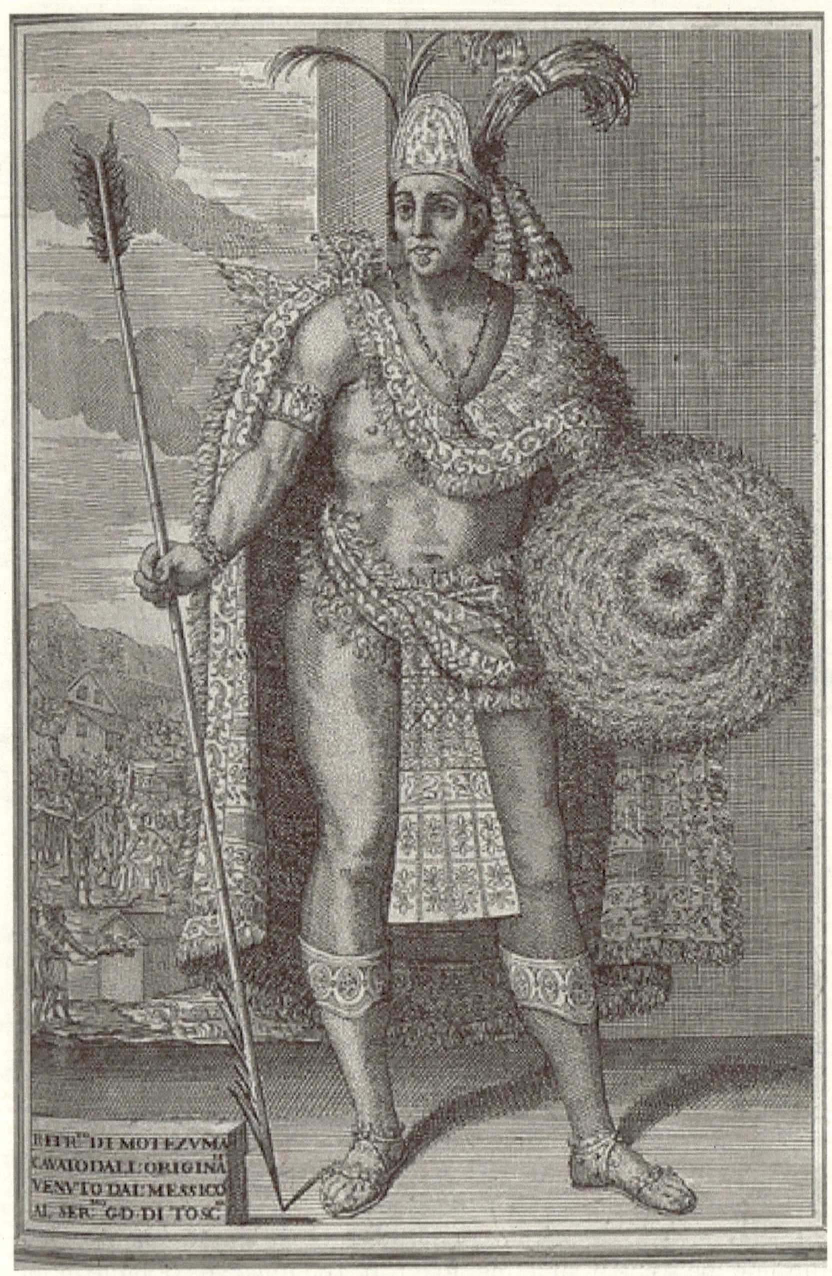

7.2. Isabella Piccini, "Motezuma" (1699). From Antonio de Solís, *Istoria della conquista del Messico*, trans. Filippo Corsini (Florence: Giovanni Filippo Cecchi, 1699). Houghton Library, Harvard University. Catalogue number 625.99.800. Public domain.

between what stirs Mitrena to fight and what ignites Motezuma emerges with clarity in the former's words "Think of us, think of your kingdom" ("Pensa a noi, pensa al tuo Regno"), against which the latter self-justifies "I think of myself, I think of my outrage" ("Penso a me, penso al mio sdegno"). When the three voices unite at the end of the scene, Fernando and Motezuma each imagine their opponent singing "O ruthless fate! O strict Heavens!" ("O sorte spietata! O rigido Ciel!"), leaving only Mitrena to deliver these words as a tragic description of her current state. The incompatible messaging with which Mitrena and Motezuma participate in the trio with Fernando underscores their discordant attitudes towards conquest in moments of immediate warfare. Mitrena's plea for collectivity rubs against Motezuma's self-serving motivation to duel. Actions and words work separately in Motezuma's ability to cope with defeat. Only at the opera's conclusion and in the moment of his final lament does Motezuma adopt the perspective of his wife that considers the lasting effects of historical memory.

If Vivaldi's opera is born from a figure who laments his fate but survives its effects, how successful are his cries of revisionist historiography? To the advantage of *Motezuma*'s overcome sovereign, laments are personal for the sake of the political in how they critique the mechanisms of storytelling passed down throughout the generations. Near the conclusion of the opera, just before the Spanish troops proudly triumph in the Mexican piazza – where they are accompanied by a parade of enslaved natives and other spoils – the defeated Aztec reflects on the lingering stain his failure will impress onto historical memory. In act 3, scene 10, the once godlike monarch articulates his decline into a counterexample of political heroism:

Stelle vinceste. Ecco un esempio al Mondo
della vostra incostanza. Ecco un Monarca,
che solo si vantava
di possanza simil ai vostri Dei
ludìbrio della plebe
reso scherzo d'ognun, vinto, ed oppresso.
Fatto servo ben vil dell'altrui glorie
argomento felice a nuove storie. (3.10.57)

(Stars, you won. Here is an example to the world
of your inconstancy. Here is a monarch,
who alone boasted of mightiness
similar to your gods,
made a plaything of commoners,

a joke among everyone,
defeated and oppressed.
He is made a simple servant of others' glories,
a happy topic for new stories.)

Recalling the language of exemplarity ("ecco un esempio"), Motezuma's invocation of the power of historical record appears self-aware in its recognition of how histories are assembled, authorized, and made available to posterity. Such attachment to the language and experience of loss further erodes Motezuma's sense of identity in his next utterance: "Where is my daughter? Where is my throne? I am no longer a father, a king I am no more" ("Dov'è la Figlia? Dov'è il mio Trono? / Non son più Padre; più Rè non sono"; 3.10.57). Musically dramatized in the words "figlia," "trono," and "padre" are octave leaps Motezuma makes from high notes to low notes – sonic manifestations of the emperor's collapse from power.

After a final thwarted attempt to refuse Fernando's authority, Motezuma accepts the joining of Aztec and Spanish bloodlines via his daughter's marriage. He views her union with Fernando's brother Ramiro not as the end of his empire but as the beginning of a new chapter in its history. In tones of pause and introspection, Motezuma sings alone the opera's final historical prophecy: "From your gods great truths are born. Mexico falls, it is true, but then it will rise again" ("Ne' vostri Dei gran verità si scorge. / Cade il Messico è ver, ma poi risorge"; 3.12.60). A farewell formed at the crossroads of shame and disappointment, Motezuma's final lament doubles as an expression of empowering resistance. While the opera's concluding image – as per the conventions of *opera seria*[50] – is that of a happy marriage between Mexican and Spanish genealogies, what remains in the listener's ear is Motezuma's gift of the non-narratable, "a momentary glimpse of what history looks like from the perspective of the losers."[51] It is not New Spain that will triumph, but Mexico that will rise again.

Coda: The Afterlives of History- and World-Making Masculinities

To return to the lament that initiated this analysis, the nobleman who reacted negatively to the world premiere of Vivaldi's *Motezuma* in Carpentier's novel, wherein "el indiano" rises from his seat shouting "False, false, false, all is false" ("¡Falso, falso, falso; todo falso!"),[52] has every reason to question the opera's poetically licensed reception of history. When accused of disrespecting the past, the figure of Vivaldi in *Concierto barroco* defends opera's natural right to invent and recreate, scoffing back: "Opera is not a historian's business … Don't bug me with history in theatre. What matters here is the poetic illusion" ("La ópera no es cosa de historiadores … No me joda con la Historia en materia de teatro. Lo que cuenta aquí es la ilusión poética").[53] The Afro-Cuban servant Filomeno observes his still outraged Mexican master, and thus seeks to remind him of the liberating potential of theatrical fiction:

> ¿Y qué se busca con la ilusión escénica, si no sacarnos de donde estamos para llevarnos a donde no podríamos llegar por propria voluntad? … Gracias al teatro podemos remontarnos en el tiempo y vivir, cosa imposible para nuestra carne presente, en épocas por siempre idas.[54]
>
> (And what does one look for in scenic illusion if not to remove ourselves from where we are in order to be transported to where we could not reach by our own will? … Thanks to the theatre, we can travel back in time and live in periods forever gone, an impossible feat for our present flesh.)

Neither the composer nor the servant is misled in his defence of the creative arts: musical-poetic illusion is as vital to the historical fantasies of Carpentier's fictional Vivaldi as it is to the ambitious hopes of Vivaldi's fictional Motezuma.

While *Motezuma* is only one example of how fascinations with the New World played out on the Baroque stage, there remain many others awaiting critical dialogues with discourses from early modern ethnography, anthropology, cartography, and political history. Just as *Motezuma* attempts a revision of the global past that lends sympathetic attention to the heroes who have suffered harm, so too does critical examination of historical operas and their afterlives afford spectators the opportunity to trace revised accounts of power and authority, and listen carefully to the stories they have to tell.

NOTES

1 "¿Y, para usted, la Historia de América no es grande ni respetable?"; Carpentier, *Concierto barroco*, 104. Here and henceforth all translations are my own, unless otherwise indicated.

2 Carpentier, *Concierto barroco*, 67.

3 Shohat and Stam, *Unthinking Eurocentrism*, 3.

4 Cusick, "'There Was Not One Lady,'" 36–7.

5 "L'opéra est affaire de femmes. Non, pas une version féministe; non, pas une libération. Tout au contraire: elles souffrent, elles crient, elles meurent";

Clément, *L'opéra, ou la défaite des femmes*, 24. Translation is from Clément, *Opera, or the Undoing of Women*, 11. See also McClary, *Feminine Endings*, 80–111.

6 Updated editions of the Italian translation appeared in 1704, 1715, and 1733, the year of *Motezuma*'s premiere in Venice. Chávez-Bárcenas, "Vivaldi's *Motezuma*," 291n9. For other source materials for the opera, see Espíndola Mata, "*Motezuma*, la ópera mexica."

7 Keen, *The Aztec Image*, 179.

8 For "historiography and patriotism" in the case of Spain, see Cañizares-Esguerra, *How to Write the History of the New World*, 130–203.

9 The emphasis throughout this article is on *Motezuma*'s libretto, since what remains of the original score is, unfortunately, incomplete, save for the still intact second act. On the assembly of the opera's texts, Steffen Voss has suggested that "the three acts were most probably originally preserved as separate volumes, for otherwise it is difficult to explain how complete gatherings from the end of Act I and the start of Act III have been lost"; "Antonio Vivaldi's Dramma per Musica *Motezuma*," 2.

10 Whittaker, "Performing Masculinity," 13.

11 Carrigan, Connell, and Lee, "Toward a New Sociology of Masculinity," 552.

12 My use of the term "envoice," to refer to the means through which characters are endowed with authorial vocality, draws upon Carolyn Abbate's study "Opera; or, the Envoicing of Women." For similar applications of this term, see Heller, *Emblems of Eloquence*, 263–94; Cusick, "Re-Voicing Arianna."

13 Horodowich, *The Venetian Discovery of America*, 173–218, at 175. Barbara Mundy has similarly noted how, in maps of the Aztec capital, "the houses of Tenochtitlan appear in careful rows on canals, making the city look like Venice. The Aztec city clearly evoked this maritime nation in the minds of Europeans"; "Mapping the Aztec Capital," 25.

14 Chapelle Wojciehowski, *Group Identity*, 301.

15 Hester, "Baroque Italian Epic," 272.

16 Quint, *Epic and Empire*, 9–10.

17 Maehder, "Alvise Giusti's Libretto *Motezuma*," 63.

18 Olivas, "Reinterpreting the Conquest of Mexico," 136.

19 Ingraham, So, and Moodley, "Introduction: Opera, Multiculturalism, and Coloniality," 9.

20 Welch, *A Theater of Diplomacy*, 2.

21 Bokina, "Deity, Beast, and Tyrant," 63.

22 Feldman, *Opera and Sovereignty*, 6.

23 Heller, "Venice's Mythic Empires," 36–40; Rosand, *Opera in Seventeenth-Century Venice*, 110–24.

24 Heller, "Venice's Mythic Empires," 41.

25 Locke, *Music and the Exotic*, 258–60.

26 Quint, *Epic and Empire*, 104.

27 Wiegman, "Unmaking," 40.
28 Koestenbaum, *The Queen's Throat*, 187.
29 Giusti, *Motezuma*, 1.1.9. Henceforth, citations from this work will be incorporated into the text (listed by act, scene, and page number).
30 Dufendach, "'As If His Heart Died,'" 633.
31 Bates, *Masculinity, Gender and Identity*, 8.
32 Schiesari, *The Gendering of Melancholia*, ix.
33 Polzonetti, *Italian Opera*, 109.
34 Waling, "Rethinking Masculinity Studies," 91.
35 Berggren, "Sticky Masculinity," 15.
36 Berlant, *The Female Complaint*, 19.
37 Comay, "Paradoxes of Lament," 257.
38 Roof, *What Gender Is*, vii.
39 Schrock and Schwalbe, "Men, Masculinity, and Manhood Acts," 281.
40 Curry Woods, *Weeping for Dido*, 11.
41 Kimmel, "Invisible Masculinity," 29.
42 Strohm, *Dramma per Musica*, 18.
43 McClary, "Soprano Masculinities," 40 and 41. Feldman's analysis of the castrati's "bravura singing" at the technical level as a "measure of victory and defeat" (*The Castrato*, 134) resonates with *Motezuma*'s representation of conquest in performance.
44 McClary, *Desire and Pleasure*, 90.
45 Feldman, *The Castrato*, 80.
46 Dame, "Unveiled Voices," 144.
47 McClary, *Desire and Pleasure*, 116.
48 Chávez-Bárcenas, "Vivaldi's *Motezuma*," 292.
49 Springer, *Armour and Masculinity*, 160.
50 Maehder, "Alvise Giusti's Libretto *Motezuma*," 72.
51 Quint, "Voices of Resistance," 116.
52 Carpentier, *Concierto barroco*, 102.
53 Carpentier, *Concierto barroco*, 102, 103–4.
54 Carpentier, *Concierto barroco*, 110.

WORKS CITED

Abbate, Carolyn. "Opera; or, the Envoicing of Women." In Ruth A. Solie, ed., *Musicology and Difference: Gender and Sexuality in Music Scholarship*. Berkeley: University of California Press, 1993, 225–58.

Bates, Catherine. *Masculinity, Gender and Identity in the English Renaissance Lyric*. Cambridge: Cambridge University Press, 2007.

Berggren, Kalle. "Sticky Masculinity: Post-structuralism, Phenomenology and Subjectivity in Critical Studies on Men." *Men and Masculinities* 17.3 (2014): 231–52.

Berlant, Lauren. *The Female Complaint: The Unfinished Business of Sentimentality in American Culture*. Durham, NC: Duke University Press, 2008.

Bokina, John. "Deity, Beast, and Tyrant: Images of the Prince in the Operas of Monteverdi." *International Political Science Review* 12.1 (1991): 48–66.

Cañizares-Esguerra, Jorge. *How to Write the History of the New World: Histories, Epistemologies, and Identities in the Eighteenth-Century Atlantic World*. Stanford: Stanford University Press, 2001.

Carpentier, Alejo. *Concierto barroco* [1974]. Mexico City: Lectorum, 2003.

Carrigan, Tim, Bob Connell, and John Lee. "Toward a New Sociology of Masculinity." *Theory and Society* 14.5 (1985): 551–604.

Chapelle Wojciehowski, Hannah. *Group Identity in the Renaissance World*. Cambridge: Cambridge University Press, 2011.

Chávez-Bárcenas, Ireri E. "Vivaldi's *Motezuma*: The Conquest of Mexico on the Venetian Operatic Stage." In Elizabeth Horodowich and Lia Markey, eds., *The New World in Early Modern Italy, 1492–1750*. Cambridge: Cambridge University Press, 2017, 288–308.

Clément, Catherine. *L'opéra, ou la défaite des femmes*. Paris: Grasset, 1979.

– *Opera, or the Undoing of Women*, trans. Betsy Wing. Minneapolis: University of Minnesota Press, 1988.

Comay, Rebecca. "Paradoxes of Lament: Benjamin and Hamlet." In Ilit Ferber and Paula Schwebel, eds., *Lament in Jewish Thought: Philosophical, Theological, and Literary Perspectives*. Berlin: De Gruyter, 2014, 257–75.

Curry Woods, Marjorie. *Weeping for Dido: The Classics in the Medieval Classroom*. Princeton: Princeton University Press, 2019.

Cusick, Suzanne G. "Re-Voicing Arianna (and Laments): Two Women Respond." *Early Music* 27.3 (1999): 437–49.

– "'There Was Not One Lady Who Failed to Shed a Tear': Arianna's Lament and the Construction of Modern Womanhood." *Early Music* 22.1 (1994): 21–43.

Dame, Joke. "Unveiled Voices: Sexual Difference and the Castrato." In Philip Brett, Elizabeth Wood, and Gary C. Thomas, eds., *Queering the Pitch: The New Gay and Lesbian Musicology*. London: Routledge, 2006, 139–53.

Dufendach, Rebecca. "'As If His Heart Died': A Reinterpretation of Moteuczoma's Cowardice in the Conquest History of the Florentine Codex." *Ethnohistory* 66.4 (2019): 623–45.

Espíndola Mata, Laura Elizabeth. "*Motezuma*, la ópera mexica de Antonio Vivaldi y Girolamo Giusti." *Investigación Teatral: Revista de artes escénicas y performatividad* 11.18 (2020): 121–44.

Feldman, Martha. *The Castrato: Reflections on Natures and Kinds*. Berkeley: University of California Press, 2016.

– *Opera and Sovereignty: Transforming Myths in Eighteenth-Century Italy*. Chicago: University of Chicago Press, 2007.

Giusti, Alvise (Luigi). *Motezuma, drama per musica*. Venice: Marino Rossetti, 1733.

Heller, Wendy. *Emblems of Eloquence: Opera and Women's Voices in Seventeenth-Century Venice*. Berkeley: University of California Press, 2004.

– "Venice's Mythic Empires: Truth and Verisimilitude in Venetian Opera." In Victoria Johnson, Jane F. Fulcher, and Thomas Ertman, eds., *Opera and Society in Italy and France from Monteverdi to Bourdieu*. Cambridge: Cambridge University Press, 2007, 34–52.

Hester, Nathalie. "Baroque Italian Epic from Granada to the New World: Columbus Conquers the Moors." In Elizabeth Horodowich and Lia Markey, eds., *The New World in Early Modern Italy, 1492–1750*. Cambridge: Cambridge University Press, 2017, 270–87.

Horodowich, Elizabeth. *The Venetian Discovery of America: Geographic Imagination and Print Culture in the Age of Encounters*. Cambridge: Cambridge University Press, 2018.

Ingraham, Mary I., Joseph K. So, and Roy Moodley. "Introduction: Opera, Multiculturalism, and Coloniality." In Mary I. Ingraham, Joseph K. So, and Roy Moodley, eds. *Opera in a Multicultural World: Coloniality, Culture, Performance*. London: Routledge, 2016, 1–17.

Keen, Benjamin. *The Aztec Image in Western Thought*. New Brunswick, NJ: Rutgers University Press, 1971.

Kimmel, Michael S. "Invisible Masculinity." *Society* 30 (1993): 28–35.

Koestenbaum, Wayne. *The Queen's Throat: Opera, Homosexuality, and the Mystery of Desire*. New York: Poseidon Press, 1993.

Locke, Ralph P. *Music and the Exotic from the Renaissance to Mozart*. Cambridge: Cambridge University Press, 2015.

Maehder, Jürgen. "Alvise Giusti's Libretto *Motezuma* and the Conquest of Mexico in Eighteenth-Century Italian *Opera Seria*." In Michael Talbot, ed., *Vivaldi, "Motezuma" and the Opera Seria: Essays on a Newly Discovered Work and Its Background*. Turnhout: Brepols, 2008, 63–80.

McClary, Susan. *Desire and Pleasure in Seventeenth-Century Music*. Berkeley: University of California Press, 2012.

– *Feminine Endings: Music, Gender and Sexuality*. Minneapolis: University of Minnesota Press, 1991.

– "Soprano Masculinities." In Philip Purvis, ed., *Masculinity in Opera: Gender, History, and New Musicology*. London: Routledge, 2013, 33–50.

Mundy, Barbara E. "Mapping the Aztec Capital: The 1524 Nuremberg Map of Tenochtitlan, Its Sources and Meanings." *Imago Mundi* 50 (1998): 11–33.

Olivas, Aaron Alejandro. "Reinterpreting the Conquest of Mexico for an Enlightenment Audience in Vivaldi's Opera *Motezuma* (1733)." In Jimena Rodríguez and Manuel Pérez, eds., *Amicitia fecunda: Estudios en homenaje a Claudia Parodi*. Madrid: Iberoamericana, 2015, 135–51.

Polzonetti, Pierpaolo. *Italian Opera in the Age of the American Revolution*. Cambridge: Cambridge University Press, 2011.

Purvis, Philip, ed. *Masculinity in Opera: Gender, History, and New Musicology*. London: Routledge, 2013.

Quint, David. *Epic and Empire: Politics and Generic Form from Virgil to Milton*. Princeton: Princeton University Press, 1993.

– "Voices of Resistance: The Epic Curse and Camões's Adamastor." *Representations* 27 (1989): 111–41.

Roof, Judith. *What Gender Is, What Gender Does*. Minneapolis: University of Minnesota Press, 2016.

Rosand, Ellen. *Opera in Seventeenth-Century Venice: The Creation of a Genre*. Berkeley: University of California Press, 1991.

Schiesari, Juliana. *The Gendering of Melancholia: Feminism, Psychoanalysis, and the Symbolics of Loss in Renaissance Literature*. Ithaca: Cornell University Press, 1992.

Schrock, Douglas, and Michael Schwalbe. "Men, Masculinity, and Manhood Acts." *Annual Review of Sociology* 35 (2009): 277–95.

Shohat, Ella, and Robert Stam. *Unthinking Eurocentrism: Multiculturalism and the Media*. New York: Routledge, 2014.

Springer, Carolyn. *Armour and Masculinity in the Italian Renaissance*. Toronto: University of Toronto Press, 2010.

Strohm, Reinhard. *Dramma per Musica: Italian Opera Seria of the Eighteenth Century*. New Haven: Yale University Press, 1997.

Voss, Steffen. "Antonio Vivaldi's Dramma per Musica *Motezuma*: Some Observations on Its Libretto and Music." In Michael Talbot, ed., *Vivaldi, "Motezuma" and the Opera Seria: Essays on a Newly Discovered Work and Its Background*. Turnhout: Brepols, 2008, 1–18.

Waling, Andrea. "Rethinking Masculinity Studies: Feminism, Masculinity, and Poststructural Accounts of Agency and Emotional Reflexivity." *The Journal of Men's Studies* 27.1 (2019): 89–107.

Welch, Ellen R. *A Theater of Diplomacy: International Relations and the Performing Arts in Early Modern France*. Philadelphia: University of Pennsylvania Press, 2017.

Whittaker, Kate. "Performing Masculinity/Masculinity in Performance." In Philip Purvis, ed., *Masculinity in Opera: Gender, History, and New Musicology*. London: Routledge, 2013, 9–30.

Wiegman, Robyn. "Unmaking: Men and Masculinity in Feminist Theory." In Judith Kegan Gardiner, ed., *Masculinity Studies and Feminist Theory*. New York: Columbia University Press, 2002, 31–59.

8 Male Courtly Feeling and the Historical Performativity of Shyness in *A Midsummer Night's Dream*

TIFFANY HOFFMAN

Summary: This paper contends that the trait of modesty stereotypically aligned with female erotic restraint became emotionally reconfigured as a male virtue guiding public performative displays of masculine civility. The article turns to the representation of Bottom and the other mechanicals to illuminate the prehistory of modesty as a male theatrical affect that began developing experientially through the English stage and other correlative sociopolitical venues, including the court. The Shakespearean theatre promoted the cultivation of male modesty as a publicly induced performative feeling that could either sustain or come to threaten the successful construction of masculinity. In this way, the stage further contributed to modern psychological and medical understandings of shyness as a theatrically ceded emotion born of modesty, as that state evolved in relation to performance anxiety and dramaturgical pressures surrounding the public display of male bodies and selves.

When Helena finds herself confronted by an angry and abandoned Hermia, she retorts back: "have you no modesty, no maiden shame, / No touch of bashfulness?" and then, in light of the harsh array of insults Hermia hurls at her, she proceeds to ask: "what, will you tear / Impatient answers from my gentle tongue?" (3.2.285–7).[1] Helena's words bring to light the emotional contours characteristic of both her and Hermia's maidenly dispositions, predicated as they are on a sense of modesty that operates in tandem with the other related emotional states of shame and bashfulness to curb the "gentle tongue" and inhibit the emboldened dictates of lively female action. It is all the more perplexing, when, by the fifth act of the play, Duke Theseus compares the "tongue-tied simplicity" and timidity of the mechanicals to the "modesty" he has witnessed during a courtly encounter (5.1.101–4). Paralysed by fear and unable to speak in his presence, the "great clerics," as he describes them, who greet the duke shiver, turn pale, and "make periods in the midst of sentences" (5.1.93–6).

A Midsummer Night's Dream, as Ronda Arab observes, takes as one of its central preoccupations the overarching question of "what it is to be a man." The play deals directly with the fomentation of cultural definitions of manliness at a pivotal time when conceptions of masculinity were beginning to be reconfigured, moving away from a battlefield ethos characterized by isolated acts of heroism and violence towards a new ideal of "gentleman-like civility" defined in the social world of the court. The mechanicals, as Arab suggests, exhibit an "intensely-felt pressure" to prove to the elite courtly audience that they are "made men," capable of the same codified behaviours conditioning aristocratic gentlemen.[2] However, as their stage fright reveals, they ultimately fail in this endeavour, displaying the effeminizing range of fear, modesty, and vocal reserve, sculpting the bashful affective parameters of early modern female identity. Shakespeare's representation of fearful bashfulness as a lived experiential facet of the tongue-tied mechanicals in *A Midsummer Night's Dream* invites a broader investigation into the emotional culture of modesty and shyness in early modernity that this article seeks to illuminate. During this especially formative time in the history of masculinity, the play reflects the social and cultural movements that led the quality of modesty to shift away from its traditional encoding in the emotional life of women to eventually dovetail with "competing ideologies of the ontology of manhood" in the early modern period.[3]

Theseus' observation that the stage replicates the same affective conditions fostering the arousal of modesty at court speaks to the cultural movements emerging in early modernity that allowed for the flourishing of shyness and for its emotional evolution in men as a controversial psychological state that, if not regulated, could threaten the stable construction of masculine identity. The play stages a dynamic interplay between the court and the commercial theatre – two parallel social spheres, or emergent "publics," where the cultural formation of early modern manhood was being renegotiated.[4] Shakespeare's portrayal of the bashful stage-frightened mechanicals, and his overblown depiction of Bottom as an emboldened player – whose performance of Pyramus is preconditioned by an earlier dream of himself as a modest and refined courtier – reveals how shyness began developing as a male emotion in response to shifting gender norms and new modes of embodiment, performativity, social interaction, and judgment shaping the development of masculinity in the court and theatre. As the article contends, it was out of these analogous early modern patriarchal social environments, centred on corresponding modalities surrounding the public performative construction of masculinity, that shyness began to emerge as a complex affect in relation to modern notions of performance anxiety.

Modest Men and Courtly Encounters

At the turn of the sixteenth century, economic and political changes began motivating a movement away from the medieval militaristic and aristocratic household in the country to the court. The move to a more quasi-urban way of life led to a transformation of the image of manhood in the Renaissance, as Jennifer Vaught maintains, inaugurating a pronounced dispositional shift in the aristocracy, "from a class of violent warriors to more civilized courtiers with comparatively little militaristic experience."[5] Men were no longer competing for honour through chivalric feats; instead, they fought for office in the gentlemanly social world of *Civil Conversation*. Taught to elite men through tracts on manners, civil conversation was the art of presenting oneself in a courteous fashion during a social encounter. Tracts on male conduct promoted the cultural formation of masculinity by detailing new forms of embodiment and social comportment geared towards constructing a civilized version of the Renaissance gentleman. Giovanni Della Casa (1503–1556) explains that "dirty, foul, repulsive or disgusting things are not to be done in the presence of others, nor should they even be mentioned." The repugnant effluents of the lower body, mouth, and nose are brought to the fore: "It is an indecent habit practised by some people who, in full view of others, place their hands on whatever part of their body it pleases them. Similarly, it is not proper for a well-mannered gentleman to prepare to relieve his physical needs in the presence of others." While eating and conversing, men must "abstain during that entire time from spitting, coughing and, even more, from sneezing ... there are also some who cough or sneeze so loudly that they deafen everybody. And some who are so indiscreet in such actions that they spray those near them in the face." As Della Casa maintains, "all of these vulgar manners are to be avoided because they are bothersome to the ear and to the eye."[6] Masculine identity was being crafted and sustained in the court through refined bodily techniques as well as new technologies of social interaction, and was now understood as "a function of one's (actual or potential) proximity to bodies possessing publicness," wherein male selves became subject to intense forms of visibility and judgment.[7] The spectacularized display of proper comportment held open the competitive capacity to advance one's social reputation and political status. As Della Casa mentions, there are "many men who, though not worthy of high praise in other things, nevertheless are or have been highly esteemed only by reason of their pleasant manner. Thus helped and sustained, they have attained high rank."[8] Male prowess was no longer evaluated by an untamed, violent, bloody or scarred body, but rather by the public display of what Mikhail Bakhtin identifies as a closed bodily *habitus* governed by developing intrapsychic controls over its own somatic impulses.[9] In order to advance socially and politically, men now had to demonstrate superior rule over themselves so that their government of others would be deemed prudent.

A temperate ideal was encouraged as the cornerstone of an attractive male image geared towards sociopolitical promotion. As Thomas Wright declares, while "in great assemblies, or at such times as most men mark our action, words, and gestures, then if a man have occasion of choler, lust, pride, fear, or such like passion, if he refrain but a little, all those will at least suspect that he permitteth not his passions to whollie overrune him."[10] Challenges to aristocratic masculinity "included challenges to the ideal of the closed controlled body and the idea that evident corporeal passions reflected a degenerate or not fully developed manhood."[11] Cultural medical tracts of the period therefore sought to recondition unruly passions and bodily expressivity. In *The Touchstone of Complexions*, for instance, Levinus Lemnius (1505–1568) explains to men predisposed to cold complexions – who "have faltering tongues, and nothing ready in utterance, a soft and womanish voice [and who] ... are fearful and timorous" – how to "frame themselves to a very commendable order and civil behavior." He explains the marks and tokens of a gentleman:

> His manner and conversation, honest and virtuous, his nature quiet, courteous, subject to no ill affections ... In him plentifully appeareth humanity, gentlenesse, frugality, equity, modesty, and a continent moderation of all affections. He is not brought into fear, but suffereth all the discommodities of life with a minde stoute, cheerful, invincible ... And not only in the inward mind of man do these ornaments and gifts of nature appear, but even in the outward show, shape, and behavior of the body there is evidently perceived a comely grace and portly dignity ... The head not aslope, the port and state of the body bolt upright, the tongue prompt and ready, able to pronounce and deliver out words of gallant utterance.[12]

As Lemnius describes, it is the sense of modesty that works to temper unruly male affections in public so that a disciplined and confident demeanour – evinced especially during conversation – can be achieved. The quality of "modest shamefastness" already held widespread cultural currency as a form of psycho-emotional regulation that maintained female chastity and defended against shame and social dishonour by acting as a curb on unethical sexual impulses in women. The conduct author Barnabe Rich (ca. 1540–1617) explains modesty as that specific emotion through which "a women guides herself by the zeale of her honor and the bridle of shamefastness."[13] Women's fear of shame, explains Richard Braithwaite, "serveth as a restraint to withhold them from those abillimentes that breed suspect of honesty. For bashfulness it is that moderates their thoughts, makes them modest in their speeches, temperate in their actions, and warie in all their deliberations."[14] Having been linked with female restraint, the *bridle of shame* – through which maids felt their bodily, vocal, and sexual instincts to be literally held fast or inhibited by the emotion – began taking on a new association with male civility, affect, and behaviour at court.

The implementation of novel forms of bodily and emotional control went hand in hand with what Norbert Elias describes as advancing thresholds of embarrassment in court society. There is now, as Elias suggests, a heightening of the "feeling of shame when one's own functions are exposed to the gaze of others."[15] The possibility of humiliation, infamy, and publicly offensive behaviour became a growing concern of the courtier, whose successful construction of politically ready masculinity was now being socially judged through his own ability to publicly act out a range of scripted behaviours before other men as well as curb his natural brutishness. Men now required, according to Thomas Elyot, the cultivation of shame as "a bridle for the continent restraint of wayward appetites."[16] Wright likewise notes that in many men "there is great resemblance and affinity with other beasts." Shamefastness it is that "aids the civil gentleman and prudent politician in restraining their inordinate motions, [so that he may win] a gracious carriage of himself, and [render] his conversation most grateful to men."[17] Once considered an affective trait that categorically defined female sexual difference, modesty was becoming emotionally reconfigured as an intrapsychic facet of masculine experience; indeed, regarded as a virtuous state – an obvious affective marking of a male *sense of shame* that governed the successful performance of civilized masculinity at court. As cultural mandates for male conduct and categories of publicity and judgment became more stringent, however, modesty began to infiltrate the emotional functionality of the courtier in an extreme and threatening way.

Bashful Courtiers and Theatrical Performance

Stefano Guazzo likened the courtly world of civil conversation to a "stage, we the players present the comedie, and the gods the lookers on."[18] The courtier was like a player who consciously shaped his social role to please the audience that watched him perform. As a facet of his political advancement, the courtier had to be constantly restraining his own brutish impulses and self-reflectively analysing his socially codified behaviours in relation to an extended audience of others. The courtier, notes Anna Bryson, "must scrutinize himself in the constant awareness of a social audience whom he may offend."[19] As the courtier's web of actions grew more complex, fears of shame and social degradation – "the fear that one's behavior will cause others to express disdain or withdraw their approval" – were becoming rampant in the psychical life of the courtier, to the extent that the moderate level of modesty upheld as a sign of male virtue and control became unruly.[20] Turning excessive, the curb of shame undergirding the courtier's social performance advanced into the very state that it was supposed to protect against – an emasculating and degenerate display of modest shamefastness. William Fiston explains that "shamefastness is a virtue so as it be moderate; but to be overbashful and ashamed to show his face is a fault also."[21] Noticing the high levels of performative pressure, fear, and anxiety at court, conduct authors began posing continual objections to over-bashfulness and warned the gentleman not to be so self-consciously concerned with the judgments of others. James Cleland likewise advises the courtier against "a foolish shamefastness in hanging down of his head," stuttering, and "blushing at every light word."[22] As the bridle of shame developed disparagingly through the court in relation to an excessive state of modesty, the insulting term *shy colt* became widely applied to bashful courtiers, who – akin to uncivilized beasts – unable to rule their passions, displayed an inordinate level of inhibition and timidity during conversation with other men.[23]

The idea of the public performative self has been most fully expounded by Erving Goffman, who drew upon the ideas of symbolic interactionism to develop his dramaturgical analysis of social life where face-to-face encounters were conducted like a performance on stage and social actors became careful to monitor the impressions they gave of themselves to others. Sociologist Susie Scott has built upon Goffman to develop her dramaturgical account of shyness, suggesting how the shy person simply begins to feel as if he cannot carry off the performance convincingly.[24] Goffman's performative art of impression management may seem a universal characteristic of human society;

however, as Stephen Mennell has noted, Elias would argue that the extent to which the sensitivity to shame and public humiliation in court society, and its link to the struggle for political prestige, had become exceptional, fostered an affective atmosphere of fear and inhibition amongst the noblemen drawn to it.[25] As if noticing the performative pressure placed on the courtier, Antoine de Courtin advises his readers "that having performed our formalities and paid those respects [to] a person of quality ... we are afterwards not to show any awe or timorousness before him but speak freely and ingeniously to him." Finding social timidity to be grounded in the gentleman's "immoderate desire of being exact" and experiencing too great a pressure to present the proper public role, the courtier could become vocally and somatically incapacitated and "rigid" with the fear of disgrace. Appearing "ridiculous to everybody," as Courtin notes, the courtier's bashfulness led to a behavioural breakdown in the performative constitution of controlled manhood, as worries over how the self was appearing and fears of embarrassment during conversation began taking over the mind, body, and voice of the subject.[26]

Eve Sedgwick has suggested that shame be considered the preeminent theatrical emotion; yet shyness – which takes as its starting point the capacity to think about and imagine oneself through the eyes of others, and which can therefore come to fruition only through an anticipated or actualized audience of gazing spectators – may be more accurately rendered in dramaturgical terms. The histrionically aroused contours of male modesty, wherein the performative capabilities of the courtier began to disintegrate before an audience of onlookers into a gestural display of inhibiting bodily and vocal expressions – enacted through stereotypically feminized forms of stuttering, blushing, and gaze aversion – inevitably gave rise to the conceptual development of shyness and its modern counterpart of "performance anxiety."[27] The early modern evolution of a performative phenomenology of shyness comes more obviously to the fore when Shakespeare compares "a bashful lover" to "an unperfect actor upon the stage / who with his feare is put besides his part."[28] *A Midsummer Night's Dream* illuminates the emotional reconfiguration of shyness as a performative category of emotional experience that was developing through the early modern theatre, but which began stretching experientially into the public domain of the court. Advancing through the emotional life of the Shakespearean theatre was a modern form of shyness, which became ideologically, affectively, and conceptually refined in relation to the novel phenomenon of stage fright and in response to the all-male stage's corresponding investment in the performative construction of masculinity.

Players, Publicity, and Performance Anxiety

It is from within the performative social context of the court that Duke Theseus' observation emerges, wherein he compares the stage fright of the mechanicals to the extreme modesty he has witnessed during a courtly encounter:

Where I have come great clerks have purposed
To greet me with premeditated welcomes,
Where I have seen them shiver and look pale,
Make periods in the midst of sentences,
Throttle their practiced accent in their fears,
And in conclusion dumbly have broke of,
Not paying me a welcome,
And in the modesty of fearful duty
I read as much from the rattling tongue
Of saucy and audacious eloquence.
Love, therefore, and tongue-tied simplicity
In least speak most to my capacity. (5.1.93–105)

Like the courtiers and the clerics who encounter the duke in his elite sociopolitical world, the mechanicals now find themselves overcome by the same bashful fear of losing face while under the duke's scrutiny. Tongue-tied before an audience of elite spectators, Quince "loses his grip upon the punctuation of his speech when faced with an actual audience," as Evelyn Tribble observes. Just as Starveling-as-Moonshine "is so disconcerted by the audience that he simply repeats his lines": "this lantern doth the horned moon present." Further comments render him dumb until Lysander instructs him to continue: "Proceed moon" (5.1.235, 239, 250).[29] The performance of *Pyramus and Thisbe* is upended by a series of cajoling interruptions from the courtly audience that bring to light the harsh emotional realities of the playhouse as an emerging public sphere marked by new forms of male publicity, performativity, and social judgment, and which therefore operated as an analogous patriarchally encoded cultural site to the court that fostered socially anxious modes of feeling as it worked to redefine masculinity as a dramatically constituted category.

The public playhouse – predicated as it was on the codification of male performance – operated like the court as a symbolic order possessing the capacity to successfully instate a player's emergence into the realm of full manhood. The nascent conceptualization of the stage as an emergent site for the genesis of masculinity is brought to the fore by the mechanicals during their first rehearsal. It is here where they are given their parts and where they express both their excitements and anxieties regarding the stage as a public domain that could either engender one's manhood or endanger its very constitution. When Flute is given the part of Thisbe, he is first thrilled because he thinks Thisbe is a brave "knight," and so playing him would secure his transition from youth to manhood. However, when it becomes apparent that Thisbe is, in fact, the woman's part, Flute is dejected because he "has a beard coming" (1.2.39, 41–2). Coppelia Kahn has observed that Shakespeare's "male characters are engaged in a continuous struggle, first to secure a masculine identity, then to be productive in it."[30] For Flute to take on the role of Thisbe would return him to a state of infantile regression and pre-pubescent effeminacy, rather than propel him into the arena of adult masculinity that his coming beard signifies.[31] Bottom suggests that he could more confidently take on the role of Thisbe because his performance of her would be exactly that – a performance – more obviously illusory in terms of his own status as a grown man. However, when he is offered the part of Pyramus, Bottom initially feels threatened and questions whether "Pyramus [is] a lover or a tyrant?" Bottom is hesitant about acting out Pyramus because playing him might potentially pose a challenge to his "chief humor [which] is for a tyrant," and a lover is more effeminate and emotional (1.2.19, 24). Although Bottom evinces a common form of actorly exhibitionism and narcissistic vanity, demonstrated through his self-gratifying ability to play any part, he evokes a range of typically male roles built upon earlier paradigms of violence, aggression, and heroic manhood more suited to his "humor," in large part because he feels that playing the "condoling" role of Pyramus will put his masculine identity in jeopardy (1.2.35). As he proclaims, "I could play Erecles rarely," or "a part to tear a cat in to make all split" (1.1.25). Quince must reconfirm to Bottom that Pyramus will pose no threat to his manhood; moreover, since Pyramus is a "a sweet-faced man; a proper man … a most lovely gentlemanlike man," whose character is shaped from emergent ideals of gentleman civility at court, Bottom's ability to confidently perform this new image of masculine perfection on the courtly stage holds out the potential to reshape and secure his identity in light of shifting cultural definitions of manliness (1.2.77–9). It is only after Quince validates Pyramus as a paragon of the new ideal of a what a man should be that Bottom agrees to play him, confirming, "well, I will undertake it" (1.2.80).

As Meredith Skura observes, "from Bottom's point of view, the play is primarily a means of pleasing the duke," and his performance of Pyramus does hold out an opportunity for an otherwise impossible encounter as well as conversational exchange with him.[32] Undergirding the theatrical meeting between Bottom and the duke is Shakespeare's repositioning of the stage as a complementary site that began to reflect the performative production of masculinity at court. The idea of the theatre as an evaluative space for male performance and validation is reconfirmed through Bottom's growing awareness that in order to garner promotion and esteem, along with the structuration of masculinity it affords – indeed, to become, as Bottom renders it, a "made man" earning sixpence a day – he must be able to fluidly speak with Theseus and perform before him the representation of elite masculinity encoded in the gentlemanly character of Pyramus (4.2.17, 20). Bottom's encounter with the duke illuminates the interrelational dynamics between the court and the theatre, and speaks to Paul Yachnin's claim about how the heterogeneity of the commercial playhouse began to offer "a corresponding advancement in the social condition of private people," proffering to them a new opportunity for "theatrical publicity" that allowed them to appear before and converse with elite members of society, perform before them, as well as share in the dialogic political life of the court by discussing and voicing their opinions about matters in the plays. The theatre in this way came to replicate the social, political, and gendered conditions of the early modern court, where masculine subjectivity was being redefined in relation to emergent forms of male theatricality and publicity, conversation, and social judgment. For, as Yachnin further maintains, Shakespeare crafted a theatre of "popular judgment" in which the people in the audience "were encouraged to judge the characters and the actions unfolding before them," and which, by extension, would have included assessment of the performance capabilities of the male actors themselves.[33]

If the courtier was a kind of player, the player, by extension, also reflected the courtier in his constant exposure to scrutiny. The actor, as Henry Chettle observed, is "publicke in every ones eye, talkt of in every vulgar man's mouth"; "no man need be more warie in his doings," for, according to John Earle, "the eyes of all men are upon him."[34] The extremity of visibility shaping the playhouse and the attention placed on the male actor would have held open the unique possibility for conferring theatrical publicity, as Yachnin observes.[35] On the other hand, the public nature of the theatre and its implementation of a culture of popular judgment and dialogic interaction likely led to the widespread emotional conditioning of fear, anxiety, and shame – performative emotions born from the possibility of negative theatrical discourse and appraisal.[36] Skura analyses the socio-emotional conditions of the theatre in psychoanalytic terms, maintaining that the playhouse was indeed a public domain that could fulfil the actor's "grandiose narcissism"; however, in this respect, it could also reopen "narcissistic wounds." Like a baby who looks to his mother, the male actor "looks not only to his role but also to his audience to fill his emptiness, to feed and sustain him with the attention and applause that he strives for"; but in this way, the object of admiration could potentially become a target for derision. The more "grandiose the original self-image, the worse the humiliation: the opposite of fame is shame."[37] By re-encoding the social, emotional, and gendered dynamics of the court through the space of the stage, *Dream* resituates the theatre as a corresponding site for male identity formation with the potential to arrest the genesis of masculinity through the intrapsychic production of modesty, performance anxiety, shyness, and their emotional transfiguration into stage fright – an infantilizing and effeminizing arrangement of male feelings generated through the playhouse, and in relation to its status as a preeminent performative platform affectively structured around male forms of publicity and social judgment.

Stage Fright, Tied Tongues, and Maternal Mouths

Psychoanalyst Steven Aaron equates acting to a bi-directional site of feeding. The actor feels a pressure to "feed the audience a good performance, while he is all too painfully aware of how much he depends on them to be fed with their applause, approval and recognition."[38] These "underlying oral incorporative fantasies" transform the stage into a narcissistic location that can return the player to the "oceanic bliss of maternal nurturance and holding, milk to drink, a cradling embrace, and a reassuring gaze."[39] As Kahn explains, the successful development of male identity is formed in this maternal space and depends in large part on the reciprocal gaze of the mother, and her own ability to allow her son "to experience a sense of magical omnipotence like that he enjoyed at the breast, [while] also help[ing] him to move from the kind of primitive identification with her that he began to experience in fantasies of incorporating and merging with her."[40] If the mother were to deprive her son of her gaze or too severely or prematurely remove him from her breast, she would cause a crisis of masculine identity formation, provoking a deep narcissistic wound or internalized state of rejection. At rehearsal, Bottom's worry over pleasing the duke and gaining his favour is extended to concerns over offending the future cohort of mothers in the elite audience. The artisans express nervousness that the women will "hang us, every mother's son" – a phrase that positions the stage as the maternal nexus of male individuation (1.2.70).

Displaying early signs of performance anxiety and fears of shame and infamy at rehearsal, the mechanicals believe that their performance will be so lifelike that it will frighten the ladies in the audience to the extent that they will negatively evaluate their performance. As Quince tells Bottom when he indulges his own narcissistic ability to play the lion's part: "an you should [roar] too terribly you would fright the Duchess and the ladies that they would shriek ... and if you should fright the ladies out of their wits they would have no more discretion but to hang us" (1.2.71–3). The artisans understand timidity as part of a feminine emotional response pattern, and so they make an attempt to qualify their own burgeoning fears of rejection by projecting their state of dread onto the women. In this way they further attempt to reconfigure the stage as a masculinizing entity and vehicle of sexual differentiation that will reconfirm their manhood via the generation of male forms of boldness and audacity. To protect themselves against the disfavour of the ladies, they next decide to insert a series of set-pieces that will reveal the truth behind their own theatrical illusion so that the women won't be scared or offended. The end result is that when they do arrive on stage, and *try* to speak to the audience, they simply deconstruct the entire performance along with their own acting capability, appearing tongue-tied and ridiculous. Hippolyta herself – though decidedly not afeard by the players – insults the mechanicals who are not able to carry off the performance of masculinity their roles attenuate, declaring, "this is the silliest stuff that ever I saw" (5.1.209). Her harsh theatrical rejection, and the mockery of the other courtiers, actualizes the mechanicals' earlier performance anxiety, provoking their extreme fear and modesty on the stage before the duke. They are not only emasculated by their stage fright and the exhibition of timidity they had earlier attributed to the women, they are also grossly infantilized. For, instead of validation and metaphoric feeding with maternal applause and recognition, the harsh insults of the female spectators, in particular, arouse in the artisans a developmentally regressive terror that replays on the stage the masculine crisis of being prematurely "detached from the supporting mother, of starving, and drying out (thirst and hunger not yet being separated), or even of suffocating."[41] As Skura observes, the remnants of this intrapsychic process come to the emotionalized surface in "adult state fright – or in everyday shyness ... [where] the actor is overcome by general paralysis ... feelings of being trapped, dryness of mouth, blushing ... the actor forgets his lines" or cannot speak.[42]

The performance of *Pyramus and Thisbe* serves not to foment or propel the artisans into manhood as they had expected, but instead threateningly deconstructs it. Through their stage fright they are emasculated, infantilized, turned into everything but men. They become "lesser-beasts," as Arab observes, whose modesty and fear are out of control and emotionally unregulated to the point at which Quince's bashfulness transforms him on the stage into a bridled, vocally inhibited, and tongue-tied "shy colt" nervously stopping and stuttering as he speaks.[43] When Quince is unable to get out his words, Lysander mockingly calls out how "he hath rid his prologue like a rough *colt*: he knows not the stop ... he hath played on this prologue like a child on a recorder: a sound, but not in government" (5.1.119–23; emphasis mine). The entire episode, as Theseus has pointed out, reproduces the performative conditions that arouse the modest courtier's shyness at court.

The feminization of the mechanicals is further rendered through the affective channelling of their frightful experience on stage through Hermia's dream – itself an unconscious product of the inhibiting bodily constraints internally developed through the biocultural conditioning of female modesty. Hermia's dream, as Norman Holland explains, is a psychical product of her earlier display of boldness before her father and the duke, as they reiterate to her the strictures accompanying the patriarchal imperatives of a forced marriage to Demetrius, whom she must marry or "live a barren sister ... / Chanting faint hymns to the cold fruitless moon" (1.1.73–4).[44] In the presence of these two men, Hermia bypasses the inhibiting expression of bashful reserve placed upon her "gentle tongue" to plead her thoughts and speak with regard to her own choice of Lysander (3.2.287). Her desire for him outweighs her culturally mandated emotional display of vocal restraint and shyness in the presence of men; as she asserts, "I know not by what power I am made bold, / Nor how it may concern my *modesty*" (1.1.59–60; emphasis mine). Despite her earlier boldness, however, the cultural enforcement of female shame seems to condition the patriarchally imposed dictates of her chastity in the wood, where her modesty takes precedence, now operating as a curb on her sexual impulses. After having eloped with Lysander, Hermia decides instead to safeguard her virtue for an arranged marriage and commands him, "gentle friend, for love and courtesy, / Lie further off in human modesty / Such separation ... becomes a virtuous bachelor and a maid" (2.2.62–5). The effect of her dream – grounded upon the constraints of maidenly inhibition – is a sexually repressive nightmare. As Hermia cries out:

> Help me, Lysander ...
> To pluck this crawling serpent from my breast!
> Ay me for pity. What a dream was here?
> Look how I do quake with fear.

> Methought a serpent ate my heart away,
> And you sat smiling at his cruel prey. (3.1.150–60)

Conditioned by Hermia's "enforced chastity," her dream produces a traumatic vision of herself engaged in a coerced marital union with Demetrius – whom she later refers to as a "serpent," an "adder" with a double tongue (3.2.190, 71–3). In her dream this serpent is crawling at her breast but, not being fed there, it must eat its way through her heart instead. The maternal image of a crawling baby, which might come from such an unwanted union – rejected at its mother's breast – is transformed into a hostile oral possession of the kind that appears to recapitulate the arresting affective development of fear and modesty in the mechanicals. For the same range of emotions aroused by the harsh judgments of the ladies and courtiers is rendered in terms of an aggressive oral wounding, and effected through a series of ridiculing insults delimited through the mirror image of the "serpent's tongue" – which Puck later on explains to be a token of the audience's "offense," negative theatrical judgment, and "reprehension" (5.1.424, 414, 420). Lysander's ensuing rejection of Hermia, and his cruel smiling as he watches this dream scene of maidenly fear born from the strictures of modesty, replays his own lack of pity for and mockery and inevitable rejection of the spectacularized, tongue-tied mechanicals, as the performative contours of their masculinity devolve before his gaze into an effeminizing exhibition of bashful timidity. Hermia's dream reflects a much broader affective transference moving through early modern culture. As the virtuous affect structure of fear, shame, and modesty, undergirding maidenly experience, made its way into the new public spheres of court and theatre, it became redeveloped within the sphere of male emotionality, where it could either secure or destroy the performative construction of masculinity.

Bashful Bottoms, Lovers, and Bridled Asses

Bottom is the only mechanical who does not appear even remotely fazed by the reprehension of the ladies, the duke, and his courtly entourage when onstage; however, like any great actor, this does not mean that he has not been confronted with the horrifying spectacle of his own public humiliation. Although Bottom proudly proclaims at rehearsal that his acting will be impeccable and his performance of Pyramus "will move storms" (1.2.23), his dream in the wood exposes the mounting pressure and anxiety he feels over performing the gentlemanly role of Pyramus before the duke. Bottom's unconscious worry that his encounter with Theseus will result in the kind of effeminizing modesty and "tongue-tied simplicity" that Theseus himself recounts as having witnessed at court is replayed here through the range of tropes of castration, which reconfirms the stage as a performative nexus of masculine subject formation (5.1.104). The fear of shame and performance failure is everywhere apparent in Bottom's dream, as Titania presents herself as a dominating matrix ready to emasculate Bottom. The inherent threat to the development of Bottom's masculinity that the stage proffers is reflected in the nightmarish rendering of the cropped bleeding thighs of bumblebees and in the state of passivity, impotence, and corporeal inhibition that Bottom himself begins to feel when the queen holds him fast in her arms, tightly encircling his body as the ivy wraps itself around a woodbine tree (3.1.160; 4.1.41–3). Bottom experiences an almost paralysing, suffocating state of physical inhibition and repression, so strongly that it externalizes the internal affective manifestation of the state of modest shamefastness and sexual restraint that maids like Hermia would have felt. As if the affective parameters of Hermia's modesty have somehow released themselves into the intrapsychic workings of Bottom's dream, Titania inflicts the emotional strictures of "enforced chastity" at the same time that she sexually arouses Bottom through a process of eroticization – as she next tickles and scratches his body, and "coys" his "amiable cheeks," while calling upon her fairies to bridle him: "tie up my lover's tongue and bring him silently" (4.1.2; 3.2.190–1). Titania evokes Bottom's equine status as a facet of the extreme and unregulated emotional component of modesty he begins to feel. In his dream, Bottom becomes physically metamorphosed into a bridled shy colt, sharing in the emasculated, animalized emotional community of the other mechanicals as they perform before the duke on the courtly stage. Rather than having his masculinity and fame stabilized through public performance, Bottom imagines his manhood to be devastatingly arrested, challenged, and threatened, as he dreams of a total breakdown in his theatricalization of Pyramus – a most "proper gentleman," but also an over-emotional and condoling lover (1.2.77). In his nightmare, Bottom is converted from man, to ass, to bashful lover. He envisions himself to be a great stage player who, out of modesty and fear, is "put beside his part"; as he stands before Titania tongue-tied, bridled, inhibited, shy, blushing, struck dumb, he cannot move or speak (Sonnet 23, v. 2).

Bottom's dream expresses his latent fear not only that he will freeze on stage but also that he will experience an even more humiliating form of public shame. Underlying his stage fright is the danger of theatrical failure and audience disapproval if he lets his character slip through the release of his involuntary motor discharges. Disturbances of the gastrointestinal tract are among the most common symptoms of performance anxiety and most dreaded attributes of stage fright. Many actors stay off the stage for years because of the "dread fear of accidentally expelling flatus during a performance."[45] Moreover, as Aaron further observes, the actor's response to the reality of the audience's disapproval is oftentimes itself rendered in terms of his own shameful disgust with himself and the "mess that he is producing."[46] This seems to be a deeply unsettling possibility that Bottom fears could happen to him, as he comes to envision Titania as a maternal figure who feeds him. As Louis Montrose observes, "Titania treats Bottom as if he were both her child and her lover. And she herself is ambivalently nurturing and threatening, imperious and enthralled. She dotes upon Bottom and indulges in him all those desires to be fed, scratched, and coddled that make Bottom's dream into parodic fantasy of infantile narcissism and dependency."[47] Despite Bottom's earlier nightmare of stage fright and his own overwrought modesty brought on by a threatening and dominating Titania-as-lover, the return to the maternal sphere here is codified by the fairy queen's portrayal of a sensitive and admiring mother. The episode does not evoke an oral fixation that is expressed as hostile, or deprived and abruptly taken away, but rather instates the right balance of maternal gazing, discipline, and audience reassurance that would allow for male identity to successfully individuate away from the mother. As Gail Kern Paster explains, as Titania gains control over Bottom's natural functions and processes, she "gives off paradoxical messages of love and discipline," creating in him a contradictory somatic apparatus of bodily restraint, "retention and release."[48] After inculcating in Bottom an emasculating state of shyness, Titania next feeds him a range of aphrodisiacs – purple grapes, ripe green figs, apricots, and mulberries – all of which, as Paster observes, were fruits that heightened erotic desire at the same time as they doubled in the early modern medical culture as laxatives (3.1.157–8). But as Paster also clarifies, despite its purported threat of uncontrolled excretory impulse and release, a scene of public humiliation never occurs in Bottom's dream, as it shifts in imagination from a tremulous stance of stage fright accompanied by possible scatological shaming into a highly stylized and convincing performance of courtliness, bodily enclosure, control, and modest and civilized masculinity.[49]

Bottom next envisions himself as a courtier in Titania's court, appearing neither shy nor ungoverned – as one would expect an ass might be – as he encounters the queen and her fairy attendants. Titania herself seems to celebrate her transcendent purging and refinement of

Bottom's "mortal grossness" so that that the looming threat of flatus is entirely controlled, as Bottom next displays the aesthetic civility and bodily restraint demanded of the performing courtier (3.1.151). In what appears to be a parody of the exaggerated deference of the kind demanded of the gentleman in the performative world of civil conversation, Bottom encounters Titania's attendants with an almost absurd reverential politeness, as he greets "Monseur Cobweb … good monsieur, good master Mustardseed" (4.1.19–20). The other fairies are shown bowing before him; indeed, their polite cast of modesty towards Bottom is so exaggerated that they themselves appear shy, to the extent that Bottom must instruct them to "leave off your courtesy" just as he desires to speak to and make further acquaintance with the others who "show him courtesies" (3.1.165, 4.1.20). As many have pointed out, Bottom appears "more modest and sensible as an ass than as a human being," and he speaks and interacts in Titania's courtly world "with the reserve one would anticipate from a virtuous lady."[50] Paster argues that Bottom's dream necessitates the alteration of the subject's "affect structures in service to emergent norms of civility and refinement."[51] The courtier's latent fear of appearing timid and shy before a group of onlookers still percolates in the back of Bottom's mind; for instance, when he recalls to Mustardseed how "that same cowardly giantlike oxbeef hath devoured many of gentleman" (3.1.183). Overall, however, the development of the affect structure of shame and modesty that Titania inculcates seems, over the course of Bottom's nightmare, to have become more properly internalized to the point at which his regulated modesty now begins to act as a governing rather than a disabling and excessive emotional force over him. He is able, as Arab observes, "to perform with gentlemanlike civility when he is conducted into Titania's court."[52] As an ass, Bottom's baser beasty impulses appear curbed through his psychological deployment of the tempered level of modesty necessary to successfully perform the highly codified version of proper masculinity that the role of Pyramus demands. He next turns in his dream into a paragon of civilized maleness that brings to mind the picture of the suave courtier outlined earlier by Lemnius, as he demonstrates the emboldened social comportment, male modesty, civility, and bodily control that allows him to move gracefully and converse fluidly amongst Titania's courtiers.

Of course, when Bottom finally does appear on stage in the grand space of the royal court it is as if the intrapsychic inculcation of modesty through his dream-vision has had little to no developmental effect. Performing before the duke, he demonstrates a stance of histrionic pride and obliviousness that precludes him from appearing shy, tongue-tied, or stage frightened like his compatriots. In his ignorance, Bottom's performance of masculinity appears ridiculous as he presents an overblown caricature of gentlemanlike civility. His overt boldness towards the duke comes across as entirely unregulated – yet no less theatrically damaging and animalizing – so that Theseus himself judges his performance in deplorable and degenerate terms, mockingly conceding that Bottom has proven "an ass" after all (5.1.285).

Shyness: A Male Dramaturgical Affliction

Despite Bottom's failure to achieve a performative stance of masculine control and perfection, what his dream ultimately illuminates is how the pressure to perform successfully – whether conscious or not – had become an inordinate concern of the early modern male. Bottom's dream calls attention to the way the experience of modesty, traditionally associated with erotic restraint and displays of feminine bashfulness, began undergoing a gendered reconfiguration as it made its way into the emotional and psychical life of the Renaissance gentleman.

Dream's filtration of the courtier's emotional life through the player's necessitates a broader understanding of the way the performative pressures of the early modern court gave way to a theatrical phenomenology of shyness that became further cemented through the performative praxis of the all-male stage. Possessing the capacity to become unregulated and extreme, modesty began to lose its ethical status as an emotional virtue, transforming into an affliction in relation to a novel theatrical ontology of bashfulness as a male pathology born of the public performative dimensions of the playhouse and court alike. As the physician Timothy Bright explains, "the same cause [bashfulness] which stirreth blushing in melancholicke men, forceth them to auoide assemblies, and publike theatres – [this is from] the opinion and fancy of some disgrace from others, who are greatly displeased with themselues."[53] The Shakespearean stage helped to advance an idea of early modern manhood already evolving in the court circle as a gendered category virtuously conditioned through the curb of modesty and the public performance of civilized masculinity. However, in this regard, it also fostered the development of a more complex emotional definition of modesty as a potentially destabilizing feeling that could challenge the proper development of a man's identity. Modesty therefore progressed medically through the period in response to male displays of bashfulness largely undergirded by burgeoning anxieties concerning the public performance and visibility of male bodies and selves.

NOTES

1 All quotations from the play are from the Oxford edition of *A Midsummer Night's Dream*.
2 Arab, *Manly Mechanicals*, 94–5.
3 Arab, *Manly Mechanicals*, 95.
4 On publics, see Yachnin, "The Reformation of Space."
5 Vaught, *Masculinity and Emotion*, 172.
6 Della Casa, *Galateo*, 34–5.
7 King, *The Gendering of Men*, 4.
8 Della Casa, *Galateo*, 32.
9 On the closed body, see Bakhtin, *Rabelais and His World*.
10 Wright, *The Passions*, 36–40.
11 Arab, *Manly Mechanicals*, 17.
12 Lemnius, *Touchstone of Complexions*, 104, 26.
13 Rich, *My Ladies Looking Glass*, 22, 44.
14 Brathwaite, *The English Gentlewoman*, 172.
15 Elias, *Civilizing Process*, 1:69–70, 80.
16 Elyot, *The Book Named the Governor*, 1.9.27.
17 Wright, *The Passions*, 48–9.
18 Guazzo, *Civil Conversation*, 2:118.
19 Bryson, *From Courtesy to Civility*, 111.
20 Mennell, *An Introduction*, 85–6.
21 Fiston, *Good Manners*, sig. Br–v.
22 Cleland, *Heropaideia*, 5.5.177.
23 The epithet "shy" had been used throughout early modernity to describe horses that were overly fearful, skittish, and unruly. In a seventeenth-century translation of the Tusculum Disputations, the translator likens Cicero's grief to the feeling "shy colts" get when they "admit into their mouths the curbed bit"; Cicero, *The Five Days Debate at Cicero's House in Tusculum*, 196. In Chapman's 1611 version of Homer's *Iliad*, Aeneas uses the word "shy" to describe his horse's state of unruliness: "keep thou the reines, and guide thyself thy horse … then with a stranger under whom, they will be much more shye grow restic"; *The Iliad of Homer*, 68.
24 On this iconic theory, see Goffman, *The Preservation of Self*. On the dramaturgy of shyness, see Scott, "The Red, Shaking Fool," 91–110.
25 Mennell, *An Introduction*, 85–6.
26 Courtin, *Rules of Civility*, 2:10.
27 Sedgwick understands shame as a feeling of self-disgust in which one's own gaze turns inward; see *Touching Feeling*, 35–66. On the pattern of symbolic self-awareness inherent in shyness, see Leary, "Shyness and the Self." Although shyness has a well-understood clinical link to the development

of modern "social anxiety disorder," this contemporary diagnosis grew out of the emotion's inherent status as a state of "performance anxiety," as psychologist Magdalena Chec observes in her article "Contemporary Views on Shyness," 77–84. See also Moran's *Shrinking Violets*, where he notes that shyness seems to have "flourished after the arrival of modern systems of manners" (19). Moran, however, does not focus on the emotion's evolution out of the male court and excludes ideas of performativity, largely omitting early modernity in his cultural history of the emotion.

28 Shakespeare, Sonnet 23, "A Bashful Lover," vv. 1–2. See also Shakespeare's related characterization of Duke Vincentio as a "shy fellow" who does not like to be "staged to the people's eyes"; *Measure for Measure* 3.1.372; 1.1.68.
29 Tribble, *Cognition in the Globe*, 119.
30 Kahn, *Man's Estate*, 1.
31 On beards and the performance of masculinity, see Rycroft, *Facial Hair.*
32 Skura, *Shakespeare*, 112.
33 Yachnin, "Reformation of Space," 262, 266, 270.
34 Quoted from Skura, *Shakespeare*, 53.
35 Yachnin, "Reformation of Space." See also Deutermann, Hunter, and Gurnis, *Publicity and the Early Modern Stage*, who link theatrical publicity with ideas about celebrity.
36 Though they do not explore these specific playhouse emotions, see Arab, Dowd, and Zucker, *Historical Affects*. This study offers a sustained historicist approach to the affective life of the Shakespearean theatre.
37 Skura, *Shakespeare*, 18–20.
38 Aaron, *Stage Fright*, 98. On animality and stage fright, see also Rideout, *Stage Fright*. For another psychoanalytic approach, see Triplett, *Stage Fright*.
39 Skura, *Shakespeare*, 19.
40 Kahn, *Man's Estate*, 5.
41 Skura, *Shakespeare*, 19.
42 Skura, *Shakespeare*, 19.
43 Cicero, *The Five Days Debate*, 196.
44 Holland, "Hermia's Dream," 369.
45 Aaron, *Stage Fright*, 95.
46 Aaron, *Stage Fright*, 79, 95.
47 Montrose, "Shaping Fantasies," 68.
48 Paster, *The Body Embarrassed*, 139.
49 Paster, *The Body Embarrassed*, 139–40.
50 Wyrick, "The Ass Motif," 445; Allen, "Bottom and Titania," 108.
51 Paster, *The Body Embarrassed*, 116.
52 Arab, *Manly Mechanicals*, 16.
53 Bright, *Treatise of Melancholy*, 173.

WORKS CITED

Aaron, Stephen. *Stage Fright: Its Role in Acting*. Chicago: University of Chicago Press, 1986.

Arab, Ronda. *Manly Mechanicals on the Early Modern English Stage*. Selinsgrove: University of Susquehanna Press, 2011.

Arab, Ronda, Michelle Dowd, and Adam Zucker. *Historical Affects and the Early Modern Theatre*. New York: Routledge, 2015.

Allen, John. "Bottom and Titania." *Shakespeare Quarterly* 18.2 (1967): 108–17.

Bakhtin, Mikhail. *Rabelais and His World*. Trans. Helene Iswolsky. Bloomington: Indiana University Press, 1984.

Brathwaite, Richard. *The English Gentlewoman*. London, 1631.

Bright, Timothy. *A Treatise of Melancholy*. London, 1586.

Bryson, Anna. *From Courtesy to Civility: Changing Codes of Conduct in Early Modern England*. Oxford: Clarendon, 1998.

Cicero, Marcus Tullius. *The Five Days Debate at Cicero's House in Tusculum*. London: Abel Swalle, 1683.

Chec, Magdalena. "Contemporary Views on Shyness – a Literature Review." *Archives of Psychiatry and Psychotherapy* 21.3 (2019): 77–84.

Cleland, James. *Heropaideia, or The institution of a young noble man*. Oxford, 1607.

Courtin, Antoine de. *The Rules of Civility*. London, 1671.

Della Casa, Giovanni. *Galateo: A Renaissance Treatise on Manners*. Trans. Konrad Eisenbichler and Kenneth R. Bartlett. Toronto: Centre for Reformation and Renaissance Studies, 2009.

Deutermann, Alison K., Mathew Hunter, and Musa Gurnis. *Publicity and the Early Modern Stage: People Made Public*. Cham, Switzerland: Palgrave Macmillan, 2021.

Elias, Norbert. *The Civilizing Process*. Ed. Edmund Jephcott. Oxford: Blackwell, 1983.

Elyot, Thomas. *The Book Named the Governor*. Ed. S.E. Lehmberg. London: 1531; London: Everyman, 1962.

Fiston, William. *The School of Good Manners*. London, 1609.

Goffman, Erving. *The Preservation of Self in Everyday Life*. New York: Doubleday, 1959.

Guazzo, Stefano. *The Civil Conversation*. Trans. George Pettie. London: R. Watkins, 1581.

Holland, Norman. "Hermia's Dream." *The Annual of Psychoanalysis* 7 (1979): 369–89.

Homer. *The Iliad of Homer Prince of Poets*. Trans. George Chapman. London: Printed [by Richard Field] for Nathaniel Butter, 1611.

Kahn, Coppelia. *Man's Estate: Masculine Identity in Shakespeare*. Berkeley: University of California Press, 1981.

King, Thomas. *The Gendering of Men 1600–1750: The English Phallus*. Madison: University of Wisconsin Press, 2004.

Leary, Mark. "Shyness and the Self." In Ray Crozier and Lynne Alden, eds., *The International Handbook of Social Anxiety*. New York: John Wiley, 2001, 219–23.

Lemnius, Levinus. *The Touchstone of Complexions*. London, 1633.

Mennell, Stephen. *Norbert Elias: An Introduction*. Dublin: University College Dublin Press, 1992.

Montrose, Louis Adrian. "Shaping Fantasies: Figurations of Gender and Power in Elizabethan Culture." *Representations* 2 (1983): 61–94.

Moran, Joe. *Shrinking Violets: The Secret Life of Shyness*. New Haven: Yale University Press, 2017.

Paster, Gail Kern. *The Body Embarrassed: Drama and the Disciplines of Shame in Early Modern England*. Ithaca: Cornell University Press, 1993.

Rich, Barnabe. *My Ladies Looking Glass*. London: Printed [by John Legat] for Thomas Adams, 1616.

Rideout, Nicholas. *Stage Fright, Animals, and Other Theatrical Problems*. Cambridge: Cambridge University Press, 2006.

Rycroft, Eleanor. *Facial Hair and the Performance of Masculinity*. New York: Routledge, 2019.

Scott, Susie. "The Red, Shaking Fool: Dramaturgical Dilemmas in Shyness." *Symbolic Interaction* 28.1 (2005): 91–110.

Sedgwick, Eve K. *Touching Feeling: Affect, Pedagogy, Performativity*. Durham, NC: Duke University Press, 2003.

Shakespeare, William. *A Midsummer Night's Dream*. Ed. Peter Holland. Oxford: Oxford University Press, 1994.

– *Shakespeare's Sonnets Never Before Imprinted*. London: G. Eld, 1609.

Skura, Meredith. *Shakespeare, the Actor, and the Purposes of Playing*. Chicago: University of Chicago Press, 1993.

Tribble, Evelyn. *Cognition in the Globe: Attention and Memory in Shakespeare's Theatre*. New York: Palgrave, 2011.

Triplett, Robert. *Stage Fright: Letting It Work for You*. Chicago: Nelson Hall, 1983.

Vaught, Jennifer C. *Masculinity and Emotion in Early Modern English Literature*. New York: Ashgate, 2008.

Wright, Thomas. *The Passions of the Minde*. London: Printed by Valentine Simmes for W. Burre, 1601.

Wyrick, Deborah. "The Ass Motif in *The Comedy of Errors* and *A Midsummer Night's Dream*." *Shakespeare Quarterly* 33.4 (1982): 432–48.

Yachnin, Paul. "The Reformation of Space in Shakespeare's Playhouse." In Angela Vanhaelen and Joseph P. Ward, eds., *Making Space Public in Early Modern Europe: Performance, Geography, Privacy*. London: Routledge, 2013, 263–80.

9 Latin Epigrams and Early Modern Sexual Knowledge: Or, How Jonson Read His Martial

IAN FREDERICK MOULTON

Summary: This article explores the role of Latin commentaries on Martial's epigrams as a medium for the transmission of sexual knowledge among an educated, mostly male elite in early modern Europe, focusing in particular on the example of Ben Jonson. Martial's poetry was highly regarded in early modern humanist culture, and unexpurgated editions with detailed commentary circulated widely. These commentaries frankly explicate the wide range of nonprocreative sexual behaviours represented in Martial's poems, including homoeroticism, oral sex, and masturbation – activities seldom openly discussed in vernacular literary culture. Martial epitomizes a Roman model of masculinity that valorizes sexual penetration; he writes openly of his desire for both women and young men; and he is critical of nonpenetrative male sexual activity. English dramatist Ben Jonson's copious manuscript annotations to Martial record his response to the sexual content of both the poems and their commentary and demonstrate the impact that ancient ideas of male sexuality could have on an early modern readership.

It is a commonplace that early modern elite masculinity was shaped by a sustained cultural engagement with models of behaviour from classical Antiquity. Classical Latin texts in particular were at the heart of the humanist project of modernizing the world by returning to the core beliefs, values, and knowledge of the ancient world.[1] The speeches of Cicero, the poetry of Virgil and Ovid, the histories of Tacitus and Livy, the plays of Terence, not to mention the rediscovery of the Greek philosophy of Plato – these were the building blocks of early modern pedagogy and the foundation of elite masculine cultural values. Formal education was based on the learning of Latin grammar, and the acquisition of rudimentary Latin literacy remained an expected attribute of an elite man.

In general, early modern humanists tried very hard to see their classical intellectual heritage as congruent with Christian revelation. Stoic ethics, Platonic idealism, Ciceronian notions of civic virtue – all were seen as supportive of Christian culture and civilization. But, as the humanists were well aware, some of the ideals and values expressed in classical texts were very much at odds with Christian doctrine, as well as with the social customs and beliefs of early modern Europe. These points of friction between classical learning and early modern culture were particularly acute in the discourses of what would come to be called sexuality. What sort of sexual behaviour was proper? What actions were shameful or forbidden? What role should sexual representation play in literary culture? All these issues were dealt with very differently in classical Antiquity than in early modern Christian Europe. No author's works highlighted these differences more than the poems of Martial.

Written in the first century AD, Martial's twelve books of Latin epigrams contain dozens of texts dealing frankly with a wide range of sexual behaviours, including homoeroticism, oral sex, anal sex, and masturbation. Martial's poems describe and explore a pre-Christian sexual morality and economy that was in many ways alien to early modern Europe. They presented their readers with a range of sexual attitudes, identities, and vocabularies that were foreign, but that could nonetheless sometimes seem familiar. They spoke openly and in detail of things seldom articulated in early modern literary culture, and they took a point of view that was often well outside of orthodox early modern thinking about sexual activity. Early modern commentaries on Martial's lewd epigrams explained in detail the meaning of Roman sexual vocabulary like *irrumare, fellare, cunnilingus*, and *pedicare*. They defined sexual identities like *drauci, tribades*, and *cinaedi*. And by doing so, they created a significant cultural space for discourse about illicit and non-procreative sexual practices.

Besides transmitting information about illicit sexuality, these commentaries on Martial can be seen as a fundamental site in the encounter of the early modern world with the world of Antiquity. By bringing ancient Roman sexual mores into the Christian world of early modern Europe, they mark a cultural fault line, a limit case of the humanist project of building a new intellectual culture on the foundations of the Greco-Roman past. In the case of Martial, there was no "renaissance": Roman sexuality was rediscovered, but not reborn. The mores, habits, and ways of thinking that constitute the Roman sexual economy often directly contradict early modern, Christian ways of understanding sexuality.[2] Scholars and educated readers could explore these differences, but not reconcile them. Thus early modern scholarly discourse around classical Latin poetry allows us to trace the conflict between ancient sexual mores and the sexual culture of Renaissance Europe, in particular in the area of appropriate elite masculine behaviour.

Early modern commentaries on canonical Latin writers like Virgil or Martial were copious texts, often providing dozens of lines of exposition for every word in the original poem (fig. 9.1). Many pages in commented editions have only ten or twenty lines of the author's poetry in large font, surrounded by the densely printed text of the commentary. The vast bulk of most commentary is explication – every notable word in the primary text is annotated and various synonyms are given. Sometimes etymologies are provided, as well as definitions. Proper names are identified, references to historical and mythological figures are explained. In some cases, uses of the word in question by other canonical classical writers are cited, sometimes at length. The overall effect is to create a book designed to be studied in detail rather than read for pleasure.[3]

Classical authors were valued more for their style and linguistic features than for their moral content or literary value. As a world language increasingly divorced from local European vernaculars, Latin was taught through intensive study of exemplary texts. Whereas modern readers of Virgil or Terence tend to emphasize the texts' literary or cultural significance, in the early modern period the primary value of classic Latin texts was linguistic – they provided an opportunity to learn vocabulary and to emulate points of phrasing and style in a language that educated men were required to learn and use, and that was no one's mother tongue. Cicero was the author most often studied and published because his prose style was to be emulated above all others. What Cicero had to say was valued, but the way he said it was valued more. The same was true of Virgil in poetry. The dramatist Terence was widely studied because his plays were believed to provide elegant examples of day-to-day spoken Latin, to be emulated by those early modern readers – students, scholars, lawyers, clerics – who still used Latin in conversation.[4] In general, classical texts were reproduced, copied, and reprinted because of their pedagogical and philological value. This had been the case since late Antiquity. As Jürgen Leonhardt observes, "it is clear that we would know virtually nothing about the classical literature of the Romans if that literature had not found its way into the body of language models that constituted a core component of language instruction."[5]

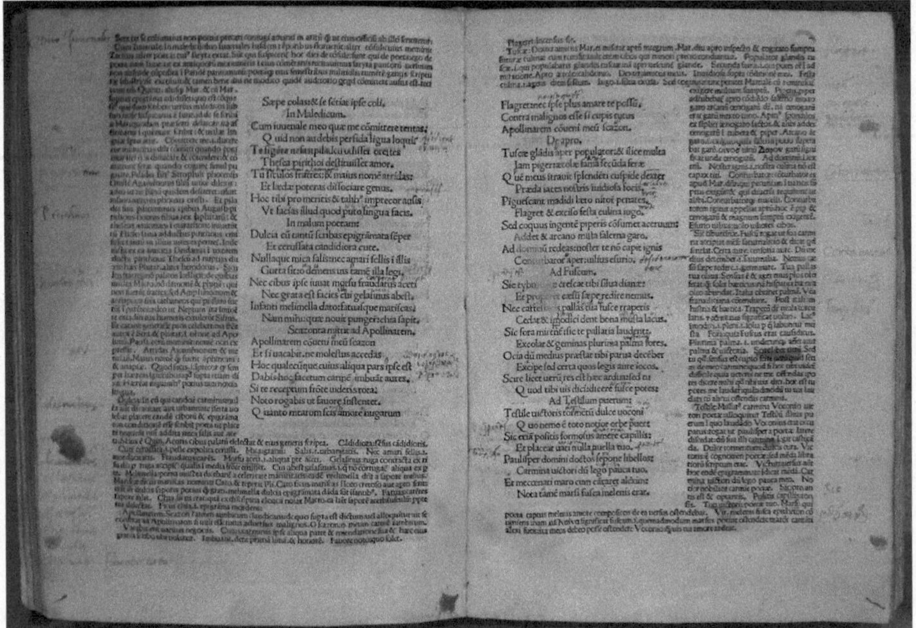

9.1. Martial, *Epigrams* (Milan, 1490). Page of text with printed commentary and handwritten marginalia. From the collections of the Archivo del Gobierno de Aragón. Photo: Escarlati (Wikimedia) Creative Commons Attribution-Share Alike 3.0 Unported licence.

If Martial survived Antiquity, it was because of his style and vocabulary. Though Martial was never on a par with Virgil or Horace as a model of poetic elegance, his usefulness as a linguistic model is clear. He supplies example after example of concision in diction and thought, and his pithy descriptions of social life provide a fascinating source of vocabulary not found in the elevated styles of epic poetry, political oratory, or philosophical prose. And since Martial's texts are all short, they are admirably suited to in-depth, close-grained linguistic and philological analysis.

Marcus Valerius Martialis first came to Rome from Iberia in AD 64, when he was in his early twenties.[6] If he ever wrote any other sort of poetry than epigrams, no trace of it has survived. In the course of his career he published twelve books of epigrams, each containing between

82 and 118 poems: there are 1,172 in all.[7] He also wrote a collection praising games at the newly built Colosseum and two volumes of short verse written to accompany gifts of food, trinkets, and luxuries.

Obscenity and offensive, sexually explicit language are a key component in Martial's overall understanding of epigrams as a genre. In epigram 1.35, he insists that collections of epigrams *must* contain some obscene material:

> these little books
> are like husbands with their wives:
> they cannot please without a cock.
> …
> The law demands that jesting verses
> cannot please unless they itch.[8]

The range of sexual behaviours Martial addresses is comprehensive: oral sex, anal sex, masturbation, voyeurism, male and female homoeroticism, sex with slaves and minors, the sexual habits of the elderly, bestiality – Martial describes it all.

While poems on sexual topics are an essential element of Martial's work, they represent a minority of his output. His epigrams cover a wide range of topics – flattery and praise of patrons, mockery of social misfits, complaints about rival poets, attacks on pomposity, poems in praise of the simple pleasures of life, laments on the death of friends, and much more. Eroticism is not cordoned off or separated from the larger world of social and cultural interaction. Variety is part of the attraction of the genre: serious poems are juxtaposed with comic ones; rude poems on bodily functions are followed by poems flattering the emperor or other dignitaries.[9] Some of the poems are insightful masterpieces of wit and concision. Others are not. Martial cheerfully admits that the quality of his poems is uneven: as he writes near the outset of his first book: "Here you will read good things, some mediocre things, and even more bad things. A book is not made any other way."[10]

Of all the ancient literary genres, epigram is by far the rudest, not only in its sexualized subject matter but also in the offensiveness of its language. Again and again the crudest terms are used: *mentula* and *cunnus*, rather than *penis* and *sinus*, to describe male and female genitalia; *culus*, rather than *podex*, for the buttocks and anus. The words for sexual acts are also unfailingly offensive: *futuo* (fuck), *irrumo* (fuck in the mouth), *pedico* (fuck in the ass), and so on. As Martial himself suggests, these are all terms that were found more commonly in bawdy theatrical mimes or graffiti than in respectable poetry.[11] Martial's epigrams frequently place their subjects in erotic situations and describe them in sexualized language. Perhaps more importantly, they insist that eroticism is a natural and fundamental part of broader social discourse and social interaction more generally.

Although Martial was criticized for his occasional obscenity, his epigrams were highly regarded in early modern humanist culture for their wit, humour, and rhetorical concision. While his works were often expurgated or published selectively, they were never banned as a whole, and his status as an important canonical writer was solid throughout the early modern period, declining only in the eighteenth century when Enlightenment taste came to value Greek literature over Latin. Joseph Addison, for example, criticized the "wrong artificial Taste" that admired "little fanciful Authors and Writers of Epigram," and remarked that "a Reader of plain common Sense … would neither relish nor comprehend an epigram of *Martial*."[12]

It was not so in the sixteenth century. Martial's epigrams were the primary model for English writers of epigrams from Thomas More to Ben Jonson, John Davies, and Robert Herrick.[13] Martial's wit was especially valued in early seventeenth-century France, and his more polite verse was consistently held in high esteem by the Jesuits as a model of style. Saint Ignatius himself commissioned an expurgated edition of Martial for teaching rhetoric.[14]

As expressed in his epigrams, Martial's sexual attitudes seem relatively typical of an upper-class Roman male.[15] Based on surviving evidence, which is largely drawn from the writing of elite male authors, the Roman sexual economy was predominantly based on a hierarchical dynamic of dominance and submission. In this discourse, sexual relations were thought of primarily in terms of the penetration of one person's body by that of another. Males were by definition active and penetrating, females passive and penetrated.[16] There was a definite hierarchy of sexual activities based on which bodily orifice was penetrated.[17] It was more shameful to be penetrated in the anus than in the vagina, and most shameful of all to be penetrated in the mouth. Although males as well as females were potentially available for penetration, the bodies of adult, freeborn, citizen males, like Martial, were considered, legally and socially, to be ideally impenetrable. While beating was a common punishment for women, children, and slaves, it was illegal to beat a freeborn male citizen.[18] This superior position in sexual, social, and legal hierarchies depended on men's status as freeborn adult citizens, rather than on their masculine gender alone. A man who was a slave had no legal or social authority over a freeborn female, for example, and his body was theoretically more available for sexual penetration than hers was.

The "proper" sexual role for freeborn adult male citizens was to penetrate the bodies of social inferiors – women, boys, girls, slaves, and prostitutes of either gender. Married women were off limits, as were youth of either gender from freeborn citizen families. In Plautus' comedy *Curculio* a young male citizen is given the following advice:

> No one is forbidden to walk on the public road,
> but don't cut a path through fenced-off ground.
> As long as you abstain from the wife, the widow, the virgin,
> young men, and freeborn boys, love whoever you like.[19]

Because by law and custom freeborn boys were considered inappropriate sexual objects, there was less of an open culture of pederasty in Rome than in ancient Greece.[20] But there was little stigma against male homoerotic activity so long as social hierarchies were respected. Martial's epigrams frequently treat young male bodies as objects of desire. An adult, freeborn man would naturally have sexual relations with slave boys or male prostitutes, but in those relationships he was expected to take the penetrative role. For an adult, freeborn male citizen to allow his body to be sexually penetrated was a shameful act that could entail effeminization, shame, and loss of status.

Marriage was an essential social structure that ensured the generation of legitimate citizen children, but there was little social expectation that a married Roman man would have sex only with his spouse. Children born out of wedlock were illegitimate, but could be adopted – and adoption was a common Roman practice, especially among the upper classes. While extramarital sex for men was not scandalous in itself, having sex with other men's wives could be harshly punished. Augustus' Julian Law of 18 BCE made sex with a married woman a public offence and imposed severe penalties on convicted adulterers among the upper classes.[21]

The ruthless logic of this system is due in part to the homogeneity of the sources that describe it – almost all our information about Roman sexuality comes from public writing by privileged men like Martial, Cicero, and Virgil. In the absence of other voices, this way of thinking about sexuality can seem more monolithic than it may have been in practice. Though it is clear that the system was well understood and generally accepted by the elite men who dominated Roman society, it is unlikely that the sexual economy I have sketched here was the only way that Romans thought about sexual matters. Indeed, if Martial's poetry is any indication of social realities, there were plenty of people who broke the rules.

So for Martial, proper male sexual activity consists in penetrating the bodies of social inferiors: women, boys, slaves. Sex is seen as a fundamentally aggressive act, and the pleasure for both partners is dependent on this aggression: in epigram 7.58, Martial implies that women disdain "unwarlike bedchambers" ("imbellicos thalamus"). Penetration is always effeminizing, putting the persons penetrated in a female role, whatever their biological sex. In terms of sexual morality, the gender of the person being penetrated is immaterial; Martial writes openly of his desire for boys and young men as well as for women. He jokes about being married, but most scholars think it is unlikely that he ever had a wife.[22] Martial sees it as natural for young women to take pleasure in being vaginally penetrated, but older women's sexuality repulses him, and he mocks adult males who enjoy being anally penetrated. Since Martial believes men should naturally take the sexual initiative, he sees sexually aggressive women as unnatural. Women who have sex with other women (*tribades*) are criticized for acting like men and are usually imagined to penetrate their partners, either with their clitoris, their hands, or some implement.[23]

Like many Roman writers on the subject, Martial finds oral sex repulsive in any capacity – the physical contact of the mouth with the genitals seems to him fundamentally unclean and degrading, almost analogous to consuming urine or feces.[24] Men who aggressively penetrate the mouths of others (*irrumatores*) are bad enough, but people who willingly take someone else's genitals in their mouth are simply disgusting. As epigram 11.95 puts it,

> Whenever you encounter the kisses of cock-suckers, Flaccus,
> Just imagine that you're putting your head in a toilet.[25]

With the possible exception of himself, Martial finds sexually active older people to be pathetic. Sex is for the young and healthy. Martial is also critical of masturbation, at times seeing male masturbation as a shameful waste of procreative potential.[26]

As strange, disturbing, or offensive as these attitudes may seem to later readers, none of them posed any sort of threat to Roman society or civic morality. However shocking Martial might seem, his writings were not particularly revolutionary or subversive – especially if they were seen, as he wished them to be, in the socially acceptable context of rude street mimes and the carnivalesque games of Floralia and Saturnalia.

Many of Martial's sexual attitudes echo the common tropes of early modern male sexual discourse: hostility towards sexually aggressive women, especially older women; revulsion at the idea of oral sex; disgust for adult men who let themselves be penetrated and for any form of sex between women; and contempt for masturbation. But Martial's frequent endorsement of adult male desire for sex with younger males goes against the early modern prohibition and persecution of such activity, and his general sexual frankness goes well beyond the norms of respectable early modern writing. So while Martial's ridicule of many forms of sexual activity could be read sympathetically in the early modern period, his praise of certain forms of male homoeroticism and the explicit nature of his sexual discourse also made him dangerously and attractively wicked. It is easy to see how his poems might appeal to the elite young men who read him in Latin. In addition, Martial's poems are brief, witty, and strikingly phrased – easy to memorize or to copy quickly on any loose piece of paper that came to hand.

Latin commentary on sexually explicit poems constituted an important site for the early modern transmission of sexual knowledge, especially about transgressive or nonprocreative forms of sexual activity. This discourse, though relatively widespread among those literate in Latin, has arguably been overlooked by scholars of the period. Classical scholars and Latinists tend to dismiss early modern commentaries as derivative or pedantic (they often are); scholars of vernacular literature downplay the importance of editions of Latin verse in early modern literate culture.

While expurgated editions of Martial became the norm by the eighteenth century, in the earliest days of printing, unexpurgated Latin editions of Martial were common – eighteen editions of the epigrams were published before 1500, each containing the complete text of all the poems.[27] Most of these editions were published in Italy, but in the sixteenth century publication of Martial spread more widely; Martial was published in Lyon beginning in 1502 and in Paris beginning in 1528.[28] The first edition published in England appeared in London in 1615. Most early modern editions of Martial came with copious Latin commentary.[29] In the unexpurgated editions of Martial, these commentaries deal frankly with the sexual content of Martial's texts, elucidating varieties of illicit and nonprocreative sexual behaviour seldom discussed openly in early modern literary culture. They define terms and describe sexual activities, as well as identifying sexual subtexts or innuendos.

Martial in Latin was readily available in early modern England. Writing Latin epigrams was a standard feature of the curriculum in early modern English schools. Students would either be given a theme on which to compose an epigram of their own, or they would be asked to paraphrase or vary an epigram from Martial or some other ancient author.[30] In 1550, for example, Martial was studied daily by three of the four forms in Winchester College.[31] Continental editions of Martial were numerous, and many ended up in English collections. A complete and unexpurgated octavo edition of Martial, with marginal commentary, was published in London in 1615, printed by Felix Kingston and William Welby, and edited by Thomas Farnaby (1575?–1647).[32] Though it was not a particularly distinguished volume from an editorial perspective, it was serviceable, portable, and convenient. This edition was reprinted in London in 1633, and again in Amsterdam in 1644.[33]

Dramatist and poet Ben Jonson took a particular interest in Martial as an author and in epigrams as a genre.[34] He owned a copy of Farnaby's edition, and indeed was the editor's personal friend.[35] In August 1623 he gave the book to his friend Richard Briggs, graduate of St John's College, Cambridge, and headmaster of a school in Norfolk, who may have been the brother of Henry Briggs, an important mathematician.[36] Jonson wrote a short letter to Richard Briggs on the back of the volume's title page (fig. 9.2). He alludes to his friendship with Farnaby and, echoing Martial's dictum that epigrams "cannot please without a cock," he proudly notes that Farnaby's edition is "uncastrated":

> It is the Martial of my Farnaby. Not the Martial of the Jesuits, castrated, unmanned, and Martial entirely without Martial. This gives you Martial manly and intact, not less chaste but more virile.[37]

He also points out the value of Farnaby's commentary on the text and insists that Briggs read the book "all the way through."[38] Clearly Jonson values Martial's poems on sexual matters and sees them as a crucial and integral part of his achievement. His contention that Martial is "chaste" suggests that while his writing discusses sexual matters in explicit detail, his morality conforms to the best models of upper-class Roman men.

Besides Farnaby's 1615 London edition, Jonson owned at least two other unexpurgated editions of Martial: a folio edition published in Paris in 1617, including multiple commentaries by various editors, and a 1619 edition published in Leiden in the Netherlands.[39] According to David McPherson, this last volume contains "the most interesting annotations of any book in Jonson's library." Most of the annotation in the volume consists of underlining and pointing of various kinds. Almost every poem in the first five books of the volume is underlined, with manicules, stars, or cloverlike symbols in the margins (fig. 9.3). In comparison with such marking, textual comments by Jonson are relatively rare, though still numerous. Annotations in books 6–12 are

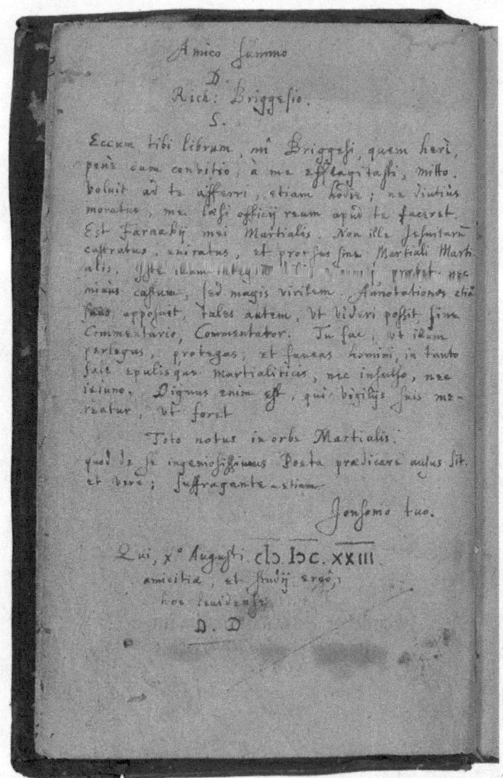

Amico summo
D.
Rich: Briggesio.
S.
Eccum tibi librum, mi Briggesi, quem heri,
pene cum convitio, à me efflagitasti, mitto.
Voluit ad te afferri, etiam hodie; ne diutius
moratus, me laesi officij reum apud te faceret.
Est Farnabij mei Martialis. Non ille Jesuitarum
castratus, enervatus, et prorsus sine Martiali Martialis. Iste illum integrum [illegible] praebet. nec
minus castum, sed magis virilem. Annotationes etiam
suas apposuit, tales autem, ut videri possit sine
Commentario, Commentator. Tu fac, ut illum
perlegas, protegas; et faveas homini, in tanto
sale epulisque Martialitiis, nec insulso, nec
ieiuno. Dignus enim est, qui vigiliis suis me-
reatur, ut foret
Toto notus in orbe Martialis.
quod de se ingeniosissimus Poeta praedicare ausus sit.
et vere; suffragante etiam
Jonsonio tuo.
Qui, X° Augusti CIƆ.IƆC.XXIII
amicitiae, et studij ergo,
hoc lucidenter
D. D.

9.2. Ben Jonson's letter to Richard Briggs, handwritten on sig. A1v in Martial, *Epigrammaton* (London, 1615). From the collections of the Folger Shakespeare Library, STC 14792 copy 1, sig. A1v. Image: Folger Shakespeare Library. Creative Commons Attribution-ShareAlike 4.0 International License (CC BY-SA 4.0).

less frequent than in the earlier books. Book 13, Martial's *Xenia*, which contains poems to accompany gifts of food, is annotated throughout, with English translations given for all the food items. Book 14, the *Apophoreta*, a collection of poems to be included with inedible gifts such as togas, jugs, and monkeys, is not annotated at all. Martial's introductory book dealing with spectacles in the Colosseum is annotated, as is most of the volume's front matter. Many of the annotations, especially in the later part of the volume, note similarities between the poem annotated and another poem elsewhere in the volume.

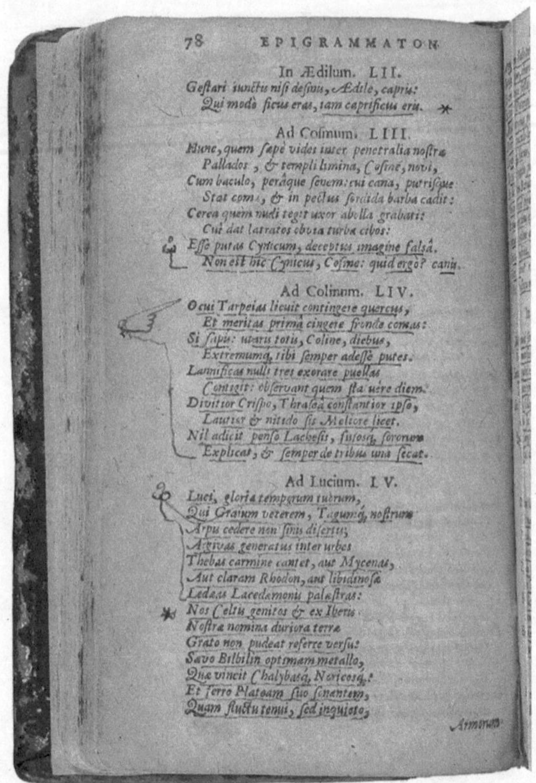

78 EPIGRAMMATON

In Ædilum. LII.

Gestari iunctis nisi desinis, Ædile, capris:
Qui modò ficus eras, iam caprificus eris.

Ad Cosmum. LIII.

Hunc, quem saepè vides inter penetralia nostrae
Pallados, & templi limina, Cosme, novi,
Cum baculo, peràque senem: cui cana, putrisque
Stat coma, & in pectus sordida barba cadit:
Cerea quem nudi tegit uxor abolla grabati:
Cui dat latratos obvia turba cibos:
Esse putas Cynicum, deceptus imagine falsâ.
Non est hic Cynicus, Cosme: quid ergò? canis.

Ad Colinum. LIV.

O cui Tarpeias licuit contingere quercus,
Et meritas primâ cingere fronde comas:
Si sapis: utaris totis, Coline, diebus,
Extremumque tibi semper adesse putes.
Lanificas nulli tres exorare puellas
Contigit: observant quem statuere diem.
Divitior Crispo, Thraseâ constantior ipso,
Lautior & nitido sis Meliore licet.
Nil adicit penso Lachesis, fusosque sororum
Explicat, & semper de tribus una secat.

Ad Lucium. LV.

Luci, gloria temporum tuorum,
Qui Graium veterem, Tagumque nostrum
Arpis cedere non sinis disertis;
Argivas generatus inter urbes
Thebas carmine cantet, aut Mycenas,
Aut claram Rhodon, aut libidinosae
Ledaeas Lacedaemonis palaestras:
Nos Celtis genitos & ex Iberis
Nostrae nomina duriora terrae
Grato non pudeat referre versu:
Saevo Bilbilin optimam metallo,
Quae vincit Chalybasque, Noricosque:
Et ferro Plateam suo sonantem,
Quam fluctu tenui, sed inquieto,

Armorum

9.3. Ben Jonson's copy of Martial, *Nova Editio* [*Epigrams*] (Leiden, 1619), p. 78, with typical handwritten annotations. From the collections of the Folger Shakespeare Library, PA 6501.A2 1619 Cage. Image: Folger Shakespeare Library.

It is not always clear why Jonson underlines particular texts in the volume – indeed, the underlining is so frequent in some sections that almost all the words on a given page are underlined. But his marginal textual comments give fascinating evidence on how Jonson understood Martial – a poet he greatly admired and emulated in his own epigrams. As Bruce Boehrer has demonstrated, Jonson's handwritten commentary on Martial's obscene verse clearly demonstrates his detailed engagement with Martial's representation of sexuality.[40] Boehrer convincingly argues that Jonson's frequently negative attitude to sexuality in his own plays and poems is rooted in his reading of Martial.

Reading Jonson's written notes in his 1619 edition in light of the printed commentary in the other editions of Martial he owned allows us to see the ways that Jonson works with the scholarly tradition to come to his own understanding of Martial – and in particular Martial's treatment of nonprocreative or forbidden sexual practices.

For example, in epigram 2.28, Martial mocks a man named Sextillus for his unorthodox sexual preferences:

> Laugh a lot at the one who calls you a queen, Sextillus.
> Give him the middle finger.
> But you're not a bugger, Sextillus, nor a fucker either.
> And Vetustina's hot mouth does not please you.
> I confess you're none of these things, Sextillus. So what are you?
> I don't know. But you know there are two possibilities left.[41]

The humour of this poem lies in its play of crude language and coy understatement. Rude terms like *pedico* (bugger, sodomite) and *fututor* (fucker, copulater) are used openly, without euphemism, and yet Martial refrains from mentioning exactly what two activities Sextillus might enjoy – leaving it up to the reader to fill in the blanks.

As early modern commentators recognized, the poem gives a comprehensive economy of Roman sexuality. There are a set number of possibilities for pleasure, and the choice of pleasure determines one's identity.[42] *Pace* Foucault, Martial clearly classifies people in terms of their sexual roles: for example, throughout his work Martial defines three different Roman sexual identities associated with male homoeroticism: the *paticus*, the *draucus*, and the *cinaedus*. A *paticus* is anyone who is anally penetrated, including those who are penetrated against their will (this term in its feminine form can also describe females anally penetrated in heterosexual sex). A *draucus* is a man who anally penetrates others, not so much for his own pleasure (which in Martial's terms would be normative male behaviour), but to service his partner. A *cinaedus* is a *paticus* who enjoys being anally penetrated and is often a prostitute, making a living by selling his sexual services. *Cinaedus* derives from the Greek κινειν (to move), though the word originally referred to dancers, many of whom worked as prostitutes.[43] There is also evidence that *cinaedus* was used as a general term of abuse: Catullus, for example, uses it in a disparaging reference to a friend's mistress.[44]

Sextillus might be a *cinaedus*. Alternatively, he might enjoy penetrating others, either anally (which would make him a *pedico*), vaginally (which would make him a *fututor*), or orally (which would make him an *irrumator*). But Vetusina's "hot mouth" holds no attraction. So, what is left? It is assumed that Sextillus must have some sexual activity he enjoys. In Martial's conceptual universe, abstinence is not an option.

Martial does not say what Sextillus does. He assumes we know. But since our sexual economy and sexual categorizations differ from those of ancient Rome, we don't.

Ben Jonson thought he did. In the margin of his 1619 copy of Martial's epigrams,[45] he wrote:

F<u>ella</u>tor
<u>Cunni</u>ling

Jonson assumes that Sextillus must enjoy licking other people's genitals – a sexual activity that Martial considers utterly debased and disgusting. This disgust is presumably part of the reason that Martial chooses to leave the activity unnamed.

Jonson may have learned his answer to the question of Sextillus' predilections from another edition of Martial he owned. In his Paris 1617 edition, printed marginal commentary on this poem by Lorenzo Ramirez de Prado (1583–1658) uses the Roman economy of sexual activities to deduce the answer:

> [Martial] writes of Sextillus, who was a cock-sucker and cunt-licker … There are six crimes involving impurity. First, to be a cinaedus: second, a paedico: third, a fututor: fourth, a mouth-fucker: fifth, a cock-sucker; sixth, a cunt-licker. He has said that Sextillus does not do the first four, and says that he knows two possibilities remain, that is the obscenities of sucking and licking … He accuses a certain Coracinus of the same crime – see epigram 4.43.[46]

Epigram 4.43 parallels 2.28 by saying that, while Coracinus is not a *cinaedus*, he is instead a *cunnilingus* (much worse).

But Ramirez and Jonson's answer to the riddle of Sextillus' pleasures is not the only one. Jonson's 1617 Paris edition of Martial also prints commentary by Domizio Calderini (1446–1478),[47] who has another interpretation. Calderini assumes that Vetusina's "hot mouth" is her vulva. If so, Sextillus is not interested in cunnilingus.[48] Instead the two possibilities mentioned in the poem's final line must be fellatio and masturbation. Calderini goes on to discuss the etymology of both terms:

> "To masturbate" is derived from a Greek word; for Greeks say "μασροπευω" to combine the notions of seduction and caressing.[49] Thus Romans say "masturbate" to describe the shameless handling of the penis. "Fellatio" is derived from young goats and lambs, who are said to "fellate" the udders

of their mothers when they suck milk. This word is used by Varro in reference to rustic matters. Clearly, Solinus often uses "fellare" in reference to lambs, and Pliny uses it to refer to goats. Some say that "fellare" does not refer to animals sucking, but derives from a Greek word, which is a laughable opinion. The Greek term means "to contaminate the mouth." Suidas believes this on evidence from Aristophanes.[50]

In the London 1615 edition, Farnaby's marginal commentary on 2.28 gives yet another reading. He notes that Sextillus "does not find the mouth of a fellatrix pleasing"[51] – to support this interpretation, he helpfully gives cross-references to Juvenal's tenth satire, line 238, which mentions the "breath" from a whore's "skilled mouth," and to Martial 2.62 (2.61 in modern standard numbering), which attacks a man whose "perverse tongue licked men's middles."[52] As to the two possibilities, he speculates that Sextillus "could also fuck people in the mouth; the other possibility I do not know."

All these commentators, including Jonson, are using Martial as a way to explore, expand, and disseminate their sexual knowledge. Latin poetry and Latin commentary provide an occasion and a medium to discuss sexual activities seldom addressed in surviving vernacular texts from the early modern period: in particular, oral sex, anal sex, and masturbation.

At times, Jonson even finds a sexual subtext in poems not usually seen as prurient, finding eroticization where other readers might not. One of Martial's most famous epigrams, in the early modern period and now, is 1.32:

Non amo te, Sabidi, nec possum dicere quare:
hoc tantum possum dicere, non amo te.

I do not love you, Sabidius, and I cannot say why:
This much I can say, I do not love you.

In the late seventeenth century, a catchy translation of this epigram became a common English nursery rhyme:

I do not like thee, Doctor Fell,
The reason why, I cannot tell.
But this I know, and know full well,
I do not like thee, Doctor Fell.

(Doctor John Fell was the dean of Christ Church, Oxford, who was said to have asked a disgraced student, Tom Brown, for the translation as a test.)[53] This epigram is often chosen even today for inclusion in elementary instructional texts for those learning to read Latin.[54] It is also regularly included in early modern expurgated editions of Martial.

This text is usually understood as describing the common situation in which a person feels an inexplicable antipathy to someone – a bad feeling that is impossible to define or attribute to any one aspect of someone's appearance or character. Jonson read it more precisely. In the margin of his 1619 Martial he writes next to the poem (fig. 9.4):

> fellator
> sive cunnilinge
> vid Lib. iii, epi. xvii.[55]

Jonson believes that the speaker dislikes Sabidius because he puts people's genitals in his mouth – and therefore has foul-smelling breath. As evidence, he points to epigram 3.17, another poem attacking a man named Sabidius:

> A tart, passed around several times at dessert,
> savagely burned our hands with its excessive heat.
> But Sabidius' gullet burned more. So right away
> he blew on it with his jowls three or four times.
> Certainly it cooled, and seemed ready to admit our fingers,
> But no one could touch it. It was shit.[56]

Clearly Sabidius' breath is not good.

The connection between these two epigrams, as well as Jonson's interpretation that Sabidius' foul breath comes from oral sex, is laid out in detail in the editorial commentary by Lorenzo Ramirez de Prado printed in Jonson's 1617 Paris edition of Martial.[57] After a lengthy discussion of the unknowability of the reason why the speaker finds Sabidius objectionable, Ramirez suggests there may be an identifiable reason after all:

> Another interpretation is that he is suggesting that there is some burning shame in Sabidius, something profoundly wrong, but what it is, he cannot say. It seems to me, however, the suggestion is that Sabidius' shame is to have an unclean mouth. Epigram 17 of book 3 makes me suspect this, insomuch as no one will touch a burning hot tart, served at dessert, after Sabidius has blown on it with his jowls three or four times. When the burning heat has subsided, none of the dinner guests dares to touch the tart because this unclean man has breathed on it. Perhaps the dinner guests smelled a pungent odour because he was a cunt-licker, or a cock-sucker.[58]

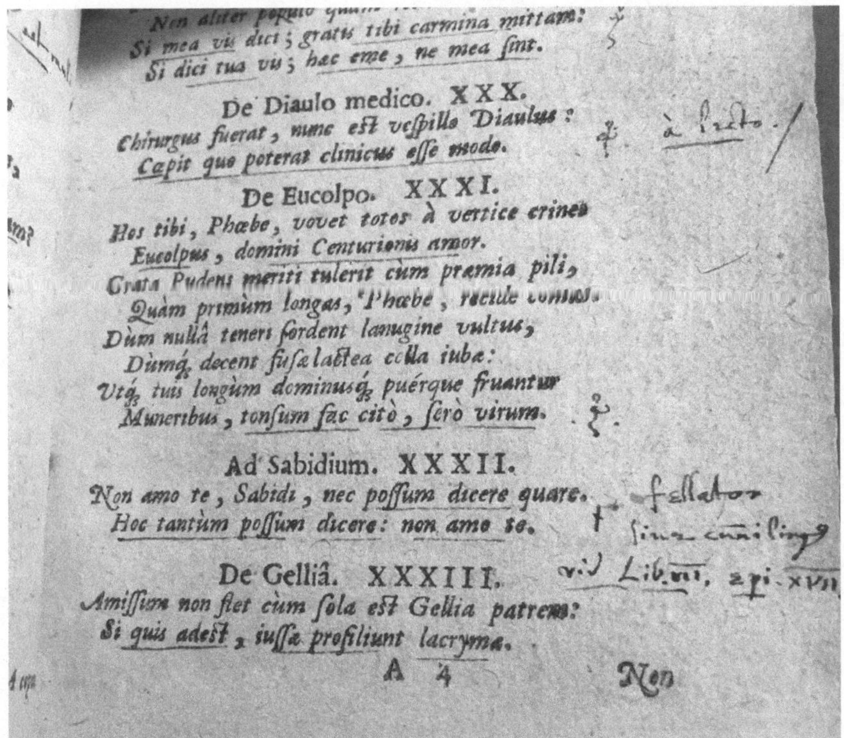

Non aliter populo
Si mea vis dici; gratis tibi carmina mittam:
Si dici tua vis; hæc eme, ne mea sint.

De Diaulo medico. XXX.

Chirurgus fuerat, nunc est vespillo Diaulus:
Cœpit quo poterat clinicus esse modo.

De Eucolpo. XXXI.

Hos tibi, Phœbe, vovet totos à vertice crines
Eucolpus, domini Centurionis amor.
Grata Pudens meriti tulerit cùm præmia pili,
Quàm primùm longas, Phœbe, recide comas.
Dùm nullâ teneri sordent lanugine vultus,
Dùmq; decent fusæ lactea colla iubæ:
Vtq; tuis longùm dominusq; puérque fruantur
Muneribus, tonsum fac citò, sérò virum.

Ad Sabidium. XXXII.

Non amo te, Sabidi, nec possum dicere quare.
Hoc tantùm possum dicere: non amo te.

De Gelliâ. XXXIII.

Amissum non flet cùm sola est Gellia patrem:
Si quis adest, iussæ prosiliunt lacrymæ.

A 4 Non

9.4 Ben Jonson's annotations to epigram 1.32: "fellator / sive cunnilinge / vid Lib. iii, epi. xvii." Martial, *Nova Editio* [*Epigrams*] (Leiden, 1619), sig. A4r. From the collections of the Folger Shakespeare Library, PA 6501.A2 1619 Cage. Photo: Ian Moulton.

Jonson's own writings often show a horrified fascination with similar moments, when food and excrement are mixed.[59]

Jonson's annotations clearly show the attention he paid to Martial's descriptions of illicit sexual behaviour. One must, however, place Jonson's interest in context. Jonson's annotations to some of Martial's obscene poems are detailed and explicit, but overall his annotations do not put any special emphasis on Martial's sexual poems. There are many sexually explicit poems he leaves unannotated, and his interest in Martial's nonsexual poems is easily as strong as his interest in the sexual ones. As I have argued elsewhere, in the early modern period, sexually explicit material was not always separated out from other areas of discourse and inquiry as it often is in modern and post-modern culture.[60] Like his letter to Briggs, Jonson's annotations suggest that he saw Martial's obscene poems as an integral part of the totality of his work. A book is not made any other way.

Jonson seems to have annotated each book systematically, and his annotations drop off rapidly after book 5. There is no way of knowing why he did not annotate the entire volume. If he is particularly interested in anything, it is the Latin names for various foodstuffs found in Martial's *Xenia* – the book of verses to accompany edible gifts. Not surprising, perhaps, as Jonson's "enduring fascination with alimentary matters" is well documented.[61]

Jonson, of course, wrote epigrams himself – 133 of them, all published in his 1616 folio *Workes*.[62] In the epistle dedicating his epigrams to the Earl of Pembroke, he calls them "the ripest of my studies," and they are given pride of place in the *Workes*, appearing at the head of all of Jonson's collected verse.[63] Although he valued his own epigrams and clearly loved Martial, in one respect Jonson's epigrams differ sharply from his classical model. Jonson attacks flatterers and fops, gamblers, hypocrites, and cowards. He praises statesmen and fellow poets, and King James. But none of the 133 epigrams contain any rude language or explicit description of sexual activity. In the terms of his own letter to Briggs, Jonson's verses are castrated – there is no cock in them at all. An early modern book is made no other way.

In the preface to his first book of epigrams, Martial justified his crudeness by appealing to the example of his predecessors and by comparing his rude verses to bawdy performances, typical of Roman festivals:

> I would apologize for the unrestrained realism of my words (that is the language of epigram) if I were the one who set the example. But this is how Catullus writes, and Marsus, and Pedo, and Gaetulicus, and anyone who is read all the way through. If there is anyone so exceedingly stern that he will not accept plain Latin on any page he reads, he can be content with my epistle, or even with my title. Epigrams are written for those who watch the games at Floralia. Let Cato not come into my theatre, or if he does come in, let him watch.[64]

The Floralia was a springtime festival in honour of the fertility goddess Flora, celebrated with the performance of bawdy farces, known as mimes.[65] The Floralia mimes were usually performed by prostitutes and often involved striptease.[66] Legend has it that the moralist Cato once voluntarily left the theatre at the Floralia so that the performers would not feel intimidated by his stern presence.[67] Martial's story of Cato's departure argues that carnivalesque licence has an important social function, one that should be recognized and honoured even by the most upright of citizens.

Always a good classicist, Jonson models the dedicatory epistle to his epigrams on Martial's preface, but with an important difference. He concludes by saying that he will not attack individuals by name in his verse: he would rather they remained masked. Reticence of all kinds is to be valued:

> I would rather know them by their vizards [masks], still, than they should publish their faces, at their peril, in my theatre, where Cato, if he lived, might enter without scandal.

Jonson, unlike Martial, wants Cato's approval.

NOTES

1 For a recent overview of the importance of classical antiquity to early modern intellectual culture, see Ruggiero, *Renaissance*, 6–9, 209–10.
2 On the transition between classical modes of sexuality and Christian ones, see Harper, *From Shame to Sin*.
3 Jones, *Printing the Classical Text*, 102.
4 A similar function was fulfilled by Erasmus' *Colloquies* and Cicero's familiar letters: Leonhardt, *Latin*, 219–20.
5 Leonhardt, *Latin*, 103.
6 On Martial's life, see Sullivan, *Martial*, 1–55.
7 This is the total from the twelve books of epigrams. If poems from other sources are added, the total is closer to 1,600. See Sullivan, *Martial*, 53n64.
8 "sed hi libelli, / tanquam coniugibus suis mariti / non possunt sine mentula placere. / … / lex haec carminibus data est iocosis, / ne possint, nisi pruriant, iuvare." For Latin text, references to Martial are to the 1993 Loeb Classical Library edition, edited by D.R. Shackleton Bailey. Unless otherwise indicated, all translations from Martial are my own. In translating Martial's Latin I have tended to use crude English terms that reproduce the rudeness of his Latin word-choice. For example, while "cunnilingus" is a relatively polite English term – because of its "scholarly" derivation from Latin – in the original Latin the term literally means "cunt-licker" and is just as rude. If any are offended, I apologize: as Martial would say, "lasciva est nobis pagina, vita proba" (epigram 1.4).
9 On the role of juxtaposition in Martial's epigrams, see Fitzgerald, *Martial*, 106–38.

10 Martial, epigram 1.16: "Sunt bona, sunt quaedam mediocria, sunt mala plura / quae legis hic: aliter not fit, Avite, liber."
11 On sexual graffiti, see Milnor, *Graffiti and the Literary Landscape*, 122–6, and Beard, *The Fires of Vesuvius*, 238–40.
12 Addison, *Spectator* 70. See also Leonhardt, *Latin*, 266–7.
13 Coiro, *Robert Herrick's "Hesperides,"* 48–59, 73–5, 83–9.
14 Sullivan, *Martial*, 270–4.
15 On Martial's attitudes on sexual matters, see Sullivan, *Martial*, 185–210.
16 Williams, *Roman Homosexuality*, 7, 16–17; Skinner, *Sexuality in Greek and Roman Culture*, 195; Walters, "Invading the Roman Body."
17 Parker, "The Teratogenic Grid." Parker's structuralist analysis of Roman sexuality in this article is insightful and influential, though his 2017 conviction on child pornography charges has led to a debate on the ethical status of his scholarship.
18 Livy, *History of Rome*, 10.9.4; Walters, "Invading the Roman Body," 37.
19 Plautus, *Curculio*, lines 35–8: "Nemo ire quemquam publica prohibet via: / dum ne per fundum saeptum factias semitam, / dum ted abstineas nupta, vidua, virgine, / iuventute et pueris liberis, ama quid lubet." See also Skinner, *Sexuality*, 196.
20 On the differences between Greek and Roman attitudes to sex between males, see Williams, *Roman Homosexuality*, 62–95.
21 Williams, *Roman Homosexuality*, 116, 119–24.
22 Sullivan, *Martial*, 25–6.
23 Epigrams 1.90, 7.67, 7.70.
24 Williams, *Roman Homosexuality*, 197–203. Richlin, *The Garden of Priapus*, 26–7.
25 "Incideris quotiens in basia fellatorum, / in solium puta te merger, Flacce, caput." In his Loeb edition of Martial's *Epigrams*, Appendix A (3.329–30), Shackleton Bailey argues convincingly for an emendation of the word "solium" ("tub") in the second line to something closer to "lasanum," "chamber pot" or "close-stool." Epigram 12.62 includes "cock-suckers" and "cunt-lickers" in a list of people you wouldn't want to kiss.
26 Epigram 9.41. See also Sullivan, *Martial*, 190–1.
27 There are eighteen distinct editions of Martial's epigrams listed in the *Incunabula Short Title Catalogue*: http://www.bl.uk/catalogues/istc. Shackleton Bailey identifies three particularly influential early editions: Ferrara, 1471, Rome, 1473, and the first Aldine edition, Venice, 1501. See Martial, *Epigrammata*, XII.
28 On sixteenth-century French editions of Martial, see Hausmann, "Martialis, Marcus Valerius," 257–8.
29 Sullivan, *Martial*, 264–7.
30 Hudson, *The Epigram in the English Renaissance*, 148. British Library Add. MS 4379, written by a boy named William Badger around 1565, contains

examples of Latin epigrams he wrote as exercises at Winchester College under the tutelage of headmaster Christopher Johnson.

31 Hudson, *The Epigram in the English Renaissance*, 147.

32 STC 17492.

33 A copy is in the Huntington Library, 600625.

34 On Martial as a model of authorship for Jonson, see Loewenstein, *Ben Jonson and Possessive Authorship*, 124–32.

35 Folger STC 17492 copy 1. On Jonson's relationship with Farnaby, see McPherson, "Ben Jonson's Library and Marginalia," 68.

36 *Dictionary of National Biography*: Henry Briggs (1561–1630).

37 "Est Farnibii mei Martialis, / Non ille Jesuitarum castratus, / eviratus, et prorsus sine Martiali Martialis. / Iste illum integrum tibi, virumq praebet; / nec minus castum, / sed magis virile"; Folger Shakespeare Library, STC 14792 copy 1, sig. A1v.

38 "Annotationes etiam suas apposuit, tales autem, ut videri possit, sine / Commentario Commentator. Tu fac, ut illum perlegas, protegas; et faveas homini, in tanto sale epulisque Martialiticis, insulso, nec ieiuno"; Folger Shakespeare Library, STC 14792 copy 1, sig. A1v.

39 McPherson, "Ben Jonson's Library," 67–70.

40 Boehrer, "Renaissance Classicism and Roman Sexuality."

41 "Rideto multum qui te, Sextille, cinaedum / dixerat et digitum porrigito medium. / sed nec pedico es nec tu, Sextille, fututor, / calda Vetustinae nec tibi bucca placet. / es istius nihil es, fateor, Sextille. quid ergo es? / nescio, sed tu scis res superesse duas."

42 On Roman male sexual identities and roles, see Williams, *Roman Homosexuality*, 163–224.

43 Adams, *Latin Sexual Vocabulary*, 194.

44 Catullus 10, line 24. Adams, *Latin Sexual Vocabulary*, 132.

45 Folger Shakespeare Library, PA 6501.A2 1619 Cage.

46 "Sextillum notat, quod fellator & cunnilingus esset … Impuritatis sex sunt scelera: primum, cinaedum esse: secundum: paediconem: tertium, fututorem: quartum, irrumatorem: quintum, fellatorem: sextum, cunnilingum. Negat Sextilium quatre habere priora, & dicit eum scire duos superesse, hoc est, fellandi & lingendi turpitudinem … Eodem sale perfricat Coracinum quemdam, lib. 4. epigr. 43"; Martial, *Epigrammatum*, 150.

47 On Calderini as an annotator of Martial, see Sullivan, *Martial*, 265.

48 "Calda bucca. in vulva: qua non es cunnilingus."

49 Calderini is mistaken. There is debate over the etymology of "masturbation," but it has Latin, not Greek, roots. See Adams, *Latin Sexual Vocabulary*, 208–11.

50 "Duas res. in fellationem: & masturbationem. Masturbari a verbo graeco tractum est; nam graeci μασροπευω dicunt lenoncinio & blanditiis

conciliare. Unde masturbari dixerunt latini per eo quid est virilia impudenter tractare. Fellare: ab haedis & agnis tractum: qui fellare dicuntur ubera matris: cum lac sugunt. hoc verbo usus est Varro in re rustica: in agnis Solinus frequentativo scilicet fellito: In haedis & Plinius. Dicitur autem non a felle animali: quod sentire est ridiculum: sed a verbo graeco. quod est os contaminare: ita interpretat Suidas testimonio etiam Aristophanis."

51 "Nec tibi placet fellaticis bucca, ep. 62. l. II. & artificis halitus oris. Iuven. 10 sat. 238 vers"; STC 17492, sig. E4v.

52 "lambebat medios improba lingua viros"; STC 17492, sig. E4v.

53 *Encyclopedia Britannica* (1911), "Brown, Thomas (English Satirist)."

54 For example, Moreland and Fleischer, *Latin*, 125; Hendricks, *Latin Made Simple*, 105.

55 "Cocksucker or cunt-licker"; Folger Shakespeare Library, PA 6501.A2 1619 Cage, sig. A4r.

56 "Circulata diu mensis scribilita secundis / urebat nimio saeva calore manus; / sed magis ardebat Sabidi gula: protinus ergo / sufflavit buccis terque quaterque suis. / illa quidem tepuit digitosque admittere visa est, / sed nemo potuit tangere: merda fuit."

57 The connection between the two poems based on the fact that both describe a character named Sabidius was made by several other commentators on Martial, including Pietro Crinito in his 1607 Paris edition. See Boehrer, "Renaissance Classicism," 375–6.

58 "Alius sensus est, quo innuit aliquod summum esse in Sabidio flagitium, quod nefas sit, id est, non possit dici. Videor autem subodorate id flagitium esse, quod Subidius impuri oris, suspicari me facit epigramma 17, lib. 3. quot cum scribilitam ardentem, secundis mensis allatam, nemo tangeret, hic idem Sabidius terque, quaterque buccis suis sufflavit, & remisso ardenti calore, nemo ex convivius ausus est tangere, quod insufflata ab hoc impuro homine, fortè cunnilingo, vel fellatore, conviviis *virus* fuit"; Martial, *Epigrams*, 76.

59 Boehrer, *The Fury of Men's Gullets*, 2–4.

60 Moulton, *Before Pornography*, 13–15.

61 Boehrer, *The Fury of Men's Gullets*, 3.

62 Jonson, *The Workes of Benjamin Jonson*, 765–818.

63 Jonson, *Workes*, 767.

64 "lascivam verborum veritatem, id est epigrammaton linguam, excusarem, si meum esset exemplum: sic scribit Catullus, sic Marsus, sic Pedo, sic Gaetulicus, sic quicumque perlegitur. si quis tamen tam ambitiose tristis est ut apud illum in nulla pagina latine loqui fas sit, postest epistula vel potius titulo contentus esse. epigrammat illis scribuntur qui solent spectare Florales. non intret Cato theatrum meum, aut si intraverit, spectet." Martial, *Epigrams*, bk. 1, introductory epistle.

65 See also, for example, epigram 1.4, lines 5–6; epigram 3.86, line 4.
66 Adams, *The Latin Sexual Vocabulary*, 5.
67 Valerius Maximus, *Memorable Doings and Sayings*, bk. 2, ch. 10.8.

WORKS CITED

Adams, J.N. *The Latin Sexual Vocabulary*. Baltimore: Johns Hopkins University Press, 1982.

Addison, Joseph. *The Spectator* 70 (Monday, 21 May 1711).

Beard, Mary. *The Fires of Vesuvius: Pompeii Lost and Found*. Cambridge, MA: Harvard University Press, 2010.

Boehrer, Bruce Thomas. *The Fury of Men's Gullets: Ben Jonson and the Alimentary Canal*. Philadelphia: University of Pennsylvania Press, 1997.

– "Renaissance Classicism and Roman Sexuality: Ben Jonson's Marginalia and the Trope of *Os Impurum*." *International Journal of the Classical Tradition* 4.3 (1998): 364–80.

Catullus. *Catullus. Tibellus. Pervigilium Veneris*. Ed. and trans. F.W. Cornish, G.P. Goold, et al. Cambridge, MA: Harvard University Press, 1988.

Coiro, Ann Baines. *Robert Herrick's "Hesperides" and the Epigram Book Tradition*. Baltimore: Johns Hopkins University Press, 1988.

Fitzgerald, William. *Martial: The World of the Epigram*. Chicago: University of Chicago Press, 2007.

Harper, Kyle. *From Shame to Sin: The Christian Transformation of Sexual Morality in Late Antiquity*. Cambridge, MA: Harvard University Press, 2013.

Hausmann, Frank-Rutger. "Martialis, Marcus Valerius." In P.O. Kristeller et al., eds., *Catalogus Translationum et Commentariorum: Medieval and Renaissance Latin Translations and Commentaries*, vol. 4. Washington, DC: Catholic University of America Press, 1980, 249–96.

Hendricks, Rhoda A. *Latin Made Simple*. New York: Doubleday, 1992.

Hudson, Hoyt Hopewell. *The Epigram in the English Renaissance*. Princeton: Princeton University Press, 1947.

Jones, Howard. *Printing the Classical Text*. Utrecht: Hes and DeGraff, 2004.

Jonson, Ben. *The Workes of Benjamin Jonson*. London, 1616.

Leonhardt, Jürgen. *Latin: Story of a World Language*. Trans. Kenneth Kronenberg. Cambridge, MA: Harvard University Press, 2009.

Livy. *History of Rome. Vol 4. Books 8–10*. Trans. B.O. Foster. Cambridge, MA: Harvard University Press, 1926.

Loewenstein, Joseph. *Ben Jonson and Possessive Authorship*. Cambridge: Cambridge University Press, 2002.

Martial. *Epigrams*. Ed. and trans. D.R. Shackleton Bailey. 3 vols. Cambridge, MA: Harvard University Press, 1993.

– *Epigrammata*. Ed. D.R. Shackleton Bailey. Stuttgart: Tuebner, 1990.

– *Epigrammaton Libri*. Ed. Thomas Farnaby. London, 1615.
– *Epigrammatum*. Ed. Josephus Langius. Paris, 1617.
– *Nova Editio*. Ed. Petrus Scriverius. Leiden, 1619.
McPherson, David. "Ben Jonson's Library and Marginalia: An Annotated Catalogue." *Studies in Philology* 71.5 (1974): 1–106.
Milnor, Kristina. *Graffiti and the Literary Landscape in Roman Pompeii*. New York: Oxford University Press, 2014.
Moreland, Floyd L., and Rita M. Fleischer. *Latin: An Intensive Course*. Berkeley: University of California Press, 1977.
Moulton, Ian Frederick. *Before Pornography: Erotic Writing in Early Modern England*. New York: Oxford University Press, 2000.
Parker, Holt N. "The Teratogenic Grid." In Judith P. Hallett and Marilyn B. Skinner, eds., *Roman Sexualities*. Princeton: Princeton University Press, 1997, 47–65.
Plautus. *Casina. The Casket Comedy. Curculio. Epidicus. The Two Menaechmuses*. Ed. and trans. Wolfgang de Melo. Cambridge, MA: Harvard University Press, 2011.
Richlin, Amy. *The Garden of Priapus: Sexuality and Aggression in Roman Humor*. New York: Oxford University Press, 1992.
Ruggiero, Guido. *The Renaissance in Italy: A Social and Cultural History of the Rinascimento*. New York: Cambridge University Press, 2014.
Skinner, Marilyn B. *Sexuality in Greek and Roman Culture*. Malden, MA: Blackwell, 2005.
Sullivan, J.P. *Martial: The Unexpected Classic: A Literary and Historical Study*. New York: Cambridge University Press, 1991.
Valerius Maximus. *Memorable Doings and Sayings*. Ed. and trans. D.R. Shackleton Bailey. Cambridge, MA: Harvard University Press, 2000.
Walters, Jonathan. "Invading the Roman Body: Manliness and Impenetrability in Roman Thought." In Judith P. Hallett and Marilyn B. Skinner, eds., *Roman Sexualities*. Princeton: Princeton University Press, 1997, 29–43.
Williams, Craig A. *Roman Homosexuality: Ideologies of Masculinity in Classical Antiquity*. New York: Oxford University Press, 1999.

Contributors

Sara E. Díaz is an Associate Professor of Modern Languages and Literatures at Fairfield University, where she teaches all levels of Italian culture, language, and literature. Her research on marriage, gender, and comedy in late medieval and early modern Italian literature has led her to the prolific seventeenth-century author and performer Margherita Costa. She has edited and translated Costa's 1641 farce, *The Buffoons*, with Jessica Goethals for "The Other Voice in Early Modern Europe" series and is currently completing a critical edition and translation of Costa's 1639 *Lettere amorose* (*Love Letters*) for the same series.

Kate Driscoll is Assistant Professor of Italian and Romance Studies at Duke University. She received her PhD from the University of California, Berkeley (2020) in Italian Studies and Renaissance and Early Modern Studies. Her research engages broadly with questions of authorship, audience, and reception in early modern Italy and Europe. She has published various interdisciplinary articles on questions of voice and lament in chivalric romance epic, women readers of this genre, and the representation of female ambassadors in Tasso and Vivaldi. She is currently finishing a book on the female readers, patrons, and performers who dialogued with Torquato Tasso (1544–1595).

Konrad Eisenbichler, CM, OMRI, FRSC, is professor emeritus from the University of Toronto. His research focuses on the intersection of literature, politics, and religion in early modern Italy. He is the author of *The Sword and the Pen: Women, Politics, and Poetry in Sixteenth-Century Siena* (Notre Dame, 2012), which won the Ennio Flaiano International Prize for Italian Studies, and *The Boys of the Archangel Raphael: A Youth Confraternity in Florence, 1411–1785* (Toronto, 1998), which won the Howard R. Marraro Prize. His more recent works include a translation of Giovan

Maria Cecchi, *Five Plays for the Archangel Raphael* (CRRS, 2020), and the collection *Premodern Masculinities in Transition* (Boydell & Brewer, 2024), which he co-edited with Jacqueline Murray.

Tiffany Hoffman is a research fellow with the Centre for Renaissance and Reformation Studies at the University of Toronto. She also serves as book review editor for *Emotions: History, Culture, Society* (Brill). She works on the history of emotions, gender, psychoanalysis, religion, and embodiment. She has held research fellowships at the Osler Library for the History of Medicine (McGill University), and with the Australian Research Centre for the History of Emotions (University of Western Australia). She has published articles on Shakespeare and emotions, and is currently completing a book project, *Performing Shyness: Masculinity, Religion, and Emotion on the Shakespearean Stage.*

Ian Frederick Moulton is President's Professor of English and Cultural History at Arizona State University. He has published widely on the representation of gender and sexuality in early modern European literature. His books include *Before Pornography: Erotic Writing in Early Modern England* (Oxford, 2000) and *Love in Print in the Sixteenth Century: The Popularization of Romance* (Palgrave, 2014). His most recent monograph, *Clever Little Books: Martial's Epigrams and Sexual Knowledge in Early Modern Europe*, is forthcoming from the University of Toronto Press.

Marco Piana (PhD, McGill University) is a Learning and Development Lead at Egale Canada. While his educational work focuses on equity, diversity, and inclusion, his scholarly research focuses on gender, otherness, and religious identity in the medieval and early modern Catholic world. He has held fellowships at the University of Calgary, the University of Toronto, and the Centre for Renaissance and Reformation Studies (Toronto) and was a Visiting Assistant Professor in Italian at Smith College. Among his latest publications, we find *Strange Encounters in the Italian Baroque* (a special issue of the journal *Quaderni d'italianistica*, 2021) and the co-edited volume *Idealizing Women in the Italian Renaissance* (CRRS, 2021).

James M. Saslow is professor emeritus of art history, theatre, and Renaissance studies at City University of New York, where he was a founder of the Center for Lesbian and Gay Studies. His work focuses on the early modern period, with special interests in gender and homosexuality. His pioneering survey, *Pictures and Passions: A History of Homosexuality in the Visual Arts* (1999), received two awards from the Lambda

Literary Foundation. His book *The Medici Wedding of 1589: Florentine Festival as "theatrum mundi"* received the Phyllis Gordan prize from the Renaissance Society of America (1996).

Laura Ackerman Smoller is Professor of History at the University of Rochester. She is the author of *History, Prophecy, and the Stars: The Christian Astrology of Pierre d'Ailly* (Princeton, 1994) and *The Saint and the Chopped-Up Baby: The Cult of Vincent Ferrer in Medieval and Early Modern Europe* (Cornell, 2014), winner of the 2016 *La corónica* International Book Award, as well as many articles and chapters on medieval eschatology, astrology, saints, and miracles. A Guggenheim Fellow (2004–5) and holder of a fellowship from the National Endowment for the Humanities (2022–3), Smoller is also a fellow of the Medieval Academy of America.

Steven F.H. Stowell is Associate Professor of Art History at Concordia University, Montreal. His research focuses on the devotional experiences of Italian Renaissance art, and relationships between art and discourses on gender and sexuality. He is the author of *The Spiritual Language of Art: Medieval Christian Themes in Writings on Art of the Italian Renaissance* (Brill, 2015); his research has also been published in the journals *Word & Image* and *Dante Studies*.

Tara White is a 2020 alumna of the Syracuse University Florence MA Program in Italian Renaissance Art. She is an art historian with a passion for social history, queer theory, and cross-cultural exchange. Her main research interest is gender and sexuality in early modern Europe, especially Italy and France in the sixteenth and seventeenth centuries. Her most recent research focuses on early modern conceptions of masculinity within women who had sexual relationships with other women.

Anne L. Williams is Assistant Professor of Art History at the University of Hong Kong and the recipient of the 2024 National Endowment for the Humanities Rome Prize at the American Academy in Rome. Her research addresses late medieval and early modern male sanctity, humour, and rhetoric. She is the author of *Satire, Veneration, and St. Joseph in Art, c. 1300–1550* (Amsterdam University Press, 2019), as well as articles published in *Gesta*, *IKON*, and the *Journal of Historians of Netherlandish Art*.

Index

Acteon, 98, 141, 144–6, 157–9, 162
Addison, Joseph, 226
affectations, 125–6, 129–30. *See also* behaviour; manners
Agamemnon (king), 98
aggression, 3–4, 207, 228; oral, 212; sexual, 228
Albertucci de' Borselli, Girolamo, 83–6, 90n29
Alexander the Great, 14–15
Ambrose (saint), 30, 44, 64
Amor (god), 98, 103, 105, 127. *See also* Cupid
androgyny, 7, 11, 52, 66, 68
Angelico (fra), 27, 40–2
Antist, Vicente Justinian, 85–6, 92n51
Antoninus of Florence (saint), 83, 90n28, 101
anxiety, 3, 6–7, 10, 78, 80, 119, 201, 204–10, 212, 214, 217–18n27
Apollo, 98
Aquinas, Thomas (saint), 58, 64
Aretino, Pietro, 126
Ariosto, Ludovico, 9, 120, 124, 136n32, 149–51, 183
Aristotile da Sangallo, 37
Aristotle, 55. *See also* philosophy, Aristotelian
armour, 150, 188
arts, martial, 4, 126
attire, 89n20, 125–6, 149. *See also* clothes; gloves; shoes; stocking
Augustine (saint), 30, 44
Avicenna, 55, 58. *See also* philosophy, Aristotelian

Bakhtin, Mikhail, 3, 4, 6, 202
Bartolommeo (fra), 55
bashfulness, 199–200, 203–6, 211–13, 216
bathing, 9, 36, 38–9, 42–3, 141, 143–4, 148, 150, 152, 157, 162
baths, bathhouses, 38–9, 47n54, 150–2, 160
beard, 11, 101–2, 130, 207
Beatis, Antonio de', 54
beauty, comeliness: earthly, 98; feminine, 129, 149, 152; ideal, 7; male, 4, 7, 12, 14, 42–3, 45, 52, 54–5, 57–60, 66, 68, 70, 107, 120, 123–30, 132
behaviour, 4–5, 8–10, 12, 68, 150, 181–2, 184, 200, 202–5, 221, 223; sexual, 79, 150, 222, 225, 229, 233, 237
Bernard of Clairvaux (saint), 61, 64
Bernardino of Siena (saint), 80, 82, 89n20, 90n29
Bilanzoni, Francesco (castrato), 184

bisexuality, 15, 17n7
body, 5–6, 10, 52–5, 59–60, 64, 66, 68, 70, 77, 88n6, 103–5, 123, 126–7, 147–8, 158, 184, 188, 201–2, 213, 226–7; female, 6, 102, 107, 152–3, 160–1, 181; of Jesus/Christ, 6, 12, 59, 66, 100–5, 107; male, 3, 6, 16, 78, 162n10, 176, 178. *See also* corporeality; hair; skin
Bordone, Paris, 25, 29, 38
Borselli, Girolamo. *See* Albertucci de' Borselli, Girolamo
Botticelli, Sandro, 13
Bourdeille. *See* Brantôme
boy, child, 39, 79, 88n6, 183, 227–8, 240n30
Bradamante (female warrior, fictional), 149–51, 162n10, 162n11, 163n13
Brantôme, Pierre de Bourdeille, seigneur de, 9, 142, 149–51, 159
bride, *sponsa*, 14–15, 55, 57, 60–2, 64–6
bridegroom, *sponsus*, 14–15, 57, 60–2, 64–5, 70
Briggs, Richard, 230–1, 238
brotherhood, 31, 33, 38, 42–3, 45
Buonarroti, Michelangelo, 14, 27, 36–8, 59
Buonarroti, Michelangelo (the Younger), 120
Butinone, Bernardino, 40
Butler, Judith, 5, 10, 141, 145–8, 161, 181

Calderini, Domizio, 234, 241n49
Caraglio, Giovanni Jacopo, 154–5
Carpentier, Alejo, 171–3, 192–3
Castiglione, Baldassare, 8, 11, 119, 152
Castiglione, Branda (cardinal), 32
Castiglione, Francesco, 88n6
Castiglione Olona, 23–4, 28, 31–2, 44
castration, 213
castrato, 184, 195n43. *See also* Bilanzoni, Francesco
Cato, 238–9, 242n64
Catullus, 233, 238
celibacy, 7, 78, 80, 87
Cervantes, Miguel de, 11
Chapman, George, 217n23
chastity, 59; Christian, 99; clerical, 78–80, 86; female, 144, 146, 203, 211–13; male, 98, 103, 230
choler, 202
Christ. *See* Jesus
Chrysostom (saint), 64
Cicero, 217n23, 221, 223, 227
cinaedus, 222, 233–4, 241n41, 241n46. *See also* sex, same-sex male
clothes, 25, 40, 89n20, 111n35, 128–9
confraternity, brotherhood (association), 35–6, 40, 42
corporeality, 6–7, 213. *See also* body; skin
Cosimo I (grand duke of Florence), 64
cosmetics, 120, 125–9, 132–3
Costa, Margarita, 5, 8–9, 117–33
courtier, 119, 127–8, 131, 200–1, 203–6, 208, 210–12, 214–16
Courtin, Antoine de, 205
Cresti, Domenico, called Passignano, 38
cuckold, 150–1
cunnilingus, 222, 234, 239n8, 241n46, 241n48
Cupid, 97–8, 100, 104–5, 107, 108n4, 108–9n13, 152. *See also* Amor

Dati, Carlo, 134n16
Davies, John, 226
de Moya, Pedro (Petrus Muya), 82–6, 92n53
del Sarto, Andrea, 27, 35, 38

della Bella, Stefano, 120, 122, 127–8
Della Casa, Giovanni, 119, 126, 201–2
desire, erotic, 214; same-sex, 16, 126
Diago, Francisco, 85–6, 92n51
Dido, 10, 98, 183
Diomede, 98
Dominic (saint), 7, 77–8, 80–7
draucus, 222, 233. *See also* sex, same-sex male
Durantino, Guido. *See* Fontana, Guido
dwarf, 120, 122–5, 129, 131–2, 136n32

effeminacy, 8, 53, 68, 80–1, 86, 118–19, 125–8, 130–3, 207
Elyot, Thomas, 203
emotions, 4, 9–11, 17, 177, 181–3, 185, 199–200, 203, 205–13, 215–16, 217–18n27
eroticism, 3, 6, 8, 12–14, 25, 27, 38, 43, 45, 54, 78, 80–1, 86–7, 98, 107, 149, 154, 159, 161, 166n72, 189, 213–14, 216, 226
eunuch, 68
expectations, cultural/social, 3–4, 9, 11, 78, 227

Farnaby, Thomas, 230, 235
Farnese, Orlando, 120
fashion, sartorial, 89n20, 119, 126–31
fear, 179–80, 200, 202–6, 208, 210–15; fearlessness, 182
fellatio, 222, 234–7, 241n50
femininity, 5, 8, 10, 118, 147–8, 157, 161; masculine femininity, 68, 141–62
Ferdinando II (grand duke of Florence), 131, 134–5n21
Ferrer, Vincent (saint), 7, 77–87, 90n29, 90n31
Ficino, Marsilio, 66, 68
Flamini, Giovanni Antonio, 84–6, 90n29
Fontana (family), 148, 160, 162; Camillo, 160; Flaminio, 160; Guido, 160; Nicolo, 160; Orazio, 160
Foucault, Michel, 5, 233
Francis (saint), 78, 105, 112n35
Francis I (king of France), 54, 152–3, 164n31
fraternity, fraternal bonds, 36, 42–3, 45
Frederick the Great (king of Prussia), 181
Freud, Sigmund, 4, 60, 125
fricatrix, 150–1, 163n18. *See also* sex, same-sex female

Ganymede, 8, 117, 125–7, 130–2, 136n42, 137n49, 137n57, 137n59
Gebersweiler, Catherine von, 106
gender bending, 158, 185
genitals, 59, 68, 148, 150, 159–61, 225, 228, 234, 236. *See also* penis
Gentile da Fabriano, 31–3
Gerson, Jean, 55
Ghirlandaio, Domenico, 25, 27, 43
Giotto, 40
Giraldi, Lilio Gregorio, 99, 108n4
girl, young woman, 173, 188, 227–8
Girò, Anna, 185
Giusti, Alvise (Luigi), 174, 176–8, 188
gloves, 120, 124–5, 129
Gonzaga (dukes of Mantua), 160
Gonzaga, Ludovico, 157
Gonzaga, Paola, 157
Graf, Urs, 59
Graun, Carl Heinrich, 181
grooming, 11, 152
guild, 35–6. *See also* confraternity

hair, man's, 55, 58–9, 100, 123, 130, 150; woman's, 52, 153, 158, 163n13. *See also* beard

Hephaestion, 14–15
hermaphrodite, 68, 129
heterosexuality, 43, 126. *See also* sex, heterosexual
Hilary (saint), 64
Hippocratic theory, 54
homoeroticism, 14, 43, 53, 70, 80–1, 86–7, 126, 145, 149, 222, 225, 227, 229, 233, 235
homosexuality, 8, 14, 16, 43, 45, 53, 125
homosociality, 13, 25, 38–40, 42, 44, 87
Horace, 224
Housebook Master, 59, 61
humanism, 125, 221–2, 226
humours, humoral theory, 157–9, 161, 207

impotence, 184, 213
Incarnation, Christ's, 6, 65–6
Innocent VIII (pope), 34
intersex, 148
intimacy, 7, 9, 25, 30, 38–9, 89n23, 91n43, 142, 145, 147, 151, 158–60

James I (king of England), 238
James the Great (saint) 71n19
Jerome (saint), 44
Jesus/Christ, 6–7, 12–14, 25, 29, 30–5, 39–42, 44, 54–5, 57–62, 64–6, 68–70, 78, 80, 90n31, 99–107
Johannes de Caulibus, 71n31
John the Baptist (saint), 7, 12, 14–15, 25, 29, 38, 42, 44–5, 52–5, 57, 59–60, 62, 64–6, 69–70, 71n19
John the Evangelist (saint), 7, 15, 55, 57, 66, 71n19
Jonson, Ben, 12, 226, 230–9
Julius II (pope), 11, 97, 99

Landucci, Luca, 39
language, body, 9; explicit, 225, 233, 238; legal, 90n26, 187; military, 78; mystical, 63–4, 68; of loss, 177, 192; of love, 132; offensive, 225; sexualized, 226
Lanino, Bernardino, 154, 156
Leonardo da Vinci, 6, 11–12, 38, 52–5, 57–60, 62, 64–70
Lippi, Filippino, 25
Livy, 221
Lorde, Audre, 10
love, 10, 12, 15, 30, 42, 68, 98–9, 102–3, 106–7, 122–3, 127, 129–32, 145–6, 149–50, 158–9, 162n7, 163n16, 163n20, 173, 211, 227; brotherly, 31, 42; Platonic, 99; self-love, 125; stories, 172. *See also* sex
lover, beloved, 10, 14, 59, 81, 120, 123, 125, 127, 129–32, 158, 184, 205, 207, 213–14
Loyola, Ignatius of (saint), 226
Lucian, 99, 159, 163n18, 163n20, 165n59
lust, 68, 79–80, 88n6, 98, 101, 103, 150–1, 159, 202

Maenads, 98
make-up. *See* cosmetics
maleness, 3, 11, 68, 215
manhood, 68, 174, 182, 184, 200–2, 205–7, 210, 213, 216
manliness, 78, 200, 207
mannerisms, 117, 129–30
manners, 125, 201. *See also* affectations; behaviour; mannerisms
Mantegna, 27, 32, 34–7
Mantuanus, Baptista, 99
Martial, 12, 164n23, 222–39
martyr, martyrdom, 55, 78
Martyr, Peter (saint), 82–3, 90n28
Mary (mother of Jesus), 60–1, 65, 71n19, 78, 98, 100, 102, 107, 109n14
Mary Magdalene (saint), 57
Masaccio, 25, 28, 34–7, 43–4

masculinity, 3–11, 66–8, 78–80, 86–7, 97, 118–20, 124–6, 128, 130–2, 141–62, 173–84, 200–16, 221–9; clerical, 7, 78; construction of, 5, 118, 181–3, 200–1, 203, 205, 212; crisis of, 209–10; elite, 11–12, 15, 119, 130, 160, 200–1, 206, 208, 221–3, 226–7, 229; feminine, 66, 68, 79, 124, 129, 131–2, 158; heteronormative, 126, 132; holy, 7, 54–5, 70, 107; non-normative, 68, 119, 131, 178; performative, 5, 10–11, 78, 145–8, 161, 181, 184, 200–16, 218n31. *See also* maleness; manhood; manliness
Masolino da Panicale, 13, 23–5, 28, 31–4, 36–7, 40, 43–4
Master GK, 141, 143, 153, 157, 161
Maximilian I (emperor) 102
Mazzi, Maria Serena, 39
Medici (family), 118, 120–1, 123, 126, 131. *See also* Cosimo I; Ferdinando II
Medici, Giuliano de', 8
Medici, Margherita de', 120
Michelangelo. *See* Buonarroti, Michelangelo
Mignon, Jean, 153–4
Milan, Pierre, 141–2, 151–2, 161
Miller, Massimiliano, 184
misbehaviour, 79, 203
misogyny, 15, 118, 132–3
mistress, 10, 233
modesty, 160, 165n70, 199–200, 202–6, 209–16; false modesty, 118, 122, 216
Monteverdi, Claudio, 183
More, Thomas, 226
Musacchio, Jacqueline, 160

nakedness, nude, nudity, 9, 12, 14, 25, 27, 35, 38, 43–4, 55, 66, 107, 111n35, 157, 188
narcissism, 125, 207, 209–10, 214
Narcissus, 8, 117, 125–7, 130–2, 137n49, 137n57, 137n59
Neoplatonism, 60, 66, 68, 98, 100
Nesi, Giovanni, 42
Nicolay, Nicolas de, 149, 151, 160
noblesse d'épée, 4
noblesse de robe, 4
nude. *See* nakedness

obscenity, 225–6, 232, 234, 237–8
Origen, 60
Ottoboni, Pietro, 175
Ovid, 98–9, 151–2, 157, 183, 221

Parmigianino, 141, 144, 146, 157–9, 161
Pasquini, Bernardo, 175
Passignano. *See* Cresti, Domenico
Passion, Christ's, 100, 102, 104–6
passion, erotic/emotional, 3, 149–50, 152, 159, 173, 185, 202, 204
paticus, 233. *See also* sex, same-sex male
patriarchy, 132, 173, 177, 201, 206, 211
pederasty, 227
penis, 110n23, 150, 159, 225, 234. *See also* phallus
Penni, Luca, 143, 153–4, 157, 161
Perugino, 25, 55–6
phallus, phallic, 66, 150. *See also* penis
philosophy, Aristotelian, 6, 52, 54–5, 66, 68, 78, 158
Piccini, Isabella, 188, 190
Pico della Mirandola, Gianfrancesco, 12, 97–107, 108n4, 108n9
Piero della Francesca, 25
Pisanello, 31–3
Plato, 98, 173, 221
Platonism, 222. *See also* Neoplatonism
pride, 42, 121, 127, 189, 202, 215

Primaticcio, Francesco, 152, 161
prints, erotic, 154
prostitute, prostitution, sex work, 47n54, 233
Pulci, Luigi, 124, 136n32

Ramirez de Prado, Lorenzo, 234, 236
Ranzano, Pietro, 77–8, 80–7, 90n28
Raphael (Raffaello Sanzio), 60, 64, 153–4
relations, same-sex, 39, 84, 89n19, 163n19. *See also* desire; homosexuality; sodomy
restraint, bodily, 214–15; sexual, 132, 199, 203, 213–16
Rinuccini, Alamanno, 42
Rocca Sanvitale, 144, 146, 157, 162
Rocke, Michael, 39, 43, 89n19
Rosso Fiorentino, 59, 62
Rubens, Pieter Paul, 38, 159
Rubin, Patricia, 25, 38
Rustici, Gian Francesco, 54

Sacchis, Giovanni Antonio de', called Pordenone, 63
Salimbeni, Jacopo and Lorenzo, 29–31, 33
Salvadori, Andrea, 123, 127, 135n28, 136n30
Salviati, Francesco, 38
Sanvitale, Giangaleazzo, 157
Sappho, 98, 151, 164n22
satire, 126, 131–2
Savonarola, Girolamo, 12, 39, 100–1, 105–7, 109n14
science, Galenic, 158
Sebastian (saint), 7, 13–14, 55, 68
self-fashioning, 5, 118, 181
sensuality, sensual imagery, 36, 42–3, 59, 103, 105, 152, 159–60, 164n31
sex, active role, 7, 9, 78, 88–9n14, 142, 146–7, 149–51, 153, 159, 161–2, 163n19, 226; anal, 79, 222, 225–6, 228, 233, 235 (*see also* sodomy); bestiality, 225; heterosexual, 39, 233; masturbation, 79, 88n6, 221–2, 225, 228–9, 234–5, 241n49, 241n50; oral, 222, 225–6, 228–9, 232–6; passive role, 4, 7, 9, 68, 78–81, 86, 88–9n14, 142, 153, 163n19, 165n58, 165n59, 226; penetrative, 91n41, 150–1, 159, 226–9, 233; same-sex female, 141–54, 157–62, 162n4, 163n16, 163n18, 163n20, 164n22, 164n23, 228 (see also *tribade; fricatrix*); same-sex male, 39, 68 (see also *cinaedus; draucus; paticus;* sodomy); vaginal, 226, 228, 233
sex work. *See* prostitute
sexuality, 4–5, 44–5, 54, 59, 222–3, 227, 232; Christ's, 59; deviant, 8; female, 9, 228; Roman, 222, 226–8, 232–3, 240n17; transgressive/illicit, 12, 222
Shakespeare, William, 3, 6, 205, 208, 218n28
shame, 10, 192, 199, 203–5, 208–15, 217n27, 222, 226–8, 236; shameless, 228
shoes, 120, 129
shyness, 10, 200–1, 204–5, 209–11, 214, 216
skin, 25; tone, 9, 54, 147, 157–9, 161
slave, enslaved people, 174, 191, 225–8
Sodoma, 14–15
sodomy, sodomite, 7, 39, 43, 77–87, 88n10, 89n19, 89n20, 91n39, 91n40, 233. *See also* sex, anal; sex, same-sex male
soldier, 4, 38, 44, 65, 79, 127, 131, 174, 180
Solís, Antonio de, 174, 178, 188, 190
Stewart, Alan, 80

Stigliani, Tommaso, 175
stocking, hose, 25, 33–4, 36–8, 40, 42, 126–7
Stoicism, 4, 222
Strozzi, Zanobi di Benedetto, 40
sword, 120, 124, 127, 188
syphilis, 129, 152

Tacitus, 221
Tasso, Torquato, 183
temptation, 6, 12, 14, 78–81, 86, 98, 103, 105, 111n35
Teoli, Antonino, 87
Terence, 221, 223
Thisbe, 98, 206–7
timidity, 10, 200, 202, 204–5, 210, 212
Torrigiano, Pietro, 36
transgender, 14
transgression, 8, 12, 124, 126, 128–9, 131, 145, 229
Traub, Valerie, 145–7
tribade, 150–1, 159, 163n18, 165n58, 222, 228. *See also* sex, same-sex female

van Meckenem, Israhel, 59
Varagine, Jacobus de, 62, 105
Vasari, Giorgio, 23, 28, 32, 34–40, 54–5, 64
Venus, 97–8, 100, 103–7, 108n4, 108–9n13, 110n23, 125
Virgil, 221, 223, 224, 227
virginity, 80–2, 85–6, 188
virility, 4, 91n41, 159, 184, 188
virtue: Ciceronian, 222; civic, 222; feminine, 6, 211; masculine, 52, 199, 204; religious, 6, 68, 70, 78, 80
Vivaldi, Antonio, 9–10, 171–7, 183, 185, 191–3
vulnerability, 10, 123, 132, 177, 188

war, 173–4, 178–9, 189, 191
warrior, 4, 11, 184, 189, 201; female warrior, 149 (*see also* Bradamante)
womanhood, 173
womanish, 10, 118, 202
women, sexually aggressive, 228–9
Wright, Thomas, 202–3
Wtewael, Joachim Anthonisz, 159

youth (age), youthfulness, 8, 12, 59, 66, 68, 125–7, 130, 132, 207
youth (person), young male, 5–8, 12, 34–5, 38–9, 43, 55, 59, 66, 68, 70, 77, 79–82, 86–7, 89n20, 90n31, 98, 103, 120, 125, 227–9

zerbino, 119–21, 126–30, 132–3, 134n16, 136n42, 137n50, 137n57
Zwingli, Huldrych, 14, 55